ANCIEN[illegible]S

ABOUT

MYSTICISM

AND

HOLLYWOOD

AND THE

MUSIC INDUSTRY

COMPILED AND WRITTEN BY:

WILLIAM JOSIAH SUTTON

PRINTED IN THE UNITED STATES OF AMERICA

BOOKS WRITTEN BY WILLIAM JOSIAH SUTTON:

Vol. I: *Beware It's Coming - The Antichrist 666*
Vol. II: *The New Age Movement and The Illuminati 666*
Vol. III: *The Real Truth About UFO's and The New World Order Connection*
Vol. IV: *Ancient Prophecies About Mysticism and Hollywood and The Music Industry*
Vol. V: *Ancient Prophecies About The Dragon, The Beast, and The False Prophet*

TABLE OF CONTENTS

2. The Secret Societies of Freemasonry and the Illuminati are just a Continuation of Sufism (Islamic Mysticism).
3. There are Three Different Beasts in the Prophecies of the Book of Revelation.
4. Shocking Revelations from the Sufi Teacher Idries Shah about the Rosicrucians, the Freemasons, and the Illuminati.
5. The Game of Chess was an Invention of Sufism.
6. A Mystical Marriage with Allah.
7. Dag Hammarskjöld, former UN Secretary General, was a Sufi.
8. Sufi Masters communicate with Jinns (Demons).
9. "Use not Vain Repetitions, as the Heathen do."
10. Albert Pike, Past Grand High Priest and Sovereign Grand Commander of Masonry and His Connection with the Kabbalah.
11. The Kabbalah is Jewish Mysticism a.k.a. Jewish Theosophy in which both Sufism and Freemasonry are rooted and grounded.
12. Madonna, Roseanne, Elizabeth Taylor, and Barbra Streisand openly admit to being involved in the Kabbalah (Jewish Mysticism).
13. The Holy Scriptures forbid the Teaching of the Doctrines found in the Kabbalah.
14. Iõannes Paulus Secundo (John Paul II in Latin) adds to 666.
15. Western Buddhists and a Sufi discover how Similar their Beliefs are.
16. Hazrat Inayat Khan, a Musician, Poet, and Sufi Master, brings Sufism to America.
17. Hazrat Inayat Khan founded the First Sufi Order in San Francisco in 1910.
18. Hazrat Inayat Khan, Granddaddy of the "Flower Children" and the "Hippie Movement."
19. Western Sufism (introduced by the Poet, Musician, and Sufi Master, Hazrat Inayat Khan) not only kindled the "Hippie Movement," but also other Non-Muslim Orders Throughout the World.

19. "Gangsta Rap" and "Gospel Rap."
20. More about John Lennon's War on Christ and His People.
21. Megadeth and the Promotion of Anarchy through their Music.
22. *Antichrist Superstar's* Marilyn Manson and the Promotion of Anarchy.
23. The Dangers of Computer Games.
24. Sufism and Kabbalism are promoted in Children's Books and Movies.
25. How Jesus is calling His People, who are tired of being Evil, to Him.
26. "Him that cometh to Me I will in No Wise cast out."
27. Theocratic Forms of Government have enslaved Masses.
28. Jesus will soon put an End to the Pied Piper's Communal Scheme.
29. The Destruction and the Cleansing of the World by Fire.
30. Understanding the Correct Doctrine about the Thousand-Year Reign of Christ.
31. When Satan will finally be Destroyed.
32. There is coming a New Heaven and a New Earth.
33. The Kingdom of Christ will be Forever.

SOURCES

1. *The Holy Bible*, King James Version, Cambridge University Press, NY.
2. *Publisher's Weekly*, January 9, 1995.
3. *Publisher's Weekly*, October 13, 1997.
4. *The Oxford Illustrated Encyclopedia of Peoples and Cultures*, ed. Hoggart, Oxford University Press, Oxford/NY, 1992.
5. *New York*, November 6, 1995.
6. *An Original Man: The Life and Times of Elijah Muhammad*, Clegg III, St. Martin's Press, NY, 1997.
7. *Newsweek*, October 30, 1995.
8. *The Black Muslims in America*, Lincoln, William B. Eerdmans Publishing Company, Grand Rapids, MI, & Africa World Press, Inc., Trenton, NJ, 1994.
9. *Malcolm X: As They Knew Him*, Gallen, Carroll & Graf Publishers, Inc., NY, 1992.
10. *The Sufis*, Shah, The Octagon Press, London, 1977.
11. *Captain Sir Richard Francis Burton*, Rice, Charles Scribner's Sons, NY, 1990.
12. *The Way of the Sufi*, Shah, The Octagon Press, London, 1980.
13. *The World Book Encyclopedia*, World Book, Inc., Chicago, 1994 and 1997 editions.
14. *Dictionary of Mysticism and the Esoteric Traditions*, Drury, ABC-CLIO, Inc., Santa Barbara, CA, 1992.
15. *A Dictionary of Comparative Religion*, ed. Brandon, Charles Scribner's Sons, NY, 1970.
16. *Man, Myth and Magic*, ed. Cavendish, Marshall Cavendish Corporation, NY, 1995.
17. *The Encyclopedia of Religion*, ed. Eliade, Macmillan Publishing Company, NY, 1987.
18. *The Two Babylons*, Hislop, Loizeaux Brothers, Neptune, NJ, 1959.
19. *World Religions*, Bowker, DK Publishing, Inc., NY, 1997.
20. *Encyclopedia of Gods*, Jordan, Facts on File, Inc., NY, 1993.
21. *The Muslim Almanac*, ed. Nanji, Gale Research Inc., Detroit, 1996.

22. *The Meaning of The Holy Qur'ãn*, Abdullah Yusuf 'Ali, Amana Corporation, Brentwood, MD, 1993.
23. *Nelson's Illustrated Encyclopedia of Bible Facts*, ed. Packer/ Tenney/White, Jr.,Thomas Nelson Publishers, Nashville/ Atlanta, 1995.
24. *The Mythic Image*, Campbell, Princeton University Press, NJ, 1974.
25. *The Encyclopedia Americana*, Grolier Inc., Danbury, Conn., 1991, 1995, and 1996 editions.
26. *New Catholic Encyclopedia*, McGraw-Hill Book Company, NY, 1967.
27. *The World's Religions*, Clarke, Reader's Digest Association, Inc., Pleasantville, NY, 1993.
28. *Webster's New World Dictionary of the American Language*, ed. Guralnik, Simon & Schuster, NY, 1980.
29. *A Dictionary of World Mythology*, Cotterell, G.P. Putnam's Sons, NY, 1979.
30. *Encyclopaedia of Buddhism*, ed. Malalasekera, published by the government of Ceylon, 1971.
31. *The American Heritage Dictionary*, Based on the New Second College Edition, Dell Publishing Co., Inc., NY, 1983.
32. *The New York Times Magazine*, May 5, 1996.
33. *The New York Times*, November 3, 1997.
34. *The Arizona Republic*, Thursday, March 27, 1997.
35. *Time*, October 13, 1997.
36. *People Weekly*, December 8, 1997.
37. *Tales from the Land of the Sufis*, Bayat/Jamnia, Shambhala Publications, Inc., Boston, MA, 1994.
38. *The Koran With Parallel Arabic Text*, transl. by N. J. Dawood, Penguin Books, London/NY, 1995.
39. *God Has Ninety-Nine Names*, Miller, Simon & Schuster, NY, 1996.
40. *The Rise of Islam*, Child, Peter Bedrick Books, NY, 1993.
41. *The New Encyclopaedia Britannica*, Micropaedia, Encyclopaedia Britannica, Inc., Chicago, 1997.
42. *Encyclopaedia of Freemasonry and Its Kindred Sciences*, Mackey, 33°, The Masonic History Company, Chicago/NY/London, 1921.

43. *Young's Analytical Concordance to the Bible*, Young, William B. Eerdmans Publishing Company, Grand Rapids, MI, 1970.
44. *Origins of Astrology*, Lindsay, Barnes & Noble, Inc., 1971.
45. *The Decline and Fall of the Roman Empire*, Vol. I, Gibbon, Encyclopaedia Britannica, Inc., Chicago, 1952.
46. *Strong's Exhaustive Concordance of the Bible*, Strong, Abingdon Press, 1890.
47. *The Encyclopedia Americana*, International Edition, Grolier Inc., Danbury, Conn., 1991.
48. *World Religions From Ancient History to the Present*, ed. Parrinder, Facts on File Publications, NY, 1971.
49. *Beware It's Coming-The Antichrist 666*, Sutton, WFG, Inc., TX, 1980.
50. *Mythology of All Races*, ed. MacCulloch, Cooper Square Publishers, Inc., 1964.
51. *The Dictionary of Classical Mythology*, Grimal, translated by A.R. Maxwell-Hyslop, Basil Blackwell Ltd., Oxford/NY, 1986.
52. *Dictionary of Symbols*, Liungman, ABC-CLIO, Inc., Santa Barbara, CA, 1991.
53. *The Oxford English Dictionary*, Oxford University Press, Oxford, 1933.
54. *The Concise Encyclopedia of Islam*, Glassé, Harper San Francisco, NY, 1989.
55. *Larousse Encyclopedia of Archaeology*, ed. Charles-Picard, Larousse and Co., Inc., NY, 1972.
56. *The Cambridge Illustrated History of Archaeology*, ed. Bahn, Cambridge University Press, NY, 1996.
57. *The Holy Koran*, translated by Ali, Ahmadiyyah Anjuman Isha'at Islam, Lahore, Inc., U.S.A., Columbus, OH, 1991.
58. *Insect Attack*, Lampton, The Millbrook Press, Brookfield, CT, 1992.
59. *Insects of The World*, Wootton, Facts on File, Inc., NY, 1984.
60. *Grasshoppers and Mantids of The World*, Preston-Mafham, Facts on File, Inc., NY, 1990.
61. *Billboard*, February 24, 1996.
62. *The Prophecies of Daniel and The Revelation*, Smith, Southern Publishing Association, Nashville, TN, 1944.

63. *National Geographic Magazine*, September 1980.
64. *Ayatollah Khomeini*, Gordon, Chelsea House Publishers, NY, 1987.
65. *The Ottomans*, Wheatcroft, Penguin Group, NY/London, 1993.
66. *The Great Controversy*, White, Pacific Press Pub. Assoc., 1939.
67. *Time*, November 24, 1997.
68. *The Masonic Report*, McQuaig/Shaw, published by C.F. McQuaig.
69. *The Extraordinary Life & Influence of Helena Blavatsky, Founder of the Modern Theosophical Movement*, Cranston, G.P. Putnam's Sons, NY, 1993.
70. *The Encyclopaedia Judaica*, Keter Publishing House Jerusalem Ltd., 1972.
71. *Kabbalah*, Scholem, Keter Publishing House Jerusalem Ltd., Jerusalem, 1978.
72. *Jewish Perspectives on Christianity*, ed. Rothschild, The Crossroad Publishing Company, NY, 1990.
73. *Reborn in the West-The Reincarnation Masters*, Mackenzie, Marlowe & Company, NY, 1995.
74. *The Path to Enlightenment*, ed. Mullin, Snow Lion Publications, Inc., NY, 1995.
75. *Newsweek*, November 28, 1994.
76. *What's On In Las Vegas*, November 18/December 1, 1997.
77. *A Dictionary of Non-Christian Religions*, Parrinder, The Westminster Press, Philadelphia, 1971.
78. *An Illustrated Encyclopaedia of Traditional Symbols*, J. C. Cooper, Thames and Hudson, Ltd., London, 1978.
79. *U.S. News & World Report*, March 23, 1998.
80. *Burton: Snow Upon the Desert*, McLynn, John Murray Publishers, Ltd., London, 1990.
81. *The Occult Illustrated Dictionary*, Day/Kay/Ward, Oxford University Press, London/NY, 1976.
82. *The New Age Encyclopedia*, Melton, Gale Research Inc., Detroit, MI, 1990.
83. *Harper's Encyclopedia of Mystical & Paranormal Experience*, Guiley, Harper San Francisco, NY, 1991.
84. *Hollywood and the Supernatural*, Steiger/Steiger, St. Martin's Press, NY, 1990.

85. *Mormonism – Shadow or Reality?*, Tanner/Tanner, Utah Lighthouse Ministry, Salt Lake City, UT, 1987.
86. *The Book of Mormon*, translated by Joseph Smith, published by The Church of Jesus Christ of Latter-day Saints, Salt Lake City, UT, USA, 1981.
87. *Abingdon Dictionary of Living Religions*, ed. Crim/Bullard/Shinn, Abingdon, Nashville, TN, 1981.
88. *Mormonism's Temple of Doom*, Schnoebelen, Triple J. Publishers, Idaho Falls, ID, 1987.
89. *The Encyclopaedia Britannica*, Macropaedia, Encyclopaedia Britannica, William Benton, Pub., 1983.
90. *The Encyclopaedia Britannica*, Encyclopaedia Britannica, Inc., 1973.
91. *Harper's Encyclopedia of United States History*, Harper & Brothers Publishing, NY, 1905.
92. *New Age Magazine*, April 1986, The Supreme Council 33°, Ancient & Accepted Scottish Rite of Freemasonry, Southern Jurisdiction, USA.
93. *Mackey's Revised Encyclopedia of Freemasonry*, Mackey, 33°, Macoy Publishing and Masonic Supply Co. Inc., 1946.
94. *The Religion of Ancient Egypt and Babylonia*, Sayce, T & T Clark, 1902.
95. *Newsweek*, October 20, 1997.
96. *The Joy of Sects*, Occhiogrosso, Doubleday, NY, 1994.
97. *Morals and Dogma of the Ancient and Accepted Scottish Rite of Freemasonry*, Pike, The Supreme Council of the 33° for the Southern Jurisdiction of the U.S.A., 1871.
98. *Free the Masons Ministries Newsletter*, March 1992, P. O. Box 1077, Issaquah, WA, 98027.
99. *The Facts on File Dictionary of Religions*, ed. Hinnells, Facts on File, Inc., NY, 1984.
100. *Essence*, November 1995.
101. *Life*, March 1993.
102. *The Los Angeles Times*, January 1, 1998.
103. *Utne Reader*, March/April 1994.
104. *National Geographic Magazine*, July 1972.
105. *The Mystical Year*, Time-Life Books, Alexandria, VA.

106. *Rosicrucian Questions and Answers with Complete History,* Lewis, Rosicrucian Press.
107. *The Illustrated Encyclopedia of Active New Religions, Sects, and Cults*, Beit-Hallahmi, The Rosen Publishing Group, Inc., NY, 1993.
108. *The Book of Enlightened Masters*, Rawlinson, Open Court, Chicago, 1997.
109. *Encyclopedia of Associations: International Organizations*, ed. Eldridge, Gale Research Inc., Detroit, MI, 1993.
110. *People Weekly*, May 11, 1998.
111. *The New York Times*, March 1, 1998.
112. *Dictionary of Symbolism*, Biedermann, Facts on File, NY, 1992.
113. *The Interpreter's Bible*, ed. Buttrick/Bowie/Scherer, Abingdon Press, NY/Nashville, 1956.
114. *Revelation: Its Grand Climax at Hand!*, Watchtower Bible and Tract Society of New York, Inc., International Bible Students Association, Brooklyn, NY, 1988.
115. *A Biographical Dictionary of Film*, Thomson, Alfred A. Knopt, NY, 1995.
116. *65 Years of the Oscar*, Osborne, Abbeville Press Publishers, NY, 1994.
117. *A New Standard Bible Dictionary*, ed. Jacobus, Funk & Wagnalls Co., NY, 1936.
118. *The Age of Fable*, Bulfinch, The Heritage Press, NY, 1942.
119. *The Encyclopedia of World Biography*, McGraw-Hill, NY, 1973.
120. *Congressional Record – House,* 10770, November 24, 1947.
121. *National Review*, October 27, 1989.
122. *Encyclopedia of the American Left*, Buhle/Buhle/Georgakas, Garland Publishing, Inc., NY/London, 1990.
123. *The New Age Movement and The Illuminati 666*, Sutton, The Institute of Religious Knowledge, TN, 1983.
124. *The Rolling Stones Chronicle: The First Thirty Years*, Bonanno, Henry Holt & Co., NY, 1990.
125. *And The Beat Goes On*, Boeckman, Robert B. Luce, Inc., Washington, 1972.
126. *Mysteries of the Unknown: Mystic Places*, Time-Life Books, Alexandria, VA.

127. *Dictionary of Pagan Religions*, Wedeck & Baskin, Philosophical Library, Inc., NY, 1971.
128. *Encyclopedic Handbook of Cults in America*, Melton, Garland Publishing Inc., NY/London, 1986.
129. *Man, Myth & Magic*, ed. Cavendish, Marshall Cavendish Limited, NY/London, 1983 & 1985 editions.
130. *Encyclopedia of the Unexplained*, Cavendish, McGraw-Hill Book Co., NY, 1974.
131. *Dictionary of Mysticism and The Occult*, Drury, Harper & Row Publishers, San Francisco, 1985.
132. *USA Today*, June 12–14, 1998.
133. *The Legacy of John Lennon*, Noebel, Thomas Nelson Publishers, Nashville, TN, 1982.
134. *The Encyclopedia of Parapsychology and Psychical Research*, Berger, Paragon House, NY, 1991.
135. *The Rolling Stone Illustrated History of Rock & Roll*, ed. DeCurtis/Henke, Random House, Inc., NY, 1992.
136. *The Penguin Encyclopedia of Popular Music*, ed. Clarke, Penguin Group, 1989.
137. *If I Can Dream: Elvis' Own Story*, Geller, Avon Books, NY, 1989.
138. *The Marshall Cavendish Illustrated History of Popular Music*, Cavendish, Marshall Cavendish, NY, 1989.
139. *The New Rolling Stone Encyclopedia of Rock & Roll*, ed. Romanowski/George-Warren, Rolling Stone Press, 1995.
140. *Imagine: John Lennon*, Solt/Egan, MacMillian Pub. Co., NY, 1988.
141. *The Beatles*, Stokes, Rolling Stone Press, 1980.
142. *The Lives of John Lennon*, Goldman, Bantam Books, NY/Toronto/London, 1988.
143. *The Harmony Illustrated Encyclopedia of Rock*, ed. Clifford, Harmony Books, 1992.
144. *Circus, America's Rock Magazine*, February 28, 1994.
145. *Cyclopedia of World Authors*, Magill, Salem Press, 1958.
146. *The Marxist Minstrels: A Handbook on Communist Subversion of Music*, Noebel, American Christian College Press, Tulsa, OK, 1974.

147. *USA Today*, October 1, 1996.
148. *The New Age Dictionary*, Jack, Japan Publications, Inc., NY, 1990.
149. *Time*, February 24, 1997.
150. *Computer Gaming World*, December 1996.
151. *The Ultimate Beatles Encyclopedia*, Harry, Hyperion, NY, 1992.
152. *Encyclopedia of Mormonism*, ed. Ludlow, Macmillan Publishing Company, NY, 1992.
153. *The International Encyclopedia of Secret Societies & Fraternal Orders*, Axelrod, Facts on File, Inc., NY, 1997.
154. *L.D.S. Reference Encyclopedia*, Brooks, Bookcraft, Inc., Salt Lake City, UT, 1960.
155. *The American Heritage Dictionary of the English Language*, New College Edition, ed. Morris, Houghton Mifflin Company, Boston, 1976.
156. *The Rockefeller's: An American Dynasty*, Collier/Horowitz, New American Library, NY, 1976.
157. *People Weekly*, May 23, 1988.
158. *Time*, May 16, 1988.
159. *Dialogue: A Journal of Mormon Thought*, Volume 27, Fall/Winter 1994, Dialogue Foundation, Salt Lake City, UT.
160. *The God Makers*, Decker/Hunt, Harvest House Publishers, Eugene, OR, 1984.
161. *The Spiritualists*, Brandon, Alfred A. Knopf, NY, 1983.
162. *Time*, August 24, 1998.
163. *Newsweek*, August 24, 1998.
164. *Mormon Doctrine*, McConkie, Bookcraft, Salt Lake City, UT, 1966.
165. *Who Really Wrote the Book of Mormon?*, Cowdrey/Davis/Scales, Vision House Publishers, Santa Ana, CA, 1977.
166. *No Man Knows My History*, Brodie, Alfred A. Knopf, NY, 1957.
167. *History of the Church*, Smith, Deseret Book Co., Salt Lake City, UT, 1965.
168. *Mormonism and Masonry*, Goodwin, P.G.M., Published by the Grand Lodge F. & A.M. of Utah, 1938.
169. *The Council of Fifty and Its Members 1844–1945*, Quinn, Brigham Young University Studies, Vol. 20, Winter 1980.
170. *Dialogue: A Journal of Mormon Thought*, Summer 1986, Dialogue Foundation, Salt Lake City, UT.

171. *Evidences and Reconciliations*, 3 Volumes in 1, Widtsoe, Bookcraft, Inc., Salt Lake City, UT, 1960.
172. *Journal of Discourses*, Vol. 13, Young, Horace S. Eldredge, 42 Islington, London, 1871.
173. *The St. Clair Banner*, September 17, 1844.
174. *The Sword of Laban as a Symbol of Divine Authority and Kingship*, Holbrook, Brigham Young University, March 24, 1992.
175. *Council of Fifty in History and Theology: An Inquiry into the Role of the Government of God in the Last Days*, Esplin, Spring 1971, Brigham Young University.
176. *Joseph Smith and World Government*, Andrus, Deseret Book Co., Salt Lake City, UT, 1963.
177. *The Complete Writings of Thomas Paine*, ed. Foner, The Citadel Press, NY, 1945.
178. *The Wayne Sentinel*, September 26, 1828.
179. *The Historical Record*, Vol. VI, Jenson, May 1887.
180. *Old Mormon Palmyra and New England*, Holzapfel/Cottle, Fieldbrook Productions, Inc., CA, 1991.
181. *Articles on the Authorship of the Book of Mormon*, copied from *The American Journal of Psychology*, Prince/Schroeder.
182. *The Septuagint with Apocrypha: Greek and English*, Brenton, Zondervan Publishing House, Grand Rapids, MI, 1980.
183. *Coil's Masonic Encyclopedia*, Coil, 33°, Macoy Publishing and Masonic Supply Company, NY, 1961.
184. *Mormonism and Masonry*, McGavin, Steven & Wallis, Inc. Publishers, Salt Lake City, UT, 1947.
185. *Confessions of John D. Lee*, reprint 1880 edition, Lee, Modern Microfilm Co., Salt Lake City, UT.
186. *A Book of Mormons*, Van Wagoner/Walker, Signature Books, Salt Lake City, UT, 1982.
187. *The City of the Saints*, Burton, Alfred A. Knopf, NY, 1963.
188. *A New Encyclopaedia of Freemasonry* , Waite, P.M., P.Z., Wings Books, NY, 1970.

CHAPTER I

THE MYSTICAL TEACHINGS OF THE NATION OF ISLAM (BLACK MUSLIMS)

"The Revelation of Jesus Christ, which God gave unto him, to shew unto his servants things which must shortly come to pass; and he sent and signified it by his angel unto his servant John:

"Who bare record of the word of God, and of the testimony of Jesus Christ, and of all things that he saw.

"Blessed is he that readeth, and they that **hear** the words of this prophecy, and **keep** those things which are written therein: for the time is at hand." Revelation 1:1–3.

CHAPTER I

This volume is based in the prophecies found in the book of Revelation which are prophesying against the hidden teachings of **MYSTICISM** and the world religions who have been promoting its secret doctrines. We shall trace the origins of mysticism and its development in lands found on both sides of the Atlantic. On the documented pages of this volume, we shall study the origins of Hinduism, Islam, Sufism, Zoroastrianism, Buddhism, Mormonism, Kabbalism, and the New Age "Hippie Countercultural" Movement and how they all have their own version or plan to sweep everybody into a "**MYSTICAL**" and "**COMMUNAL**" **WORLD GOVERNMENT**. Not only will this volume expose the hidden teachings of these above religions, but we will also expose how certain celebrities from Hollywood and the Music Industry have helped mysticism (spiritualism) experience a revival and how they made the New Age and New World Order schemes acceptable among multitudes today.

This volume will also focus on the various **revolutions** against Bible-believing Christians in the world today which are, as I write, being perpetrated by the various agencies and disciples of the New Age and the New World Order, the Papacy and their revivals, and the Muslims. In Revelation, Chapters 17 and 18, it warns of a short-lived "**universal bond of union**" of all religious bodies who do not make the Holy Scriptures and its Author their supreme rule of life and the basis for their faith in God. This attempt to unite the world today under a one-world religion and a one-world government (although it sometimes comes to us with a Christian label) is not being led by the **Spirit of Christ**, but "**is that spirit of antichrist**, whereof ye have heard that it should come; and even now already is it in the world." 1 John 4:3. Apostate Christians from both the Catholic and the Protestant Churches are today joining hands with pagan idolaters who worship the **forces of nature as gods** instead of nature's God, the Creator of heaven and earth. Those who are ignorant of the warnings found in the book of Revelation about modern Babylon are attempting today to re-establish nothing less than just another Tower of Babel. This great spiritual apostasy from Him, who has created both heaven and the earth, will lead the inhabitants who join Satan's mystical union, not into world peace as proposed, but into folly and world anarchy. It shall be shown that Jesus has been misrepresented and His Gospel has been mingled with pagan doctrines by both Roman Catholics and Protestants on both sides of the Atlantic. However, we will also see what one must do "to escape all these things that shall come to pass, and to stand before the Son of man." Luke 21:36.

In this volume, we shall have an in-depth study of the prophecies and their historical content about the **THREE WOES** which would come upon those who mingled mysticism and its philosophies with the worship of God. About 514 years before it began, the God of Abraham, Isaac, and Jacob told the apostle John in A.D. 95–96 that the **FIRST** and **SECOND WOES** would first come upon the apostate Jews and Roman and Byzantine Christians who lived between A.D. 610–1840 in the Old World. After we study in this volume what mysticism actually is and just who God used to punish **Old World** citizens for practicing it, then we will look at the prophecies of the coming judgments upon the people of the modern world for doing the same things. However, before these final woes fall upon the inhabitants of both the Old and New World, God is sending out a message to flee the coming destruction of Babylon the Great, which is symbolizing the whole apostate world.

The prophecy about the three woes is found in Revelation 8:13, and it reads as follows: "And I beheld, and heard an angel flying through the midst of heaven, saying with a loud voice, **WOE, WOE, WOE,** to the inhabiters of the earth by reason of the other voices of the trumpet of the three angels, which are yet to sound." The prophecies about these **THREE WOES** actually begins in Revelation, Chapter Nine, where the "**first woe**" was delivered by the **Arabian Saracens (A.D. 610–1258)** and the "**second woe**" started with the rise of the **Ottoman Empire in the year A.D. 1299. WE ARE STILL**

LIVING IN THE TIME OF THE SECOND WOE. The second woe will continue until the seventh angel sounds his trumpet. However, reader, when the "**third woe**" is pronounced by the **seventh angel, Christ's plan of salvation will have already closed.** In Revelation 11:14–19, we read:

"**THE SECOND WOE IS PAST; AND, BEHOLD, THE THIRD WOE COMETH QUICKLY.** And the **seventh angel** sounded; and there were great voices in heaven, saying, **The kingdoms of this world are become the kingdoms of our Lord, and of his Christ; and he shall reign for ever and ever.**

"And the four and twenty elders, which sat before God on their seats, fell upon their faces, and worshipped God, Saying, We give thee thanks, O Lord God Almighty, which art, and wast, and art to come; because thou hast taken to thee thy great power, and hast reigned.

"**And the nations were angry**, and thy wrath is come, and the time of the dead, that they should be judged, and that thou shouldest give reward unto thy servants the prophets, and to the saints, and them that fear thy name, small and great; and shouldest destroy them which destroy the earth.

"And the temple of God was opened in heaven, and there was seen in his temple the ark of his testament: and there were lightnings, and voices, and thunderings, and an earthquake, and great hail."

As we shall surely see, "**mysticism a.k.a. spiritualism**" is coming today in the name of Hinduism, Buddhism, Zoroastrianism, Confucianism, Judaism, Catholicism, Protestantism, Islam, Freemasonry, Sufism, Illuminism, the Kabbalah, Mormonism, Satanism, Hollywood, the Music Industry, the New Age Movement, the New World Order, **and especially in the name of the United Nations**, just to name a few. They all are demanding a communal government to be set up.

***Publisher's Weekly*, January 9, 1995,** on page 33 had an announcement to the bookstores throughout the United States **to clear some shelf space for Sufism, which is rapidly growing in popular appeal**. This lengthy article by Bob Summer states that during the 70's and 80's spiritual seekers outside of mainstream Christianity and Judaism focused their energy and quest for exotic practices towards Buddhism, especially Zen and Vedanta, but now there is an increasingly widespread attraction to Sufism in America. Summer quotes an editor-publisher of a book publishing company for Sufi books who called **Sufism the "third wave," and that it is "the enlightened tradition of Islamic mysticism."**

Additionally, on page 48 of *Publisher's Weekly*, October 13, 1997, Rahel Musleah wrote a lengthy article appealing to bookstores and their readers to seek **Jewish mysticism** by accessing the mysteries of the **Kabbalah**. Musleah stated that **Jewish mysticism** has come out of the closet and it fits in with the resurgence of interest in Buddhism, **New Age spirituality**, and various contemplative practices. He says the Kabbalah has also developed a practical or magical side that includes the use of amulets, charms, rituals, and combinations of letters and numbers. **Celebrities like Roseanne and Kirk Douglas, who have embraced the Kabbalah, are doing what they can to entice their fans to do the same.**

It is not just Roseanne and Kirk Douglas who have attracted multitudes (who are ignorant of the Hebrew-Jewish prophets' warnings against mysticism) to the Kabbalah, but Shirley MacLaine, Elizabeth Taylor, Barbra Streisand, and Madonna have all come out of the closet and are now publicly urging their fans to access the mysteries of **mysticism**. While Roseanne, Kirk Douglas, Elizabeth Taylor, Barbra Streisand, and Madonna are busy promoting Jewish mysticism, John Travolta, Kirstie Alley, and Patricia Presley have been busy promoting Scientology, a religious system based on the teachings of the late science-fiction writer, L. Ron Hubbard (1911–86). Travolta's Church of Scientology is centered around a type of psychotherapy called Dianetics. **Scientology is nothing less than a blend of Hinduism, Buddhism, and pseudo-Christianity (Gnosticism) which, like all practices of mysticism, is based in the doctrine of an immortal soul.** Scientologists call these immortal souls "Thetans" who supposedly progress towards enlightenment by rebirth and reincarnation.[1]

We will look more into Hollywood's and the Music Industry's efforts to promote mystical knowledge throughout this volume. We will show with documented pages how **mysticism, especially Sufism, is**

[1]***The Oxford Illustrated Encyclopedia of Peoples and Cultures*, Vol. 7, ed. Hoggart, 1992, p. 276.**

causing Black Christian pastors to worry about how many Black young people have crossed over the gulf that separates occultism from Christianity to embrace Islam. Mysticism, since the Tower of Babel, has been used to both integrate or separate human beings, and some of its most sought-after gurus have been from the entertainment field. In this chapter, we will be investigating into the Black Separatist movements of the early 20th century, the founding of the Nation of Islam, and Louis Farrakhan, the former calypso singer, and what he is involved with as we continue.

While the reader will recognize what mysticism and its historical origin actually are, at the same time we will also look at how the ancient, Hebrew prophets in the Old Testament and Jesus and His apostles in the New Testament warned of the dangerous consequences one will pay for practicing these sciences of the occult, which the news media and the gods and goddesses of Hollywood and the Music Industry openly promote. We will look at how the **news media is the vehicle which has carried ancient mystical knowledge throughout the U.S.** and how Shirley MacLaine, Barbra Streisand, John Travolta, Richard Gere, Harrison Ford, Muhammad, Michael Jackson, Gautama Buddha, Louis Farrakhan, Cat Stevens, the Dalai Lama, John Paul II, H. P. Blavatsky, Sir Richard Burton, Elvis Presley, Orson Wells, H.G. Wells, the Beatles, Mahatma Gandhi, Marilyn Manson, Paramahansa Yogananda, Maharishi Mahesh Yogi, Benjamin Franklin, Hitler, Simon Magus, St. Francis of Assisi, Attila the Hun, Zoroaster, Madonna, Jezebel, Joseph Smith, John D. Rockefeller, Jr., St. Dominic, Muhammad Ali, John Denver, Tonya Jackson, Mary Baker Eddy, Dag Hammarskjöld, Dennis Weaver, Genghis Khan, Clint Eastwood, Khomeini, Karl Marx, George Bernard Shaw, George Orwell, Hazrat Khan, Vilayat Inayat Khan, David Carradine,Willie Nelson, Princess Diana, Jalal ud-din Rumi, Bruce Lee, Carl G. Jung, Jeanne Dixon, Eleanor Roosevelt, Lindsay Wagner, Baalam, Plato, Rudolph Steiner, Annie Besant, George Lucas, Roseanne, Idries Shah, Nimrod, Walt Disney, Charles Manson, Aleister Crowley, Roger Bacon, Haile Selassie, Adam Weishaupt, Tina Turner, Jean Houston, Joan Quigley, Nancy Reagan, Bob Marley, Carlos Santana, Wallace Fard, Deepak Chopra, Rolling Thunder, Tom Laughlin, Sylvester Stallone, Timothy Leary, John and Yoko Lennon, Meher Baba,

Nostradamus, Brad Pitt, Steven Seagal, the Beastie Boys, Dionne Warwick, Alec Guinness, Baba Ram Dass, Marcus Garvey, Goldie Hawn, Lance Burton, David Copperfield, Betty Ford, Laurie Brady, Carroll Righter, Steven Spielberg, Steven King, Carlos Castaneda, the Who, Dick Gregory, Edgar Cayce, Elizabeth Clare Prophet, Joyce Jillson, Kush, José Argüelles, Anton LaVey, Elizabeth Taylor, Merv Griffin, Crosby, Stills, and Nash, AC/DC, Alice Cooper, and the Rolling Stones are just a few names who have promoted either Sufic, Hindu, Buddhist, Jewish, Christian, or Native American mysticism or Satanism. This is not a gossip columnist writing, but these above names have openly in the past or have presently stated that they have been advocates of mysticism, mythology, or occultism.

Since the time of Moses, some of the above names have founded world religions, religious centers, or have written books, songs, or made movies promoting mysticism. Devotees of mysticism seek to be brought into a spiritual union with their favorite deity or gods, saints, ancestors, or even UFOs in hopes of being empowered by them so that they may communicate supernatural knowledge to them or be possessed by them. Devotees of mysticism do this so they, too, can perform extraordinary physical feats and miracles, escape from the cycle of birth, death, and rebirth (karma and reincarnation), or become awakened to Self-Realization beliefs.

Perhaps my reader is a Hindu or a Buddhist, a Taoist or a Muslim, a Catholic or a Protestant, a Jew or a Mormon, or a Freemason. The astonishing documented facts in this book, which reveal how **the Dragon has deceived the whole human race through the use of mysticism, have not been written by a bigoted mind, but with a sincere desire that the whole human family will become awakened to these facts and not only put away their hostilities against one another, but all deceptions from mysticism as well!**

It has been Satan's chief work to divide the human race into different religions and hate factions in an effort to divide and conquer us. This invisible Foe has been most successful in his effort to annihilate the human race by using religion. More people have died in the name of religion than for any other reason. **However, it has been foretold in the book of Revelation that Satan will attempt to unite all religions and all governments in these last**

days against the God of Abraham and His Christ by using the power of mysticism and force. Those who do not join with this union shall suffer much persecution. In Revelation 13:16, 17, it is prophesied that mysticism (Babylon the Great) through its various religious and political channels will cause those who reject its claims to be cut off from the societies of the world. Those who make the Bible the basis for their faith will not be able to buy or sell very soon.

"And he causeth all, both small and great, rich and poor, free and bond, to receive a mark in their right hand, or in their foreheads: And that no man might buy or sell, save he that had the mark, or the name of the beast, or the number of his name." Revelation 13:16, 17.

As we have seen on the news today, we have hate factions from the different races who are bent on destroying each other. During my lectures, I personally have been confronted by White Skinheads, Black Skinheads, and Brown Skinheads. The mystic Louis Farrakhan, the Black Muslim Supremacist, can be quoted as saying **that the entire White race was the accidental creation of a mad, Black scientist named Yakub**.[2] The lengthy article in the *New York* magazine went on to point out that Farrakhan's Black Supremacist ideas stem from Farrakhan's involvement with the **Nation of Islam, which traces itself back to Freemasonry**.

According to *The World Book Encyclopedia*, there is a Black Masonic organization which was set up by Afro-Americans and is called "**Prince Hall Freemasonry**."[3] They are devoted to the same ideals as other Masons, and they have their lodges scattered throughout the United States. However, they soon became recruiting depots for Islamic mysticism around the years before the Great Depression and when the Marcus Garvey and Noble Drew Ali Black Separatist movements were in their heyday. The Black Supremacist and Separatist movement of the Nation of Islam emerged out of these three movements.

It should be noted here that both the order of Freemasonry and the religion of Islam did not recognize the Nation of Islam as their own. Black Muslims are, in their own right, the same as White

[2]***New York*, November 6, 1995, p. 24.**

[3]***World Book Encyclopedia*, Vol. 13, 1997, p. 267.**

Separatist groups, like the Aryan Nation or the KKK. Both Black and White Separatist groups claim to be the superior race, while the Mexican nationalist's prejudice stems from Mexico's loss of land in the American Spanish War. Today, American cities are facing problems from White Nationalists, Black Nationalists, and Spanish-American, racial, separatist organizations spreading their hate propaganda at those who are not of their persuasion. **THE SEGREGATED STREET GANGS, WHICH HAVE MADE THE CITIES INTO WAR ZONES, ARE EVEN WORSE.** Nonetheless, the Holy Scriptures warn:

"If ye fulfil the royal law according to the scripture, Thou shalt love thy neighbour as thyself, ye do well: But if ye have respect to persons, ye commit sin, and are convinced of the law as transgressors." James 2:8, 9.

However, these dangerous racial groups continue and are threatening to cause America to fall from within. Americans can no longer ignore this very serious problem and think it will just pass away. **For decades now, conspirators from communist-run organizations, as well as these racial orders, have worked to divide Americans into different hate factions.** We shall see this is true espeially in Chapters Eight and Nine of this volume. Jesus warned, "Every kingdom divided against itself is brought to desolation; and every city or house divided against itself shall not stand." Matthew 12:25.

The news media makes big money off crime and social unrest and have made heros out of the worst criminal-minded people who have ever lived. This produces copycats among the ignorant and the immature. *The Jerry Springer Show* thrives on showing sexual perversion, occultism, racial conflicts, and violence which often takes place during his programs. The more the fists swing, the more hair is pulled, and the more the blood flows the better the program unless, of course, it is Jerry Springer's. Hollywood is freely allowed to promote teen-age violence on the screen and also makes heros out of young murderers and gangbangers. Now, we are even witnessing small children who act out (in real life) what they see on the screen.

Farrakhan or White Supremacist leaders manufacture and stir up racial hatred while they are allowed to use the news media as their vehicle to spread their wacky ideas to the public. Amazingly, both the Black and White racially-motivated groups are claiming to be morally right and use religion to justify their actions. Farrakhan and his Nation of Islam are as dangerous to the public safety and stability of the United States as are the KKK. **The Nation of Islam mainly derived out of an offshoot of the Masonic Order which was founded by Blacks and called itself the Moorish Science Temple.** It was founded in 1913 by a Black mystic named Noble Drew Ali in Newark, New Jersey, and had established temples in Chicago, Detroit, and Harlem.[4] Like the members of the "**Mystic Shrine**" (the Shriners), these members of the Moorish Science Temple publicly wore their **red fezs**[5] as a sign of their religious order.

During the first decades of the 20th century and prior to the Great Depression, Marcus Garvey also started a "Back-to-Africa" movement among Blacks. According to the October 30, 1995, issue of *Newsweek* on page 43, Marcus Garvey was the first to start mass-urban, Black marches. He was a Black Separatist and even invited Ku Klux Klan leaders to speak at his marches, and insisted the Klansmen were "better friends of the race" than other Whites. Both the Marcus Garvey **"Back-to-Africa" movement** and Noble Drew Ali's Freemasonry-based Moorish Science Temple prepared the way for the founding of the Nation of Islam.[6]

Another Black Separatist movement which was influenced by Marcus Garvey (1887–1940) is the Rastafarian movement, whose Black Supremacist ideas are centered around the worship of the former emperor of Ethiopia, Haile Selassie I a.k.a. Ras Tafari (1892–1975), whom they deem as divine. This Jamaican cult is world famous for its reggae music, particularly that of Bob Marley (1945–81), and for the use of marijuana as an aid to receive a "mystical experience" while practicing the enchantment of meditation. The Rastafarians also try to use the Bible to show that they

[4]*An Original Man: The Life and Times of Elijah Muhammad*, Clegg III, 1997, p. 19.

[5]*New York*, November 6, 1995, p. 24.

[6]*Ibid.*, November 6, 1995, p. 24.

are the Ten Lost Tribes of Israel and express their sense of brotherhood through certain symbols and their hairstyle, known as "dreadlocks."[7]

The Marcus Garvey and Noble Drew Ali movements started developing before the worst economic crisis in the United States. The 1929 crash left multitudes in desperate financial trouble, especially among the Black ghettos of Detroit and Chicago, and, like the people of Germany at that time, the poor Black people were vulnerable for some kind of a self-proclaimed Deliverer to come and sweep them away into perdition.

Some African-American scholars, however, argue that Freemasonry is centered in the Egyptian mysteries (mysticism), and **that the White Freemasons stole their entire intellectual tradition from the Blacks**. With this idea in mind, intellectual Blacks, who are calling themselves Afrocentrists,[8] also point out how the ancient Greeks borrowed their knowledge from the Blacks as well. **Some Afrocentrists are trying to recycle pagan, Egyptian mysticism or Egyptology within Islam as a means to combat Christianity and to recruit Blacks out of the Christian churches.**

The Nation of Islam (Black Muslims) was actually founded by a mysterious foreigner and mystic named Wallace D. Fard who came to America in 1930. **This same Wallace Fard claimed that he was the incarnation of the god Allah**[9] and announced himself to the Detroit police as "the Supreme Ruler of the Universe."[10] Fard taught his disciples that **Allah was a Black god, and that the devil is the White man.**[11] He also stated that the Blacks were the original people on earth and that their race was trillions of years old and once had ruled the earth under the banner of Islam.[12] Fard claimed to have come from the Holy City of Mecca as a Savior of the Black race from the

[7] ***The Oxford Illustrated Encyclopedia of Peoples and Cultures*, ed. Hoggart, Vol. 7, p. 258.**

[8] ***New York*, November 6, 1995, pp. 24, 95.**

[9] ***The Black Muslims in America*, Lincoln, p. 68.**

[10] ***Ibid.*, Lincoln, p. 13.**

[11] ***Ibid.*, Lincoln, p. 69.**

[12] ***An Original Man: The Life and Times of Elijah Muhammad*, Clegg III, p. 20.**

Ancient Prophecies About Mysticism

It is true what some African-American scholars have stated about European Freemasonry. Freemasons did, indeed, borrow heavily from the black Egyptian mysteries which are centered around the black sun-god Osiris. Two of the most powerful, cultural influences in the religion of astrology, which developed outside of Mesopotamia, were those of the Egyptians and the Greeks. In the Egyptian version, Osiris the sun-god, who is pictured above, conquered the world by using ***MUSIC*** *and* **ELOQUENCE**. *His weapons were his musical talents and the influence he gained from playing his eloquent music. After Osiris conquered the world, he divided it into "ten kingdoms." This is also found in the myth about Poseidon in Greek mythology. Poseidon had ten sons of whom Atlas was the eldest. In the myth, the god Poseidon gave Atlantis to his ten sons who divided Atlantis into "ten kingdoms." As pointed out in Volume Three,* The Real Truth about UFO's and The New World Order Connection, *the book of Revelation foretold that the seven-headed Dragon with his "ten horns" would attempt to unite the whole world both religiously and politically, dividing it into "ten divisions." (See Daniel 2:41–43 and Revelation 17:12–14.) This fulfillment of Bible prophecy, which is unveiling itself right before our very eyes, can be seen today in the New Age and New World Order schemes. The Club of Rome, who are the geographical planners of the New World Order, back in 1974 planned that the world in the next millennium would be divided into "ten zones." New Agers believe that the UFOs, which have been sighted in the heavens, are the ancient gods that visited ancient Atlantis and helped the Atlanteans develop a Utopian or Golden Age. New Agers believe that these ancient astronauts (UFOs) are going to land on this planet and usher in another Golden Age of Atlantis with a socialist government, dividing it into ten divisions as ancient Atlantis. Above, the black god Osiris is shown with his bull horns and his ankh. The Israelites were fooled into worshipping him at Mt. Sinai when they made a golden calf which symbolized Osiris. Today, his symbol, the ankh, is often worn by those of the rock culture who make their heros of the entertainment field into Osiris's and Isis's, his goddess and consort.*

blue-eyed devils. Fard spread his doctrines of Black supremacy and White hatred like fire among ghetto Blacks, and within three years he developed an organization so effective that he was able to withdraw almost entirely from active leadership. He had set up a temple, a University of Islam, a Muslim Girls Training Class, and a military unit called "**the Fruit of Islam**" in which Black men would be trained for the use of firearms against police. Fard had chosen ministers to serve under him, and one of his first was a Black Freemason named Elijah Poole, who was originally from Georgia. His name was changed to **Elijah Muhammad, and he became Fard's most trusted lieutenant**. After making Elijah Muhammad his chief minister of the Nation of Islam, **Fard a.k.a. God (Allah) disappeared in 1934**.[13]

Real Islam teaches that Allah is God, and Muhammad I was his Messenger. However, the **black Muslims were taught that Wallace D. Fard was God (Allah) and, amazingly, that Elijah Poole (Muhammad) was his Messenger**.[14] In spite of it all, Fard, who was not a Black man but had straight hair and was fair-skinned,[15] disappeared as mysteriously as he came, leaving Elijah Muhammad in control of the whole Nation of Islam.

Later, the mystery of the incarnation of Allah in the person of Wallace D. Fard began to unfold itself. A police and FBI background check revealed that this same impostor was born in New Zealand or Portland, Oregon, on February 25, 1891, to either Hawaiian or British and Polynesian parents and had lived outside the U.S. He used several different aliases like Fred Dodd or Wallace Ford, and this so-called god Allah abandoned his family of a wife and son before making his way to America. He turned up in Los Angeles during World War I and opened a cafe. In November 1918, he was arrested for assault with a deadly weapon and managed to be released; but on January 20, 1926, Fard was arrested again for violating the California Prohibition Law and, a month later, was again jailed for selling narcotics in his cafe. He was sentenced to a prison term of six months to six years at San Quentin. Following his release in 1929, he left for

[13]*The Black Muslims in America*, Lincoln, pp. 11–15.

[14]*Ibid.*, Lincoln, p. 16.

[15]*An Original Man: The Life and Times of Elijah Muhammad*, Clegg III, p. 21.

Chicago where he mingled with the Garveyites and Noble Drew Ali's Moorish Science Temple members as he made his way to Detroit.[16] Police and FBI mug shots of Wallace Fard a.k.a. Wallace Ford are displayed in Claude Andrew Clegg III's book, *An Original Man: The Life and Times of Elijah Muhammad*, between pages 110 and 111.

Nevertheless, Fard's Nation of Islam continued and, after a struggle, Elijah Poole (Muhammad) became its chief minister and wholeheartedly promoted Fard's kinky, macabre, and false religion for some 40 years until he died in 1975. According to *U.S. News & World Report,* prisons have become an active recruiting ground for Muslim missionaries.[17] In 1947, the Nation of Islam recruited a man who was still in prison for a list of criminal charges[18] and who would become the Nation of Islam's number-one spokesperson and recruiter of Farrakhan and Cassius Clay (Muhammad Ali). His name is **Malcolm X a.k.a. Malcolm Little**.

After his release from prison in 1952, Malcolm X became the Honorable Elijah Muhammad's most trusted lieutenant as Muhammad was to Fard. However, after spreading White hatred and death to the White devils for over a decade, in 1962 and 1963 Malcolm started to see the folly in following Elijah Muhammad and began a campaign against him. Malcolm's loyalty to Muhammad began to weaken when he found out that the **Honorable Elijah Muhammad hadn't been so honorable**.

After Elijah Muhammad's television interview with Mike Wallace and Louis Lomax on a New York television program on July 10, 1959, where he stated that all Black members of Islam are God, Allah is supreme, the devil is the White man, and the Whites are a doomed race,[19] Malcolm X continued to say and do things that would excite the news media to put him under their spotlight. This, of course, would excite the Nation of Islam's counterpart, the infamous KKK.

[16]*An Original Man: The Life and Times of Elijah Muhammad*, Clegg III, pp. 19–21.

[17]*U.S. News & World Report*, March 23, 1998, p. 38.

[18]*Malcolm X: As They Knew Him*, Gallen, p. 14.

[19]*The Black Muslims in America*, Lincoln, p. 69.

They, too, would say and do things to get the news media's spotlight to turn and shine on them. However, it was in 1962 that Malcolm's faith in the Nation of Islam's Black reform movement started to weaken and some of its secret sins began to be revealed. Its Honorable Elijah Muhammad was exposed in 1962 as an adulterer and had six illegitimate children while leading the members of the Nation of Islam's moral reforms. **It was Malcolm X who publicly exposed Elijah Muhammad which caused members of the Chicago Mosque No. Two to leave.** However, Malcolm continued to promote Elijah Muhammad's hate propaganda against Whites and Black Supremacist ideas, but made the biggest blunder of his career as a Black propagandist when President Kennedy was assassinated on November 22, 1963. Malcolm X made fun of Kennedy's death, which he was warned by his boss to be quiet about. This episode caused the media spotlight that was centered on him to cease. Instead, the media spotlight turned and began to focus on Muhammad Ali, who Malcolm recruited into the Nation of Islam in the early part of 1964. In March of 1964, Malcolm announced his break with Elijah Muhammad and the Nation of Islam and began to form his own Black reform movement. In that same month of March, Malcolm told *Ebony* magazine that Black Muslim leaders would try to kill him because of some of the things he knew.

On April 20, 1964, Malcolm went to Mecca to visit the Muslim shrine and was astonished to see how many blue eyes were Muslims and began to change his mind about promoting Black supremacy and death to the Whites.[20] However, his propaganda about White injustice continued, and **Malcolm developed a Black reform movement called Organization of Afro-American Unity which was committed to bringing civil rights among Black Americans instead of focusing on racial hatred and bigotry**. When Malcolm departed from the Nation of Islam and denounced its beliefs, he was looked upon by his former brethren in the Nation of Islam as being used by the Devil to divide Black people. He in turn called Elijah Muhammad a "hypocrite" and actually made war on the Black Muslim community **by stating that he "had lost**

[20]***Malcolm X: As They Knew Him*, Gallen, p. 20.**

his mind" and was foolish enough to have embraced the "blood-bath" teachings of Elijah Muhammad.[21] On February 21, 1965, Malcolm X was assassinated by a Black male later identified as Talmadge Hayer a.k.a. Thomas Hagan. On February 22, 1965, Elijah Muhammad denied that neither he or the Nation of Islam had anything to do with the slaying of Malcolm X.[22]

After Muhammad Ali was used as a recruiting tool for the Nation of Islam, which was for a short time, Malcolm X had another recruit, Louis Farrakhan, who stepped in to fill the media limelight with a continuation of Elijah Muhammad's White hate propaganda that Malcolm stopped preaching at the cost of his life. Now, **Farrakhan has emerged as the leader of this bizarre movement** after the Nation of Islam split in 1977, which was after Elijah Muhammad went to his grave to await his reward.

In 1985, Libya's leader Kaddafi (Qaddafi) lent Farrakhan $5 million, interest-free, to finance POWER, a Black economic development project; and, at a **POWER** rally in New York, Farrakhan again showed his continued bigotry by calling the city of New York the "capital of the Jews."[23]

After his father's death, the son of Elijah Muhammad (Warith Deen Muhammad) also denounced the racial bigotry, doctrines, and worldly lifestyles of his father and his staff; and, because of it, he feared for his life.[24] In an exposé for *The Chicago Defender*, **Warith accused the Nation of Islam of being "ruthless and frantic" and not beyond killing opponents.**[25] Since this statement, Warith has merged 250,000 members of the Nation of Islam into Sunni Islam, leaving 20,000 who chose to go with Farrakhan.[26] In January of 1995, Qubilah Shabazz, who is

[21]*An Original Man: The Life and Times of Elijah Muhammad*, Clegg III, p. 232.

[22]*Malcolm X: As They Knew Him*, Gallen, pp. 23–24.

[23]*Newsweek*, October 30, 1995, p. 35.

[24]*An Original Man: The Life and Times of Elijah Muhammad*, Clegg III, pp. 222–223.

[25]*Ibid.*, Clegg III, pp. 223–224.

[26]*New York*, November 6, 1995, p. 95.

the daughter of Malcolm X, was arrested for plotting to murder Farrakhan in revenge for what she thought was his role in her father's death.[27]

However, Farrakhan continued to teach the Fard-Elijah Muhammad Black Supremacist doctrines while, at the same time, he preached that the Whites (Freemasons) stole their intellectual wisdom from the Black Egyptians. This statement, however, is not as luney as Farrakhan projects himself. **It is true that the ancient Greek mystics, like Plato, did borrow their mystical knowledge from not only the Black Egyptians, but also from the Black Cushites who originated from the Hindu Cush area in India during the post-Flood Era and migrated into the Land of Shinar (Mesopotamia). The most learned Muslim Sufi teachers boast that all mystical knowledge originated with the Black race.**

Idries Shah is one of the most-read Sufi authors in the West. Shah points out in his book, *The Sufis*, that **Captain Sir Richard Burton**, the famous British secret agent of the 19th century who also was a socialist, diplomat, explorer, linguist, translator, scientist, occultist, and author, made a startling statement when he revealed that **"Sufism was the Eastern parent of Freemasonry."**[28]

This well-known author was a real James Bond of the last century. However, he wore a **red fez**, as well, for Sir Richard Burton himself belonged to the secret combination of political and religious Islam. **Burton was a White Sufi master**[29] **who was determined to spread Sufism throughout the world. It was this same British secret agent and Master Sufi, Sir Richard Burton, who came to the United States in 1860 to visit Brigham Young in Utah. After the murder of Joseph Smith in 1844**, Young became the successor of the founder of Mormonism. Joseph Smith, Brigham Young, and their church leaders under them **were all Freemasons** at Nauvoo, Illinois, before Joseph Smith and his brother were murdered by an angry mob at a Carthage jail there. **Sir Richard Burton**, who was a **secret agent** for the British government and also a **Sufi master**, was sent to Utah to

[27]***Newsweek*, October 30, 1995, p. 35.**

[28]***The Sufis*, Shah, p. 182.**

[29]***Captain Sir Richard Francis Burton*, Rice, p. 152.**

investigate this new religious phenomenon of the 19th century called Mormonism. The Sufi master was intrigued with this **communal living** and Christian religion which practiced the Muslim doctrine of polygamy and religious syncretism and also because of their stand and position outside the pale of the United States proper.[30] While Mark Twain rejected the Book of Mormon with sarcasm and ridicule, the Sufi master of Islamic mysticism from England saw it as a valid religious testament and had appreciated the genius and inspiration of its author. After meeting with Brigham Young, Sir Richard Burton afterwards compared Brigham Young with the head of the Assassins and called him "the Old Man of the Mountain," and praised Brigham Young's fight with the sword of the Lord and his few hundred guerrillas who were against the mighty power of the United States.[31]

We will begin to study Joseph Smith's connection with Freemasonry and his secret combination to overthrow the United States government and the world by using Freemasonry shortly.

Today, it is Idries Shah who is hailed among occult intellectuals as one of Sufism's most prolific writers and teachers. **Shah publicly acknowledges that the Masons, indeed, borrowed their ideas from Sufism, which is Islamic mysticism a.k.a. Sufi Illuminism.** Like Jewish mysticism, Islamic Illuminism has also come out of the closet. Like Farrakhan, Shah points out how white mystics borrowed their mystical knowledge (which is, by the way, forbidden in the Bible) from the **Black mystics**. The Sufi teacher and author points out on pages 187 and 188 that the word "**black**" is also another word for **Egypt** and is said to have derived from the color of the soil. He goes on to state that the Black Art is thought by many to mean nothing more than "the Egyptian Art" or "the Art of Understanding."

Amazingly, Shah also points out that a Shriner must be a Mason, and their "Masonic ritual" is based upon a myth connected with the Muslim Temple in Mecca, which is the holiest shrine (the Kaaba) to the people of Islam. The Kaaba has a sacred, black stone for black is a symbol for wisdom. The shrine at Mecca, which is covered by a huge, black velvet canopy, is a cubical

[30]***Burton: Snow Upon the Desert*, McLynn, p. 172.**

[31]***Captain Sir Richard Francis Burton*, Rice, pp. 335-336.**

temple and was rebuilt in A.D. 608 when Muhammad was 35 years old. The Kaaba was built with 31 courses of stone and wood (along with the addition of Earth and Sky) numbering to "33," which is the origin of the 33° Shriner Mason.[32]

What really astonished me about the secret and historical information that **Idries Shah was exposing to his readers in his books was how the secret society of the Illuminati, like Freemasonry, had developed out of Sufism (Islamic mysticism) as well**. The term **Illuminism** was used in Sufic, occult literature to describe its hidden, secret teachings centuries before the founding of the notorious **Illuminati of Bavaria on May 1, 1776**. The reknown Sufi teacher and author points to another famous English occultist, scientist, philosopher, and Sufi student who lived before Sir Richard Burton entered history as a Sufi master, and shows how **Sufi Illuminism had influenced the founding of the secret society of the Rosicrucians**. This famous Englishman was **Roger Bacon**. Ironically enough, Bacon was a double agent, for he was also a member of the Roman Catholic Order of the Franciscans. Bacon secretly had been a Rosicrucian himself and is still praised today as a hero for the cause of the occult among its various secret combinations. **Roger Bacon, who died in A.D. 1292, said that Illuminism was identical with the inner teachings of all the ancient Greeks, Persians, and Egyptians, and that this Illuminism (Enlightenment) was known to Noah and Abraham, the Chaldeans, Zoroaster, Hermes, and to such pagan Greek philosophers as Pythagoras, Anaxagoras, and Socrates.** Shah says in his book, *The Way of the Sufi*, that the Franciscan and Rosicrucian Roger Bacon died wearing Arab dress.[33] In Volume Two of this series of volumes about the ancient prophecies on Time of the End (Daniel 12:4) events on pages 91–94, I pointed out that the Rosicrucians claim to be initiates of the Illuminati.

More than 50 of the names which were signed on the Declaration of Independence were either Freemasons or Rosicrucians and were much concerned with the esoteric sciences such as astrology,

[32]*The Sufis*, Shah, p. 186.

[33]*The Way of the Sufi*, Shah, p. 38.

numerology, tarot, Kabbalah, etc. Benjamin Franklin and Thomas Jefferson were not only high-ranking Freemasons, but were also expert astrologers.[34]

However, Shah spent painstaking time compiling historical records of how both occult and Christian mystics owe their knowledge about mysticism to the schools of the Muslim Sufis. Sufi Illuminism, according to Shah in *The Sufis* on page 243, was taught to the hero of magicians and alchemists, Albertus Magnus, who was another double agent and a Roman Catholic cleric that went on to inspire another Roman Catholic mystic named Thomas Aquinas. As we continue, the reader shall be absolutely astonished to see how mysticism has made its way from the descendants of Noah to those who sit in high places of the earth in our present day. Satan's greatest triumphs, however, have been accomplished by working through secret combinations (secret societies) of mysticism.

According to Shah, John of the Cross, Pope Silvester II, Laurence, Archbishop of Malfi, the Franciscan Order of the Roman Catholic Church, the Rosicrucians, Freemasonry, the Illuminati of England, France, and Germany, and the earlier Illuminati of Spain called the Alumbrados, which was founded by Ignatius Loyola some 200 years before the infamous Bavarian Illuminati – all were a development of Sufi Islam.[35] Amazingly, endorsements from ***New York Times Book Review*, *Library Journal*, *Psychology Today*, *The Listener*, *Encounter*, *The American Scholar*, *The Observer*, and *Theoria to Theory*** are on the jacket of Shah's above book.

According to Shah, even the Rosicrucians claim that their founder brought his knowledge of mysticism from Arabia, Fez, and Egypt and can be traced to the **Qadiri Sufi Order**.[36] Keeping in mind that Freemasonry and other occult, secret societies have sprung from Sufism (Islamic mysticism), let's now come back and study some more historical background behind the Nation of Islam.

When Elijah Muhammad was in his heyday, the former Freemason was telling other Black Freemasons to join the Nation of

[34]***The Occult Illustrated Dictionary*, Day/Kay/Ward, 1976, p. 56.**

[35]***The Sufis*, Shah, pp. 243–245.**

[36]***The Way of the Sufi*, Shah, p. 41.**

Islam because they had developed a much more advanced level of knowledge which was even more intriguing than the coveted 33 degrees of Masonic secret knowledge.[37] This lure, coupled with the belief that the White Freemasons stole their mystical knowledge from the Blacks and that Allah was a Black god (not a blue-eyed blonde), was just the bait Elijah Muhammad needed to lure even Black Christians away from the Son of God who taketh away the sins of the world. While the Nation of Islam also used the slavery issue forced upon Blacks by some Whites in the early stages of American history, the Black Separatists failed to mention, however, how Black Egyptians had made slaves out of God's chosen people, the Hebrews, for over 400 years.

Another important fact that Black Christian people, who are thinking about crossing over to join the Nation of Islam, need to ponder is how the God of Abraham, Isaac, and Jacob buried the ancient Egyptian army along with their Pharoah in the Red Sea for practicing the same religion that the Freemasons, Mormons, and Muslims teach and promote today. **Afro-American Christians** should also be made aware that Jesus was neither from the White or the Black race, as White or Black Separatists claim and use as a tool to gain converts. Jesus was a Hebrew Jew (a Semitic) from the tribe of Judah as the Holy Scriptures plainly reveal in Matthew, Chapter One.

White separatists who hate both the Blacks and the Jews also need to realize in their KKK or Aryan Nation meetings that the first Christians were Hebrew Jews and every prophet and apostle of Christ were from the Hebrew race, save Luke who was a Greek physician. Furthermore, the Holy Scriptures plainly state that the coming Kingdom of God after the millennium will have as its citizens people from **EVERY** kindred, tongue, and nation who made Christ Jesus their Redeemer, Saviour, and Lord. (See Revelation 14:6; 15:2–4.)

However, history is, indeed, repeating itself. **The ancient, hidden prime minister of the Egyptian religion and government was Satan himself.** He was represented visibly by the person of his Pharoah who used the mystical powers of his magicians to counterfeit the power

[37]***An Original Man: The Life and Times of Elijah Muhammad*, Clegg III, pp. 72–73.**

of God demonstrated through Moses. Again, this same god of this world is marshalling his divisions of mysticism a.k.a. Illuminism in our day for another supernatural conflict between him and the Great I Am. The events which occurred between Moses and his God and the Pharoah and his god are another shadow of things to come in our day. This time, however, the people of Spiritualism (worldwide) who reject the God of Abraham, Isaac, and Jacob shall be buried under fire and brimstone, instead of the Red Sea, if they do not repent.

The book of Revelation reveals that Satan has deceived **all nations** by the trickery and philosophies of mysticism. Satan, who is symbolized as the Dragon, will unite the adherents of mysticism against **all races** who are presently loyal to the Biblical Jesus. The terrible conflict that the ancient Hebrews went through in the days of Moses (which is recorded in Scripture) is, indeed, a prophetic view of what shall be repeated again in our day. In Psalm 105:23, we read: "Israel also came into Egypt; and Jacob **sojourned in the land of Ham**." The **Egyptians are descendants of Ham and Cush** who brought their mystical knowledge to Africa, starting from northern India. The **Cushites (Hindus)** first migrated to Mesopotamia and **Nimrod, the son of Cush,** built the first city there called **Babel**, which the **Greeks** called **Babylon**.

Today, Babylon is a symbol for the **whole world** and the God of Abraham, Isaac, and Jacob is telling His people from all races to separate themselves from its practices and its sins. As the God of Moses sent plagues on the stubborn Pharoah and his people in ancient Egypt, so will this same God today bring plagues upon people in this modern world who remain stubborn and will not repent of their sorceries, fornications, thievery, murders, etc., etc. In this volume, we will study how these prophetic and monumental events are, indeed, materializing right before our very eyes!

We have briefly studied how Islamic mysticism (Sufism) and its daughter, the mystical Order of Freemasonry, had spawned a Black Supremacist group calling themselves the Nation of Islam. Another secret society which Freemasonry spawned was the Order of the Elus Cohens, which was founded by a French mystic named Jacques Martinez de Pasqually (1727–74), and the well-known mystical/esoteric author Louis-Claude de Saint-Martin (1743–1803) was a member. There are three well-known divisions of the Illuminati that developed out of Sufi Illuminism via the Order of Freemasonry and the secret society of the Rosicrucians. They were the secret society of the Illuminati founded by Louis Claude de Saint-Martin; then shortly afterwards, the Order of the Illuminati of Bavaria which was founded May 1, 1776, in Ingolstadt, Germany; and also the Rosicrucians themselves whose real name is the Illuminati.

Another secret society that was not so well-known and which also derived out of Sufi Illuminism was none other than the German Thule Society of which **Adolf Hitler was a member** and was groomed for his mission in life. All this is documented in Volume Three, *The Real Truth About UFO's and the New World Order Connection.*

Mormon scholars acknowledge that Louis-Claude de Saint-Martin had migrated from France to the French republic of Haiti in the Caribbean in 1774. Saint-Martin became one of the most learned teachers of Illuminism and his esoteric influence (**Martinism**) had spread to America before the founding of both the Illuminati of Bavaria and the United States.[38] **Today, Martinism is considered one of the highest levels of occult knowledge.** As pointed out in Volume Two, *The New Age Movement and The Illuminati 666*, there were 15 orders of the Illuminati set up in America before July 4, 1776! Sufism, Islamic mysticism, and Freemasonry owe their crafts, however, to the hidden, secret doctrines of the prophet Zoroaster (600 B.C.) who is believed to be the father of the ancient Kabbalah, which is Jewish mysticism. Zoroaster blended Judaism with ancient, Oriental witchcraft. We shall study about Zoroaster and his enormous contribution to all modern mystical knowledge shortly.

As the mystic prophet Zoroaster blended Spiritualism with Judaism (which developed the Kabbalah), so did the mystic prophet Joseph Smith blend the teachings of the Kabbalah and Egyptian mysticism with the Christian faith. This next chapter will prove that the Mormon hierarchy are Spiritualists who have now developed into one of the most secretive, mystical orders of Spiritualism a.k.a. Illuminism in the world. We will see how the Mormons have their own version of a one-world government and how they are determined to unite the world under their secret priesthood known as the Order of Melchizedek.

[38]***Dialogue: A Journal of Mormon Thought*, Vol. 27, Fall/Winter 1994, p. 10.**

CHAPTER II

THE MYSTICAL TEACHINGS OF JOSEPH SMITH AND THE PARALLELS BETWEEN THE ILLUMINATI PLAN AND MORMONISM

"For the Lord spake thus to me with a strong hand, and instructed me that I should not walk in the way of this people, saying, Say ye not, A confederacy, to all them to whom this people shall say, A confederacy; neither fear ye their fear, nor be afraid. Sanctify the Lord of hosts himself; and let him be your fear, and let him be your dread.

"And when they shall say unto you, Seek unto them that have familiar spirits, and unto wizards that peep, and that mutter: should not a people seek unto their God? for the living to the dead?

"To the law and to the testimony: if they speak not according to this word, it is because there is no light in them."

Isaiah 8:11–13, 19, 20.

CHAPTER II

As already established, mysticism's foundation was laid in the belief of an immortal soul, and all of mysticism's doctrines are built upon this belief. As pointed out in Volume Three of this series of books which are based on the prophecies of the Time of the End events found in the books of Daniel and Revelation, the New Age bestselling author, **Brad Steiger**, has published more than 100 books on mysticism. He is considered one of the New Ager's most respected authorities on the occult and the supernatural. Steiger presented compelling evidence about Hollywood's fixation with the occult and the supernatural. Steiger's books not only promote Spiritualism, but also biographies about the movie careers of Valentino, Judy Garland, and also Jim Thorpe. Steiger's book about Valentino was made into a movie. According to *The New Age Encyclopedia*, it says Brad Steiger's book, *Revelation: The Divine Fire* (1973), "became a virtual encyclopedia of New Age mysticism as it was emerging in the early 1970's."[1] According to the same *New Age Encyclopedia*, **it was Steiger who helped make popular among New Agers the idea that human beings had previous lives before they were born and had originally come from the stars**. Elvis Presley, as we shall see, adopted this belief. Another New Age author who made popular this notion that humans had previous lives and originally came from the stars is the "**Beverly Hills shaman,**" **Lynn Andrews**. Andrews has been compared to Carlos Casteneda and his supposed mystical experiences he had with a Yaqui sorcerer named Don Juan. However, Lynn Andrews is a New Age feminist and writes about her shamanistic journeys while under the influence

[1]***The New Age Encyclopedia*, Melton, p. 291.**

of a Cree Native American Indian and sorceress (medicine woman) named Whistling Elk.[2] Another Native American Indian who was brought under the Big Screen spotlight was a sorcerer (medicine man) named **Rolling Thunder**. Rolling Thunder, a Shoshone, served as a consultant on the 1971 film, ***Billy Jack***. This film helped popularize not only karate, but also New Age/Native American shamanism. Tom Laughlin, who played the half-breed, shaman, and ex-Green Beret Billy Jack, said that he would not have undertaken the ceremony with the seven-foot rattlesnakes in the movie if Rolling Thunder had not been present.[3] Like the Steigers, the Mormons believe in the doctrine of a premortal existence as well. According to the *Encyclopedia of Mormonism,* Vol. 1, p. 234, the Latter-day Saints believe that a Father and a Mother in heaven created spirit children to inhabit this planet and other worlds. Not only did Joseph Smith (1805–1844) teach that mankind has an eternal spirit that is engaged in a process of becoming a god, but he claimed that he had been visited by numerous extraterrestrial beings (spirits), two of whom (according to *Mormon Doctrine*, page 396) were the Father and the Son, when he was just 14½ years old in 1820. Later, Smith claimed another extraterrestrial visitor named Moroni, who supposedly was an advanced human being, visited him on September 21, 1823, and told him of some hidden gold plates. What really caught my attention about Smith was that he later became a Freemason.

Joseph Smith stated the following: "**I was with the Masonic Lodge and rose to the sublime degree**."[4] A record that **Smith** was also **initiated** as a **Master Mason in 1842** is also found in the book, *Mormonism and Masonry*, written by S.H. Goodwin, Past Grand Master of the Grand Lodge F. and A.M. of Utah.[5] Smith became a Master Mason about **15 years after** he supposedly found his famous gold plates (which he translated) in 1827.[6] **Smith and Sidney Rigdon** both were quickly communicated the **Entered Apprentice, Fellow Craft, and Master Mason initiation** by the **Deputy Grand Master**

[2]***Harper's Encyclopedia of Mystical & Paranormal Experience*, Guiley, pp. 18, 19.**

[3]***Hollywood and the Supernatural*, Steiger/Steiger, photograph section.**

[4]***History of the Church*, Vol. 4, p. 552.**

[5]***Mormonism and Masonry*, Goodwin, P.G.M., pp. 28, 29.**

[6]***The Book of Mormon*, third page of Joseph Smith's testimony.**

who was in league with Smith and Rigdon. Sidney Rigdon had been Smith's mentor and guru since1827.

Not only was Joseph Smith a Freemason, but so was his brother Hyrum, Heber C. Kimball, George Miller, Newel K. Whitney, **Judge James Adams**, and Brigham Young, who are all considered to be saints of the Mormon Church.[7] Although the Book of Mormon's pages are filled with warnings which condemn secret societies or secret combinations as being the inventions of Satan, Smith's and Rigdon's attitude towards secret societies had apparently changed or they had all along been camouflaged to hide their own secret revolutionary plans to establish a new religious order and a **one-world government**, which we shall soon discover in the coming documented pages.

According to *No Man Knows My History* written by Fawn Brodie on pages 280 and 329, it was **Judge James Adams**, the Deputy Grand Master of the Illinois Masonic Order who eventually became a Mormon, who actually arranged for Smith and his brethren to establish a Masonic Lodge in Nauvoo. This was done before Smith had become a Mason himself! Smith's big room over his store officially became the Nauvoo Masonic Lodge, and John C. Bennett became the Lodge's first secretary. The same night Smith became a first-degree Mason, the next night he rose to the sublime degree, and then shortly afterwards he advanced upwards to become a Master Mason. Smith and the Deputy Grand Master of Illinois officially established the Masonic Lodge in Nauvoo on March 15, 1842.

It was in Nauvoo where Joseph Smith not only became a Freemason, but formed the **"Council of Fifty" (which was not only a secret society of high priests within his church but, according to Mormon scholars, the mysterious "Council of Fifty" had several non-Mormons among them as well)**.[8] Today, this hierarchical priesthood within the LDS is known as the "**Council of Seventy**." We were told this in April of 1998 when my wife and I visited the LDS' Old Tabernacle in St. George, Utah. We were given a whole tour of the Mormon Visitor Center by some high officials in the Mormon Church who were acting as our guides. There is both an old and a new Mormon Tabernacle

[7]***Dialogue: A Journal of Mormon Thought*, Fall/Winter 1994, p. 67.**

[8]***The Council of Fifty and Its Members 1844–1945*, Quinn, 1980, p. 179.**

in St. George. As we toured the Old Tabernacle in St. George with one of our Mormon guides, we could not miss seeing the "**All-Seeing Eye**" which was proudly displayed on the upper center of the tabernacle. This well-known occult sign is not only a prominent Freemason sign, but it is also an occult sign in Hinduism as well. This eye was known to the Egyptians as the "**Eye of Ra**" **or** "**Horus**," and it is used by the people of mysticism today to show that they have the power of clairvoyance of which Smith had. This same Masonic symbol, also known as the "Third Eye," may be seen on the back of the American one dollar bill. The Egyptians used the "**Eye of Horus**" as a funerary amulet for protection against evil and rebirth in the underworld, and decorated mummies, coffins, and tombs with it.[9]

In this chapter, the reader shall learn that before Smith officially founded the Mormon Church in **1830**, he and Sidney Rigdon had already contrived a revolutionary plan to unite the world into a **one-world communist government**. According to *Dialogue: A Journal of Mormon Thought,* Summer 1986, pp. 146–149, in **1832** Smith and Rigdon established the Mormons under a communistic secret society in Kirtland, Ohio, called the **United Order** with Smith as its religious dictator. **Like the pope**, Smith claimed God had ordained him to control the masses of all people both in their temporal and religious things. This belief, however, led him to be tarred and feathered in Ohio, and then later to be murdered by a mob in Carthage, Illinois.

However, Smith claimed to the Mormons to have received his revolutionary plans from other extraterrestrial visitors (spirits) who were once famous Christian men on earth, but had reached godhood. The first of these god-men was John the Baptist who supposedly conferred the Aaronic Priesthood on Smith and his associate, Oliver Cowdery, on May 15, 1829. Then, Peter, James, and John came, along with Elijah and other prophets of God, and conferred on them the Order of Melchizedek Priesthood **of which, according to *Mormon Doctrine*, pages 476, 481, everything on earth is subject to its power and authority for these priests are considered to be gods**.

Joseph Smith can be compared with the exalted office of the pope of Rome. Today, the Mormon Church (according to *Mormon Doctrine*,

[9]***Harper's Encyclopedia of Mystical & Paranormal Experience*, Guiley, p. 197**.

The above photograph was taken in August of 1998 when we again visited the Mormon Temple and Visiting Center in Salt Lake City, Utah. These statues are supposedly depicting a visit from John the Baptist amongst Joseph Smith (left) and Oliver Cowdery (right) on May 15, 1829, on the bank of the Susquahanna River in Pennsylvania. Mormons claim that John the Baptist appeared to Smith and Cowdery to confer on them the restoration of the Aaronic Priesthood. Then, Peter, James, and John later appeared to Smith to restore the higher Order of Melchizedek. The truth is that it was Sidney Rigdon who not only stole from the Freemasons the idea for the Order of Melchizedek, but also Masonry's signs, symbols, tokens, and Temple Endowment ceremony which were incorporated into Mormonism. Freemasonry's Novus Ordo Seclorum, which means New World Order for the Ages, was altered by Rigdon and Smith to fit their version of a world takeover by Mormonism. Instead of calling it a New World Order or, astrologically speaking, New Age a.k.a. Age of Aquarius, they called this mystical union the "New Dispensation."

pages 396, 482, 578) teaches that Joseph Smith and his successors hold the keys of salvation and Mormon members, like Roman Catholics, subordinate themselves under blind obedience to their priests. We should stop here and remember that because of Lucifer's self-exalting statement, "**I will be like the most High**" (Isaiah14:14), our Lord was forced into a war with Lucifer and had to cast him down out of Heaven!

Today, we are engaged in a great spiritual war. However, God's people are **never to use physical violence against** the people whom Satan is using to try to overthrow the worship of the Biblical Jesus. "For we wrestle not against flesh and blood, but against principalities, against powers, against **THE RULERS OF THE DARKNESS OF THIS WORLD, AGAINST SPIRITUAL WICKEDNESS IN HIGH PLACES**." Ephesians 6:12.

Since the time of the Renaissance, Satan has put forth superhuman efforts by working in the **high places** of this world to bring about his last effort to completely overthrow the worship of Jesus Christ. To counteract the power of the Reformation sparked by Martin Luther, Satan used Plato's plan to re-establish the Utopian theocracy supposedly developed by the ancient Atlanteans. **This theocracy of Atlantis became the main theme of the Renaissance, and the main secret society of the occult who has been promoting it in the *high places* of this world has been the Freemasons. Today, this Atlantean plan is called "Novus Ordo Seclorum." In Latin, this means "New Order of the Ages" or "New World Order!"** It is here, as well, that the reader may find the parallels between the Illuminati plan and Mormonism and also the reason for the deadly rivalry between Freemasonry and Mormonism which also developed.

Mormons admit that many of the converts to the Mormon Church are, or have been in the past, Freemasons or have belonged to other occult societies. The Mormon apostle John A. Widtsoe admitted, **"Many members of secret societies have joined the Church of Jesus Christ of Latter-day Saints."**[10] As we will see, Joseph Smith, like Plato, planned to unite the whole world into a **communal and/or theocratic society**.

In Volume Two of this series of books which are based on the prophecies of the book of Daniel and the book of Revelation, the reader

[10]*Evidences and Reconciliations*, 3 Volumes in 1, Widtsoe, p. 113.

will find a comprehensive study of Freemasonry and how they trace their crafts and legends back to the first architect after the Flood. Masonry, geometry, and astrology are central to the Lodges of Freemasonry. Learned Master Masons are taught that the origin of their crafts can, indeed, be traced back to Babel's first builder who was Nimrod and, as we saw, also Hermes (who was actually Cush, the son of Ham, who was the father of Nimrod). It can also be proven without any doubt that not only was Smith a wizard himself, but it was actually Sidney Rigdon, Smith's guru, who stole the whole myth about the famous gold plates (from which the Book of Mormon supposedly derived) and the Priesthood after the Order of Melchizedek from the Freemasons. My Mormon reader, it will be shown that it was Rigdon who founded Mormonism, not your prophet.

Another astonishing thing that I discovered about Joseph Smith was his attitude towards the non-Mormon community and how he adopted Muhammad's attitude towards non-believers. Like Muhammad, Smith told the Mormons, "Thus you will waste away the Gentiles by robbing and plundering them of their property; and in this way we will build up the kingdom of God." "**I will be to this generation a second Mohammed, whose motto in treating for peace was 'the Alcoran or the Sword.' So shall it eventually be with us –'Joseph Smith or the Sword!'**" (Quoted in *No Man Knows My History*, Brodie, pp. 215, 230, 231) What this American Muhammad instilled in his Mormon disciples is what actually came upon them, especially in Far West, Missouri, and in Nauvoo, Illinois, before they fled to the Salt Lake area.

This writer and his wife have also been taken on a tour at the Salt Lake City Mormon Temple while holding lectures about the New Age and New World Order conspiracy in that area in the early 1990s and then again in 1998. As we approached the temple, my eyes immediately recognized and focused on how the main **Mormon Temple also displays prominent Masonic signs and symbols**. There on the outside wall of the Salt Lake Temple, as on the dollar bill, you may see the Masonic **All-Seeing Eye with astrological symbols of the sun, moon, and stars, the beehive, and two right hands clasped in fellowship**.

Reader, the Mormon Temple in Salt Lake City is the denomination's ritual center; like the Muslim Shrine in Mecca, only members may enter sacred places within the temple.[11] There is, however, a Visitor

[11]***Abingdon Dictionary of Living Religions*, ed. Crim/Bullard/Shinn, p. 424.**

Center that is set aside where a movie is shown about the history of the Mormon people and some of the beliefs of Mormonism which are allowed for the Gentile eye to view are revealed.

According to William Schnoebelen, who was a former Mormon, Master Mason, and Wiccan High Priest, he says: "**The most bizarre and distinctive doctrines of the LDS Church are revealed in the temple ceremony .**"[12] When my wife and I were at the Temple Visitor Center of the Mormons in St. George, Utah, we were at first delighted with the Christ-centered beliefs which our Mormon leaders were relating to us as they showed us around their complex. However, after spending about four hours with our Mormon guides and questioning their beliefs about Jesus and who he was to them, we began to hear from their lips (towards the end of our visit) of doctrines that are found on the pages of New Age literature. Although Mormons are seemingly against the New Age and the New World Order as they told us, nevertheless, they are, indeed, wrapped up in some of their most disturbing philosophies.

We were told by our guides that God the Father has a wife who is our Mother. Immediately, I asked, "Who is our Mother?" However, we did not receive a satisfactory answer and my question was quickly switched to something else. Since the early 70s, I have studied the evolution and spread of the pagan concept of a Mother Goddess who was even worshipped by the apostate Hebrews and the Indians of North and South America. To the ancient Hebrews, this Mother Goddess was worshipped as **Ashtoreth**, the **Queen of Heaven**; and to the pagan Egyptians, she was known as **Isis**. To the pagan Greeks, she was known as **Aphrodite**; to the Romans, she was known as **Juno** or **Diana**; and to the Babylonians, this astrological Mother Goddess was the great goddess of war and sex named **Ishtar**. This Mother Goddess was Kali to the Hindu, and to the ancient Mexicans, she was **Coatlicue**.

According to the *Encyclopedia of Mormonism*, Vol. 1, p. 961, Mormons do, indeed, believe in the pagan belief of a Heavenly Mother and Father. After hearing with my own ears from the Mormons that they believe in a Mother who helped create mankind, then I began to realize why so many occultists from different secret societies have

[12]***Mormonism's Temple of Doom*, Schnoebelen, p. 9.**

joined the Mormon Church. Not only do the Mormons believe that human beings pre-existed as spirits among the planets and stars, as we saw, but they teach that Jesus and Lucifer were spirit brothers!

William (Bill) Schnoebelen, who had been a high priest of Wicca witchcraft, shows his readers with good documentation of how the pagan ceremonies of the Church of Wicca and Freemasonry are almost identical with that of the Temple Ceremony which he participated in at the Salt Lake Mormon Temple. This may sound strange to my Christian reader who has never witnessed to a witch or someone involved in Spiritualism, but, believe it or not, they do not worship the Devil in white magic witchcraft and they think that what they are practicing is from God. On pages ten and eleven of *Mormonism's Temple of Doom*, its author tells his readers that this is what he believed, as well, and that witches and Freemasons are also initiated into an Order of Melchizedek Priesthood. **Schnoebelen also goes on to tell his readers that before he became a Mormon, the head of the Druidic witches in North America told him that the highest form of witchcraft was practiced in Mormon temples.**

When William and his wife entered the Salt Lake Temple as Mormons, they already knew that they would be involved in highly occultic, religious activities. They said as soon as they entered the Salt Lake Temple, which is off limits to not only non-Mormons but also to Mormons who have not been cleared by the priesthood, they said the atmosphere was electric and they felt strange, heavy vibes.[13] After presenting their "temple recommends" (passes), the Schnoebelens were separated and escorted to two separate dressing areas to prepare for the first rite of the Mormon Temple Ceremonies. This first rite was, according to Schnoebelen, called "**the Shield**." William was told to remove all his clothes, and then his naked body was covered in a thin, white poncho/sheet which is called a "shield." **William said that nudity in a religious ceremony was not new to him, and the shield which the Mormons used was also identical to the one he had worn when going through his initiation into the witchcraft Melchizedek Priesthood. He said the only difference between the shield worn by the Mormon and that**

[13]*Mormonism's Temple of Doom*, Schnoebelen, p. 11.

of the Wiccan who were being initiated into the priesthood of Melchizedek was the color of the shield. This shield was black in witchcraft.

However, according to Schnoebelen, there is also a religious hierarchy among witches; the lower degrees of witchcraft wear a black shield during their rites while those of the higher degrees of witchcraft wear white as they advance in the various degrees of the knowledge about the occult.

The next step of their initiation into the Mormon Temple rites at Salt Lake was the "**Washing and Anointing**." After receiving "the shield," Schnoebelen said he was led into a little cubicle where his body was first washed and then anointed with olive oil. This is also done among the people of witchcraft in the belief that the anointing of all the various openings of the body is necessary to keep out evil spirits. Amazingly, Schnoebelen said that the only difference between this Mormon Temple rite and that of the people of witchcraft was that the witches anoint male to female with more intimate contact.[14] **Witches claim that they do not worship demons and what they are doing is not evil; they think that they can control evil spirits by practicing these protective rites so they can make them do their bidding.** Among the people of mysticism, the practice in Temple Ceremonies of protecting oneself from demons is known as having **talismanic influences**. This dangerous practice, however, comes under the heading of **necromancy in the Holy Scriptures**; and not only is this satanic practice forbidden in the Bible (Deuteronomy 18:11), but Schnoebelen warns us that witches have suffered terrible things and even death while trying to **communicate with or control evil spirits**. Nevertheless, witchcraft lures ignorant human beings into believing that they can conjure and control spirits and use their power without being hurt in the process.

After being washed and anointed, Schnoebelen was given his **temple garment**, which was of one piece and extended below his knees. Masonic markings of sacred significance were found on this temple garment of the Mormons and were stitched over the left and right breast, the navel area, and the knee. **This garment,**

[14]***Mormonism's Temple of Doom*, Schnoebelen, pp. 11, 12.**

he was told by the Mormon priest, would protect him from the Destroyer until he had completed his mission on earth.[15] Schnoebelen said that he was amazed to see what these Masonic signs were that were stitched on their temple garment. Schnoebelen goes on to explain that he had not only been initiated as a High Priest into Wicca witchcraft, but also into the Blue Lodge, York and Scottish rites, and all the way to the Shrine, which is as high as most Masons go in the United States; then, and only then, was he considered worthy to receive the "continental degrees" from such arcane European Masonic systems such as the **Ordo Templi Orientis**, the Rite of Memphiz and Mitzraim, **Martinism**, and Palladium Masonry. After graduating to this level in the occult, he realized the profound links between Lucifer-worship, Wicca, and Masonry.[16]

As pointed out in Volumes One, Two, and Three of this series, **Lucifer a.k.a. Satan hides the worship of himself in the religion of astrology**. He is the ancient, chief sky god of the peoples of both the ancient and modern worlds. Today, he is being worshipped by the ignorant as such on both sides of the Atlantic. However, in modern witchcraft, like Wicca, they are first taught among the lower ranks to worship a Mother Goddess and a male horned-god named **Pan**; then, as they pass through the various degrees of witchcraft, they are finally conditioned to be told that it is really Lucifer who is the god behind all gods. The ancient Israelites worshipped this heavenly Mother and Father as **Ashtaroth (Ashtoreth)** and **Baal** as seen in Judges 2:12, 13.

Both Freemasonry and Wicca witchcraft are founded in the philosophies of astrology, as well as all of their occult signs and symbols. One of Lucifer's most prominent signs of his religion of astrology is found on the temple garment of the Mormon Church and on the Temple Building itself. **It is the compass and the square!** The compass is stitched over the left breast of the Mormon temple garment and the Schnoebelens were told while they were members of Wicca that this represented their Mother Goddess. The compass is used to describe a circle in geometry;

[15]***Mormonism's Temple of Doom*, Schnoebelen, p. 12.**

[16]***Ibid.*, Schnoebelen, pp. 12, 13.**

hence, the circle is the consummate symbol of the Goddess in Wicca[17] of whom the Roman Catholics today also worship ignorantly as Mary, the Queen of Heaven. The square, which symbolizes the horned-god Pan in Wicca witchcraft, is stitched over the right breast of the Mormon temple garment. Pan is also worshipped among occultists everywhere as the god of music. **For years, early Mormons denied borrowing** their Temple endowment from Freemasonry. However, today they admit to this, but point out that Smith had access to the Kabbalah, the major source of Masonic dogma, before he became a Mason.

William Schnoebelen goes on to show in his booklet how other disturbing doctrines in the Mormon Church, such as the LDS concepts like **"eternal marriage," plural marriage (polygamy),** sacred oaths, secret signs and grips, and their evolution to godhood (become as gods) taught by Joseph Smith, were all borrowed from ancient witchcraft. Joseph Smith's connection with the black art of divination before he supposedly found the gold plates was well-known among his neighbors in New York. **Smith was known as a "Glass Looker," which is a 19th-century expression for a "Crystal Ball Gazer**," at least one year before he supposedly found the gold plates.

In the book, *Mormonism – Shadow or Reality?*, the Tanners, who are former Mormons, show that they have found documents which show that Joseph Smith was arrested for being an impostor, and for assault and battery charges in 1826 in which the Justice of the Peace Albert Neely called him a "**Glass Looker**."[18] A photocopy of a receipt that Joseph Smith paid for court charges is seen in the above book.

According to the Book of Mormon, Joseph Smith was given another name by the Lord. In Alma 37:23, we read: "And the Lord said: I will prepare unto my servant **GAZELEM**, **a stone**, which shall shine forth in darkness unto light." (Emphasis mine.) Mormonism claims that **Joseph Smith had a peepstone a.k.a. seerstone which he used to find the plates and, after finding the gold plates, he also found two other seerstones which are known among Mormons as the Urim and Thummim**.[19] Smith received his **first peepstone**

[17]***Mormonism's Temple of Doom*, Schnoebelen, p. 13.**

[18]***Mormonism – Shadow or Reality?*, Tanner/Tanner, p. 33.**

[19]***Mormon Doctrine*, McConkie, p. 819.**

while he was digging a well for a man named Clark Chase. As he and his friends were digging, they found a chocolate-colored, somewhat egg-shaped stone which Smith identified as a **seerstone** a.k.a. peepstone.

Earlier, Smith (**Gazelem**) learned the practice of divination from his father, Joseph Sr., who was a **water witch**. Joseph Jr. switched from using the witch hazel rod for divining to the peepstone, which was found in the well he was digging for Clark Chase. Reader, it was through the **spirit of divination that the Book of Mormon** was partly produced. His wife Emma and some of his close associates said that Smith would divine by putting his seerstone into a hat and, then, by placing his face down inside the hat to look at the stone, he would draw the hat close around his face to exclude the light. In the darkness, he claimed to be able to see spiritual light from the stone. A piece of something resembling parchment would appear and on that appeared the writing.

It was in **1826, before Smith publicly claimed to have found the gold plates and the Urim and Thummim in 1827**, that he was arrested for fraud for claiming to be able to divine for hidden treasure or money by using this magical stone. **Gazelem** (Smith) had earlier earned a reputation as a **diviner** and **necromancer** and people came to seek him, employing him to look for buried treasure or money.

One of the witnesses for Smith during his trial was Deacon Isaiah Stowell (Stowel), who appeared before the Justice of the Peace Albert Neely; however, he confirmed all that was said about Joseph Smith's ability to divine. He swore that the prisoner possessed all the power he claimed and declared that he could see things 50 feet below the surface of the earth, as plain as the witness could see what was on the justice's table. He described many different circumstances to confirm his words. Later, another witness was brought in by the name of Mr. Thompson, an employee of Mr. Stowell. Thompson said Smith had told Mr. Stowell that years ago a band of robbers had buried on his land a box of treasure, and they had by a sacrifice **placed a charm over it** to protect it so that it could not be obtained except by faith, accompanied by certain **talismanic influences**. Mr. Stowell went to his flock and selected a fine, vigorous lamb and **resolved to sacrifice it to the demon spirit** who guarded the coveted treasure. It was brought out during this trial that Mr. Stowell might be seen **on his knees at prayer near the pit, while Smith**, with a lantern in one hand to dispel the midnight darkness, might be seen **making a circuit around the spot and sprinkling the blood from the lamb upon the ground as a propitiation to the spirit that thwarted them**. They then proceeded to excavate the pit, but **the treasure still receded from their grasp and it was never obtained**. This account is so lengthy that this writer, because of limited space, has to condense these historical facts. It was said that these scenes occurred some four years before Smith found the golden bible or the Book of Mormon by the aid of his luminous stone. **Joseph Smith's talismanic interests were seen in** *The Chenango Union* of Norwich, New York, on May 3, 1877, as reprinted in *A New Witness For Christ in America*, Vol. 2, pp. 366–367, and may be seen in its entirety on pages 32–44 in *Mormonism – Shadow or Reality?*. When Smith and his brother were murdered by an angry mob at a Carthage, Illinois, jail, **Joseph had a Jupiter talisman,**[20] which was used for invoking **the pagan Roman god**, among his belongings.

According to *No Man Knows My History*, pages 19 and 31, the *Palmyra Reflector* of that day wrote that Smith's interest in **invoking spirits** and money-digging was excited by his **first mentor**, who was a vagabond **foretuneteller named Walters**, whose mantle fell on young Smith after he left his area. Smith went on to claim that he had numerous visits from extraterrestrial visitors from heaven as well. **He said that not only was he visited by a spirit named Moroni, but was also visited by the prophet Mormon, Elias, Elijah, Moses, John, James, Peter, John the Baptist, Jesus, God the Father, and numerous others.**[21]

After the Mormon Church was organized, Smith used this same stone in an attempt to predict the future. He said he had a revelation from God that the Mormons were to move and gather themselves in Jackson County, Missouri. **Joseph Smith said Jackson County is where the original Garden of Eden was located**, and he claimed to have found the remains of an **altar** which was originally built by **Adam**. Amazingly, Smith also claimed that **Noah built his ark near the Carolina coastline**. Joseph Smith even went as far as to claim that his powers as a seer (diviner) extended beyond the earth. However, this claim is just another fact that proves that Joseph Smith was a false prophet.

[20]***Dialogue: A Journal of Mormon Thought*, Fall/Winter 1994, p. 96.**

[21]***Encyclopedia of Mormonism*, ed. Ludlow, Vol. 2, 1992, pp. 885, 886.**

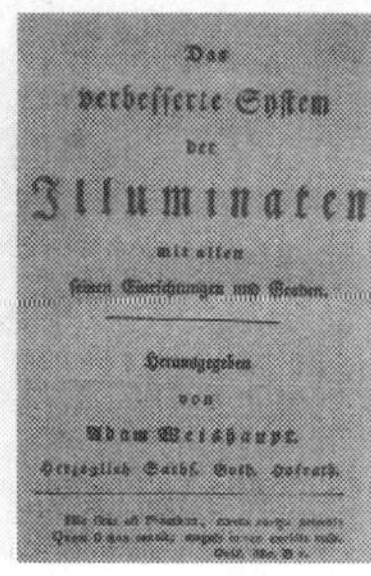
Das
verbesserte System
der
Illuminaten
mit allen
seinen Einrichtungen und Graden.

Herausgegeben
von
Adam Weishaupt.
Herzoglich Sachs. Goth. Hofrath.

As we shall see as we continue, Joseph Smith later developed into an occult revolutionary, and he and his mentor and guru, Sidney Rigdon, planned to overthrow the United States government and then the world. The above portrait is of Adam Weishaupt, the real father of all world revolutions since the French Revolution. The Weishauptian Plan to overthrow Christianity and all governments became the blueprint which early Mormonism and the various branches of Communism, Socialism, and Marxism modeled. Before Weishaupt founded the secret society of the Bavarian Illuminati on May Day, 1776, he belonged to the Order of the Quest which was a secret society of Sufism (Islamic mysticism) which can be traced back in history to a Sufi shaykh named Suhrawardi (1153-1191). Between A.D. 610-1840, Sufi Illuminism became the most dominant force in Spiritualism and Suhrawardi founded a school of Sufi Illuminism in Iran near Afghanistan out of which both the secret societies of Freemasonry and the Bavarian Order of the Illuminati have their roots. Sidney Rigdon, Joseph Smith's mentor and guru and Mormonism's real founder, and Joseph Smith became Freemasons themselves, however, at the displeasure of most Freemasons at that time. Rigdon and Smith and their Mormon followers became deadly rivals of the Masons because Mormon leaders borrowed from Freemasonry its political ambitions, its revolutionary scheme, and its Temple Endowment and symbols. Like Adam Weishaupt, Rigdon and Smith planned to use the Order of Freemasonry as a vehicle to carry out Mormonism's own plans to dominate the world. The Mormon hierarchy for over 100 years denied their involvement in Freemasonry until recent years. Early Mormons had even called polygamist Joseph Smith a second Muhammad. Smith tried to lead the Mormons into a Mormon revolution to bring about their own world dominance plans. Like Islam, the founders of Mormonism invented their own bible (Book of Mormon) in which to base their new religion, which, like Islam, is nothing less than a sophisticated blend of Spiritualism and the Judeo-Christian faith. Joseph and Hyrum, his brother, are considered martyrs among the Mormons, for they were murdered June 27, 1844, by the Carthage Grays militia, who were Masons, while they were awaiting their court appearance for treason. According to A New Encyclopaedia of Freemasonry *by Arthur Waite on page 82, the expulsion of Brigham Young and 1500 other Mormons from Freemasonry by the Grand Lodge of Illinois took place this same year.*

Ancient Prophecies About Mysticism

My Mormon reader, God warned our ancient brethren: "For these nations, which thou shalt possess, hearkened unto **observers of times (ASTROLOGERS)**, and unto **DIVINERS**: but as for thee, the Lord thy God hath not suffered thee so to do." Deuteronomy 18:14.

Again, the Lord warns in Isaiah 44:25 of what he does to diviners and what their knowledge is. "That frustrateth the tokens of the liars, and maketh **DIVINERS MAD; that turneth wise men backward, and maketh THEIR KNOWLEDGE FOOLISH**." Here is an example.

GAZELEM (Smith) claimed that he saw the inhabitants of the moon who were of a more uniform size than the inhabitants of the earth and were about six feet in height. Their dress, said Joseph Smith, was very much like the Quaker style, and he said they lived to be very old, nearly a thousand years.[22]

For many years after Joseph Smith's death in 1844, the Mormons continued to teach that the moon was inhabited. Brigham Young, the second president of the Mormon Church, made this amazing statement: "Who can tell us of the inhabitants of this little planet that shines of an evening, called the moon?...and when you inquire about the inhabitants of that sphere you find that the most learned are as ignorant in regard to them as the most ignorant of their fellows. So it is with regard to the inhabitants of the sun. Do you think it is inhabited? I rather think it is. Do you think there is any life there? No question of it; it was not made in vain."[23]

As established, Joseph Smith was a known water witch **(diviner)** before he found his peepstone and the gold plates which supposedly were **the Book of Mormon**. It has been believed that Smith had three different scribes who wrote down the words found in the original Book of Mormon while Smith, with his face down in his hat, dictated aloud what he was reading from his peepstone. However, the reader shall discover that there were **two other scribes** besides Emma Smith, Martin Harris, and Oliver Cowdery who wrote the Book of Mormon.

One of the surprising things, however, that I found out while reading the pages of *Mormon Doctrine*, an authorized Mormon book about their church beliefs , was Smith's blasphemy against God. Smith taught

[22]***Mormonism – Shadow or Reality?*, Tanner/Tanner, p. 2.**

[23]***Journal of Discourses*, Vol. 13, BrighamYoung, p. 271.**

that **God himself was once as we are** now and is an exalted man now enthroned in heaven. The Biblical doctrine, which teaches that God was God from all eternity, Smith **refuted** to his Mormon brethren. Smith said that God himself dwelt on this earth, as did Jesus Christ, and that **Mormons have got to learn how to be gods themselves and to be kings and priests to God.**[24] Smith went on to teach that all of mankind were spirits before they received mortal bodies. He is recorded as saying that these spirits, which existed before the world was created, also had different classes or ranks and some spirits were more noble and intelligent than others. Early Mormon leaders also taught that the "more noble" or choice spirits were born to be Mormons, while the Negro is considered to have been more unfaithful than any of the spirits who were given human bodies.[25]

The following is from *Mormon Doctrine* whose author is Bruce R. McConkie, who was a prominent LDS leader. It reads: "Those who were less valiant in **pre-existence** and who thereby had certain spiritual restrictions imposed upon them during mortality are known to us as the **negroes**. **Such spirits are sent to earth through the lineage of Cain, the mark put upon him for his rebellion against God and his murder of Abel being a black skin**."[26]

This same Bruce R. McConkie goes on in his *Mormon Doctrine* about the Black race. He states the following:

"Though he was a rebel and an associate of Lucifer in **pre-existence**, and though he was a liar from the beginning whose name was Perdition, Cain managed to attain the privilege of mortal birth. Under Adam's tutelage, he began in this life to serve God.... He came out in open rebellion, fought God, worshiped Lucifer, and slew Abel....

"As a result of his rebellion, Cain was cursed with a dark skin; he became the father of the Negroes, and those spirits who are not worthy to receive the priesthood are born through his lineage. He became the first mortal to be cursed as a son of perdition. As a

[24]***Mormon Doctrine*, McConkie, p. 321.**

[25]***Mormonism – Shadow or Reality*, Tanner/Tanner, p. 263.**

[26]***Mormon Doctrine*, McConkie, p. 527.**

result of his mortal birth he is assured of a tangible body of flesh and bones in eternity, a fact which will enable him to rule over Satan."[27]

This doctrine about Cain can be found among most White Supremacist (so-called Christian) organizations and is equally as absurd and foolish as Farrakhan's statement that the White people were created by a mad Black scientist. Ironically enough, there are some Black converts found among the Mormons.

As we shall see, the Mormon Church was actually founded by Sidney Rigdon via Joseph Smith in 1830 and claims to base its beliefs or creed on the Bible, the Book of Mormon, and other volumes revealed to Joseph Smith. As we saw, Mormonism is characterized by an elaborate, hierarchical organization and ritual, and there is strict control over the lives of members, numbering about **ten million**.[28] While my wife and I visited the Mormon Visitor Center in St. George, we were told that Joseph Smith, Brigham Young, and the other founding members at Nauvoo, Illinois, were indeed Freemasons, and that today they have members of their church who belong to Freemasonry. We had already known this by reading the Tanner's book, of which they were ostracized by their hierarchy for writing. We asked about Sandra Tanner and asked if she was Brigham Young's great, great granddaughter as she had said. We were told she was, but that she had been excommunicated from the church for apostasy. We were also told, as the Tanners stated, that **Mormons, indeed, believe that they were spirits before who were given mortal bodies**. After spending these two days with the Mormon officials, this writer has come to this conclusion. Although Mormons claim that their religion is based in the Bible, they owe their entire existence as a church to the teachings of Sidney Rigdon and Joseph Smith's revelations, not from the teachings of the Holy Scriptures. As a matter of fact, Joseph Smith told his early disciples to not depend on the Holy Scriptures for religious guidance. Like the Sufi master, Smith taught that the Bible was corrupted by priests who were ignorant and careless translators,[29] and that he was now receiving new

[27]*Mormon Doctrine*, McConkie, pp. 108, 109.

[28]*The Oxford Illustrated Encyclopedia of Peoples and Cultures*, ed. Hoggart, Vol. 7, p. 207.

[29]*Mormon Doctrine*, McConkie, p. 82.

revelations from God and that the fulness of the Gospel was given to the Mormons. Smith claimed that the whole world had apostatized from God; and the Lord said that the Mormons were the True Church for the last days and all others were Gentiles.

After interviewing these top officials of the Mormon hierarchy at both the Salt Lake Temple and then again later at the St. George Tabernacle and Visiting Center and Brigham Young's Winter Home, we have observed with our own eyes and ears how our Mormon brethren are, indeed, dangerously ignorant of the Holy Scriptures and its prophecies concerning the Time of the End. However, reader, it was also observed by my wife and I how genuinely nice and polite ordinary Mormons are; they do not want to hurt anyone. Nevertheless, the Mormon Church has a religion within a religion with a secret priesthood. Its most bizarre, mystical teachings and practices are (as the former Master Mason and Elder of the Mormon Church, William Schnoebelen, pointed out) found within the Mormon Temple Ceremonies, not among the mass membership. Even Mormons have to be cleared by the priesthood before they can enter their temples. Schnoebelen, being a former high priest of the Order of Melchizedek of both the Church of Wicca and the Mormon Church, **observed that less than 25% of all Mormons ever go to their temple, and less than half of them ever return**.

When we went to the St. George Mormon Visitor Center, we were told by our guides that their attitude towards the Black race and polygamy has changed, and that now the Blacks since1978 are accepted into their priesthood. We were told that those who continue to practice polygamy are offshoots of the Mormon Church. This is, however, a far cry from what the Mormon attitude was in the days of Smith and Young. Let's again look at more historical facts about early Mormonism and the terrible violence Mormons have suffered for following the teachings of their prophet.

The name *Mormon* itself supposedly derived from an ancient prophet of God whose name was Mormon; hence, this is the origin of the name of the Book of Mormon. This belief in the Church of the Latter-day Saints evolved from Smith's claim of being instructed by an angel named Moroni who related that the prophet Mormon wrote his scriptures on gold plates. According to Mormon beliefs, this angel Moroni also told Smith where they were located and buried.[30] This appearance of the angel, according to Mormon sources, was on the night of September 21, 1823, when **Smith was only 17 years old**. According to Smith, the angel Moroni went on to tell him that there were **gold plates** buried in the Hill Cumorah near Manchester, New York. The angel stated that the plates contained an account of the former inhabitants of this continent (America), who were originally from Jerusalem and had fled its destruction by King Nebuchadnezzar of Babylon. Four years later, on September 22, 1827, Smith supposedly found the buried plates and some time later he began to translate them. We were told by our Mormon guides in St. George that these gold plates were written in Egyptian hieroglyphics. The translation of these plates was published in 1830 under the title of the **Book of Mormon**. We asked the Mormon officials where these plates are now; and we were told that after Joseph Smith translated the plates by the use of his seerstones, he supposedly returned the gold plates to the angel. Another thing we found that has definite New Age links is the Mormon's belief in Moroni. **As pointed out, the Mormons teach they were spirits before who received a mortal body and that they are spiritually advancing to become gods.** New Agers teach that human beings who have reached Nirvana or Christ-consciousness are looked upon as **masters**, and that these so-called ascended masters have a spiritual hierarchy which New Agers call the Great White Brotherhood. Like the masters of New Age Hinduism, Moroni (according to our Mormon guides) was a real human being in the past who died about A.D. 400; however, he became an angel, and then later was sent to Joseph Smith to deliver him the fulness of the Gospel of Christ via the gold plates. Reader, please keep in mind that this rebellious teenager was a known diviner and necromancer when this story was first told by Smith.

As pointed out from the quote from John A. Widtsoe, who was a Mormon apostle, Mormons have had many converts to their church who have been members of occult, secret societies. One of them was William J. Schnoebelen and having been a witch, Catholic priest, Freemason, and a Mormon, he now (after being delivered by the power of

[30]***A Dictionary of Comparative Religion*, ed. Brandon, p. 451.**

Christ from the power of the occult) feels it to be both a moral and a spiritual obligation to warn other Mormons of what he and his wife had fallen victim to for so many years. We have not met the Schnoebelens personally; but during our years of holding evangelistic meetings, we have met both men and women like them who have given themselves over to Christ to be cleansed and forgiven by Him, whose name is Holy!

I was given a copy of William Schnoebelen's booklet entitled *Mormonism's Temple of Doom* from a family of Christians that we have become friends with in the St. George area. I was very surprised to receive it, for this very eye-opening and documented booklet covered the very subject I was writing about at that time. This booklet, *Mormonism's Temple of Doom*, has shown me even more shocking things about Mormonism that I had not the slightest knowledge of and which most Mormons are not aware of as well. Only those who have participated in the Mormon Temple Ceremony, which are few, are aware of these things which we have examined. William Schnoebelen's booklet documents some other connections between Mormonism, Magick, and Masonry as they were experienced by William Schnoebelen and his wife. On page seven of this above booklet, it states that both of the Schnoebelens investigated Mormonism and joined the Mormon Church. They became True Believers and thought they " 'had a testimony' that Joseph Smith was a True Prophet, that the Book of Mormon was scripture, and that the Mormon Church was God's True Church." In the back of *Mormonism's Temple of Doom,* the reader will see photocopies of not only Schnoebelen's documents from Masonic Lodges displaying William J. Schnoebelen's name as a Master Mason and a 32° Freemason, but also a diploma from Saint Francis Seminary showing his Master Degree of Theological Studies, three Certificates of Ordination from schools of the occult, his Certificate of Baptism, and his Elder Certificate of Ordination from the Church of Jesus Christ of Latter-day Saints. These former occultists and Mormons are now very grateful to Jesus for extending His grace to them who, unwittingly, were some of His worst enemies in the past against His cause. We will see some more eye-opening things from the *Mormonism's Temple of Doom* shortly.

Naturally, the Schnoebelens were ostracized by the Mormon secret priesthood for revealing some of their most hidden secrets, as were the late Fawn Brodie, who wrote a biography about Joseph Smith, and Jerald and Sandra Tanner, who exposed not only his connection with Freemasonry and Spiritualism, but also Smith's revolutionary plans. This writer had no idea that Smith and his associates were Freemasons or of his revolutionary plans until he read the Tanner's book, *Mormonism – Shadow or Reality?*. My wife and I interviewed Sandra Tanner, who is the great, great granddaughter of Brigham Young, while we were in Salt Lake City in July of 1998. We thanked her personally for the scholarly manner in which she and her husband, through their book, helped multitudes of Mormons understand what Smith, the Mormon American Muhammad, really founded. Today, the Mormon hierarchy believes that Masonry was, in part, responsible for the death of Joseph Smith and that the Masons continued to wage war on them in an effort to destroy their political ambitions. Freemasons and Mormons have been rivals from the time of Smith's death up until 1984.[31] This deadly rivalry, which developed between the Freemasons and the Mormons, was just one of the things which the Tanners exposed in their documented book.

After ostracizing many Mormon and non-Mormon authors of the 19th and 20th centuries for accusing Joseph Smith of borrowing their Temple Ceremony and signs and symbols from the Freemasons, the Mormon leadership has now publicly admitted to this. The Mormon hierarchy now admits that Smith was a Freemason; but that he discovered that Freemasonry had apostatized from true Freemasonry, which Smith claimed to have originated with the building of Solomon's Temple. Smith told the early Mormons that the Lord appeared to him and revealed to him the true knowledge of Masonry which had been lost and, like Christianity, Smith was called to restore both of them. Hence, the Mormons believe that they possess true Masonry within their temples and, because of their **superior knowledge** of true Masonry, the Freemasons became jealous and cut off (closed up) the Mormon Lodge at Nauvoo.[32] The Mormons have

[31]*Dialogue: A Journal of Mormon Thought*, Fall/Winter 1994, pp. 71, 72, 86.
[32] *Ibid.*, p. 71.

gone even further to claim that although the Masonic institution's origin dates back many centuries, it is a perverted priesthood stolen from the Temples of the Most High and that Freemasonry is a **counterfeit** of the true Masonry of the Latter-day Saints.[33] Please keep in mind, reader, **that Freemasonry's Eastern parent is Islam**, and it has two mainstreams: the European Lodge and the American (Blue) Lodge. Albert Pike, one of the most learned adepts of Masonry, said that the **initiate of the Blue degrees** of the American Lodge is **intentionally** misled by **false interpretations**.[34] European Masons point out that King Solomon had never been a Freemason,[35] and that they use his name (Sol-om-on) to express the names for the sun-god in Latin, Hindu, and Egyptian.[36] The truth is European Masons have blended the Judeo-Christian faith into the American Lodge to attract Christian men to their order. The claim by Smith that Freemasonry originally derived from the building of Solomon's Temple has absolutely no foundation.

Now, let's look at another claim by this American Muhammad. Smith claimed that an angel named Moroni appeared to him and told him about a book written on gold plates which contained the fulness of the Gospel. According to Smith, the angel also told him that deposited with the plates were two stones in silver bows, and the stones, which were fastened to a breastplate, constituted what is called the **Urim and Thummim**.[37] The angel went on to say the stones (Urim and Thummim) were what seers in ancient or former times had used. According to Smith, God prepared the seerstones (Urim and Thummim) for the purpose of translating the book which was written on the gold plates by a prophet named Mormon. Smith said that he was told by Moroni that he should not show the plates or the stones after he received them to anyone except those whom Smith was told to do so; if he showed them to anyone else, he would be destroyed. As the angel was speaking, Smith said he was given a vision and could clearly see the place

[33]***Dialogue: A Journal of Mormon Thought*, Fall/Winter 1994, pp. 70, 71.**

[34]***Morals and Dogma*, Pike, p. 819.**

[35]***The Masonic Report*, McQuaig/Shaw, p. 13.**

[36]***Ibid.*, McQuaig/Shaw, p. 13.**

[37]***The Book of Mormon*, first page of Joseph Smith's testimony.**

where the plates were deposited. Later, Smith went to the hill which he said was conveniently located by the village of Manchester, New York. On the west side of this hill, not far from the top and under a stone of considerable size, he found the gold plates and the seerstones in a stone box. However, according to Smith, the angel Moroni told him not to remove the plates and the seerstones until four years later (1827). In 1830 after the plates were translated by Smith, the translation was entitled the Book of Mormon. The Mormons claim eight witnesses saw and touched the gold plates from which the Book of Mormon was translated by Smith.[38]

However, the former Mormon Elder and Master Mason pointed out in his booklet, *Mormonism's Temple of Doom*, that not only were **the Temple Ceremony of the Mormon Church, its priesthood after the Order of Melchizedek, and secret signs, symbols, and grips stolen from the Freemasons by the Mormons; but they also stole the idea about these mysterious gold plates from the Freemasons as well.** It just so happens that in **the Scottish Rite of Freemasonry** men are anointed **after the Order of Melchizedek, as well,** and in the 13th, 14th, and 21st degrees of the Scottish Rite, there is **a Masonic Legend of Enoch** passed on to the initiate. **It says that Enoch was led to find gold and brass plates containing ancient records in a hillside vault.**[39]

Smith went on to claim that on May 15, 1829, another extraterrestrial visitor (spirit), John the Baptist, appeared to him and Oliver Cowdery. He said that John the Baptist spoke to Cowdery and him, and they were given the Aaronic Priesthood. The Baptist, according to Smith, said that he informed them that he acted under the direction of Peter, James, and John, who held the **keys of the Melchizedek Priesthood**, and that the Melchizedek Priesthood would also be given to them. Supposedly, Peter, James, and John then appeared to Smith and Cowdery afterwards and **also ordained them as apostles**. After this, according to the Mormons, Peter, James, and John committed to them "**the keys to the kingdom, and of the dispensation of the fulness of times**."[40]

It should be noted here that the Book of Mormon throughout its

[38]***Encyclopedia of Mormonism*, Vol. 1, ed. Ludlow, p. 215.**

[39]***Mormonism's Temple of Doom*, Schnoebelen, pp. 14, 15.**

[40]***Encyclopedia of Mormonism*, Vol. 2, ed. Ludlow, pp. 885, 886.**

I took the above photograph of the "All-Seeing Eye" of Freemasonry, which is proudly displayed in the Old Mormon Tabernacle of the St. George Visitor Center. This talismanic symbol of the occult represents the power of having clairvoyance. It is used by other systems of mysticism, especially in Hinduism and Buddhism, and is known as the Third Eye. My wife and I both saw the inverted pentagram design on some of the chairs of the tabernacle. The inverted or upside-down pentagram (five-pointed star) is used in casting spells in Wicca witchcraft, and it is a dominant sign in Satanism. It represents the goat attacking Heaven.

pages **warns against joining secret societies** and that they were inventions of the Devil. (See *The Book of Mormon,* Index, page 723.) Smith lived during the time when Freemasonry was being exposed for its part in causing the French Revolution and other problems in Europe. Newspapers of that day in New York were publishing huge articles about the **terrible deeds committed by Freemasons in Europe**. A lengthy article written about how the Freemasons overthrew papal Christianity in France can be read in the *Encyclopaedia Britannica*, Macropaedia (1983 edition), Vol. 9, pages 1154, 1155. For those who have not read Volume Two of this series which exposes the rise and evolution of the Illuminati, I will again quote a portion from this article seen in the above encyclopedia for the benefit of those who have not seen it. It reads:

"Not all the **FREEMASONS** became supporters of the **REVOLUTION AND OF THE FRENCH**, but many of them did so. The moderate and constitutional demands of the **Masonic lodges** began to be accompanied by more democratic demands, and there were in Milan, Bologna, Rome, and Naples **CELLS OF ILLUMINATI**, republican freethinkers, after the pattern recently established in Bavaria by **Adam Weishaupt**." (Emphasis mine.)

As I examined the Book of Mormon, it clearly showed that it was anti-Masonic; but what became so puzzling to me was why then did Smith later become a Master Mason? Furthermore, I saw a **definite parallel** in history between the **Platonic** ambitions of the secret society of the Illuminati founded by Adam Weishaupt on May 1,1776, in Ingolstadt, Germany, and what Smith was trying to accomplish under his secret priesthood and under his New Dispensation doctrine.

As pointed out to the reader, the secret society of the Illuminati became a **secret combination** of conspirators who used the Masonic Order to camouflage themselves and their plans and purposes. According to the *Encyclopaedia Britannica*, Volume 11, 1973 edition, p. 1096, "their founder's aim was to **REPLACE Christianity** by a **RELIGION OF REASON (DEISM)**, as later did the **revolutionaries of France** and the positivist philosopher A. Comte in the 19th century." I would like to point out again to the reader that the Illuminati is where the threat of the New Age and the New World Order movements derived of which Bible-believing Christians are facing today, and there is plenty of evidence that Mormonism is just a spin-off of the same threat. Let's look at some parallels.

Interestingly enough, the Book of Mormon in Ether, Chapter Eight, also writes of **secret combinations** (secret societies) which were formed in the days of the ancient Jaredites to overthrow its government and king. According to Mormon beliefs, the Jaredites are the descendants of the prophet Jared who lived around 2200 B.C. in Mesopotamia during the era of the Tower of Babel. According to Mormon beliefs, it was the prophet Jared and his brother who were first to lead their people from the **Tower of Babel** to the Western Hemisphere.[41] Later, to escape the destruction of Jerusalem in 600 B.C., a man named Laman (an apostate Jew) and Lemuel, Sam, and Nephi (his brothers) also brought their families to ancient America. However, **according to Mormonism, the American Indians derived from Laman and his brother Lemuel**. The Lamanites became a separate nation from the followers of Nephi, the brother of Laman, and perpetually warred against them.[42]

An ancient prophet, who is supposedly the author of this book known as Ether which is found in the Book of Mormon, tells of how Akish, an earlier Jaredite and a cruel leader of a secret society, caused the death of the prophet Jared and obtained his kingdom.[43] It was said that **Akish made his fellow conspirators take a solemn oath** and swear by the God of heaven and earth that they agreed to lose their heads if they should divulge anything that their leader had made known to them. The prophet Ether, who supposedly lived during the time of Akish and the Jaredites before they annihilated each other in wars, wrote a message to warn Gentiles (non-Mormons) that because the Jaredites had formed secret combinations among themselves, this had brought about their total destruction. **Ether warns the Gentiles in a prophecy that what had happened to the ancient Jaredites shall be repeated again.[44]**

Ether supposedly warns that what happened to these ancient peoples of America will be repeated **IN OUR DAY**. In Ether 8:24 of the Book of Mormon, it states: "When ye shall see these things

[41]*Encyclopedia of Mormonism*, Vol. 1, ed. Ludlow, p. 235.

[42]*L.D.S. Reference Encyclopedia*, Brooks, pp. 260, 261.

[43]*Ibid.*, Brooks, p. 18.

[44]*The Book of Mormon*, Ether 8:20–26.

come among you that **YE SHALL AWAKE TO A SENSE OF YOUR AWFUL SITUATION, BECAUSE OF THIS SECRET COMBINATION WHICH SHALL BE AMONG YOU**." (Emphasis mine.) According to the Mormons, the Jaredites had their final battle at the site where Smith supposedly found the gold plates.[45]

In Nauvoo, Illinois, on the banks of the Mississippi River, the Mormons built a village which quickly grew into one of the largest cities in the state of Illinois. It had its own independent military force and a strong judicial system. Joseph Smith was not only the president of the Mormon Church, but he also served as mayor, commander of the Nauvoo Legion State Militia, justice of the peace, and university chancellor. Smith overreached himself by striving to establish in Illinois a Theocratic Union to be governed under his priesthood.[46] However, Joseph Smith and his brother Hyrum were arrested and jailed in Carthage, Illinois, for ordering the *Nauvoo Expositor* newspaper press to be set on fire and for treason against the government. While waiting in jail to appear before County Court, Joseph Smith at age 38 and his brother were murdered on June 27, 1844.[47] What led to this terrible and cowardly act was this.

As established, Smith was a mystic (diviner) and very learned in the crafts of Freemasonry. He became a Master Mason and had established his own Masonic Lodge in Nauvoo, Illinois, which had become the largest order of Freemasonry in the entire state and had more members than all of the other lodges combined. It should be noted Joseph Smith was the general of his own private army in Nauvoo, and he was addressed by the Mormons as **General Smith**. Smith's military and political ambitions did not end there. He went on, in an exalted opinion of himself, to imagine that he had been chosen to establish the Kingdom of God on earth. He told his Mormon disciples that he had another revelation from God and was told by him **"THAT HE WAS A DESCENDANT FROM JOSEPH OF OLD THROUGH THE BLOOD OF EPHRAIM. AND THAT GOD HAD APPOINTED AND ORDAINED THAT HE,**

[45]***L.D.S. Reference Encyclopedia*, Brooks, p. 19.**

[46]***Enyclopedia of Mormonism*, Vol. 2, ed. Ludlow, p. 860.**

[47]***The City of the Saints*, Burton, pp. 586-628.**

WITH HIS DESCENDANTS, SHOULD RULE OVER ALL ISRAEL,...AND ULTIMATELY THE JEWS AND GENTILES."[48] [sic] Smith told his followers that the Mormons have the privilege and responsibility to bear the message of the restoration of the Gospel to the world and to gather scattered Israel. Smith taught the future, literal gathering of Israel, the restoration of the Ten Lost Tribes, and that Zion (the New Jerusalem) will be built upon the American continent.[49] He went on to tell his Mormon church members that the authority with which God had clothed him **extended over all mankind**. Smith even stated, **"The sword is unsheathed and shall never return to its sheath again until all those who reject the truth and fight against the kingdom of God are swept from the face of the earth."**[50]

My Mormon reader, my wife and I have spent days and long hours at the Brigham Young University Library and other libraries in the Provo, Utah, area probing through Mormon books and records so we could document everything we are presenting to our readers. We are not anti-Mormon in the least. However, we are, indeed, most strongly opposed to your fascist-like secret priesthood of the Order of Melchizedek and their plans. This writer knows that not one in a hundred thousand Mormons understands the true plans that Joseph Smith, Sidney Rigdon, John Taylor, Willard Richards, John D. Lee, Brigham Young, Hyrum Smith, James J. Strang, and other Mormon leaders of the original **Council of Fifty** set up back in March of 1842. Are you aware that this secret society anointed Joseph Smith, then after his death Brigham Young, and later John Taylor as "**King-Priest and Ruler over Israel on the earth**"?[51] Are you aware, my Mormon reader, that Smith and his Council of Fifty planned first to take over the state of Illinois, then the United States, and then the whole world?

If the reader has any doubts to what this writer is exposing in this chapter, may I suggest to you that you make a personal visit to the Brigham Young University Library on the fourth floor and ask to see

[48]*The St. Clair Banner*, September 17, 1844.

[49]*Encyclopedia of Mormonism*, Vol. 2, ed. Ludlow, p. 461.

[50]*The Sword of Laban as a Symbol of Divine Authority and Kingship*, Holbrook, Brigham Young University, March 24, 1992, p. 37.

[51]*The Council of Fifty and Its Members 1844–1945*, Quinn, pp. 174–187.

the Special Collection files on the Council of Fifty. Ask for Brigham Young University Studies, Vol. 20, Winter 1980, Number 2, *The Council of Fifty and Its Members 1844–1945*. Also, look for *Council of Fifty in History and Theology: An Inquiry into the Role of the Government of God in the Last Days* by Ronald K. Esplin, Spring 1971, Brigham Young University.

Smith became obsessed with the idea that he was to establish the Kingdom of God and New Jerusalem here on earth. Like Adam Weishaupt, Smith planned to overthrow the world by using the secret society of Freemasonry. However, this in itself was a contradiction to the Book of Mormon for Smith had supposedly translated earlier that secret oaths and covenants with secret signs, secret words, and secret combinations of people were of the Devil.[52]

Nevertheless, according to *Council of Fifty in History and Theology: An Inquiry into the Role of the Government of God in the Last Days* written by the Mormon writer Ronald K. Esplin on pages four and 19, it was on March 11, 1844, that Joseph Smith organized the secret society of the Council of Fifty whose purpose was to take into consideration the necessary steps in establishing Smith's version of the Kingdom of God and a worldwide government. Brigham Young and Willard Richards wrote to Reuben Hedlock, the head of the Mormon Church in Great Britain, that the "**Kingdom is organized; and although as yet no bigger than a grain of mustard seed, the little plant is in a flourishing condition, and our prospects brighter than ever.**"

According to *Joseph Smith and World Government* by Andrus on pages five and six, this Kingdom of God the Mormons are to establish under their priesthood is to be both **Church and State and will, through the Mormon Church, govern and control the whole world**.

While touring the Brigham Young Winter Home and the Old Mormon Tabernacle and the Visitor Center in St. George, my wife and I brought up the question about New Jerusalem. When I asked about New Jerusalem, it was quickly answered by our Mormon guides from both centers that the Mormon Church is going to build New Jerusalem near **Independence, Missouri, and the Ten Lost Tribes of Israel, who shall reappear in these last days, shall build another**

[52]***The Book of Mormon*, Ether 8:1–26.**

temple in the Old Jerusalem area. However, I quickly pointed out from the Holy Scriptures that it plainly states in Revelation, Chapters 20 and 21, that the **God of heaven, not man, shall build us this city, and that New Jerusalem shall descend from God out of heaven**. The Mormon guides were unable to give a satisfactory reply, so the conversation again switched to something else.

It was Joseph Smith who taught the Mormons that they were to build New Jerusalem, that Christ shall reign upon this earth, and that this world will be renewed and will receive its paradisiacal glory. However, not only was Smith wrong about New Jerusalem, but also about Christ's reign upon this earth. Jesus said in John 18:36, **"MY KINGDOM IS NOT OF THIS WORLD." Like the New Holy City, THE THOUSAND-YEAR REIGN OF CHRIST WILL BE IN HEAVEN, NOT HERE ON THIS EARTH.**

The founding fathers of Mormonism had a great deal of knowledge about the secret society of the Illuminati. When my wife and I interviewed Sandra Tanner in Salt Lake City, we asked her if she knew if Smith had any connection with the Illuminati. She said she didn't know, but graciously went to her computer and found some eye-opening references about Smith and the Illuminati and told us that this Mormon literature was at BYU, which is where I went. According to *Dialogue: A Journal of Mormon Thought*, Fall/Winter 1994, p. 48, John C. Bennett, the one-time Assistant Church President, claimed that in April of 1841 Smith had commissioned him to establish a Masonic-like "**Order of the Illuminati**" in the event of Smith's death.

Smith, like Weishaupt, infiltrated Freemasonry and eventually claimed to have a more superior knowledge of Masonry as well. Again, like Weishaupt, Smith planned to use the Masonic Order as a revolutionary tool to unite the world under his secret priesthood. As Smith's Mormonism is a religion within a religion, so was Weishaupt's Illuminati a secret society or **SECRET COMBINATION** within the secret society of Freemasonry. Adam Weishaupt became an "**occult revolutionary**," as were Thomas Paine, Thomas Jefferson, and Benjamin Franklin. **Weishaupt borrowed this one-world socialist government scheme from the pagan, Greek philosopher Plato.** Adam Weishaupt, like Joseph Smith, was a **mystic** whose exalted ideas of himself led him on to try to establish a one-world government in this present world with him as its **REX (KING)**. Adam Weishaupt, the founder of the Bavarian Order of the Illuminati, died in 1811 so Smith could not have had a connection with him or with Saint-Martin, whose ideas are compatible with Mormonism. However, the historical parallels are, indeed, suspicious!

What really caught my attention about the crosslinks between Freemasonry, the Bavarian Illuminati, and that of Mormonism was when I learned that in 1850 a schismatic Mormon secret society was actually founded. They named themselves **the American Society of the Illuminati!** This secret society of Mormon Illuminism was formed in 1850 by James Strang who had been a member of the Council of Fifty on Beaver Island in northern Lake Michigan. This secret society of Mormons swore an oath to defend the Mormon Church even to the point of spilling blood. However, the American Society of the Illuminati was short-lived. James Strang, its founder, was shot and killed by one of his followers, who had been publicly whipped for refusing to compel his own wife to wear the temple garments. After Strang's death, the tabernacle which served as the secret society's headquarters was destroyed by fishermen who lived on Beaver Island.[53] Mormon scholars say John C. Bennett (former Secretary of the Nauvoo Masonic Lodge) had joined them.[54]

It was Thomas Paine's books, *Common Sense* and *The Age of Reason*, which sparked both the American and the French Revolutions. Both revolutions were provoked and carried out under the auspices of the Masonic Orders. Thomas Paine tried to destroy the credibility of the Holy Scriptures by attacking the translation of it. In his book, ***The Age of Reason***, Paine calls the Bible "**stupid**,"[55] and the Tanners point out how **Joseph Smith adopted Paine's ideas**, as well as did the early Mormon disciples of Joseph Smith. It is quite evident that the prophet of the Mormon Church knew about the conspiracy of the Illuminati revolutionary movement within Freemasonry whose

[53]*The International Encyclopedia of Secret Societies and Fraternal Orders*, Axelrod, p. 134.

[54]*Dialogue: A Journal of Mormon Thought*, Vol. 27, Fall/Winter 1994, pp. 48, 50.

[55]*The Complete Writings of Thomas Paine*, ed. Foner, p. 603.

goal was to overthrow all religions and all governments. Let's look at some more parallels between Smith's Mormonism in the New World and the occult revolution of the Illuminati in the Old World.

According to the *American Heritage Dictionary* on page 656, the name ***Illuminati*** was also used by persons who were known as "**ATHEISTS**, libertines, or radical republicans during the 18th century (such as the French Encyclopedists, **THE FREEMASONS, OR THE FREETHINKERS): THE DOCTRINES OF THE ILLUMINATI AND THE PRINCIPLES OF JACOBINISM**."[56] (Emphasis mine.)

As we have seen, the Illuminati (like Freemasonry) can be first traced back to the secret combination of mysticism known as **Sufism**, which is **Islamic mysticism**, who borrowed their mystical knowledge from the **Egyptians, Persians, Greeks, and the ancient Chaldeans of Babylonia**. We will see more documented proof of this as we continue. However, in France, the Illuminati mystics were operating under another name within the secret society of the Freemasons and were known as the **Jacobin Clubs**. It is very important that the reader understands that **not all Freemasons were supporters of the Jacobin Clubs within their secret society**. I pointed out in Volumes Two and Three of this series of studies on the Time of the End prophecies that both George Washington and John Adams themselves were engaged in warning other Freemasons about the Jacobin Clubs within their order. In Volume Three of this series, I presented with documented proof that both George Washington and John Adams were in fierce opposition with Thomas Jefferson, Benjamin Franklin, and Thomas Paine because of their involvement with the Jacobin Clubs and how they were the very ones, indeed, who helped start the French Revolution and the overthrow of papal Christianity in France. Although George Washington was a deceived Freemason, he was strongly opposed to the New World Order scheme of that day of which many Freemasons like Franklin, Paine, and Jefferson adopted. George Washington was like most Masons are today. He did not understand the historical significance of the rise and evolution of the dangerous secret society in which he had even

[56]***The American Heritage Dictionary*, ed. Morris, 1976, p. 656.**

served as **Worshipful Master. However, President Washington's warning and some of his last dying words to us were "BEWARE OF SECRET COMBINATIONS."**[57]

Voltaire, the French antichrist and hero of the French Revolution, was also a Freemason. According to *An Encyclopedia of Freemasonry and Its Kindred Sciences*, Voltaire was "initiated in the Lodge of the Nine Sisters, at Paris on February 7, 1778, **in the presence of Benjamin Franklin**."[58] "In 1734, he (Franklin) was elected Grand Master of the Provincial Grand Lodge of Pennsylvania." During this Age of Enlightenment, Franklin was also the **Ambassador of France.**[59] Just before the French Revolution broke out, Benjamin Franklin was also a minister of the French Court and in 1785, Franklin was succeeded by fellow Mason and New World Order advocate, Thomas Jefferson, who remained in that position until 1789.[60] History says that Thomas Jefferson was against the policies of both George Washington and John Adams.[61] He worked to promote the French Revolution during the years of 1785–89. He was in France before and after the fall of Bastille when a mob stormed that prison and the French Revolution, with all of its violence and anti-Christian hatred, was being perpetrated.[62] My Christian Bible-believing brethren, these same Freemasons, who were "**cells of the Illuminati**" (Jacobins), went on to legislate that there is no God and ordered the French citizens to publicly burn their Bibles in the streets.[63]

The Tanners, who are former LDS members, point out in their book that these warnings from George Washington are also found in the Book of Mormon, which supposedly traces the history of some ancient civilizations here in America long before the arrival of Columbus. The Tanners point out that Joseph Smith lived in the very same area of the

[57]***Mormonism – Shadow or Reality?*, Tanner/Tanner, pp. 70, 71.**

[58]***Encyclopaedia of Freemasonry and Its Kindred Sciences*, Vol. II, Mackey, 33°, p. 831.**

[59]***Ibid.*, Vol. I, Mackey, 33°, pp. 278, 279.**

[60]***Harper's Encyclopedia of United States History*, Vol. 5, 1905, p. 130.**

[61]***Encyclopedia Americana*, Vol. 16, 1996, p. 1.**

[62]***New Age Magazine*, April 1986, p. 55.**

[63]***The Prophecies of Daniel and The Revelation*, Smith, pp. 284, 285.**

United States where this huge scandal broke out about the Freemason's plans to overthrow the governments of the world. Newspapers of that day were publicly exposing the dangers of Freemasons after the sudden disappearance of Captain William Morgan, a Mason himself who became awakened to their secret plans. Smith was also living when Thomas Jefferson and Adam Weishaupt were still alive, so he had to have known about the Illuminati conspiracy.

This hot fire against Masonry during the early 1800s was first sparked by John Robison (1739–1805), who was also a Freemason himself and wrote a book entitled ***Proofs of a Conspiracy against all the Religions and Governments of Europe carried on in the Secret Meetings of the Freemasons, Illuminati, and Reading Societies, collected from Good Authorities***. John Robison was a Professor of Natural Philosophy at the University of Edinburgh and Secretary of the Royal Society in that city at that time. Robison published his above book in 1797 at Edinburgh and also at London. *Mackey's Revised Encyclopedia of Freemasonry* states the following about his book:

"In consequence of the anti-Jacobin sentiment of the people of Great Britain at that time, the work on its first appearance produced a great sensation. It was not, however, popular with all readers."[64]

Later, while Joseph Smith was making his debut in around the same area of upstate New York, another hot fire was kindled against this **occult revolution** by Captain William Morgan in 1823. After he wrote ***The Illustrations of Masonry***, which exposes Freemasonry's doctrines, Morgan began to suffer a series of mysterious persecutions. He was kidnapped on the evening of September 12, 1826, was taken by force to the Canadian border, and was never seen again. Morgan was murdered by the Freemasons after which many members left the Order and turned against it. The feeling against Freemasonry became so strong that many Masons, when they left the fraternity, became active workers against it. A newspaper of that day called the ***Wayne Sentinel*** became one of the biggest voices in the United States which was publishing warnings against the members of Freemasonry.

[64]*Mackey's Revised Encyclopedia of Freemasonry*, Vol. 2, Mackey, 33°, John Robison section.

Ancient Prophecies About Mysticism

At the Brigham Young University Library, my wife found on microfilm an old ***Wayne Sentinel*** article which contained anti-Masonic statements of that day. This same article was revealed by the Tanners in their book. This article said the following: "If you listen to the party which lately welcomed Don Miguel as their 'tutelar angel,'...the **FREEMASONS** have been the cause of all the 'seditions, privy conspiracies, and rebellions,' which, **FOR THE LAST THIRTY YEARS, HAVE AFFLICTED EUROPE**.... The Freemasons are, therefore, radically and essentially, demagogues, **JACOBINS**, conspirators, assassins, infidels, traitors, and **ATHEISTS**. Their **BAND** of union is formed of the broken cement of existing order – their secret is the watchword of sedition and rebellion – their object is **ANARCHY** and **PLUNDER** – ... unless they are suppressed, there will soon be neither religion, morals, literature, nor civilized society left!"[65] (Emphasis mine.) Amazingly, E. B. Grandin, the printer of the *Wayne Sentinel*, printed the first 5,000 copies of the Book of Mormon, according to *Old Mormon Palmyra and New England*, Holzapfel/Cottle, pp. 87, 88.

According to the book, *Mormonism and Masonry*, written by S.H. Goodwin, Past Grand Master of the Grand Lodge F. & A.M. of Utah, before the Mormon Church was founded in 1830, Joseph Smith lived in the **very heart** of the region affected by anti-Masonic excitement, as shown earlier, which was between the years 1826–1830.[66] He was familiar with exposés widely distributed at that time. Smith lived within a few miles of the center of that excitement where Captain William Morgan, the famous anti-Masonic martyr, exposed Freemasonry in Batavia, New York. Strange as it may seem, Morgan's widow (Lucinda) later became **one** of the 50 wives of Joseph's harem. Andrew Jenson, who was the Assistant LDS Church Historian, stated that Lucinda was one of the first women sealed to Joseph, according to his account in *The Historical Record*, Vol. VI, May 1887, page 233. According to *Dialogue: A Journal of Mormon Thought,* Fall/Winter 1994, p. 95, Dr. B.W. Richard saw Lucinda crying in Nauvoo over Joseph's dead body. In *The God Makers* on page 34, it points out that both Joseph Smith and Brigham Young stated that only polygamists could become gods.

[65]***The Wayne Sentinel*, September 26, 1828.**

[66]***Mormonism and Masonry*, Goodwin, P.G.M., 1938, p. 38.**

The Mystical Teachings of Joseph Smith

When the **Illuminati of Bavaria**, which was founded by Adam Weishaupt on May 1, 1776,[67] in Ingolstadt, Germany, **was exposed in 1785 and banned by the Bavarian government**,[68] it was eventually revealed that the Illuminati had continued secretly and was undetected for many years. Its leader had kept his secret society hidden by not only hiding within the walls of Masonic Lodges, but by using symbolic or code names for themselves and their locations. Adam Weishaupt used Spartacus as a code name, and his comrades, such as Von Knigge and Zwack, were named Philo and Cato, respectively. They also gave fictitious names to the countries from which they were operating. Ingolstadt, Germany, where Adam Weishaupt was located, was Eleusis. Austria was Egypt; Munich, Germany, was called Athens; and Vienna was called Rome. Adam Weishaupt's connection with Freemasonry and his secret Order of the Illuminati can be read in the *Encyclopaedia of Freemasonry and Its Kindred Sciences*, Volume 1, Mackey, 33°, on page 346.

Joseph Smith and Sidney Rigdon, whose minds were filled with **mystical knowledge and that of Freemasonry**, were also believed by 1833 to have also written the **Book of Mormon in symbolic code to hide Mormonism's real plans and purposes**. A statement written in *Articles on the Authorship of the Book of Mormon* says, **"Now in at least twenty-one chapters in seven out of the sixteen 'books' of the Book of Mormon are to be found passages, varying from several to sixty-three lines in length, plainly referring to Masonry under the guise of pretended similar organizations in ancient America."**[69]

In the Book of Mormon, even to the casual reader it is very obvious to see the parallels between the secret society of the **GADIANTON ROBBERS** and what **FREEMASONS** actually were doing throughout their history. In Helaman 7:4, 5 and Ether 8:8, 14, 16, 20 of the Book of Mormon, it tells how the **GADIANTON**

[67]***Encyclopaedia of Freemasonry and Its Kindred Sciences*, Vol. 1, Mackey, 33°, p. 346.**

[68]***The Encyclopaedia Britannica*, Vol. 11, 1973, p. 1096.**

[69]***Articles on the Authorship of the Book of Mormon*, copied from *The Amerian Journal of Psychology*, Prince/Schroeder, p. 3.**

Ancient Prophecies About Mysticism

Joseph Smith was a prophet of Spiritualism and blended the Kabbalah, Freemasonry, and Egyptian mysticism with the Christian faith. Smith was a known diviner in his state of New York before the founding of the Mormon Church in 1830. He possessed a strong talismanic influence and at his murder site in Carthage, Illinois, there was found on Smith's body a Jupiter talisman amulet, which for years was thought to have Masonic significance.[1] *Before Smith became a Master Mason in Nauvoo, Illinois, he set up a secret society known as the United Order which failed. The United Order began to be formed on April 26, 1832, and divided itself into two divisions: one in Kirtland, Ohio, and one in Missouri.*[2] *The United Order* **promoted communal living (communism)** *and to keep itself hidden, its leaders within its inner circle, like the Illuminati, selected code names which were as follows: Joseph Smith (Gazelam), Sidney Rigdon (Pelagoram), Oliver Cowdery (Olihah), Newel K. Whitney (Ahashdah), and Martin Harris (Mahemson).*[3] *It is no doubt that Smith was aware of Masonic ritual and of its hidden secret society of the Illuminati before he became a Master Mason. The spread of Spiritualism (Illuminism) via Saint-Martin (Martinism) before the founding of the United States, the excitement of John Robison's book,* Proofs of a Conspiracy, *and the establishment of 15 lodges of the Illuminati before 1776 in the Northeast of America, and John C. Bennett's claim that Smith told him to establish an order of the Illuminati are ample evidence that Joseph Smith knew of the plans of the Illuminati takeover. It is quite evident, however, that Smith had his own plans to unite the world under his own secret priesthood, the Order of Melchizedek, which he and Rigdon conveniently borrowed from the Freemasons. Smith told his disciples that Freemasonry, as well as Christianity, had apostatized from the God of Solomon. Smith claimed that he was to restore them both back to their original design, and that a "New Dispensation" was to be set up in the world by the Mormon Church. Smith claimed that by divine revelation he had received the fulness of the Gospel via the gold plates which became the Book of Mormon. Modern Mormon writers try to justify the plagiarism of the Masonic endowment ceremony by pointing out that the Masons, as well, borrowed from the Kabbalah, Egyptian rites, astrology, and the Bible.*[4]

[1]*Dialogue: A Journal of Mormon Thought*, Fall/Winter 1994, p. 96.

[2]*Ibid.*, Summer 1986, pp. 146–149.

[3]*Ibid.*, Summer 1986, p. 146.

[4]*Ibid.*, Fall/Winter 1994, p. 104.

ROBBERS had **FILLED** the "**JUDGMENT-SEATS**," – having **USURPED** the power and authority of the land, laying aside the commandments of God, and letting the guilty and the wicked to go **UNPUNISHED** because of their **MONEY**; how those of this **SECRET SOCIETY** held an office at the **HEAD OF GOVERNMENT** to rule and do according to their wills that they might get gain and glory of the world; and how the members of this secret society took **OATHS TO NOT REVEAL** any of their **SECRET PLANS**. They also took **OATHS** among them that they would not reveal their plans to **GAIN POWER**; to **MURDER**, **PLUNDER**, and lie; or to commit any other **WICKEDNESS**.

Let's now compare an **oath that Freemasons** take with that of the Gadianton robbers which is found in the Book of Mormon. In the *Masonic Hand Book* on page 183 we read: "Whenever you see any of our **signs** made by a brother Mason, and especially the **grand hailing sign of distress**, you must always be sure to obey them, even at the risk of your life. If you're on a **jury**, and the **defendant is a Mason**, and makes the Grand Hailing sign, you must obey it; you must disagree with your brother jurors, if necessary, but you must be sure **not to bring the Mason guilty**, for that would bring disgrace upon our order. It may be **perjury**, to be sure, to do this, but then you're fulfilling your obligation, and you know if you live up to your obligations you'll be free from sin." (Quoted in *The Masonic Report*, McQuaig/Shaw, p. 9.)

About three years after the Book of Mormon was published, it was also published that Smith had plagiarized the whole idea of the American Indians being descendants of the Ten Lost Tribes of Israel from a novel entitled ***Manuscript Found***, which was written by Solomon Spaulding over 20 years before Smith said he found the gold plates. The name **Nephi** , which is so central in the Book of Mormon, can actually be found in the Apocrypha.[70] The names **Moroni, Nephi, Lehi, Laman, Nephites, and Lamanites**, which are found in the Book of Mormon, and their migration to America were originally taken from Spaulding's novel. It has been alleged for over 150 years now that Sidney Rigdon is the Book of Mormon's real author, and that he designed it to be anti-Masonic so that it would be popular with the

[70]***The Septuagint with Apocrypha: Greek and English*, Benton, p. 184.**

public sentiments of that day and would also satisfy curious minds as to where the American Indians had originated. We will study about the new developments about the charge of plagiarism against the author of the Book of Mormon shortly but, before we do, let's look again in history at what led to the murder of Joseph and his brother.

The word "**fascism**" (according to *The American Heritage Dictionary*, Based on the New Second College Edition, p. 255) means "*a system of government that* ***exercises a dictatorship*** *of the extreme right, typically through the* ***merging of state and business leadership, together with belligerent nationalism***."

The above is what Joseph Smith and his Council of Fifty had set up in the city of Nauvoo. They became a separate State within the State of Illinois. However, just a little over three months after he founded the secret society of the Council of Fifty, Smith went into an untimely grave. According to the *History of the Church*, Vol. VI, pages 596–611, Joseph Smith and his brother were arrested on the charge of treason against the State of Illinois and were placed under the guard of the Carthage Greys, who happened to be their worst enemies, by order of the Governor of the State. The Governor of Illinois, at that time, was Thomas Ford, and he wrote about what Joseph Smith had developed into at Nauvoo. He said:

"It seems…that Joe Smith about this time conceived the idea of making himself a **temporal prince** as well as **spiritual leader** of his people. He instituted a new and select order of the priesthood, the members of which were to be **priests and kings temporally and spiritually**. These were to be his nobility, who were to be the upholders of his throne. **He caused himself to be crowned and anointed king and priest, far above the rest;** and he prescribed the form of an **oath** of allegiance to himself, which he administered to his principal followers."

The above was quoted in *Council of Fifty in History and Theology: An Inquiry into the Role of the Government of God in the Last Days* on page 15 by Ronald K. Esplin, Spring 1971, Brigham Young University.

Smith's secret political plans about trying to take over the whole Masonic institution to use as his vehicle to place the whole world under his version of the government of God started to unveil itself to the Freemasons; and it is not unusual that all of the men of a small town

The above picture I took on July 6, 1998, when my wife and I, along with another Christian companion, visited the Mormon Temple area of Salt Lake City. The photograph shows statues of Joseph and Hyrum Smith with the Mormon Temple in the background. A plaque at the base of one of the statues claims that Joseph Smith was the prophet of the "New Dispensation" of the Gospel of Jesus Christ. An unmistakable parallel between Adam Weishaupt's New World Order plans which were orchestrated through the Order of Freemasonry, whose French Revolutionaries were cells of the Illuminati, and that of Master Mason Joseph Smith's plans of a "New Dispensation" are most strikingly similar! Both Weishaupt and Smith used the mystical Order of Freemasonry to carry out their secret plans to unite the whole world under their secret priesthood; both claimed to be religious reformers. Adam Weishaupt died in 1811, and the Mormon Church was founded about 19 years later.

were Masons as well as high officials of the State, like Thomas Ford to whom the Smiths had surrendered themselves under the governor's pledge that he would protect them from the militia. As we saw, both Joseph and Hyrum Smith became Master Masons and were hoping to receive the protection that this secret society offered its members when under distress. According to *History of the Church*, Vol. VI, pages 602, 603, Governor Ford betrayed his trust by placing Joseph and his brother under guard at the Carthage Jail by the very men who were seeking their lives, namely the Carthage Grey militia. It was told by one of the militia men guarding the Smiths on Tuesday, June 27, at 5:30 a.m. that both Joseph and his brother would be dead before sundown that day. As pointed out, the Masons became hot over Smith's plans before he was arrested. A Mormon writer says, **"It is not surprising that they made a few departures from the ancient landmarks and introduced some changes in the procedure which brought upon them the full weight of Masonic displeasure."**[71]

An inquiry was demanded by the Bodley Lodge No. 1 of Quincy, Illinois, as to how Joseph Smith and Sidney Rigdon were given the degrees of Entered Apprentice, Fellow Craft, and Master Mason **at one and the same time**, and it was also demanded by what authority the Deputy Grand Master (Judge James Adams) initiated them! After this, the Masons demanded that Smith's Nauvoo Masonic Lodge **suspend its activities**,[72] which was ignored by the Mormons who had established other Mormon Masonic Lodges outside of Nauvoo (according to *Coil's Masonic Encyclopedia*, 1961, pages 317, 318).

What actually brought about the wrath of the State of Illinois was when Smith began to **wear his political badge** openly and announced himself as a **candidate for the office of the president of the United States**. While Joseph Smith was busy with his **secret priesthood** in an effort to bring not only the whole Masonic Lodge under the **subordination** of his "Order of Melchizedek," but the United States as well, a local newspaper in Nauvoo (where Smith's headquarters were located at that time) was exposing some of Smith's secret plans and false claims. What really **sealed his doom** was when he (as mayor of

[71]***Mormonism and Masonry*, McGavin, 1947, pp. 89, 90.**

[72]***Mormonism and Masonry*, Goodwin, P.G.M., 1938, pp. 28, 29.**

Nauvoo) ordered the town marshall on June 10, 1844, to burn the printing press and materials of the ***Nauvoo Expositor*** (which was run by former Mormons) in the street. (See *History of the Church*, Vol.VI, Smith, p. 432.) However, warrants were issued against the Smiths (Joseph and his brother Hyrum) and other leaders for treason and for the destruction of the printing press of the *Nauvoo Expositor*. When this news was discovered, Joseph and his brother Hyrum fled to Iowa, but later returned and surrendered to the authorities in Carthage, Illinois. Soon afterwards, a mob of Carthage Greys, whom Brigham Young believed were Masons,[73] started attacking the jail and shot and killed Joseph's brother Hyrum first. Then, Joseph Smith, after emptying a six-shooter smuggled to him by a visitor, gave the Masonic signal for distress and yelled out, **"OH LORD, MY GOD! IS THERE NO HELP FOR THE WIDOW'S SON!"**[74] as he was being murdered (according to John D. Lee, who was a member of the Council of Fifty). However, the mob ignored his Masonic appeal, and he was shot and fell out of a second-story jail window to the ground.

Before two years had elapsed after the death of Joseph Smith, violent, Illinois citizens forced the whole Mormon Church out of Illinois by the point of a gun; and Brigham Young led the majority to the Salt Lake in Utah. We were told by Mormon officials in St. George that a contest over who was to be the successor of the Mormon prophet soon arose. This contest was between the two highest leaders of the secret Council of Fifty; they were Sidney Rigdon and Brigham Young. **We were also told that while the leaders were trying to decide between the two, Brigham Young delivered a speech to his brethren and both his face and his voice changed into Joseph Smith's face and voice. It was immediately decided that Brigham Young would be their new prophet.**

Because of the bizarre teachings of Joseph Smith, the Mormon people were forced out of their homes in Far West and Nauvoo by the barrel of a gun. After they made their way to the Salt Lake and southern Utah, there where some who suffered the pains of starvation and died. Nevertheless, their secret priesthood's plans to overthrow the United

[73]***Dialogue: A Journal of Mormon Thought*, Fall/Winter 1994, p. 97.**

[74]***Confessions of John D. Lee*, reprint 1880 edition, Lee, p. 153.**

States government and its non-Mormon citizens continued under their new king, Brigham Young. It was at this time that the Mormons were led by their fanatical, false religious beliefs to massacre 120 men, women, and children in a wagon train which was making its way through Utah to California. My wife and I visited this historical area. It is called the **Mountain Meadows Massacre Site** and is still an embarrassment and a black cloud that is hovering over the heads of the Mormon people today. Brigham Young's White Supremacist beliefs, at that time, about the Black race and slavery; his beliefs about polygamy, his secret priesthood, and the establishment of the Kingdom of God by force; and the murder of American citizens brought the wrath of the United States upon him and the Mormon people in Utah as well.

We were told at the St. George Visitor Center that the LDS' earlier doctrines about the Black race and polygamy are no longer believed and practiced. However, they still continue to subordinate their ten million members under their secret priesthood of the **Order of Melchizedek**, and they still think that they have been chosen to establish a **"NEW DISPENSATION"** in this present world. They still think that they will build New Jerusalem near Independence, Missouri. They still believe that Joseph Smith was a prophet of God and that he was a descendant of Joseph's son, Ephraim. However, reader, if you will turn in your Bible to Revelation, Chapter Seven, you will soon discover that the **tribes of Dan and Ephraim are missing on the gates of New Jerusalem. The name *Ephraim* became synonymous for idolatry among the ancient, northern Hebrews. It was the tribes of Ephraim and Dan who were foremost in leading the ten northern tribes into idolatry, and this is why their names were removed.**

There is a strong denouncement against Ephraim given by the prophet Hosea. "Ephraim is joined to idols: let him alone." Hosea 5:17. It was because of ancient Israel's refusal to turn from Spiritualism that they are now called the Ten Lost Tribes of Israel, for Isaiah was told to prophesy "**WITHIN THREESCORE AND FIVE YEARS SHALL EPHRAIM BE BROKEN, THAT IT BE NOT A PEOPLE**." Isaiah 7:8. Not only is this doctrine about Joseph Smith being a descendant of the son of Ephraim (Joseph of Egypt) untrue, but so was his claim about having been ordained of God to translate a **new** bible (the Book of Mormon) so that a **new** religion (Mormonism) could be founded with a hierarchical priesthood (Order of Melchizedek) who would subordinate all peoples under their authority so that a **New** Dispensation would be ushered in with a **New** Jerusalem to be built in Jackson County, Missouri.

Of all the false claims found in Mormonism, none are as diabolical as the deception that Sidney Rigdon and Smith manufactured together to deceive Mormons into believing that the Book of Mormon was a new bible from God for the last days. As pointed out earlier, the myth about gold plates being stored in the earth was borrowed from Freemasonry. Long before Smith was born, there was a Masonic Legend of Enoch passed on to the initiate. Enoch was supposedly led to find gold and brass plates containing ancient records in a hillside vault.

Not only was the myth about the gold plates plagiarized to make up part of the Book of Mormon story, but so was the entire myth found in the Book of Mormon about the first settlers of America originally coming from Jerusalem. For years, this writer has heard the rumor, which actually began back in 1833, that the Book of Mormon was really a novel written by a man named Spaulding. However, this writer follows our brother Paul's advice to "**Prove all things; hold fast that which is good**," (1 Thessalonians 5:21), and I was not about to put any such statements in my books without any proof. "**SHOW ME THE MANUSCRIPT**" had been my response.

During our second visit to Utah in the midsummer of 1998 about the time my wife and I went to interview Brigham Young's great, great granddaughter, Sandra Tanner, we met another Christian couple of whom the husband's parents had been Mormons but had renounced it as a delusion. While we were visiting with them, we were also told by them that the Book of Mormon had originally been a novel written by Solomon Spaulding. Again, with this thought ("show me the manuscript") in mind, we were given two books to read. They were Fawn Brodie's *No Man Knows My History* and *Who Really Wrote the Book of Mormon?*, which was written by several other authors. After reading Brodie's biography of Joseph Smith and how he began his career, I became even more convinced that the Book of Mormon had been plagiarized from the writings of Solomon Spaulding's novel entitled *Manuscript Found,* however, not by Joseph Smith, but by his mentor and guru, Sidney Rigdon!

However, Fawn Brodie, after displaying sworn testimonies from Spaulding's friends and relatives who stated that over 20 years before the Book of Mormon was ever published Spaulding had written that the Nephites and Lamanites had originated from Jerusalem and were the descendants of the Ten Lost Tribes of Israel, seemed to have dismissed the idea that this story was stolen by Sidney Rigdon from Spaulding's novel. Nevertheless, my request to "show me the manuscript" was finally satisfied by the independent researchers and authors of *Who Really Wrote the Book of Mormon?*. Let's now look at the history behind this terrible deception.

As established, this charge of **plagiarism** of Spaulding's novel, which was blamed on the founders of Mormonism, began to first appear in the newspapers in **1833** by showing affidavits which were written by friends and family of Solomon Spaulding. This was, of course, flatly denied by Smith and his church members. However, in **1841** the original transcribed manuscript (which was written by Emma Smith, Martin Harris, and Oliver Cowdery) was sealed in the southeast cornerstone of the Nauvoo House by Smith himself as they were building it. After Smith was murdered in 1844 and the surviving Mormons were driven by force out of Nauvoo, Major Lewis C. Bidamon and his work crew in **1882** were hired to dismantle the Nauvoo House and sell the brick. As they tore down the old building, **they discovered the old, original manuscript of the Book of Mormon** in a small chest into which Smith back in 1841 had placed it.[75]

According to *Who Really Wrote the Book of Mormon?*, which was compiled by Wayne L. Cowdrey (a descendant of Oliver Cowdery), Howard A. Davis, and Donald R. Scales, on pages 171, 172, **on September 7, 1883**, Mrs. Sarah M. Kimball visited Major Bidamon and she obtained from him about **144 pages of the manuscript** which the Mormon Church possesses today. As the Mormon Church Historians' Office in Salt Lake City went to work trying to identify the various handwritings on the manuscript, they found a <u>fourth</u> that they could not identify and had labeled about 12 pages written by this unidentified writer as "**unidentified scribe**."

[75]***Who Really Wrote the Book of Mormon?*, Cowdrey/Davis/Scales, p. 171.**

While Howard Davis, one of the authors of the above book, was flipping at random through a research book on Mormonism, he spotted a photograph of an old manuscript and **it turned out to be a picture of a section from the original transcribed copy of the Book of Mormon, which had been discovered by Major Bidamon and given to Sarah M. Kimball back in 1883.** Ironically enough, the very section in the photograph of Smith's old handwritten manuscript, which was labeled by the Mormon Church as "**unidentified scribe,**" **was identified by handwriting experts to actually be Solomon Spaulding's own handwriting!**[76]

My Mormon reader, this writer also discovered something else very eye-opening from reading the documented pages of *Who Wrote the Book of Mormon?*. The authors were able to obtain copies of the original sworn testimony from Solomon Spaulding's friends and family which showed that Spaulding in 1812 had given his novel *Manuscript Found*, which was about the American Indians being descendants of the Ten Lost Tribes, to the **Patterson Print Shop in Pittsburg, Pennsylvania, for publication.** However, Robert Patterson, one of the owners, had asked for the money in advance to print the novel, but Spaulding was unable to raise the money to do so. This was all transpiring between the years of **1812–1814.**[77]

Another very interesting fact is that **Sidney Rigdon**, who was a very literate man, was born in 1793 in Library, Pennsylvania, and **lived just 15 miles south of the Patterson Print Shop!** Rigdon, who was Smith's most trusted lieutenant and mentor later on in the early stages of Mormonism, was a friend of J. H. Lambdin **who worked as a printer for Patterson's Print Shop**. Rigdon was often seen with Lambdin in the print shop by people living and working in the neighborhood at that time. **Mrs. William Eichbaum**, who at that time had worked with her father who was the Postmaster of the Pittsburg Post Office, gave a written testimony witnessing to the fact that she had often seen Lambdin from the Patterson Print Shop together with Sidney Rigdon, and they would often come together into the Post Office where she worked.[78]

[76]***Who Really Wrote the Book of Mormon?*, Cowdrey/Davis/Scales, pp. 167–189.**

[77]***Ibid.*, Cowdrey/Davis/Scales, pp. 66, 92.**

[78]***Ibid.*, Cowdrey/Davis/Scales, pp. 95, 96.**

The truth is that Sidney Rigdon was given Solomon Spaulding's manuscript to read for his opinion about it, but he never returned it. Solomon Spaulding died shortly afterwards on October 20, 1816; **thus, Rigdon was left with Spaulding's *Manuscript Found* in his possession**. According to Mrs. Amos Dunlap, who was the niece of Rigdon's wife, she stated in a written testimony to the fact that Sidney Rigdon married her aunt in Bainbridge, Ohio, where Rigdon and his wife lived from **1826–1827**. When Mrs. Dunlap visited the Rigdon home as a child, she said she saw Sidney take out a manuscript from a locked trunk and sat down by the fireplace to begin to read it when her aunt (Rigdon's wife), showing her displeasure, threatened to burn it. Rigdon responded by telling her, **"You will not. This will be a great thing some day."**[79]

At this point, I would like to remind the reader about the anti-Freemasonry excitement, which we saw earlier, that had been stirred by John Robison's book, *Proofs of a Conspiracy*, and also of another excitement which was stirring the imaginations of the people in the upper Northeast of the United States of that day. This was the discovery of many Indian mounds in that region. There was, indeed, a great interest about the trouble Freemasonry was causing, and there were many unanswered questions back then about the origin of the American Indians. Spaulding, being a literate man, saw an opportunity to pay off his debts by writing a novel about the Indians having originated from the Ten Lost Tribes of Israel. With all of the excitement as to the origin of the Indians, Spaulding thought even a novel on this subject would sell many books.

However, this notion that the American Indians originated from the Ten Lost Tribes of Israel and that Jesus visited America and witnessed to the Indians (which is found in the Book of Mormon) was, as pointed out in Volume One, *Beware It's Coming–The Antichrist 666*, on pages 92-96, first started by Joseph de Acosta, a Jesuit who in 1580 began to write about Cortez and his conquest of Moctezuma and the Aztecs of central Mexico. Moctezuma thought Cortez was Quetzalcoatl returning to take over the world. In the myth, Quetzalcoatl was worshipped by the ancient Toltecs and Aztecs as

[79]***Who Really Wrote the Book of Mormon?*, Cowdrey/Davis/Scales, p. 107.**

the "Bright and Morning Star" and was said to have been a white man with dark hair and a dark beard in his human form. Catholic monks began to imagine that this pagan god Quetzalcoatl must have been Jesus because of the similarities between the Aztec religion and that of Christianity. Spaulding visioned that all this excitement of that day would be a good base to build a novel upon, and so did Rigdon who stole Spaulding's novel.

After Spaulding's death, Sidney Rigdon went on to become a Baptist preacher for the First Baptist Church of Pittsburgh. However, on October 11, 1823, he was ex-communicated for teaching irregular doctrine.[80] After this, **Rigdon moved to Ohio, became a Campbellite preacher**, and went on to become a well-known revivalist, but had mingled Communist beliefs with the Gospel and established for himself a small Communistic colony in Kirtland, Ohio. This communal-styled living, however, was to the dismay of the founder of Campbellism. **Alexander Campbell quarreled with Rigdon over the idea of re-establishing ancient Communism**;[81] and according to *A Book of Mormons*, Van Wagoner/Walker, p. 23, in 1830 Campbell delivered a bitter scathing attack on Rigdon's economic community which he had started. From **1824–30**, Ridgon's occult-based Communistic ideas were clashing with Bible-based Christians, so he imagined that he would start a **new religion** which would be based on a **new bible**.

It was during this time that Sidney Rigdon, who at the age of 34 had developed into a very literate and cultured person, became acquainted with a very uncultured, impoverished foretuneteller named Joseph Smith, whose fame at the age of 22 as a clairvoyant in the Palmyra, New York, area had reached the ears of Rigdon just 250 miles away in Kirtland, Ohio. The authors of *Who Really Wrote the Book of Mormon?*, in their investigation into Mormonism, found old sworn statements from witnesses living at that time which linked Smith and Rigdon being together about three years before the Book of Mormon was ever published and before Rigdon officially became a member of the Mormon Church in 1830. One of these sworn statements was from **Mrs. S.F. Anderick**, who had been friends with the

[80]***Who Really Wrote the Book of Mormon?*, Cowdrey/Davis/Scales, p. 93.**
[81]***No Man Knows My History*, Brodie, p. 94.**

Smith kids when she was younger. She had been to the Smith's house several times to associate with Sophronia, who was Joseph's sister, for they were of the same age. Mrs. Anderick said in her sworn statement that she had not only seen the gold plates that Joseph Smith claimed he had found, but she also had seen Sidney Rigdon several times in the house of Joseph Smith in Palmyra, New York, in 1827. She said the plates were covered by a cloth and were six to eight inches square.[82]

Another sworn testimony was given by Lorenzo Saunders, who also hung around the Smith kids when he was young and knew the Smith kids well and had visited them often between **1827–1830** when he lived in Palmyra, New York. In Saunder's two sworn and written testimonies, he stated that he saw what Joseph claimed were gold plates. Saunders said that Smith carried them in an old glass box and that they really were **TILES** about 7 x 8" square. Saunders had also testified that **Oliver Cowdery, who he knew well, had come from Kirtland, Ohio, to Smith's home in 1827**, and that he had also met Sidney Rigdon at Smith's house in **March 1827**. Saunders testified that he saw Oliver Cowdery actually writing what was to become the Book of Mormon from Smith's house. He also stated, however, that Martin Harris didn't know that the gold plates were really just tiles. Saunders said Martin Harris "didn't know a gold plate from a brick at this time."[83]

The truth is it was actually Sidney Rigdon who was Moroni that delivered the gold plates (a revised version of Solomon Spaulding's *Manuscript Found*) into the hands of this new prophet, Joseph Smith, who he was grooming. Rigdon, who had been a revivalist in Kirtland, Ohio, had already set the stage there for the debut of his new prophet (with his new bible and his new religion of Mormonism) by predicting before the Book of Mormon was published that a new religion was coming. Rigdon had actually been preaching Mormonism before he became a Mormon.[84]

Later, Smith employed his wife, Martin Harris, and Oliver Cowdery as his scribes to produce another manuscript. Smith faked

[82]*Who Really Wrote the Book of Mormon?*, Cowdrey/Davis/Scales, pp. 133, 134.
[83]*Ibid.*, Cowdrey/Davis/Scales, pp. 127–131.
[84]*Ibid.*, Cowdrey/Davis/Scales, pp. 140–142.

that he was translating from his peepstone as to what the gold plates (tiles) had supposedly said, but instead dictated aloud from behind a curtain what Rigdon had written in a revised version of Solomon Spaulding's *Manuscript Found.*[85]

As Muhammad founded his new religion on the basis of receiving a new bible (the Koran) supposedly from an angel of God, so did Smith and Rigdon plan to start a new religion by inventing a new bible to take the place of the Holy Scriptures. It was Sidney Rigdon who stole from the Masons the myth about the gold plates being buried in a hillside. It was actually Sidney Rigdon who was the hidden author of not only the Book of Mormon, but Mormonism as well! Rigdon had revised Spaulding's novel (*Manuscript Found*) into a religious book by mingling some passages and some twisted stories from the Holy Scriptures with it, while using the Old English language to make the whole Book of Mormon appear that it had been written in Biblical times.

My Mormon reader, evidence shows that Rigdon and Smith had even fooled Joseph Smith's wife, Emma, and Martin Harris into believing that the tiles were gold plates for Smith had warned them that God had told him that no one else was to look at the gold plates but him and, if they did, they would surely die. They were allowed to hold them, but not to look into the glass box or pillowcase with which Smith had covered them. Martin Harris was also duped into believing that if he would pay for the printing of the Book of Mormon, he would be given a place next to Smith in the new church. Harris, after he left the Mormons, said, "When they had got all my property they set me out."[86] [sic] Not only did Harris leave the Mormons, but so did Oliver Cowdery and Sidney Rigdon himself after Brigham Young became the Mormon's new king. Oliver Cowdery was ex-communicated from the Mormon Church for rightly calling Smith an adulterer. He remained out of the church for ten years, but returned about fours years after Smith died and tried to sell the Mormons on the idea that he still retained the keys of the priesthood. However, he was ignored by the church hierarchy and died about two years later in 1850 at the

[85]***Who Really Wrote the Book of Mormon?*, Cowdrey/Davis/Scales, p. 129.**
[86]***Ibid.*, Cowdrey/Davis/Scales, p. 145.**

age of 43.[87] Smith's secret sexual rendezvous were kept hidden until in 1835 when they began to surface in the Fannie Alger affair. Cowdery, at that time, caught Fanny and Smith together and began to expose them publicly. This, of course, was not very pleasant for Smith, so he ex-communicated his other partner who claimed to have been conferred the keys of the kingdom of God by the spirits of John the Baptist and Peter, James, and John.

Smith was not only a victim of Spiritualism but also of unsatiable sexual desires and, to justify his illicit sexual relationships which were coming out of the closet, he simply used the errors of Abraham and Jacob who had polygamous relationships and which were recorded in the Bible. However, the God of the Bible has recorded both the good and the evil deeds that His people have committed. Plural marriages were not ordained by God for He declared through Moses: "Therefore shall a man leave his father and his mother, and shall cleave unto his wife: and they shall be **ONE FLESH**." Genesis 2:24. The apostle Paul says: "This is a true saying, If a man desire the office of a bishop, he desireth a good work. A bishop then must be blameless, the husband of **ONE WIFE**, vigilant, sober, of good behaviour, given to hospitality, apt to teach." 1 Timothy 3:1, 2.

Nevertheless, Smith, to justify his adulterous affairs, invented the idea that God had given him a revelation that the ancient practice of plural marriages a.k.a. celestial marriages was to be reinstated in the church of which caused Mormons to divide into two opposing factions. After Smith had in 1835 instituted polygamy as a revelation of God, he went so far as to even claim that God had revealed to him that he should add some **married** Mormon women to his harem. Of course, his wife Emma was outraged and embarrassed by her husband's lustful actions under the guise of religion and, after suffering terribly for years, she openly opposed Smith's doctrine of polygamy. Smith countered his wife and others who opposed him by pretending to have had another revelation from God in which he wrote that God had made polygamy a law to be obeyed and if not, one must be destroyed.[88]

It was at this time that another adulterer entered the Mormon Church

[87]***Encyclopedia of Mormonism*, Vol. 2, ed. Ludlow, pp. 335–339.**

[88]***No Man Knows My History*, Brodie, pp. 340, 341.**

who, by his talents as a doctor, made his way up through the ranks of Mormonism, even for a time bumping out Rigdon as Smith's guru and most intimate friend. His name was Dr. John C. Bennett, an abortionist who later joined the American Society of the Illuminati after he was also ex-communicated from the church. Like Smith, Bennett had an unsatiable appetite for sex and had not only seduced innumerable Mormon ladies, but became Smith's rival among them. Smith justified his adulteress affairs by marrying them, while Bennett would not. This brought accusations from the Bible-believing Christians and non-believers alike of a prostitution scandal among the Mormons in Nauvoo, and Smith was forced by pressure to rebuke Bennett. However, the real showdown between the American Muhammad and Bennett came when Smith tried to tell Sidney Rigdon's daughter that he had a revelation from God that she was to be one of his wives. However, Bennett had warned her beforehand and Nancy Rigdon not only rejected Smith's advances, but told her father.

On June 23, 1842, John C. Bennett was ex-communicated. As an act of revenge, Bennett, who had stood next to Smith in the church hierarchy, wrote a series of articles exposing Smith's plans to take over the Western states of America with his legion. Bennett went on to expose Smith's polygamous practices, along with his secret society of the Danites who swore an oath to protect Smith. Sir Richard Burton, in his book, *The City of the Saints*, on p. 227 pointed out that the Mormons speak of John C. Bennett as the ***Musaylimat el Kazzáb*** of their religion. ***Musaylimat the Liar*** tried and failed to enter into partnership with **Muhammad**. Bennett in turn called Smith everything from an outrageous libertine to a foul and polluted murderer. Bennett published his letters about Smith in America's most leading newspapers of that day. Later, he collected and revised them and produced a book entitled *The History of the Saints: or, An Exposé of Joe Smith and Mormonism.*[89]

According to *Who Really Wrote the Book of Mormon?*, pages 102, 103, Bennett (in his written testimony) affirmed and openly stated that the Book of Mormon was originally written by Solomon Spaulding and that the story of the plates was all chimerical.

There is overwhelming evidence now that Mormonism's doctrines

[89]***No Man Knows My History*, Brodie, pp. 314, 315.**

are based in polytheism (a belief in more than one god), and it is really just a sophisticated system of **Spiritualism** using the Judeo-Christian faith to hide this fact. The very first two lies of Satan, which he used to deceive Eve in the Garden of God, are presently deceiving the ten million Mormons today! Satan told Eve in his first lie, **"YE SHALL NOT SURELY DIE."** Genesis 3:5. Like the New Agers, Mormons are taught by their gurus that they shall never die because Smith said the soul (spirit) was not created by God and that they had pre-existed in the spirit world in the Cosmos before they had received mortal bodies. Satan's second lie consisted of an offer at the chance at godhood if Eve would just disobey God by partaking of the Tree of Knowledge of Good and Evil. Satan promised **"YE SHALL BE AS GODS, KNOWING GOOD AND EVIL."** Genesis 3:5. My Mormon reader, is this not what Mormons are taught and promised today?

Sir Richard Burton, who was a master of Islamic mysticism, after visiting with the Mormons frankly told their leaders that their religion was essentially an agglomeration of **Jewish mysticism**, **millennialism**, **transcendentalism**, and **Freemasonry**, plus certain **Muslim** practices; and the Mormons replied that their religion embraced all truth, "**come whence it may**."[90] In spite of this, after denying their involvement with the secret society of Freemasonry to not only other non-Mormons but to Mormon members as well, the First Presidency whispered a message on October 15, 1911, "**that because of their Masonic character the ceremonies of the temple are sacred and not for the public.**"[91]

There is some truth, however, to Smith's notion that the Masons, Jews, Catholics, and Protestants have apostatized from the Word of God, which we shall surely continue to see in the following chapters. Jesus symbolizes this worldwide apostasy from God as a Mother of Harlots who is named Babylon the Great. The Mormon Church is one of her daughters, and Jesus is telling His people who are unwittingly still members of Babylon the Great to **"Come out of her, my people, that ye be not partakers of her sins, and that ye receive not of her plagues. For her sins have reached unto heaven, and God hath remembered her iniquities." Revelation 18:4, 5.**

[90]***The City of the Saints*, Burton, p. xxix.**

[91]***Dialogue: A Journal of Mormon Thought*, Fall/Winter 1994, p. 73.**

CHAPTER III

THE MYSTICAL TEACHINGS OF ZOROASTER, BUDDHA, AND THE DALAI LAMA

"And there came one of the seven angels which had the seven vials, and talked with me, saying unto me, Come hither; I will shew unto thee the judgment of the great whore that sitteth upon many waters: With whom the kings of the earth have committed fornication, and the inhabitants of the earth have been made drunk with the wine of her fornication.

"So he carried me away in the spirit into the wilderness: and I saw a woman sit upon a scarlet coloured beast, full of names of blasphemy, having seven heads and ten horns. And the woman was arrayed in purple and scarlet colour, and decked with gold and precious stones and pearls, having a golden cup in her hand full of abominations and filthiness of her fornication:

"And upon her forehead was a name written, **MYSTERY, BABYLON THE GREAT, THE MOTHER OF HARLOTS AND ABOMINATIONS OF THE EARTH.**

"And I saw the woman drunken with the blood of the saints, and with the blood of the martyrs of Jesus: and when I saw her, I wondered with great admiration. And the angel said unto me, Wherefore didst thou marvel? **I will tell thee the mystery of the woman, and of the beast that carrieth her, which hath the seven heads and ten horns.**" Revelation 17:1–7.

CHAPTER III

Reader, Satan really has only one religion which he has used down through the centuries, both in the ancient and modern worlds, to divide people from all races so that they will war on each other. In the prophecies found on the pages of the Holy Scriptures, his power and religious influences are symbolized as a **seven-headed Dragon**. The seven-headed Dragon not only symbolizes the power and influence (spirit) of Satan in the Bible, but in prophecy it also represents Satan's number-one religion, which is **ASTROLOGY**. The seven-headed Dragon had been used by the ancient Babylonians themselves to symbolize the religion and mystical practices of astrology.[1] In Revelation 12:9, we read as follows: "And the great dragon was cast out, that old serpent, called the Devil, and Satan, **WHICH DECEIVETH THE WHOLE WORLD**: he was cast out into the earth, and his angels were cast out with him."

Before the birth of Zarathushtra (Zoroaster), Buddha, Plato, and Muhammad, the God of Abraham, Isaac, and Jacob warned the Israelites through Moses not to adopt the religious practices of the pagans who were living in Canaan. "And the Lord spake unto Moses, saying, Speak unto the children of Israel, and say unto them, I am the Lord your God. After the **doings of the land** of Egypt, wherein ye dwelt, shall ye **not** do: and **after the doings** of the land of Canaan, whither I bring you, shall ye **not** do: **neither shall ye walk in their ordinances. Ye shall do my judgments, and keep mine ordinances, to walk therein: I am the Lord your God**." Leviticus 18:1–4.

However, they ignored Him, and, as a result, the ancient Israelites were gradually seduced into worshipping the gods of astrology

[1]***The Religion of Ancient Egypt and Babylonia*, Sayce, 1902, p. 240.**

which were the sun, moon, and stars instead of Christ, the Creator of these heavenly bodies. Very few there are, indeed, who have not been deceived into following some precept from astrology's mysticism.

This book will take a look at the origins and doctrines of Hinduism, Zoroastrianism, Buddhism, Islam, Ashkenazi Judaism, papal Christianity, and mainstream Protestantism and will show the reader how all of the above have also, like the Israelites, adopted precepts which derived out of ancient, Babylonian astrology (mysticism).

Although the religion of astrology varies throughout the world, it will be shown that it has only one source. As the Old Testament Scriptures foretold that Christ or the Messiah would come to deliver His people from the Dragon's power, so did the various systems of the religion of astrology found throughout the world have their messiahs or messengers. However, reader, thinking humans must be prepared for the greatest deception coming that was ever pulled on the human race. Satan, astrology's author, was predicted in Scripture to appear in the person of Christ in these last days.

"Little children, it is the last time: and as ye have heard that ANTICHRIST shall come, even now are there MANY ANTICHRISTS; whereby we know that it is the last time." 1 John 2:18.

The God of Abraham has clearly warned the people of this planet about Satan's plans to personate Jesus Christ and how he shall condition the inhabitants of this world into accepting him as Christ. God has given us the Holy Scriptures as a guide to help us to distinguish the difference between the Christ and the Antichrist; "lest Satan should get an advantage of us: for we are not ignorant of his devices." 2 Corinthians 2:11.

As my wife and I travel on the highways and byways in the U.S. and in different parts of the world holding lectures about the Second Coming of Christ and the warnings found in the Scriptures about the Antichrist, I have been astonished to see how much confusion there is among **mainstream Christians** about just who this Antichrist is. I have heard from Protestant pastors and read from well-known Christian authors that the Antichrist will be a Jew who shall arise out of Rome.

Reader, the Antichrist first began his mission in Heaven. The Antichrist is Satan himself (not some Jew from Rome) who will appear in these days of the "**Time of the End**." Nevertheless, both Jesus and John, the penman of the book of Revelation, along with the apostle Paul, warned of human beings who would arise and say, "**I AM CHRIST, AND SHALL DECEIVE MANY**," (Matthew 24:5) "**even now are there many antichrists**." 1 John 2:18. The apostle Paul also warned of a particular human being, who he called "**THE SON OF PERDITION**" (2 Thessalonians 2:3), who is not Satan, but "even him, whose coming is **AFTER** the working of Satan with all power and signs and lying wonders." 2 Thessalonians 2:9. The apostle John said this **human impostor** would be branded with the number 666. (See Revelation 13:18.) Jesus also warned of false christs and false prophets who would arise from His day to ours. The mission of these false christs or false prophets, of course, is to usher the world into a confederacy by attempting to unite all religions and all governments into **ONE**, leaving the Biblical Jesus out. This confederacy will be molded and helped along by businessmen and religious and political leaders of this present age who will preach a gospel of peace and safety throughout this world. The apostle John prophesied that this blend of worldly businessmen (merchants) and religions (Babylon the Great; Revelation, Chapter 17) is an abomination unto the Lord, and it is a "Time of the End" **sign** to Bible-believing Christians that the arrival of this Antichrist is near. **"For when they shall say, Peace and safety; then sudden destruction cometh upon them, as travail upon a woman with child; and they shall not escape. But ye, brethren, are not in darkness, that that day should overtake you as a thief."** 1 Thessalonians 5:3, 4.

It is, indeed, very eye-opening to learn that the six major religions – Hinduism, Buddhism, Judaism, Islam, Christianity (Catholicism and Protestantism), and Confucianism – are looking for some kind of a world teacher or messiah to come and overthrow the present systems of this angry world and usher in an Age of Peace. The messiah to the Hindu is **Krishna**; to the Buddhist, he is the **fifth Buddha**; to the Muslim, he is the last Imam called **Mahdi**; to the Jew who still rejects Jesus, he is the **Messiah**; to the Christian, of course, he is **Jesus**; and to the theosophist (New Ager) who is also trying to unite all of these religions, however, he is **Maitreya Buddha**. We will study more about how to discern the difference between the Christ and the Antichrist as we continue.

Zoroaster, Buddha, and the Dalai Lama

Let's now begin to look at the documented history of three men who arose in history claiming to have had a special revelation and went on to become the founders of world religions. They are Zarathushtra (Zoroaster), Gautama Buddha, and Muhammad. We will first examine the history of Zoroaster, for many of his teachings can be found in the writings of Plato (the father of the New Age and the NWO), the Kabbalah, and also the Sufis of Islam.

Among historians, the birth of Zoroaster is still uncertain. Some historians place the birth of Zoroaster around 1200 B.C., while others think it was around the year 628 B.C. which was about 65 years before the birth of Gautama Buddha. The name ***Zoroaster*** is the Greek form of **Zarathushtra** which, to the people of the Near East, means "***He of the Golden Light***."[2]

Zoroaster (Zarathushtra) is believed to have promoted his religion in the area of northern Persia. About the time of King David of Israel or a little before, the Aryans began to invade Mesopotamia. The Aryans conquered Iran and India and occupied the lands and consequently introduced their version of mysticism upon its inhabitants. The ancient, pagan religions which were practiced in India and Persia at that time had striking similarities to the Aryan religion, as the Native American Indians and the Siberian Natives are discovering today. At the birth of Zarathushtra, the people of Persia were worshipping a pantheon of gods to which the Aryans added the worship of Mithra around 1000 B.C. It was from Persia that both Mithraism and later Zoroastrianism developed and spread together into different parts of the world with Zoroastrianism becoming the official religion of Persia. Zoroastrianism survived the overthrow of the Persian Empire by Alexander the Great and, afterwards, continued during the reign of the Caesars of the Roman Empire. However, when the Muslims invaded Persia, the Zoroastrians who survived the sword of the Saracens fled to India, and Islam became Persia's official religion after the Sassanids were defeated in A.D. 636.[3]

One of the central doctrines of Zoroastrianism is this. Zoroaster claimed that while practicing meditation (in a trance), his "**soul**" had

[2]***The World Book Encyclopedia*, Vol. 21, 1997, p. 619.**

[3]***The Concise Encyclopedia of Islam*, Glassé, p. 456.**

a "**mystical union**" with *Ahura Mazda* who was to become the chief deity of Persia. He claimed that he had received a "special revelation" and power from his god, and that he had been called by his winged-deity to announce to the world that *Ahura Mazd*a was the only supreme god.

The worship of this winged-god was to be spread throughout the known world by conducting religious wars. Zoroaster taught that the earth is a battleground where a great struggle is taking place between *Spenta Mainyu*, the spirit of good, and *Angra Mainyu*, the spirit of evil. According to Zoroaster, *Ahura Mazda* has called upon everyone to fight in this struggle, and each person will be judged at death on how well he or she fought.[4]

After experiencing many mystical visions from his god, Ahura Mazda, and wandering throughout Persia and parts of India proclaiming that his deity was the only true god, Zoroaster gained only one convert, his cousin. However, according to Zoroastrian tradition, Zoroaster was given an audience with King Vishtaspa who requested a miracle be done as proof of his spiritual claims and of the power of his god of fire. **It is believed by modern-day occultists that Zoroaster produced a heavenly fire**[5] to appear in the presence of the king; and **this fire could not be extinguished**, but would burn those who would come near. The pagan king made Zoroaster a member of his court after witnessing the power of this fire. King Vishtaspa, who was astonished by this miracle, began to help spread the religion of Ahura Mazda by building **fire temples**[6] to honor Zoroaster's fire-god.

It is interesting to note that the great test between the prophets of Jezebel, whose god was the Phoenician sun-god Baal, and Elijah, a prophet of the God of Abraham, was over bringing **fire** down from heaven. It is also interesting to note that the prophets of Baal today will demonstrate the power of the "**prince of the air**" by performing this miracle. In Revelation 13:13, 14, it warns:

"And he doeth great wonders, so that **he maketh fire come down**

[4]*The World Book Encyclopedia*, Vol. 21, 1997, pp. 619, 620.

[5]*Dictionary of Mysticism and the Esoteric Traditions*, Drury, p. 323.

[6]*Ibid.*, Drury, p. 323.

from heaven on the earth in the sight of men, And **deceiveth** them that dwell on the earth by the means of those **miracles** which he had power to do in the sight of the beast; saying to them that dwell on the earth, that they should make an image to the beast, which had the wound by a sword, and did live."

Fire is sacred to those in mysticism. Pagans are shown in the Old Testament to have caused their children to pass through the fires of Molech to see if they were acceptable to him. If they were burnt, they were not acceptable to Molech and were sacrificed. This practice was forbidden in Deuteronomy 18:10.

In Haiti, where voodoo is openly practiced, the mystics or shamans call upon their African gods and the spirits of Roman Catholic saints or deified ancestors to give them supernatural counsel and to perform extraordinary, physical feats. A photograph of a practitioner standing over a fire with it blazing over his head (without being injured by the fire or his clothes catching on fire) is found in *The Oxford Illustrated Encyclopedia of Peoples and Cultures*.[7] This is looked upon as the power of God because the God of the Old Testament saved the three companions of Daniel from the fiery furnace (Daniel, Chapter Three).

According to *A Dictionary of Comparative Religion*, **Zoroaster has been regarded as a shaman, a mystic, and a prophet**.[8] His religion, Zoroastrianism, was also based in a *dualistic* conception of the cosmos as having good spirits and evil spirits. Zoroaster named these good spirits **ahuras** and the bad spirits **daivas**.[9]

The Encyclopedia of Religion says that the above Iranian prophet belonged to a priestly order that sought "**Aryan mysticism**" a.k.a. Indo-Iranian mysticism.[10]

Zarathushtra's god of mysticism and magic was a god of fire. It is said that the Persian prophet showed evidence of the power given to him from his deity. While in prayer, **Ahura Mazda caused Zoroaster to levitate above the floor while his body became**

[7]*The Oxford Illustrated Encyclopedia of Peoples and Cultures*, Vol. 7, ed. Hoggart, p. 327.

[8]*A Dictionary of Comparative Religion*, ed. Brandon, 1970, p. 663.

[9]*Man, Myth & Magic*, Vol. 20, ed. Cavendish, 1995, pp. 2870-2872.

[10]*The Encyclopedia of Religion*, Vol. 15, ed. Eliade, 1987, pp. 556–558.

luminous and, at the same time, a flame would rest upon his head. A Buddhist mystic named Sura Acharya floated himself across a stream while sitting upon his mantle.[11] This occult phenomenon has also been claimed by mystics of the Roman Catholic Church. Both St. Cubertin and the very famous **St. Francis of Assisi were said to have so overflowed with spirituality that when they engaged in their devotions, there was no keeping their bodies down to the ground.**[12] Jesus Himself, as the reader knows, performed many signs and wonders. However, both the Old and the New Testaments warn of men who would deceive the inhabitants of this world by the power of sorcery (Revelation 18:23). **"FOR THERE SHALL ARISE FALSE CHRISTS, AND FALSE PROPHETS, AND SHALL SHEW GREAT SIGNS AND WONDERS; INSOMUCH THAT, IF IT WERE POSSIBLE, THEY SHALL DECEIVE THE VERY ELECT." Matthew 24:24.**

Zoroaster's popularity in the ancient world continued throughout the Renaissance until the Enlightenment. He was viewed as a wise man, a master of the secrets of the universe, a seer, an astrologer, a psychologist, and a wonder worker. His popularity diminished somewhat because of Islam; however, during the Renaissance and the Enlightenment Movement (Illuminism) in the 18th century, he was again rediscovered. **He was again viewed as a great and wise man, as the author of the *Chaldean Oracles,* and as probable inventor of the Kabbalah.**[13] **All modern Spiritualism, as well as Freemasonry, is based in the Kabbalah, the Jewish book of magic.** We will investigate more into the Kabbalah, and we will also see just who the Hollywood celebrities are that are publicly promoting its teachings and philosophies as we continue.

Zoroaster was viewed by some as a possible bridge between Christianity and Platonism, and, at times, as a symbol of non-Christian wisdom. The antichrist Friedrich Nietzsche saw Zoroaster as the first

[11]Todd's *Western India*, p. 277, quoted in *The Two Babylons*, Hislop, p. 258.
[12]Eusebe Salverté, p., 37, quoted in *The Two Babylons*, Hislop, p. 258.
[13]*The Encyclopedia of Religion*, Vol. 15, ed. Eliade, p. 558.

to discover the true motive force underlying the eternal struggle between good and evil.[14] **However, Zoroaster is often thought of as an Iranian prophet. This is not to be confused with being a prophet of the God of Abraham, for Zoroaster was a prophet of the occult; he was a wizard like Joseph Smith.**

Zoroaster's teachings have mainly been preserved in 17 hymns, known as *Gathas*, which are in the Yasna, part of the Avesta scripture. We can trace the doctrine of hell, the burning place of torment, to Zoroaster. **He claimed that God, who he called Ahura Mazda, (not to be confused with the God of Abraham) taught him personally through a series of visions which called him to his mission.**[15] He taught a twisted account of the Biblical record of the conflict between Christ and His angels and Satan and his angels. A person's fate depended on whose side they chose to be on.

According to Zoroaster, when a person dies his soul is immediately taken to the Bridge of Judgment. Those who have done good deeds are led to paradise, and those who are found evil in the Judgment are led to the **House of the Lie**, a place of torment.[16] Both Roman Catholics and Protestants owe their unscriptural doctrine of **"hell," the burning place of torment**, to the teachings of Zoroaster,[17] not to Jesus' teachings. This false doctrine has been one of the main reasons for multitudes to receive a false impression of God. It makes Him out to be a tyrant, and, because of this, Satan has added to his cause an untold number of atheists. **Yet, there are those who actually get irate when they find out that their beliefs about hell are wrong, for they have been programmed to actually enjoy this thought of God torturing the wicked.**

However, Zoroastrianism speaks of worshipping only one God (Ahura Mazda). It also teaches there will be a Last Judgment, a resurrection of the body, and how the good God will, in the final end, triumph over evil. Some scholars believe that the doctrines or theology of Zoroaster must have come from the God of Abraham because

[14]*The Encyclopedia of Religion*, Vol. 15, ed. Eliade, p. 558.

[15]*World Religions*, Bowker, p. 13.

[16]*Ibid.*, Bowker, p. 13.

[17]*The Concise Encyclopedia of Islam*, Glassé, p. 434.

of the similarities found in the Judeo-Christian faith and that Zoroastrianism influenced the monotheism of the Arab Muslims.[18] However, as we continue, the reader shall examine how Satan, our invisible Foe, has always confused the human race by blending the philosophies of astrology with the precepts found written in the Law and the Prophets. There is a **Mystery of Godliness**, and there is a **Mystery of Iniquity**; there is a power of God and a power from Satan. When the two are blended, human minds are led to believe this is of God. However, **the True God of Abraham never does anything in partnership with the *prince of darkness***, and it shall be shown how Satan has crosslinks in Zoroastrianism, Buddhism, Judaism, Christianity, and Islam which are, indeed, leading the whole human race to that battle of that great day of God Almighty. The Bible prophecies have warned over and over again about how human beings will be deceived into unwittingly uniting themselves with devils as did our ancestors in the past. The spirits that pagans and their shamans seek are not gods or deified saints; they are demons who have pretended to be gods.

"But I say, that the things which the Gentiles sacrifice, THEY SACRIFICE TO DEVILS, and not to God: and I would not that ye should have fellowship with devils. Ye cannot drink the cup of the Lord, and the cup of devils: ye cannot be partakers of the Lord's table, and of the table of devils." 1 Corinthians 10:20, 21.

Followers of Christ who blend mysticism or voodoo with the worship of God are under a strange delusion for the Scriptures plainly state that we are either on Satan's side or we are on Christ's side. The power from which Satan works his miracles comes from mysticism (occultism), not from God.

"Be ye not unequally yoked together with unbelievers: for what fellowship hath righteousness with unrighteousness? and what communion hath light with darkness?

"And what **concord hath Christ with Belial**? or what part hath he that believeth with an infidel?" 2 Corinthians 6:14, 15.

The Holy Scriptures clearly show that the ancient gods which our ancient ancestors worshipped and were led to even kill for were,

[18]*The Concise Encyclopedia of Islam*, Glassé, p. 434.

in reality, the worship of the cosmic Dragon (Satan) and his fallen angels who have personated themselves as gods. Once the reader learns for himself that this is true, then it shall be easy to understand why many of these so-called idols and stars from Hollywood and the Music Industry are busy promoting the precepts of Eastern religions while, at the same time, claiming to be of the Jewish or Christian faiths. A union with devils and an acceptance of their doctrines by Christians was predicted by the apostle Paul in 1 Timothy 4:1:

"Now the Spirit speaketh expressly, that **IN THE LATTER TIMES some shall depart from the faith, GIVING HEED TO SEDUCING SPIRITS, AND DOCTRINES OF DEVILS**."

The prophecy of 1 Timothy 4:1 may answer many puzzling questions in the minds of Christians as well. When Christians hear the words *occult*, *spiritualism*, or *witchcraft*, for instance, they naturally think of these words as being associated with evil. **Many Christians do not realize that the people of mysticism have among themselves, as well, a division of good and evil.** For instance, among occultists today there are two divisions of people: those who practice **black magic** and those who practice **white magic**. Occultists believe there are good witches who cast spells for the good of people, and there are bad witches who cast spells to try to kill or injure people.

However, there is no such thing as a good witch in the Judeo-Christian religion of the Bible, and all magic is from the power of the Devil. As we continue, we shall see how this occult practice of mysticism and this mixture of good and evil has, indeed, not only confused human minds about their perception of the True God, but how He has been misrepresented by erring religious leaders down through the centuries. We will again study what the prophet Zoroaster taught his followers, but first let's take a look at what the religion of astrology teaches about good and bad spirits.

In the religion of astrology, the minds of its disciples are directed to an **imaginary 360° circle** in the sky called the zodiac. As pointed out, the religion of astrology is symbolized as a ***seven-headed dragon*** in the Bible and even among astrologers themselves. It is interesting to note that, according to modern-day astrologers, the seven heads on the dragon represent the ***seven chief gods*** of astrology that serpentine their way around the 360° circle of the zodiac. Here are just some of their names in history: **Baal (Sun), Ashtaroth (Moon), Tammuz (Venus), Marduk (Mars), Nebo (Mercury), Zeus (Jupiter), and Cronus (Saturn).**[19]

Besides the seven chief gods which move around the zodiac band, astrologers believe that there are 18 good gods and 18 bad gods in fixed positions around the 360° circle of the zodiac. They are also known as "House" gods and "Room" gods. These 36 lesser gods are divided into two divisions around the zodiac and are divided 10° apart around its 360° zodiac band. When the sun-god appears in the East and travels 180° to the West, he is worshipped as a good god; but when he sinks into the ocean, the sun-god becomes an evil god as do the other remaining 18 gods positioned on the bottom portion of the zodiac. Here we find the origin of the Oriental concept of the Yin Yang **(Yin=evil, Yang=good)** and also the origin of Zoroaster's dualistic doctrines. Here is also the origin of that number of doom which Bible-believing Christians had better not be found identified with at Christ's Second Coming. If the reader will add the numbers from one to 36 together, **they will add to the number 666**.

Zoroaster's religion, as we have seen, was centered around the conflict of good spirits and bad spirits. He went on to become the founder of *Zoroastrianism* a.k.a. *Mazdaism* in ancient Persia. As we have seen, Zoroaster believed in an **immortal soul** and taught that the people of this world are to **submit** their souls only to this **supreme god** which he called **Ahura Mazda**. Zoroaster (Zarathushtra) borrowed many of his doctrines from the ancient Chaldeans who had migrated from northern India during the post-Flood Era. It shall be proven that all the religions of mysticism originated with the Chaldeans. The Chaldeans, however, worshipped a pantheon of gods and goddesses. **Anu**, the sky-god, was at the head of this pantheon. Three chief gods were under the sky-god; they were the **moon-god Sin**, the **sun-god Shamash**, and the goddess **Inanna** or **Ishtar** (Sirius). Zarathushtra struggled with the Persians to worship only one god, Ahura Mazda. However, the Persians continued to blend Aryanism with Zoroastrianism, as well.

Before the rise of both Zoroastrianism and Islam, the chief sky-god

[19]*Origins of Astrology*, Lindsay, 1971, pp. 233, 375.

to the ancient, idolatrous Arabs and ancient Canaanites of northern Israel, Lebanon, and the Syrian coastal regions was ***"IL,"* the Creator god.**[20] After the fall of the Persian Empire, the chief sky-god became Zeus, who was of Indo-European origin, to the ancient Greeks who conquered the ancient Persians.[21] Who this ancient god "***IL***" of the ancient, pagan Arabs and Canaanites actually was will be studied later when we examine the documented history of Muhammad. This will prove to be very astonishing for those who follow Allah.

This volume will focus mainly on five of the six major religions which, I might add, have gained much popularity and many converts in the United States. They are the mystical, religious orders of Hinduism, Zoroastrianism, Buddhism, Islam, and **Hasidic Ashkenazi Jewry**. Although the above religions differ in beliefs, this volume will show how all of these religious orders have something in common with Zoroastrianism and astrology which is threaded throughout all of them – the secret doctrine of astrology known as **MYSTICISM**.

Maybe it is time now to stop here and just define the word ***mysticism***. What is **mysticism**? According to *The American Heritage Dictionary*, mysticism is "*a spiritual discipline aiming at union with the divine* ***through deep meditation or contemplation***."[22] In other words, **mysticism is a practice of receiving power from a deity after the seeker loses consciousness of his immediate surroundings. He seeks methods to bring his mind (soul) into a unity with his deity, like Zoroaster did, by putting oneself into a hypnotic trance. This practice is very popular today, and it is called yoga.** The actress Lindsay Wagner, star of the ***Bionic Woman*** and numerous made-for-television movies, was introduced into the New Age Movement when she was 20 years old while she was drawn in by exploring into New Age medicine, meditation, visualization, and reading literature from the mystic-prophet Edgar Cayce.[23]

[20]*Encyclopedia of Gods*, Jordan, p. 112.

[21]*A Dictionary of Comparative Religion*, ed. Brandon, p. 662.

[22]*The American Heritage Dictionary*, Based on the New Second College Edition, 1983, p. 453.

[23]*New Age Encyclopedia*, Melton, p. 94.

Zoroaster, himself, was a mystic and a teacher of mysticism. A mystic is a person who has been initiated into secret rites and practices of the occult which center around mystical understanding. Zoroaster taught his disciples how to unite their soul (spiritual self) with ***Ahura Mazda***. I have found in my research of the six major religions of the world that all of them promote some kind of a mystical experience with their chief deity.

Mystical ideas, practices, and experiences are **central** to Hinduism, Zoroastrianism, Buddhism, Hasidic Judaism, Sufism, and pseudo-Christianity. However, it shall also be shown from Scripture that the **God of Abraham, Isaac, and Jacob forbids** any manner of these dangerous occult-based methods of seeking a union with Him.

In this volume, we will not only study how to tell the difference between the Christ and the Antichrist and what mysticism is, but we will also see the crosslinks between the New Age Movement and this New World Order scheme whose adherents are also busy in a worldwide effort to unite the world's religions and governments into a MYSTICAL UNION. We will look into the Hindu and Buddhist teachings of KARMA and REINCARNATION and see how many of the most well-known celebrities are involved in mysticism and the occult and how they are using their influences to win others.

In the next chapter, we will explore the prophecies from Revelation, Chapter Nine, which foretold the "**two woes**" upon apostate Christians and other non-Muslims of the Old World. The first two scourges (woes) were delivered by the **Arabian Muslims (Saracens)** from A.D. 610–1258 and then, again, by the **Asian Muslims (Turks)** during their first 150 years (five prophetic months). These woes were continued under the power of the Ottoman Empire which was foretold to last 391 years plus 15 days (a day, a month, a year, and an hour). We will also study the prophecies of this coming "**third woe**" on those who do not have the "**Seal of God**" in their foreheads. (See Revelation 9:12.) We will also see that Muhammad was a mystic.

It is very important for the Bible-believing Christian to have some knowledge of Zoroastrianism, Hinduism, Buddhism, Sufism, and Islam to understand why they are receiving multitudes of converts who were former Christians into their ranks. Islam is the fastest growing religion in the world; it has 1.1 billion followers. Like Zoroaster, Islam advocates ***Jihãd*** (holy wars)[24] to Islamize the whole world, while Hindus and Buddhists, on the other hand, believe in using religious propaganda. While Zoroastrianism teaches that Ahura Mazda is the supreme deity, Islam believes that it is Allah who is the sole deity in heaven and Muhammad is the last prophet to appear in this world. Nevertheless, Zarathushtra and Muhammad were not the only mystical religious leaders in history to try to unite their nations under a monotheistic society. **Pharoah Amenhotep IV** (1387–1366 B.C.) outlawed the worship of all gods **except Aton, the sun-god.**[25] However, on the other hand, Buddhists and Hindus believe in a multitude of gods, goddesses, and demons, but they believe that the gods or demons **were once human beings**.

This is religious confusion, indeed, but to be able to see how Islam and Buddhism could possibly unite one day into a religious confederacy with apostate Christians as predicted in the book of Revelation, one must understand the doctrine of **MYSTICISM**.

Unlike Orthodox Islam, however, mysticism among the Hindus and the Buddhists has a pantheistic view that the universe and its God are one vast microcosm, a **ONENESS**, and that everything is connected. Occultism teaches that man can experience a oneness with the Divine through this spiritual discipline called **YOGA a.k.a. MEDITATION. The word *yoga* comes from the Sanskrit (ancient Indic language) verbal root *yuj* meaning "*to yoke, to join*," *to yoke one thing to another*.**[26]

This Hindu view that nature and God are **ONE** is the avenue in which Satan has directed human beings to worship trees, mountains, rocks, stars, insects, animals, fowl, and humans. **God is *not* nature; He is the God *of* nature.** He is the Creator of all things. Pagans, however, are led by this subtle lie to believe that nature is God which leads them to worship the forces of nature instead of the Creator of all things.

[24]*The Meaning of The Holy Qur'ãn*, 'Ali, Surah 2:216, 217; pp. 86, 87; Surah 4:84, p. 211; *The Muslim Almanac*, ed. Nanji, p. 499.

[25]*Nelson's Illustrated Encyclopedia of Bible Facts*, ed. Packer/Tenney/White, Jr., p. 91.

[26]*The Mythic Image*, Campbell, p. 303.

Hinduism also teaches that the Divine is One God, but has many emanations of his attributes; and that all the gods, sun-gods or moon-goddesses, etc., etc., are just emanations of the One Supreme Deity. Therefore, man, being a miniature microcosm is also a god but has forgotten this and must be awakened to the fact that he too is divine and has an eternal, divine soul. Hence, it is the goal of disciples of mysticism to join their soul (spiritual self, mind) with that of their deity. New Agers call this a "mystical union" of the human soul with the Divine – **Christ-consciousness or Self-Realization**.

New Agers believe that through meditation (yoga) a human can unite his soul (mind) with the Divine and become a christ or a Buddha himself. This is also known as the **introvertive** path to enlightenment. When Hindus greet each other, they press their hands together in a praying gesture towards each other. This is known among the Hindus as the ***Anjali*** which means "***I bow to the divinity within you.***"[27]

There are two types of this mystical experience: the **EXTROVERTIVE** and the **INTROVERTIVE** paths.[28] The **extrovertive** mystic looks forward to a physical and universal, mystical union of all religions and nations under **ONE** banner. **A MYSTICAL WORLD REVOLUTION** which would force all religions and governments to unite was planned centuries ago by this chief Antichrist named Lucifer. This invisible Foe has always had his chosen few who he has used or is using to promote this secret doctrine that the nations of the world and their religions would some day be united into a world alliance. **This secret revolution by occultists to do this very thing has continued undetected by Bible-believing Christians for centuries; however, the darkness of mysticism will be laid out in the light for everyone to view.**

Occult leaders who are believed to have reached an ***introvertive*****, mystical oneness with the Divine are known as Mystics, Mahatmas, Shamans, Gurus, Buddhas, Bodhidharmas, Lamas, Imams, Taoists, or Masters**. The process in which occultists attempt to unite their soul with the will of the *cosmic one*, the author of *mysticism*,

[27] ***World Religions*****, Bowker, p. 40.**

[28] ***The Encyclopedia Americana*****, Vol. 19, 1995, p. 697.**

involves learning how to empty the conscious mind (soul) of his or her awareness of all sensations, thoughts, desires, ego, etc. until the subconscious is brought into a mystical union a.k.a. marriage with this power which occultists call **the Force a.k.a Solar Logos, the Chi, the Chakra, or the Tao**. By uniting the mind (soul) with the Force, the mystic can acquire power under a trance to overcome certain bad habits or traits of character or perform miracles by the use of magic, pyschic healing, and other occult sciences which are all an abomination unto the Lord.

The astrological sciences of mysticism are clearly exposed and condemned in the Bible in Deuteronomy 18:10–12. "There shall **NOT** be found among you any one that maketh his son or his daughter to pass through the fire, or that useth divination (**PYSCHIC**), or an observer of times (**ASTROLOGER**), or an enchanter (**YOGI, MYSTIC, SORCERER, OR ONE WHO CASTS SPELLS**), or a witch,

"Or a charmer (**HYPNOTIST**), or a consulter with familiar spirits (**MEDIUM a.k.a. CHANNELER**), or a wizard (**MALE WITCH, MAGICIAN**), or a necromancer (**SHAMAN OR ONE WHO CLAIMS TO COMMUNICATE WITH PAGAN GODS, UFOS, ANCESTORS, etc.**).

"For all that do these things are an abomination unto the Lord: and because of these abominations the Lord thy God doth drive them out from before thee." (Emphasis mine.) Deuteronomy 18:10–12.

What has been so deceptive about mysticism is that it has been blended with the worship of God. Before the birth of Islam, this subtle practice of sorcery was written on the pages of the Kabbalah, the Jewish book of magic. In Jewish circles, one who is skilled in esoteric doctrine or mysticism is called a **CABALIST (Kabbalist)**. We will look more into the origin of the Kabbalah shortly.

This doctrine of a "**mystical union**" with a deity is found in the writings of Gnosticism, which Simon Magus the sorcerer founded. This blend of occultism with Christianity is taught among the schools of the Rosicrucians. Amazingly, in the *New Catholic Encyclopedia*, this same mystical union of the soul with a deity is also taught by the Papacy.[29] On page 176 of this above Catholic encyclopedia, the Papacy

[29]*New Catholic Encyclopedia*, Vol. X, 1967, pp. 174–177.

freely admits that mysticism can be traced back to Hinduism, which influenced Plato, who later influenced early Roman Catholic writers. John of the Cross, Teresa of Avila, Thomas Aquinas, and Augustine are just some of the names in Roman Catholic history who are believed to have been mystics.

Zoroaster, Gautama Buddha, Plato, and Muhammad were all practitioners and seekers of mystical knowledge and are said to have received their revelations through the practice of *meditation* (yoga). The difference between Islamic mysticism and Buddhist mysticism is that the Muslim mystic disciplines his mind (soul) to submit to Allah only, while the Buddhist (through the practice of yoga) looks inwardly to achieve a spiritual bliss known among Buddhists as Nirvana. The Catholic mystics, however, practice meditation in hopes of having a "**mystical marriage**" with the Godhead. While the Hindus seek a **mystical union** with their chief pagan gods, the **papal mystics** who reject the worship of pagan gods **(like the Sufis of Islam) have switched the pagan understanding of this mystical union to be understood as a union of the soul with God and His saints**.

A mystic seeking to help the world receive both a physical and a spiritual union of the eternal soul is called a **Cabalist** to the Jew and to the Buddhist, he is a **Lama** or a **Bodhisattva**. To the Christian, as we have seen, he is a **mystic**; but to the **Muslim, a mystic is a Sufi**.[30]

However, contrary to popular belief, the Holy Scriptures reveal that there is no such thing as an eternal soul, and only God has immortality. (1 Timothy 1:17; 6:16). We will not receive immortality until Jesus comes. (1 Corinthians 15:51–55). When a man dies, so does his brain where the mind is located. When the brain dies, so does its thoughts. **The Holy Scriptures say there is absolutely no consciousness after death.**

"His breath goeth forth, he returneth to his earth; in that very day **HIS THOUGHTS PERISH.**" Psalm 146:4.

"For the living know that they shall die: **BUT THE DEAD KNOW NOT ANY THING**, neither have they any more a reward; for the memory of them is forgotten.

[30]***The World's Religions*, Clarke, p. 99.**

"Also their love, and their hatred, and their envy, **IS NOW PERISHED**; neither have they any more a portion for ever in any thing that is done under the sun.

"Whatsoever thy hand findeth to do, do it with thy might; **for there is no work, nor device, NOR KNOWLEDGE, NOR WISDOM, in the grave, whither thou goest**." Ecclesiastes 9:5, 6, 10.

However, the hope of Christianity is to be resurrected at the **FIRST RESURRECTION**.

"Blessed and holy is he that hath part in **THE FIRST RESURRECTION: ON SUCH THE SECOND DEATH HATH NO POWER,** but they shall be priests of God and of Christ, and shall reign with him a thousand years." Revelation 20:6.

Nevertheless, Hindus, Buddhists, Muslims, Roman Catholics, and most Protestant church members go on to believe that the human mind (soul) continues to live after death. Here we can find the origin of all beliefs found in mysticism (the occult) and in **karma and reincarnation** which are sweeping across the U.S. Let's look at how mainstream Christians, the news media, Hollywood, and the Music Industry are being used to promote the precepts of Hinduism and Buddhism. Willie Nelson, the famous country/western song-writer and singer who often braids his hair like an Indian warrior, believes he was a Texan Indian in a previous life.[31] Sylvester Stallone claims to recall a number of past lives, including one in which he said he was beheaded by a guillotine.[32]

Today, multitudes of Christians, who have ignored the Bible warnings about devils posing as gods in Psalm 106:37, 38 and 1 Corinthians 10:20, have crossed over the gulf which has separated them from pagans to grasp the hands of Hinduism, Buddhism, and Sufism while, at the same time, they have remained as members of their Christian churches. Christians are blending the precepts of Buddhism and Sufism with the religion of Jesus. How is this being done? Christians have clasped hands with Hindus, Buddhists, and the Sufis by practicing yoga (meditation) and/or by participating in martial arts. **Christian parents who are sending their children to their favorite Kung Fu**

[31]***Hollywood and the Supernatural*, Steiger/Steiger, p. 78.**

[32]***Ibid.*, Steiger/Steiger, photograph section.**

or Tae Kwon Do class have not the foggiest idea that they are also introducing their children to the sophistries of theosophy (the occult). The ever popular Kung Fu and Tai Chi excitements were born in Chinese Buddhism. We will examine the origin of karate and this writer's involvement in the past shortly.

Like Christianity and Sufism of Islam, Hinduism and Buddhism have developed into different branches and offshoots. In Revelation 17:5, God through His apostle John not only calls the religions of this world Babylon the Great, which is interpreted as meaning "**spiritual confusion**," but He also calls it a "**MYSTERY**."

According to *Webster's New World Dictionary of the American Language*, the word "***mystery***" derived from the Greek word "***mysterion***," which means "***a secret rite***," and from the Greek word **"*mystes*," which means "*one initiated into the mysteries*"** or doctrines known only to a small esoteric group.[33] Although there are various religious movements in the Mystery Religions, each act of seeking a union of the soul with a Supreme Deity, which is believed to be either a Spirit, a Light, or an abstract infinite reality like Nirvana, has one thing in common. **All mystical techniques have their beliefs based in the lie of an immortal soul.**

As already stated, Zoroaster's teachings about the conflict between good and evil are a twisted account of the real conflict between Christ and His angels and Satan and His angels. The Holy Scriptures (both in the Old and New Testaments) not only most strikingly warn of the fallen angels, but also of God's angels who are sent to protect us from Satan.

"And of the angels he saith, **Who maketh his angels spirits, and his ministers a flame of fire**." Hebrews 1:7.

"For he shall give his angels charge over thee, to keep thee in all thy ways." Psalm 91:11.

Angels of God have throughout the Bible appeared to human beings as human beings. They still do today; however, the same goes for Satan and his fallen angels. Satan appeared to Jesus in the wilderness (Matthew, Chapter Four) as an angel

[33]***Webster's New World Dictionary of the American Language*, ed. Guralnik, 1980, p. 941.**

of light sent from heaven, not as the hideous-looking Devil with horns and cloven feet. The fallen angels still have the ability to appear on this earth as humans, angels, or the gods of astrology.

Before the rise of Ashkenazi Jewry, Catholicism, and Islam, Jesus and His apostles warned of devils who would approach us to try to deceive us. These spirits of devils who are working miracles have not only appeared as God's angels, but also as a deceased prophet at such time when King Saul in his apostasy went to the channeler of Endor. This witch invoked a demon who took the form of Samuel the prophet, and this witch had a familiar spirit.

"Then said Saul unto his servants, Seek me a woman that hath a familiar spirit, that I may go to her, and inquire of her. And his servants said to him, Behold, there is a woman that **HATH A FAMILIAR SPIRIT at Endor**." 1 Samuel 28:7.

In 1 John 4:1, it warns: "Beloved, **BELIEVE NOT EVERY SPIRIT**, but try the spirits whether they are of God: because many false prophets are gone out into the world."

As we have clearly seen from the Holy Scriptures, the sciences of the occult and the worship of the gods of astrology are, in reality, the paths that lead one to obey the precepts of the **prince of darkness** instead of the **Prince of Peace**. Occultism (mysticism) is a road that leads to Endor, not to Heaven. Those who believe in an **immortal soul** have received Satan's first lie to human beings which was "**YE SHALL NOT SURELY DIE**." Genesis 3:4. Those who believe in an immortal soul are being set up in their minds to accept a spirit who can appear and sound as a dead relative, a hungry ghost, an angel from heaven, a spirit posing as an advanced human being known by occultists as a master or a bodhisattva, a god of mythology, an elf, a fairy, or even a devil posing as an alien from a UFO. These are some of the outward manifestations which Satan is using to deceive us. Let's again look at one of his (Satan's) most terrible delusions which has brought multitudes under his bewitching spell. To the Hindu, this delusion is known as Brahman; to the Buddhist, it is known as yoga; and to the Roman Catholic or Muslim, again, it is known as "**meditation**."

According to *Webster's New World Dictionary of the American Language*, the word ***hypnosis*** means "***a sleeplike condition***." Believe it or not, the word ***hypnosis*** derived from the **Greek god named *Hypnos*, the god (demon) of sleep, who was identified by the Romans as *Somnus***. The Greek word ***hypnos,*** which means "***sleep***," or the Latin word ***sopire***, which means "***to lull to sleep***," are the origin of the word ***hypnosis***, which means to put a human being "***in a state of altered consciousness***" whereas his will is controlled by another.[34] It is interesting to note that Buddha and Hindu gurus are pictured in their arts with half-closed eyes as if in a **hypnotic trance**. This hypnotic trance the mystic puts himself under is also known as being in a **state of ecstasy**. The powers of the occult are given by its author only to those who have learned its secrets through invitation by so-called masters of mysticism.

Buddhism has its origin in the teachings of a single man named Siddhartha Gautama. Gautama was born in India some 2,500 years ago in Kapilavastu in the foothills of the Himalayas in what is now Nepal.[35] Buddha's teachings are known as the *Dharma*. However, Gautama Buddha wrote no books, and there is no Buddhist equivalent of the Bible or the Koran (Qur'ãn). Gautama taught by word of mouth, preaching, and discussing. Those who heard him remembered what he said and passed it on to others. Buddha's words were not actually written down until 400 years after his death. The term ***Buddha*** is applied to human beings who have reached godhood **(enlightenment)**, and the term ***Bodhisattva*** is a person who is an advanced human being that is on his way to becoming a Buddha. At the head of the **Bodhisattvas** is someone who Buddhists call the **Avalokita** or **Avalokiteshvara**. He is believed to be the savior of those who are on their pathway to **enlightenment. The Dalai Lama of Tibet is regarded as the incarnation of this Bodhisattva.**[36] There is, however, a divided camp in Buddhism. Not all Buddhists believe in the many Buddhas

[34]***Webster's New World Dictionary of the American Language*, ed. Guralnik, 1980, p. 691.**

[35]***Man, Myth & Magic*, Vol. 3, ed. Cavendish, 1995, p. 296.**

[36]***A Dictionary of Non-Christian Religions*, Parrinder, 1971, pp. 35, 53.**

in the past, others believe there will be more in the future, but to many there is only one Buddha for this present world and that was Gautama.

Siddhartha Gautama claimed that by the practice of yoga (meditation) he reached "**enlightenment**," the ultimate truth by which people who believe in an immortal soul are freed from the cycle of rebirth, karma, and reincarnation. **A Bodhisattva is believed to have also attained enlightenment but has sworn to remain in this world to help others who are still suffering.** However, some Buddhists believe in celestial bodhisattvas and of one in particular who is said to be a beautiful young man who is coming to earth to become the next Buddha.[37]

Like the Hindus, the Buddhists are taught to invoke their celestial beings for their protection from evil. They are taught to visualize their Buddhas or Bodisattvas while in quiet meditation so they may attain a union with them.[38]

It is mind-boggling to this writer to see how some Christians are uniting themselves with Buddhism and/or practicing yoga while they claim to be Christians. In Exodus 20:3, the First Commandment says, **"Thou shalt have no other gods before me."**

Hinduism and its child, Buddhism, worship an astrological pantheon of gods and goddesses which have a hierarchy. In the religion of Hinduism, the king of the gods is Indra and the queen is Indrani;[39] and under them are Brahma, Shiva, and Vishnu. Gautama Buddha did not teach his disciples that the gods of Hinduism were false. On the contrary, Gautama claimed that he himself had been Indra in past lives and had been reincarnated as Indra 36 times.[40]

Another celestial being Buddhists worship is a Mother Goddess named Tara who supposedly is the mother of all Buddhas. A third eye that represents this idol's all-seeing nature is found on the center of this graven image's forehead. As I have shown in my last three

[37]*World Religions*, **Bowker, pp. 55, 67.**

[38]*Ibid.*, **Bowker, p. 68.**

[39]*The Mythic Image*, **Campbell, pp. 8, 40, 41, 341.**

[40]*A Dictionary of World Mythology*, **Cotterell, p. 66.**

volumes, these pagan goddeses who have been worshipped all over the world are alive and well today.

Again, instead of seeking a" **mystical union**" with their Supreme Deity, Buddhists hope to reach **enlightenment** through the practice of yoga as they think the founder of their religion did also.

Amazingly, Buddhism died out in Gautama's own native land, but had established itself in other traditions in China, Japan, Sri Lanka, Southeast Asia, and in Tibet[41] where the **great red dragon** is often displayed in the center of the various Oriental cultures. Like Hindus, Buddhists believe in demons and spirits, some of whom were molded into the likeness of graven images to guard their sacred temples. Ironically enough, Buddhism and Islam are the biggest rival religions of Christianity in America. We will see that this is true as we continue.

In Hinduism, the god Shiva was also believed to be endowed with a "**third eye**" (clairvoyance) which was a frontal eye that gave him a unifying vision. It is regarded by occultists as the seat of psychic and paranormal powers.[42] Gautama Buddha claimed that he had obtained this third eye a.k.a. celestial eye a.k.a. All-Seeing Eye which permitted him to see the life of all beings simultaneously and gave him the knowledge of the chain of the fundamental forces of existence, as well as its previous forms. This "**third eye**" is also known among Buddhists as the **eye of wisdom**. It supposedly permits the wise man to experience the Divine.[43] **This "*third eye*," also known as the "*Urna*," is one of Buddha's symbols, and he claimed to receive this enlightenment**[44] **WHILE HE PASSED THROUGH FOUR STAGES OF A MEDITATIVE (HYPNOTIC) TRANCE.**[45] Roman Catholics who practice meditation call this "***third eye***" the "***soul's eye***."[46] Here, again, are some more mystical practices which Buddhist followers say came directly from their deity.

[41]*Man, Myth & Magic*, Vol. 3, ed. Cavendish, 1995, p. 296.

[42]*Dictionary of Mysticism and the Esoteric Traditions*, Drury, p. 297.

[43]*Encyclopedia of Religion*, Vol. 5, ed. Eliade, 1987, p. 239.

[44]*An Illustrated Encyclopaedia of Traditional Symbols*, Cooper, 1978, p. 170.

[45]*World Religions*, Bowker, pp. 54–56.

[46]*Encyclopedia of Religion*, Vol. 5, ed. Eliade, 1987, p. 239.

According to the *Encyclopaedia of Buddhism*, Gautama Buddha said, **"I am the one who is worthy of being revered in this world; I am the Supreme Teacher; I am the only one who has attained the most perfect Enlightenment."**[47] Gautama is regarded by some Buddhists as superior to all other beings, both human and divine.[48] In Buddhist tradition, Gautama Buddha claimed to have talked with the Hindu god Brahma, who persuaded him to teach others the truths about what he learned that even the gods did not know.[49] **Gautama Buddha claimed to have received a transformation to Buddhahood (enlightenment) while meditating in a trance. In the occult, the term which describes this transformation is known as *metamorphosis*, which means "*a transformation, as by magic*."**[50] According to the *Dictionary of Mysticism and The Occult*, p. 52, **cryptesthesia** and **cryptomnesia** describe a condition of clairvoyance, psychic perception, telepathy, and the capacity to activate the memory while in a meditative trance. However, again, I would like to remind my readers that the Holy Scriptures written by Moses, the prophets, and the disciples of Jesus warned us of devils who personate gods, and how even Christians will unite themselves with them by receiving doctrines from them. As pointed out earlier, the power of **hypnosis** is a science of the **prince of the power of the air**; it is the same as casting a spell on someone. A witch tries to get people to do things against their will; a **hypnotist** works on the same principle. He puts his client under a spell or in a trance (sleep). This occult practice could open the door of the heart and actually invite the "**Arch Deceiver**" of mankind in while using a human agent and thus control a human being's will.

The inward practice of yoga (meditation) is nothing less than an occult teaching in which the practitioner learns to wipe away or empty his own conscious mind, which discerns what is going on around him between right or wrong and good or evil, and allows a foreign power, demon, and/or god to control the inner

[47]*Encyclopaedia of Buddhism*, Vol. 3, ed. Malalasekera, 1971, p. 357.

[48]*Ibid.*, Vol. 3, ed. Malalasekera, 1971, p. 358.

[49]*World Religions*, Bowker, p. 54.

[50]*The American Heritage Dictionary*, Based on the New Second College Edition, 1983, p. 430.

thoughts a.k.a. subconscious mind. **Meditation or yoga is self-hypnosis**, and those who practice this are conditioning their minds to be yoked to Brahma instead of to Christ.

There are, however, practitioners of mysticism (yoga) who reject the idea of uniting their souls with any deity. They will urge that they are practicing yoga to seek a blissful isolation of the soul in a transcendental state, which is known among occultists as Nirvana. **In Hinduism and Buddhism, it is believed that the soul is reborn over and over again, and each time it is reborn the soul transmigrates into another vehicle.** This doctrine promoted by seducing spirits has a metaphysical term; it is called **METEMPSYCHOSIS**. Here we can find the reason behind the belief that all the gods and demons were once men. Hindus and Buddhists are taught by their gurus or lamas that everybody is subject to the "**Wheel of Life and Death**." The Wheel of Life and Death or the "**Wheel of Metempsychosis**" represents (to those who seek mysticism) six modes of existence which are gods, demi-gods (asuras), human beings, animals, hungry ghosts, and demons.[51] According to Buddhism, after death the soul is reincarnated as one of these above until he learns to break the cycle of karma. It is taught that the souls of people who have lived an exceptionally virtuous life will be reborn as gods. Those who have lived a good life will return to earth as men and women, but it is believed that others will be reborn as animals, hungry ghosts, or denizens of hell because of their evil, sinful lives. This doctrine is not only found in Hinduism and Buddhism, but similar beliefs can also be found in the teachings of Zoroastrianism, Platonism, Neoplatonism, and certain esoteric forms of Judaism and Christianity.[52] Although the esoteric forms of Judaism and papal Christianity do differ in their beliefs about the transmigration of the soul, the large majority of both religions, like Islam as well, have this false doctrine as a basic foundation of their faiths. Let's take another historical look at the founder of Buddhism.

It should be noted that **Gautama Buddha himself was a Hindu and believed that the gods of Hinduism were once men**. His new

[51]*A Dictionary of Comparative Religion*, ed. Brandon, p. 439.

[52]*Ibid.*, ed. Brandon, p. 439.

revelation (enlightenment) was not to do away with the worship of the Hindu gods, but to show his disciples how they too can reach godhood a.k.a. Nirvana. **Buddha taught his followers to work out their own salvation instead of appealing to gods and sacrifice. Unlike Hinduism, Zoroastrianism, and Islam, Buddhism's goal is to reach Nirvana, whereas the others above seek to have a mystical marriage with their god.**[53]

Some modern Buddhists worship the founder of their religion, who was a Cushite, as a god; while other Buddhists honor Buddha as a great sage or prophet who had reached **Nirvana (godhood)** and left his teachings to guide others in how to do the same. In the traditions of Buddhism, Gautama Buddha became enlightened while he sat under a Bodhi tree as he went into a meditative (hypnotic) trance. It was there that his eyes were opened, "seeing all things as they really are."[54]

This self-worship is called Self-Realization by New Agers today. However, this same doctrine was taught before the Flood and before the rise and evolution of Hinduism or Buddhism. Its inventor taught this same doctrine to Eve in the garden. It was by using the power of hypnotism and channeling that Satan deceived Eve in the Garden of Eden. Eve was charmed (mesmerized) by the beauty of the serpent and consequently was put into a temporary, altered state of mind. Satan then channeled his voice through a serpent, perhaps a python, and made Eve think that she had hidden, latent powers within her which had to be awakened and which her Creator did not want her to learn. The serpent said that if she would disobey God by eating of the tree of knowledge of good and evil, "**YE SHALL NOT SURELY DIE**: For God doth know that in the day ye eat thereof, then **YOUR EYES SHALL BE OPENED, AND YE SHALL BE AS GODS, KNOWING GOOD AND EVIL**." Genesis 3:4, 5.

In Revelation 18:1–3, the God of Abraham, Isaac, and Jacob is warning the citizens of this world that this planet's inhabitants have unwittingly united themselves with devils. In Jewish symbolic language, the God who dwells between the cherubims calls the people

[53]***World Religions*, Bowker, p. 55.**

[54]***Ibid.*, Bowker, p. 54.**

of this world, who have turned their backs on Him and have been intoxicated by the sophistries of mysticism, as the citizens of Babylon the Great.

"And after these things I saw another angel come down from heaven, having great power; and the earth was lightened with his glory.

"And he cried mightily with a strong voice, saying, Babylon the great is fallen, is fallen, and is become the habitation of devils, and the hold of every foul spirit, and a cage of every unclean and hateful bird.

"For **ALL** nations have drunk of the wine of the wrath of her fornication, and the kings of the earth have committed fornication with her, and the merchants of the earth are waxed rich through the abundance of her delicacies." Revelation 18:1–3.

Daniel the prophet, who lived centuries before the apostle John wrote the above warning, said: "Many shall be purified, and made white, and tried; but the wicked shall do wickedly: and none of the wicked shall understand; but the wise shall understand." Daniel 12:10. The apostle John, writing under the inspiration of the Spirit of God, said in 1 John 4:2, 3: "Hereby know ye the Spirit of God: Every spirit that confesseth that Jesus Christ is come in the flesh is of God: And every spirit that confesseth not that Jesus Christ is come in the flesh is not of God: and this is that **SPIRIT OF ANTICHRIST**, whereof ye have heard that it should come; and even now already is it in the world."

The apostle went on to write later in the book of Revelation about those who are possessed with this **spirit of antichrist** and what they shall go on to do. "And the rest of the men which were not killed by these plagues **YET REPENTED NOT** of the works of their hands, **THAT THEY SHOULD NOT WORSHIP DEVILS**, and idols of gold, and silver, and brass, and stone, and of wood: which neither can see, nor hear, nor walk: Neither repented they of their **MURDERS, nor of their SORCERIES, nor of their FORNICATION, nor of their THEFTS**." Revelation 9:20, 21.

This writer is not interested in studying every doctrine of Hinduism and Buddhism, but just enough so my reader will see the dangers of uniting all religions, including Christianity, into some sort of an

International Brotherhood of religions. The ancient Israelites mingled the idolatry of Egypt, Canaan, Phoenicia, Assyria, and Babylonia into their faith in God as well. The God of Abraham denounced the Hebrews as **HARLOTS** (as in Ezekiel, Chapter 16) after they ignored His prophets' warnings to repent of their apostasies. The ten northern tribes of Israel were cast out of their land, and the tribes of Benjamin and Judah were sent to Babylon for 70 years (after Nebuchadnezzar destroyed the Holy City) because of adopting the philosophies of mysticism.

Nevertheless, Professor Robert Thurman, who is a highly respected scholar of Tibetan Buddhism and is a professor of Indo-Tibetan Buddhist Studies at Columbia University, is determined to spread his sect of Buddhism in America, especially among the rich and the famous. Thurman, who is one of America's most well-known exponents of Tibetan Buddhism, stated he believes that after Buddha received his enlightenment, he was a seething energy field and his skin was all gold.[55] Thurman went on to say that Tibetan Buddhism is probably the most difficult and exotic path with its emphasis on prostrations, visualizations, **GURU WORSHIP, AND DEITY YOGA, IN WHICH THE PRACTITIONER IDENTIFIES WITH TIBETAN DEITIES.**[56]

In *The New York Times*, an article by Kennedy Fraser entitled "Buddhism's Flowering in America: An Inside View" shows a picture of staff members of the *Tricycle* magazine having colorful masks with hideous faces of dakinis and mahakalas, which are worshipped as Tibetan deities.[57]

While conducting a series of lectures about the deceptions of the New Age and the New World Order in the Phoenix, Arizona, area in March of 1997 and just shortly after the news media in Phoenix showed UFO sightings on the evening news videos, there was an article promoting Zen Buddhism which appeared in *The Arizona Republic*. This article heading reads: "**Meditation blends in easily with many Valley religions**."[58] The swapping of the teachings of

[55]*The New York Times Magazine*, May 5, 1996, p. 48.

[56]*Ibid.*, May 5, 1996, p. 49.

[57]*The New York Times*, November 3, 1997, p. E2.

[58]*The Arizona Republic*, Thursday, March 27, 1997, p. HL2.

Jesus for the teachings of Buddha has, indeed, become a socially accepted thing today because of the influence coming from the entertainment field, news media, the sports arenas, and New Age centers. In the previous article, Buddhism is promoted by Pastor and Mrs. James Ford of the Valley Unitarian Universalist Church in Chandler, Arizona.

Buddhism with its doctrine of "**Self-Realization**," which teaches that human beings are gods but must be awakened to this fact, is "cool" among the young punk rockers and rappers who are up to their eyes in self-exaltation, drugs, and sex, for the Buddhists teach there is no God to answer to for their sins because they believe men are gods. Buddhists also teach there is no judgment for they are judged by no one; therefore, there is no need for a Saviour. However, the Messiah of the Judeo-Christian faith says through His faithful apostle John in Revelation 21:7, 8:

"He that overcometh shall inherit all things; and I will be his God, and he shall be my son. But the fearful, and unbelieving, and the abominable, and murderers, and whoremongers, and sorcerers, and idolaters, and all liars, shall have their part in the lake which burneth with fire and brimstone: which is the second death."

This lake of fire is not what Catholic and Protestant leaders have interpreted. This Scripture in Revelation 21:8 is referring to what the whole world shall look like after the thousand-year reign of Christ is over. The hell fire which Jesus and the prophets foretold is coming upon this world shall **COME FROM HEAVEN**, not from some secret place under the earth where the Devil is in charge. Peter said that the whole world will be cleansed of its sin by fire. (See 2 Peter, Chapter Three.) The word "***hell***" is symbolic and simply means ***grave***. In Greek, the word for grave is ***Hades***.

There is hardly a day that goes by in the United States without seeing something written in a national newspaper or magazine or some popular celebrity promoting Buddhism. **Buddhism is promoted by articles about the Dalai Lama's struggle with Red China to get his throne back by movies such as Bernardo Bertolucci's *Little Buddha,* Martin Scorsese's *Kundun*, which was written by Harrison Ford's wife, Melissa Mathison, and promotes the Dalai Lama story, or perhaps by Brad Pitt's new movie, *Seven Years In Tibet.***

Zoroaster, Buddha, and the Dalai Lama

In the October 13, 1997, issue of *Time* written by David Van Biema, the reader may see how serious the days are in which we live. The heading of the lengthy article, which reveals how popular Buddhism has become in America, reads as follows: "An ancient religion grows ever stronger roots in a new world, with the help of the movies, pop culture and the politics of repressed Tibet."[59] The director of ***Seven Years in Tibet***, Jean-Jacques Annaud, stated, "Buddhism is everywhere."[60] It was also revealed in this issue of *Time* that it was from a Buddhist temple that Al Gore came into some dubious campaign money.

In *The New York Times*, it was pointed out how Oprah Winfrey used her national TV program to discuss the practice of "**meditation**" with actor Richard Gere.[61] Gere is a practicing Buddhist and has made a career of proselytizing converts for the Dalai Lama. Richard Gere's movie, *Red Corner*, sent the Chinese government protesting to United States' officials.

Gere, Professor Robert Thurman (former Buddhist monk and father of actress Uma Thurman), and two others founded the **Tibet House in 1987 at the Dalai Lama's request**.[62] Harrison Ford's wife, Melissa Mathison, is listed as one of the board members. Richard Gere and Robert Thurman are the two most visible exponents of Tibetan Buddhism in America. The Tibet House has played host to many rock stars, models, movie stars like Harrison Ford, and other wealthy patrons.[63] Both Richard Gere and Robert Thurman, the first American to become a Tibetan monk, use the Tibet House, which serves as a cultural embassy for the Chinese-occupied nation, as a means to send propaganda against the brutal ***red*** army.[64] Harrison Ford, who has attended rallies at the Tibetan House, told *People Weekly* that he has advocated the cause of the Tibetan government on a number of occasions, and Ford

[59]***Time*, October 13, 1997, p. 73.**

[60]***Ibid.*, October 13, 1997, p. 74.**

[61]***The New York Times*, November 3, 1997, p. E2.**

[62]***The New York Times Magazine*, May 5, 1996, p. 48.**

[63]***Ibid.*, May 5, 1996, p. 46.**

[64]***Ibid.*, May 5, 1996, p. 48.**

went on to reveal what else he advocates by the title of his movie entitled *The Age of Aquarius*.[65]

David Van Biema, in the October 13, 1997, issue of *Time*, went on to write about the martial arts actor, **Steven Seagal, who in February of 1997 was hailed as the reincarnation of "Tulku" of the Nyingma lineage of Tibetan Buddhism, a school older than the Dalai Lama's.**[66] Van Biema wrote about singer Adam Yauch of the punk-rap group, the Beastie Boys, and how he has been a convert to Buddhism since 1992. He also wrote about singer Tina Turner's involvement with Buddhism.

In some Buddhist traditions, Gautama Buddha was the personification or equal of the Hindu god Vishnu.[67] One of the ten avatars of Vishnu's in the myth was **Krishna**, the Hindu messiah, of whom George Harrison of the Beatles is a disciple. While I was living in Hawaii, Harrison recorded a very popular song in 1970 called "***My Sweet Lord***," which later I was astonished to learn was a prayer to the god **Krishna**. I was even more astounded to learn later, after being able to distinguish occultism (mysticism) from Christianity, of just how many of Hollywood's favorite idols are also occultists!

It was not hard for me later, after studying the origin of Hinduism, to recognize how the ancient gods of the Egyptians, Hindus, and the South American Indians were exalted in the *Indiana Jones* movies played by Harrison Ford. In the *Temple of Doom*, Ford played a Hindu shaman who was out to avenge his offended god Shiva. Shiva is the Destroyer in Hinduism, and his sign is the trident just as it was for Poseidon to the Greeks and Neptune to the Romans. One of his consorts is the hideous-looking Mother Goddess Kali whose tongue is hanging from her mouth and dripping with blood. In Hinduism, Kali worshippers seek to be possessed by her spirit while he or she is in a state of trance. These Hindu shamans have been photographed while under the control of this spirit named Kali and they have been photographed

[65]*People Weekly*, December 8, 1997, p. 152.

[66]*Time*, October 13, 1997, p. 74.

[67]*Encyclopedia of Gods*, Jordan, p. 48.

showing their glazed eyes, matted hair, and with Kali's characteristic lolling tongue hanging from their mouths.[68]

In Psalm 106:37, the God of Abraham said that those who sacrificed to these heathen gods were actually sacrificing to devils, not to God.

"YEA, THEY SACRIFICED THEIR SONS AND THEIR DAUGHTERS UNTO DEVILS." Psalm 106:37.

As pointed out, Buddhism derived out of Hinduism for Gautama Buddha was a Hindu. Today, as I write, a new Hindu guru from India has arisen and is sweeping New Agers and apostate Christians in the United States into his form of mysticism. He is a medical doctor and a bestselling author who is making millions by using his medical training to promote New Age Spiritualism. He is known as the "**Hollywood guru**" for many of its well-known citizens like Madonna, Gillian Anderson, Michael Jackson, and Olivia Newton-John, just to name a few, have flocked to him. His name is Deepak Chopra.

In the October 20, 1997, issue of *Newsweek*, there is a huge article written by John Leland and Carla Power about Deepak Chopra and what he is promoting. His picture appears on the cover of the same magazine with a heading which reads: **"DEEPAK CHOPRA: SPIRITUALITY FOR SALE."** In the above magazine, it states that one of Chopra's ideas is to have a global empire.[69] According to this article in *Newsweek*, Chopra came to the United States in 1970 by riding the wave which the Beatles' guru Maharishi Mahesh Yogi (b. 1911) and his Transcendental Meditation movement had made. The Maharishi Mahesh Yogi was first introduced to world fame by the Beatles' rock group who disowned him just six months later. However, after the Beatles dropped him, Maharishi's Transcendental Meditation movement continued to grow in America as Clint Eastwood, Mike Love of the Beach Boys rock group, Mia Farrow, Merv Griffin, and other pop culture figures openly embraced TM. The above famous celebrities helped this form of Hindu Spiritualism become a household word in America.[70]

[68]***World Religions*, Bowker, p. 25.**

[69]***Newsweek*, October 20, 1997, p. 53.**

[70]***The Joy of Sects*, Occhiogrosso, p. 66.**

This guru of TM went on to establish a fully accredited university in Fairfield, Iowa, and Vedic universities in Washington, D.C., and Moscow. TM claims three million members worldwide, having close to a million members in America. Maharishi has also established medical clinics based on a "modified and simplified" form of traditional Indian medicine known among Hindus as "**ayurveda**" of which Deepak Chopra borrowed when he was an unknown.[71]

Since then, Chopra has sold more than ten million of his books and is expanding his mystical teachings by using the movies, TV series, CDs, a chain of healing centers, and by lecturing. His popularity among the ignorant of the Holy Scriptures now seems to have left the Maharishi's TM movement, the New Age prophetess Shirley MacLaine, and the Dalai Lama in the dust.

Chopra lectures around the world and is charging $25,000 a talk for people to hear him preach about meditation, karma, Nirvana, alternative medicine, alternative states of awareness, self-help, etc., etc. Ironically enough, this New Age guru has even written a movie script which he entitled ***The Lords of Light***, which is about Satan who comes to earth in the form of a spiritual cult leader who seduces the masses with Utopian promises. Chopra's critics have pointed out, however, that this "New Age healer" is not far from being what he wrote in his own movie script. William Jarvis of the National Council Against Health Fraud is not only critical about the $2,750/week Chopra charges his clients to stay at his Chopra Center for Well Being in La Jolla, California, but Jarvis warns that people like Chopra "are delusional. And when you are delusional, you think you're the messiah."[72]

[71]*The Joy of Sects*, Occhiogrosso, p. 66.

[72]*Newsweek*, October 20, 1997, p. 58.

CHAPTER IV

THE MYSTICAL TEACHINGS OF MUHAMMAD AND THE HISTORICAL FACTS ABOUT ALLAH AND HIS KAABA SHRINE

"And I saw three **unclean spirits** like frogs come out of the mouth of the dragon, and out of the mouth of the beast, and out of the mouth of the false prophet.

"**For they are the spirits of devils, working miracles,** which go forth unto the kings of the earth and of the whole world, to gather them to the battle of that great day of God Almighty."

Revelation 16:13, 14.

CHAPTER IV

Before we focus more indepthly on the prophecies which point to the Muslims, the New World Order scheme, and the Hollywood and the Music Industry connection, this writer wants to inform his readers that he was not raised in a quiet, sheltered Christian home. My childhood was just the opposite. I grew up in an atmosphere of violence, drunkenness, sex, smoky rooms, music, and sports. Although I never made it to the Big Screen as I had once thought of in my teenage years, my whole life was rooted and grounded in the Music Industry. I kept company with some celebrities from the Music and Hollywood scene from the time I was a little child up until my early 20s; and if I were to mention their names, you would recognize them in an instant.

Beginning in 1960, I became one of the regular hosts on a television program which centered around rock music and dancing. It was not *American Bandstand*, but was a show like it. Famous recording stars would come and sing and promote their latest hits. This is one of the ways I became acquainted with some of them. From the years between 1960 and 1970, I made my way by the use of music and dancing. From 1965 to 1970, I worked and managed a dance club and studio. During these years, I was also a performer. I not only demonstrated the latest dances among rock'n'rollers, but I also demonstrated and taught ballroom dancing, mainly among the upper-middle class and the rich. It was also during this time that I got involved with martial arts in which Buddhism and mysticism plays a major part. After my conversion to Christianity, I discovered to my surprise, years later, that karate actually originated from Chinese Buddhism. The grandfather of martial arts in China is Kung Fu which dates back to about A.D. 520. The martial arts are actually nothing less than a form of meditation put in action. **The universal belief in witchcraft that the universe is controlled by "the Force" a.k.a. "Ch'i," which the motion picture *Star Wars* dramatized, is the central theme in martial arts.**[1]

In the late 60s, I began to take private lessons from a three-time national champion Black Belt in Tae Kwon Do, a Korean style of karate, who just happened to wander in one day into our dance club. He was single and thought that if he could learn to dance, he could possibly find himself a wife. He was from Syria, and he was a Muslim. I assigned him a female teacher who was also at that time single. This three-time national champion Black Belt in Tae Kwon Do karate was a successful businessman and very pleasant to talk to. It was while he was taking dance lessons that I found out through his teacher that he was also a **Black Belt** in **Tae Kwon Do karate**, so a stockholder in this dance club that I managed and I immediately began to take private karate classes from him. As the months went by, we became friends; and the dance teacher who I assigned to him ended up becoming his wife.

It was also during this time in the late 60s that I was taken by this Black Belt to watch a karate tournament. Bruce Lee and Chuck Norris were there. It was Bruce Lee who can be credited for making karate so popular today. It was also Bruce Lee who opened the doors of Hollywood in the 70s and promoted Kung Fu on the Big Screen. His movie, *Enter the Dragon*, sold over $8 million worth of tickets, and back then that was a lot of money. However, it was to be his last for he died a sudden, untimely death. While it was Bruce Lee who introduced Kung Fu on the Big Screen, it was David Carradine who made not only Kung Fu karate a popular television smash, but also introduced to many American, Christian children the philosophies of Buddhism. As I look back to the late 60s and the early 70s now, it amazes me to see how often the **red dragon** is associated with the martial arts for, as we have seen in the book of Revelation, the red Dragon represents the spirit of Satan. (See Revelation 12:9.)

[1]***Harper's Encyclopedia of Mystical & Paranormal Experience*, Guiley, 1991, p. 344.**

During this time when I was involved in karate, another puzzling thing I noticed was my teacher's ring on his finger. **His ring displayed symbols of the compass and the square with a "G" in the middle.** I asked this Black Belt champion what the "G" on his ring meant. He quickly informed me that he could not tell me what it meant, for if he did he could have his throat cut from ear to ear. I, being astonished at his answer, went away wondering **WHAT IS THIS!**

Before the year 1970, I had absolutely no religious understanding about Freemasonry or of the different religions. I did not know the difference between Krishna and Buddha or Muhammad and Jesus; and, at that time, I could care less. This was occurring between the years 1967 and 1968 before the riots hit Washington, D.C. However, it was on the island of Oahu, after my conversion to Christianity in 1970, that I finally found out what the symbol on my karate teacher's ring meant. It meant that he had been a member of the International Order of Freemasonry. **The "G" in the middle of the ring stands for the Great Architect of the Universe, and those who are in the Blue Lodge in America think it means God. However, in the White Lodges of Europe the "G" symbolizes the SUN-GOD (Osiris) in Freemasonry.**[2] At that time back in the late 60s, however, I had not yet learned the connection between Freemasonry, Islam, Sufism, and the Illuminati because at that time I had absolutely no understanding of any of them. For a time, I remained puzzled about this Masonic symbol that my former Muslim karate teacher displayed on his ring.

From 1970 to 1975, I lived in Hawaii. It was there in 1970 that I began to get interested in religion. It was on the island of Oahu that I had my first actual exposure to the philosophies of Hinduism and Buddhism, which I never became a practitioner of but just a wondering observer. It was also on the island of Oahu in 1971 that I first became aware of **ILLUMINISM**, a mystical revolutionary conspiracy to unite all religions and governments under one banner. I initially learned about this occult plan to overthrow Christianity by listening to a cassette tape by the late **Myron Fagan, a former director and producer of motion pictures in Hollywood**. It should be noted that this same Myron Fagan,

[2]***The Masonic Report*, McQuaig/Shaw, p. 15.**

himself, was a **former member of the Illuminati** out of which both the New World Order and the New Age Movement today derived. Before his death in the late 60s, Myron Fagan made a recording which exposed the history of Communism and the plans of the Illuminati out of which Communism also derived. The former Hollywood director tried his best to warn American citizens that this mystical revolution of the Illuminati **(ILLUMINISM)** was being orchestrated under the auspices of Freemasonry and the United Nations.

After hearing these astonishing things, I was a little skeptical because I was soon told that the Illuminati was a hoax and that Southern Baptists claimed Freemasonry was a Christian organization. However, as I remembered that my former karate teacher was a Muslim (not a Christian) and a Freemason, naturally I wondered how a Muslim could be a member of a Christian organization. After pondering over this for some time, I wanted to prove to myself if these things I heard from the former movie producer about Freemasonry and its connection with the Illuminati were true or not. This investigation of mine began in the year 1971. Not only did I find out from encyclopedias of Freemasonry themselves that the secret society of the Illuminati had, indeed, been a secret society within the secret society of Freemasonry, but I also learned why my former karate teacher, who was a Muslim, was allowed to join. The truth is, shocking as it may sound to some, that both Freemasonry and the secret Order of the **Illuminati** have their roots in **Sufi Illuminism**, which is not only the most secretive of all the secret societies of the world, but Sufism is wrapped tightly in the green mantle of Islam. It just so happens that today the 33° Freemason is known to be a member of the "**Mystic Shrine**," which is nothing less than the mystical order of the Islamic faith today. Most Christians have heard of the Shriners and have seen their **Arabian mystical symbols** on their vehicles, caps **(fezs)**, and temples which they use to express and identify who they are. However, most American Bible-believers are puzzled as to why Shriners wear funny-looking red caps (fezs), which look similar to the fezs of the Sufi, but are adorned with sequins displaying an Arabian sword, **an upside-down moon crescent, and the five-pointed star**. The truth is this well-known ideogram of the **"crescent and the five-pointed star" is the symbol of the Islamic faith**

and is used as a symbol in Islamic countries on their national flags. William (Bill) Schnoebelen, the author of *Mormonism's Temple of Doom* and a Bible-believing Christian who was converted from Satanism, Freemasonry, and Mormonism, is quoted along with J. Edward Decker, a bestselling author and a former Mormon, in a March 1992 newsletter published by *Free the Masons Ministries.* Both Schnoebelen and Decker point out how pagan Islamic symbols were borrowed by the Freemasons and how they were woven into the fabric of our history, including the streets of Washington, D.C., where this writer was raised. It is a historical fact that the Islamic morning star or pentagram, which is a central symbol of both Freemasonry and the United States, originally symbolized Lucifer, who was worhipped by the ancients as the **FENEX or PHOENIX**[3] or **Molech** or **Remphan** in classical mythology. William (Bill) Schnoebelen, a former Wiccan High Priest and Satanist, points out that "Albert Pike, the giant of Masonic philosophy who is entombed **just 13 blocks** from the White House in the '**House of the Temple**' has identified the **pentagram (or 'Pentalpha')** as the **blazing star** … which represents the **star Sirius**."[4] The above newsletter states that "**Sirius** has been known for 5,000 years as the symbol of the **Egyptian devil, Set**; and it is regarded as a star of great evil![5]

The newsletter of March 1992 of *Free the Masons Ministries* goes on to say:

"Bill emphasized that to the magician, **the inverted pentagram has one use only, and that is to call up the power of Satan and bring the Kingdom of the Devil into manifestation on earth.**[6] Yet this very same symbol straddles the corridors of our nation's power and is 'aimed' right at the White House!

"This pentagram is found almost constantly at sites of ritual

[3]*Mythology of All Races*, Vol. 12, ed. MacCulloch, 1964, p. 54.

[4]*Free the Masons Ministries Newsletter*, March 1992; *Morals & Dogma*, Pike, pp. 14, 15.

[5]*Free the Masons Ministries Newsletter*, March 1992; *Aleister Crowley and the Hidden God*, Grant, p. 12.

[6]*Free the Masons Ministries Newsletter*, March 1992; *Man, Myth & Magic*, p. 2159.

murders; and in the notebooks of teens who have become involved in satanism and ended up killing themselves. In *The Arizona Republic*, 11/27/88, section B, an article by Bill Donovan and Mark Shaffer, talks about 3 teenage suicides. The authors quote a school administrator, 'All you have to do to know we have a large problem on our hand is to drive down the street. There are **pentagrams everywhere**, on top signs, buildings, trash dumpsters, even one that's been on the post office. **Pentagrams are five-pointed stars used as a symbol by practicing satanists.**'

"It is evident that death, destruction and carnage follow this symbol everywhere. It is a key which opens up the door of hell; at least according to sorcerers. What does the Bible say?

"This star, which has been identified even by the Bible as the accursed tabernacle of Molech, and the **star of your god, Remphan, figures which ye made to worship them...' (Acts 7:43, cf. Amos 5:25–27)** is an idolatrous image sullied by untold centuries of debauched worship; and yet it is carefully placed right upon our nation's capital.

"Every bit as staggering is the fact that this same pentagram is the central symbol of the **CONGRESSIONAL MEDAL OF HONOR**, this nation's highest military award for bravery. The **inverted 5-pointed star** within a circle is the highest form of satanic expression, representing **BAPHOMET**, The Goat of Mendes, or the embodiment of **Lucifer as god**.

"Of course, nearby the main part of Washington, D.C., is one of the most famous and distinctively shaped buildings in America, the **Pentagon**. Although most recognize the Pentagon as the nerve center of our nation's defence establishment; few realize that the **Pentagon itself is a geometric design used in magic and witchcraft as well**.

"The Pentagon, through its use of the number 5 is associated profoundly with the planet Mars and the ancient god of war, called variously Aries, Horus or Mars. (see ***A Practical Guide To Qabalistic Symbolism*** by Gareth Knight, p. 124ff) This is because Mars is the fifth planet on the magical diagram, the Tree of Life; among other reasons.

"The Pentagon is also one of the two secret symbols of the highest levels of Freemasonry, the Ancient and Illuminated Seers of Bavaria

While holding lectures in Los Angeles, I took this amazing photograph above on Hollywood Boulevard in Hollywood. Spiritualism, sex, and Socialism have ever been flowing freely from the cup of the wine of her fornication (Babylon the Great) into the minds of those who have followed after the vanity coming from Hollywood. All up and down the sidewalks of Hollywood Boulevard, the visitor may see the greatest names from the Movie and Music Industries proudly displayed in the middle of the pentagram. I was almost undone when I came across the well-known Baptist preacher's name, Billy Graham, engraved in the middle of the pentagram.

I was also disturbed when I read in the nationwide bestseller, The Rockefeller's: An American Dynasty, *that the prophet of the Interchurch Movement, John D. Rockefeller, Jr., was a hidden supporter of both Billy Sunday and Billy Graham.*[1] *By the time of his death, John D. Rockefeller, Jr. contributed nearly $75 million to Interfaith organizations in an effort to unite the world into a one-world religion along with a one-world Socialist government. John D. Rockefeller, Jr. camouflaged his true intentions by professing the Baptist religion, but his international, Socialist ambitions were also seen when he contributed $8.5 million to establish the modern Tower of Babel, which is calling itself the United Nations. His bizarre religious intentions were seen in 1930 when he gave $26 million towards the construction of an Interfaith Church in Morningside Heights, New York, in which the figures of Confucius and Moses, Hegel and Dante, Muhammad, and even Darwin are proudly displayed on the arches of the main portal of this Gothic edifice.*

[1]*The Rockefeller's: An American Dynasty*, Collier/Horowitz, pp. 149–153.

(aka the Illuminati)–the other being the Pentagram. It may be observed that **every pentagram has a pentagon within it**; and that every proper pentagram can fit perfectly point-to-corner within a pentagon."[7] [sic]

In the Royal Arch Masonry, the pentagon is also known as the "**Keystone**," which is a symbol of the phallus, and it is the Kabbalistic sign of a man.[8]

Since I published *The New Age Movement and The Illuminati 666* back in 1983, I have discovered in my research of the origin of mystical understanding (Illuminism) that both Sufism and Freemasonry are, indeed, rooted and grounded in the ancient philosophies of the Kabbalah, the Jewish book of magic. The Kabbalah had derived much of its mystical philosophies from the Persian prophet Zoroaster, who earlier borrowed from the ancient Aryans and Chaldeans. Before the rise of Islam, teachers (masters) of mysticism (the occult), which is found in the Kabbalah, were known as Cabalists. Although the Jews and the Muslims have been deadly enemies, the reader shall discover in this chapter that the most learned Sufis claim to be in contact with an **immortal Sufi master whom they call *KHIDR*, who the Sufis believe is a Jew**.[9] We will study more about this so-called immortal Sufi master after we see how Sufism was brought into the United States.

In Islam, the mystical traditions are taught by the ***pir*** a.k.a. ***shaykh***.[10] Sufism was influenced by the Kabbalah because Muhammad was as well. Later, the Freemasons borrowed much of their mystical teachings from the Islamic Sufis. Both the spread of Zoroastrianism and the Kabbalah can be credited to the ancient Persians.

Before the birth of Islam, apostate Hebrews blended Zoroastrianism with the worship of the God of Abraham while living under the Persian Empire. We will see more eye-opening facts about the Kabbalah and how its mystical teachings are being promoted today by Hollywood's most prominent celebrities as we continue.

[7]*Free the Masons Ministries Newsletter*, March 1992.

[8]*The Masonic Report*, McQuaig, p. 51.

[9]*The Way of the Sufi*, Shah, p. 114.

[10]*Tales from the Land of the Sufis*, Bayat/Jamnia, pp. 175, 176.

As the Illuminati was a secret society within the secret society of Freemasonry, so is the Sufi master (shaykh) a member of the secret intelligentsia and esoteric school within Islam. Just as the Cabalists are the mystics and poets of Judaism, so are the Sufi masters the mystics and poets of Islam.[11] We have already seen from Sufi masters that both Freemasonry and the secret society of the Illuminati of Bavaria borrowed many of their ideas and occult symbols from Sufism, but let's look a little deeper into the origin of the Masonic Order of the "**Mystic Shrine**" and the "**FEZ**" the Shriners proudly wear and are even sometimes buried in.

J. Edward Decker, co-author of *The God Makers*, writes the following about the origin of the Masonic red fez worn by the Shriners from one of his bestselling tracts entitled "*FREEMASONRY: Satan's Door to America?*" The article reads as follows:

"When the average American thinks of Masonry, the thoughts are of Children's Burn Centers and Hospitals, and the Shrine Circus, where handicapped children are often carried to the front row seats in the strong arms of weeping men who are wearing the **Red Fezes** of their fraternity. Rarely do we see a parade without these same Shriners driving up and down the parade route in their little cars and motorcycles, **wearing clothes out of the Arabian nights**, bringing laughter to the children lined up along the way.

"On more serious occasions, such as the laying of public building cornerstones or at the funeral service of a Lodge member, **these same men, dressed in somber attire, wearing their ornate sashes, medallioned chains of office and ceremonial aprons, will perform with solemn dignity the rites handed down through the centuries of their ritual secrecy. 'Good Men,' they say, 'becoming better.'**

"Yet, once you get past the good-old-boy fraternal act, the **funny red hats of the Shriners** and the sheltered reputation of the local, Blue Lodge Masonic groups, there is something beyond the colorful mask, an aura of mystery, power and intrigue, complete with undertones of false gods, blood oaths, conspiracy and back room politics.

"The Fez itself is an example of the double meaning behind most of Freemasonry's facade. Worn and even carried to the grave with

[11]*Man, Myth & Magic*, Vol. 18, ed. Cavendish, 1995, p. 2495.

pompous dignity, the history of the **Fez** is barbaric and anti-Christian. In the early 8th century, Muslim hordes overran the **Moroccan city of Fez, shouting, '*There is no god but Allah and Muhammed is his prophet.*' There, they butchered almost 50,000 Christians.** These men, women and children were slain because of their faith in Christ, **all in the name of Allah, the same demon god to whom every Shriner must bow in worship (and proclaim him the god of his fathers) in the Shrine initiation ceremony.**

"The Shriners' blood oath and confession of Allah as God is found in the secret ritual book, ***THE MYSTIC SHRINE, An Illustrated Ritual of the Ancient Arabic Order of Nobles of the Shrine*** (1975, pp. 20–22). But the 'Allah' of Islam is **NOT** just another word for God. It is a specific **'god' of the Quraish tribe in Mecca**. The initiate swears that he will be obligated to this **'most powerful and binding oath,'** ***in advance*****, and that he may never retract it.**

"During the butchering of the people of Fez, the streets literally ran red with the blood of the martyred Christians. **The Muslim murderers dipped their caps in the blood of their victims as a testimony to Allah.** These blood stained caps eventually were called **Fezes** and **became the Muslim badge of honor.** The Shriners wear that same red Fez today. The greatest tragedy is that the **Fez** is often worn by men who profess to be Christians themselves. **It must cause God to weep**." [sic]

Reader, shortly we will study the historical record of the rise and evolution of Muhammad, Islam, and of its god Allah in this volume. However, it is very important that the Bible-believing reader first understands what the **secret order** of the Sufis is, along with their history, because **Sufism developed into the most learned and most powerful schools of Oriental Spiritualism on earth after the death of Muhammad in A.D. 632**. The first Sufis were influenced by the ascetic practices of Roman Catholic monks in Syria, by the father of the Kaballah, Zoroaster (Zoroastrians) of Persia, and by Hindu Vedanta philosophy.[12]

Sufism claims that they were the actual scribes (Companions) of Muhammad who developed the Qur'ãn (Koran). According

[12]***The World's Religions*****, Clarke, p. 85.**

The above picture shows a Shriner proudly wearing his Islamic red "fez" of the Order of the Mystic Shrine of Freemasonry. According to The Encyclopedia of Secret Societies & Fraternal Orders, *Axelrod, pages 224 and 225, the Shriners were originally set up by 13 Master Masons in 1871 in NYC as a drinking club. The true name of this elite branch of Masonry is the Imperial Council of the Ancient Arabic Order of Nobles of the Mystic Shrine. The Shriners certainly show the origin of Freemasonry in their Order. Their Lodge is known as a Temple and some of the ornaments of their Temples include both the Bible, the Koran, and a foot-square Black Stone after the Black Stone in the Kaaba in Mecca. Shriners claim that their rituals and ceremonies date back to the son-in-law of Muhammad, the Caliph Ali. However, today most Masons are unaware of just where the fez originated and why their Order of the 33° is centered in Islamic mysticism. The name "Fez" is the name of the city of Morocco in which the blood of thousands of Catholic Christians flowed in its streets when the invading Arab Muslim armies swarmed out of Arabia into Morocco and Egypt like waves of locusts destroying those who would not worship Allah and accept Muhammad as his messenger. The conquering Muslims dipped their caps into the blood of their conquered Catholic foes as an expression of praise and thanks to their God Allah for giving them the victory. Many Shriners are completely ignorant about where their fez originated and spend as much as $1000 decorating them with gold and tiger claws. They are, however, an offense to the Orthodox Muslims.*

to *The Encyclopedia of Religion,* the Sufis are an elite group among Muslims a.k.a. 'People of the Bench,' the intimates of the prophet Muhammad who gathered at the first mosque in Medina.[13]

We studied earlier how both Adam Weishaupt of Germany and Joseph Smith of New York had their own versions of a one-world government plan to unite the world under their dominion, and now it is time to look at Sufism's version. To begin this study, let's take a historical look at the **Koran (Qur'ãn), which is Islam's scriptures**.

According to *The Meaning of The Holy Qur'ãn*, the scriptures written in the Koran were first compiled by Muhammad's **Companions** to whom he verbally communicated his revelations.[14] The Prophet of Islam's **Companions** asked Muhammad questions, and his answers are said to have been carefully stored in the memory of the **Companions** and were afterwards written down. In the next generation, Muslim scribes who helped in the development of the Koran, who were known as the **Tabiun**, were those who had not personally conversed with the Prophet, but had conversed with the **Companions** and learned from them. **Subsequent generations always went back to establish a chain of evidence through the Tabiun and the Companions.**[15]

As the mystic Joseph Smith claimed to have received his revelations and authority from God via extraterrestrial visitors, so did Muhammad claim to have been supposedly visited by an angel. However, this angel is the most powerful of all angels now. He took Lucifer's place in Heaven and had appeared to both Daniel and John as they received visions to write their very famous books. According to the **Companions**, Muhammad told them that the **angel Gabriel had visited their prophet and verbally delivered to Muhammad what is now written in the Koran**.[16] However, although the Koran seemingly accepts Jesus Christ as a True Prophet of God, it at the same time rejects His Divinity.

In *The Meaning of The Holy Qur'ãn*, it teaches that Jesus was no

[13]***The Encyclopedia of Religion*, Vol. 14, ed. Eliade, pp. 104, 105.**

[14]***The Meaning of The Holy Qur'ãn*, 'Ali, p. xv.**

[15]***Ibid.*, 'Ali, p. xv.**

[16]***The Koran With Parallel Arabic Text*, translated by Dawood, 1995, p. ix.**

more than a messenger, and it plainly states that those who call Jesus the Son of God – "**ALLAH'S CURSE BE ON THEM**."[17] Today, there are multitudes of Christians who are beginning to think that the Islamic faith is also another Christian religion for the last days. However, it should be understood by Christians who have attended Muslim schools or mosques (or who are thinking about it) that most Muslims are violently opposed to anyone who claims that **Jesus is the Son of God** and have put multitudes of Byzantine Catholics in the grave for believing this truth. When the Muslims went forth to convert the known world to Islam, they used the point of the sword and all that was needed for a non-Muslim to be spared the sword was to become a Muslim and chant the "**shahada**," which is today chanted **"There is no god but God (Allah), and Muhammad is his messenger."**[18]

It is also a matter of public notice, however, that the Muslims for centuries have fought and killed each other as well over the various interpretations of the Koran and what Muslims call the ***Hadith***, which are traditions relating to the deeds and utterances of their **Star** of Islam (Muhammad). Qaddafi of Lybia publicly announced that the Muslim's traditions have been so corrupted and misinterpreted by self-serving Muslim scholars that they could no longer be regarded by the devout as binding. He also said that the Koran could not be interpreted by such suspect sources, and that the Koran itself should not be interpreted at all. **Qaddafi wants an Islamic revolution that would purify the Islamic faith.**[19]

It is very eye-opening to learn what Muslims think about Satan. The Muslims not only reject the Deity of Jesus, but they also reject the record in Revelation, Chapter 12, about Christ's pre-existence as Michael, Christ's war with Satan (the seven-headed Dragon) in Heaven, and how Satan a.k.a. Lucifer (the day star) was cast out with one third of the angels. In *The Meaning of The Holy Qur'ãn*, it states that the reason why Allah cast Satan out of

[17]*The Meaning of the Holy Qur'ãn*, 'Ali, Surah 4:171, p. 239; Surah 5:75, p. 272; Surah 9:30, p. 446.

[18]*The World's Religions*, Clarke, p. 86.

[19]*God Has Ninety-Nine Names*, Miller, pp. 218, 219.

Heaven was because he refused the command from Allah to bow before Adam like the other angels had done.[20]

Another eye-opening claim by the Sufi Muslims which sent me flying into Islamic encyclopedias and Sufi books to see if this was true is their proclamation that their ancient wisdom about mysticism extends far back in time before the birth of Muhammad. Sufis boast that they were using the term "**Illuminism**" to signify the advanced teachings in their ancient schools of mysticism **long before** the founding of the secret societies of the **Rosicrucians**, the **Freemasons**, the **Illuminati**, and the New Age Movement's notorious **Theosophical Society**. Amazingly, mysticism to the ancient Buddhist was also called Enlightenment, but to the Sufi it was **ILLUMINISM**. After learning this, I began to more fully understand why the 33° Freemasons wear costumes in parades which reflect the Sufi Muslim culture and why the famous secret agent and **Sufi Master Sir Richard Burton** came to Utah from England to visit Brigham Young in 1860 during his struggles with President James Buchanan and the United States government.

According to *The Encyclopedia of Religion*, the name of these secret schools of Sufi Illuminism **traces back to a famous Sufi teacher named Suhrawardi a.k.a. Shaykh al-Ishrãq (master of illumination) who lived and died (A.D. 1153–1191) about one hundred years before the rise of Osman** a.k.a. Othman and his Ottoman Empire.[21] Suhrawardi called his school of mystical teachings **Ishrãqiyah (Arabic for illumination)**, which developed two major currents of thought known among the Sufi shaykhs. These were the ***exoteric*** **(falsafah)** thought, which deals with Greek, scholastic philosophy mainly deriving from Aristotle and Plato, and ***esoteric*** **('irfãn)** thought, which deals with the metaphysical teachings of Eastern religions which are centered in the beliefs of **Self (spiritual) Realization a.k.a. yoga**.

Suhrawardi founded his school of Illuminism in Persia (Iran) long after the Muslim invaders conquered the followers of Zoroaster, but before Sultan Osman founded the Ottoman Empire in A.D. 1299.

[20]*The Meaning of The Holy Qur'ãn*, 'Ali, Surah 7:11–18, pp. 347, 348.

[21]*The Encyclopedia of Religion*, Vol. 7, ed. Eliade, 1987, pp. 296–298.

Suhrawardi published several books on exoteric and esoteric philosophy, one of which was entitled *Theosophy of Illumination*, which was based on **imaginal thinking and the metaphysical experiences of receiving light**. Sufi shaykhs wrote that it was from the **"Orient" (the East)**, the sacred place from which the sun rises, that both spiritual and cosmic illumination **originates**. This metaphysical illumination was, according to Suhrawardi, passed on to the initiate of Sufism from a cosmic hierarchy of radiant angels of light and by the **prophet Idris**. Sufism claims that at the head of this cosmic hierarchy of angels is **Gabriel** who, if one is worthy, will reside in the innermost part of the soul of each human being, issuing directions concerning his or her internal and external acts.[22] **Sufis claim that this is how Muhammad received the Koran.** We will see documented history about this as we continue.

Let's take time here to compare the similarities between Hindu mysticism and that of Islam. Instead of seeking to invoke pagan gods through the practice of yoga (meditation) as the **Hindu mystic** does, the **Sufi mystic** thinks he is seeking a spiritual union with what he believes is the Judeo-Christian God, His angels, and His saints through this practice of **meditation**. Reader, the only differences between Hindu mysticism and Islamic mysticism are the **names of their deities and saints**. Both practice meditation which leads the practitioner to place one self under a trance, to be put under a spell, or to self-hypnotize the mind. This, says the Hindu yogi, is how his deity Kali possesses his body. **However, the Holy Scriptures have shown us that these gods and goddesses are demons.** Those who ignore the Bible warnings about Spiritualism and continue to practice yoga are opening their heart to be possessed by Spiritualism's founder. **The God of Abraham, Isaac, and Jacob forbade all these sciences of mysticism.** After He destroyed the Pharoah and his men in the Red Sea and wrote the Ten Commandments with his own finger, the same God that dwelleth between the cherubims told Moses: **"There shall not be found among you any one that maketh his son or his daughter to pass through the fire, or that useth divination, or an observer of times, or an ENCHANTER, or a witch, Or a charmer,**

[22]***The Encyclopedia of Religion*, Vol. 7, ed. Eliade, 1987, pp. 297–300.**

or a consulter with familiar spirits, or a wizard, or a necromancer. For all that do these things are an abomination unto the Lord: and because of these abominations the Lord thy God doth drive them out from before thee." Deuteronomy 18:10-12.

An **enchanter** is one who **invokes spirits**, and this practice lies at the center of all forms of mysticism found on both sides of the Atlantic. The technique used to invoke spirits is called **YOGA a.k.a. MEDITATION. The first yogi on this side of the Flood, according to the ancient mystics, appears to trace back in time to none other than Hermes, who Sufis identify as the prophet Idris.[23]** **Hermes** was actually the founder of all Eastern religions and **Oriental mysticism**. The esoteric sciences, dating back to the days of antiquity, of the mystical prophet Idris a.k.a. Hermes became known as **Hermetism**. To the ancient Greeks, this god of writing, whose symbols were the stylus, the caduceus, and the swastika, was the prophet-god Hermes from whom the Sufis borrowed heavily.

After the death of Muhammad in A.D. 632, his successors within a hundred-year span had replaced Zoroastrianism with Islam, which had extended its religion during the era of the Persian Empire from northern India to Greece and Egypt. Islam within its first hundred years had also replaced much of Eastern papal Christianity, which was known as the Byzantine Empire before it split from papal Rome in the closing days of the 11th century. The Arabian-invading Muslims, who were also known as the Saracens, with the point of the sword persuaded the mixed people in this Mediterranean region to exchange their worship of Ahura Mazda (the god of fire) and his prophet Zoroaster and the worship of Jesus as the Son of God for Allah and his prophet Muhammad. Those who refused went into untimely graves or had to pay the local Muslim leader a tax to not only save their property, but their lives as well!

As we continue, we shall have an in-depth study into the shocking history of the worship of Allah and his Star of Islam, Muhammad. We will examine more about the origins of Islamic doctrines which are found in the Qur'ãn (Koran). We will also look at the amazing prophecies that are now history about Islam

[23]***The Encyclopedia of Religion*, Vol. 7, ed. Eliade, 1987, p. 298.**

and what **Islam** is predicted to do in the near future to **those who do not have the Seal of God** as foretold in **Chapters Seven and Nine** of the book of **Revelation**. However, first we need to understand more about Sufism (Sufi Illuminism) and to see with documented history how **Sufism amalgamated into their order all mystical traditions of the ancient known world and how Sufism in the West split and developed into non-Muslim secret societies from which Freemasonry and Adam Weishaupt's secret society of the Illuminati borrowed heavily**. Let's now take another look at Muhammad and some brief historical facts about how he founded Islam which now has a membership of **1.1 billion**.

Like the Illuminati Enlightenment Movement of the 18th century and Joseph Smith later, Muhammad's ambitions were to unite the whole world into a one-world communal government as well, however, under the power of his Islamic religion. Instead of the Novus Ordo Seclorum or the New Dispensation, Muhammad called this mystical union of all religions and nations an **UMMA**. After a 12-year military struggle with the Meccans of Arabia, Muhammad fled with his band of disciples to Medina in the year A.D. 622. Muslims commemorate this date as ***the Hijra*** which **begins their Islamic calendar.**[24] From A.D. 622 to A.D. 631, Muhammad, however, was determined to make all of Arabia an Islamic State, and he warred again with Arabians, Jews, and Christians in Mecca who rejected him as a prophet. As his plan to take Mecca and then all of Arabia began to materialize, in A.D. 629 **Muhammad sent letters and messengers to the kings of Persia, Yemen, and Ethiopia and to Emperor Heraclius of the Byzantine Empire inviting them to accept Islam**. After being rejected, he set his face to conquer these lands, as well, by military force.

When Muhammad gained more converts in Arabia, he returned to Mecca and finally conquered them, and by A.D. 631 the entire population in Mecca who survived the sword converted to Islam.[25] After putting the Jews of Khaybar to the sword in A.D. 629 and conquering Mecca, Muhammad suddenly died of a fever in A.D. 632. This threw the Muslims into confusion. **While Muhammad lived,**

[24]***The Koran with Parallel Arabic Text*, translated by Dawood, p. xv.**

[25]***Ibid.*, translated by Dawood, p. xvi.**

the Muslim Arabs were united. They had established their first *Umma* (Islamic communal community) at Medina which became a model or symbol of what Muslims were determined would extend into all parts of the world.

To continue this effort to make the world into an entire Muslim State, Abu Bakr was chosen to be the first **caliph** (successor) to continue the spread of Islam. The Koran promises Muslims who fight and die for the spread of the religion of Islam that their sins will be forgiven and they will go to Heaven.[26] However, at the death of Muhammad, the **Arabian Muslims** never united under one government. This would not happen until the **Asians (Turks)** became the dominant power in Islam. During this time, Zoroastrianism of the Persians and the Eastern Roman Catholic powers (the Byzantine Empire) had all but exhausted each other's strength from waging wars against each other, and the Muslims saw their chance to conquer both of them.

While Muslim armies were conquering the Persian and Byzantine Empires, which had for centuries controlled the Mediterranean nations, **Sufi shaykhs were studying and borrowing both the mystical and academic knowledge of the nations which the Muslims had overthrown. This was especially true when Islam extended its borders to Greece and to Alexandria in Egypt. By A.D. 751, Islam had conquered the peoples from Spain to central Asia.**[27]

Sufism, however, traces its mysticism to Ali, Muhammad's cousin and son-in-law, who in turn was initiated by Muhammad. Islamic tradition states that Muhammad on the 27th of the Islamic month of Rajab, after leading Abraham, Moses, Jesus, and other prophets in prayer, was carried from Mecca to Jerusalem **on a horselike beast with a female head called *al-buraq*.**[28] **He was then carried by the al-buraq from the rock on the Temple Mount in Jerusalem, which is now marked by the Dome of the Rock shrine, to the presence of Allah.**[29] After receiving honor

[26]*The Rise of Islam*, Child, p. 12.

[27]*Ibid.*, Child, p. 12.

[28]*World Religions*, Bowker, pp. 164, 165.

[29]*Ibid.*, Bowker, pp. 164, 165.

from his god, Muhammad was said to have been given a green robe (mantle) before returning to Mecca the next morning. According to Sufism, this green mantle given to Muhammad is known as the ***Khirqa*** and was presented to Ali, Muhammad's cousin, as an indication that he was permitted to guide and teach others the spiritual path of Islam. It is said that Ali gave four of his brethren – Hasan and Husayn (two of his sons), Komail, and Hasan Basri – the same authority. These above Sufis are referred to as the four **Pirs** (masters) to which true Sufism traces its origin.[30]

Athens and Alexandria had been known for centuries as the learning centers of both Oriental and Occidental Illuminism in the ancient world, and one of Greece's most honored gods before the rise of the Roman Empire and the Papacy was also **Hermes, the patron of science, the scribal arts, and mysticism**. However, Hermetic wisdom, also referred to as mysticism, flourished for centuries in ancient Babylon, Persia, and Egypt before Alexander the Great had overthrown the Persian Empire, which had earlier destroyed the Babylonian Empire. Mysticism began spreading its philosophies to the known world from the Chaldean city of Nimrod. There have been multitudes, since the passing of Nimrod's day at Babylon, who have carried the knowledge of Hermetic wisdom to all parts of the world. However, mysticism's most noted apostles were Cush, Nimrod, Zoroaster, Buddha, Plato, and, as we shall surely see, Muhammad! This prophet of Islam was, indeed, one of mysticism's most noted apostles. It is also very eye-opening to learn that the secret society of Freemasonry, with its Islamic Order of the "**Mystic Shrine**" of the 33° and its lesser degrees, **traces the origin of their mystical teachings (crafts) to Hermes and Nimrod**.[31]

Who really was the god Hermes, and how does the name ***Hermes*** fit in with the traditions of Islam and Freemasonry? The name ***Hermes*** did not originally derive from the Greeks, but came from the Babylonian Chaldeans who invented the ancient religion of astrology, which is the worship of the sun, moon, and stars. The pagan Romans worshipped

[30]*Tales from the Land of the Sufis*, Bayat/Jamnia, p. 11.

[31]*Encyclopaedia of Freemasonry and Its Kindred Sciences*, Mackey, 33°, 1921, Vol. I, p. 322; Vol. II, p. 513.

this god and prophet of occult literature as Mercury and, like in the Babylonian version of astrology (mysticism), Mercury (***Hermes***) was one of **the seven chief gods of the astrological pantheon of Rome**.

As pointed out in my first two volumes, in the 19th century Alexander Hislop stated with good documentation in his book, *The Two Babylons*, on pages 25 and 26 that the ancient Chaldeans called Kush, who was the father of Nimrod, by the name of ***Hermes***. **The Chaldean name of *Hermes* is a compound name: "*Her*" means "*Ham*" and "*Mes*" means "*out of*," "*to draw forth*," or "*son of*." Hence, Hermes was simply the son of Ham of whom Moses said was Cush (Kush) who begot Nimrod. (See Genesis 10:6, 8.) The ancient Egyptians worshipped this god of writing as Thoth.**

To the Sufi, Hermes a.k.a. Idries was the first prophet of mysticism (occultism) on this side of the Flood. Not only do Islam and Freemasonry trace the origins of their mystical traditions to this prophet of occultism, but **all New Age secret societies of Spiritualism exalt Hermes as the god of wisdom and writing and the founder of mystical understanding as well.** According to the *New Encyclopaedia Britannica*, **"Hermetism was extensively cultivated by the Arabs, and through them it reached and influenced the West."**[32]

The Moabites and the Babylonians knew Hermes as ***Nebo*** or ***Nabu***[33] (which means "*height*"),[34] and they worshipped and named their sacred mountain after him. Moses viewed the Promised Land from **Mt. Nebo** in Moab. (See Genesis 34:1–12.)

Nebo (or sometimes spelled Nabu), the equivalent of **Hermes** to the Greeks, **Mercury** to the Romans, **Bel** to the ancient Babylonians, or **Thoth** to the Egyptians, was also worshipped as the father of all occult sciences. One Mesopotamian tradition has Nebo as the son of Marduk. Nabu's chief temple, which was called the "Firm House," was at Borsippa, a city near Babylon. **Nabu (Nebo) was the god of writing and wisdom, and his symbol was the pen or stylus.**[35]

[32]***The New Encyclopaedia Britannica*, Micropaedia, Vol. 5, 1997, p. 875.**

[33]***Encyclopedia of Gods*, Jordan, p. 174.**

[34]***Young's Analytical Concordance to the Bible*, Young, p. 689.**

[35]***Encyclopedia of Gods*, Jordan, p. 174.**

It just so happens that a prophet to the Muslims is called a "Nabi."[36] Both of the names *Nabi* and *Abu,* so common among Muslims, originally were names of heathen deities. Abu was a minor vegetation god among the Mesopotamian people.[37]

Babel, which was called Babylon by the Greeks, ruled the known world twice in the past: once under its original architect and founder, Nimrod (Genesis, Chapter 11), and then again by King Nebuchadnezzar. Nimrod journeyed from the East and settled in the plain known as Shinar. He became not only this world's first hunter and warrior-king after the Flood, but he was also the world's first founder and architect of the first metropolis which God destroyed by confusing the language of Babel's inhabitants, thus causing them to scatter throughout the world. As world history records, the second time Babylon controlled the known world was under King Nebuchadnezzar. Nebo (Nabu), the god of writing, is incorporated into Nebuchadnezzar's name. Keeping in mind that the gods of astrology were, in reality, Satan and his fallen angels, it should be noted that this very famous king of Babylon was, indeed, at first fooled into worshipping the hidden Prime Minister of this world of whom the devil worshippers of **Kurdistan** and **Armenia** call ***Sheitan*** (which in **Chaldean is *Teitan*** in Greek transliterations). Teitan, using the Greek numerical system, adds as follows:

T	E	I	T	A	N	
300	**5**	**10**	**300**	**1**	**50**	**= 666**

The God who dwells between the cherubims used both the pagan nations of Assyria and Babylon to punish the apostate Israelites for connecting themselves with the sophistries of mysticism (Spiritualism) in their day. After a long history of idolatry and a persistent refusal to turn away from Spiritualism, our Lord used the people of Spiritualism as his instrument to destroy both the northern and southern divisions of ancient Israel. This will be repeated in our day among both Roman Catholics and Protestants who have blended the precepts of mysticism with the worship of Jesus. The same God of the Old Testament is the same God of the

[36]***The Facts on File Dictionary of Religions*, ed. Hinnells, p. 226.**

[37]***Encyclopedia of Gods*, Jordan, p. 1.**

New Testament. Spiritualism a.k.a. mysticism is still an abomination unto the Lord.

Again, I would like to point out the warning from Jesus written by the apostle John in Revelation 17:5 about the **"MYSTERY" of BABYLON THE GREAT** which has intoxicated the minds of the people of this world from Noah's day on this side of the Flood to our time. **The word "MYSTERY" in Bible prophecy has no private interpretation. It most strikingly means "MYSTICISM" which had re-emerged again through ancient Babylon's founding fathers after the Flood.**

Moses and Micah the prophet both point out respectively in Genesis, Chapter Ten, and Micah, Chapter Five, that it was Nimrod, the son of Kush (Cush), who not only built ancient Babylon (Babel), the capital city of Babylonia, but also ancient Nineveh, the capital city of Assyria, as well. These two cities became the two most powerful capitals of Mesopotamia. Nimrod was the world's first mystic-king, hunter, and architect after the Flood. He was the **great rebel** who led the **great rebellion** against God at Babel. The Holy Scriptures clearly point to ancient Babel, which the ancient Greeks called Babylon, as to where the birth of the religion and sciences of mysticism were born. Astrology and mysticism are one in the same, for the philosophies of mysticism are, indeed, based in ancient astrology.

Amazingly enough, astrology (also known as Chaldean wisdom) was anciently symbolized as a **RED SEVEN-HEADED DRAGON. The "seven heads" symbolize the seven chief gods of ancient, pagan, Chaldean and Semitic religions which were later adopted by the Greeks and Romans. They are the Sun (Baal), Moon (IL), Venus (Tammuz), Mars (Marduk), Mercury (Nebo), Jupiter (Zeus), and Saturn (Cronus).**[38] This is why the apostle John was given a vision of Satan representing a seven-headed Dragon in Revelation, Chapters 12, 13, and 16. This is why Jesus through the pen of John said, **"And they WORSHIPPED THE DRAGON which gave power unto the Beast."** Revelation 13:4. We shall see more of the historical origin of who the

[38]***Origins of Astrology*, Lindsay, 1971, pp. 233, 375.**

ancient Chaldeans were and how, indeed, all religions of mysticism, including the Muslims and Catholics, have borrowed their most cherished religious observances from them.

The Babylonians, Hindus, Persians, Greeks, central Asians, and Romans all had their **own versions** of this religion of astrology which directed the inhabitants of this world to not only abandon the worship of the Creator of the sun, moon, and stars, but to follow the subtle delusions of the author of astrology and the first apostate who began his rebellion against God in Heaven. ***Lucifer***, whose name means **"*day star*" a.k.a. "Son of the Morning"** (Isaiah 14:12), is symbolized in the book of Revelation just **13 times** as a cosmic seven-headed Dragon because he not only invented astrology, but was worshipped as astrology's cosmic gods as he camouflaged himself as **Baal, Sin, IL, Nebo, Bel, Shamash, Ishtar, Tammuz, Cronus, Zeus, Jupiter, Brahma, Krishna, Shiva, Vishnu, Osiris, Isis, Horus, Quetzalcoatl, Kulkulcán, etc., etc**. Although the gods of astrology worldwide do trace to the legends of Nimrod and his family, all the pagan gods were, **in reality, Satan and his fallen angels personating them**. All the pagan gods on both sides of the Atlantic are just a **recollection** of the **original gods** of the Babylonians.

It is eye-opening, indeed, to study how ancient, pagan rulers often claimed to be the personification or the incarnation of the chief deity of their land. All over the world, kings were considered to be gods as was **Attila (d. 453)**, the most feared barbarian star of the Huns. **This mystic-king Attila claimed to be the personification of Marduk (Mars), the god of war.** It was the war-like Goths and Vandals who helped bring about the fall of the Western Roman Empire in A.D. 476. However, these Gothic barbarians fled from Attila who became the terror of the world in his heyday.

Attila was presented an ancient sword which was uncovered by a shepherd. It was spread abroad that this sword was the sword of Mars. The way Attila wielded it in battle convinced his peers of that time that this supernatural sword had been reserved alone for his invincible arm. Barbarian and superstitious princes confessed that they found it hard to gaze with a steady eye on the supposed divine majesty of the king of the Huns. The king of the

Huns was not only dreaded as a warrior-king, but he was also dreaded because **he (Attila) was a magician (sorcerer).**[39] Jesus warned His people who will remain loyal to Him in these last days of this "**Time of the End**" in which we live that men would rise up claiming themselves to be christs or prophets from God, and they would have the power to work miracles which would deceive the very elect of God, if possible. Read and compare Matthew, Chapter 24, with 2 Thessalonians, Chapter Two.

The seven-headed Dragon (Satan) has again and again deceived human beings through the miracles produced by mysticism, which has derived from the esoteric sciences of astrology. Every plan and purpose the True God has used to turn the inhabitants of this world from following (worshipping) the Dragon has down through the ages of mankind been counteracted or counterfeited by our witty foe by using his **magi** or **sorcerers like Attila. Did not the Pharaoh use the *magicians* to counteract the power of God in Moses' day?**

Often Satan has been successful in tricking human beings into believing that he is God Himself. For instance, let's first look at some of the Old Testament names for God and then compare some of the names of gods that Satan was worshipped as in ancient mythology (astrology). ***JAH* or *JEH*** is the abbreviation of ***JEHOVAH* (YAHWEH)**, and one of the other ancient, Hebrew names for God is ***EL***. Hebrews, to identify with God, sometimes combined the name ***EL*** when they named their children or towns, like ***Elijah* (*God is Jah*)** or ***Elishah* (*God is Saviour*)** or ***Bethel* (*House of God*)**. Another ancient, Hebrew word, which in the Holy Scriptures identifies the True God of Abraham, is the ancient Hebrew word ***Adonai (Lord)***. King David named his fourth son ***Adonijah*** which means in Hebrew "***Jah is my Lord***." It is interesting to note that the name ***Jesus*** was translated from the Greek word **IĒSOUS** and from the Hebrew word ***Jehoshua***.[40]

I	Ē	S	O	U	S		
10	8	200	70	400	200	=	888

[39]***The Decline and Fall of the Roman Empire*, Vol. I, Gibbon, 1952, p. 547.**

[40]***Strong's Exhaustive Concordance of The Bible*, Strong, 1890, p. 37.**

Let's now compare well-known names of gods in the religion of astrology with the original Hebrew, Greek, and Latin names for the Godhead. Let's see how the Dragon cleverly turned and confused multitudes from worshipping the True God by borrowing and twisting the ancient names for God and then applying them as names for deities in which he camouflaged himself in the various systems of mysticism.

Biblical Names	Ancient Mysticism
EL	IL
Elohim	Ellil (Enlil)
Yahweh (Jehovah)	Jove (Jupiter)
Adonai	Adonis
Iēsous (Jesus)	Zeus

When I first began my research in world religions on the island of Oahu, Hawaii, back in 1970, I never dreamed that I would make my life's career in writing and lecturing on this very important knowledge. I never dreamed that I would reach hundreds of thousands of people of various races and of different faiths as they read my books, listened to me on the radio or cassette tapes, or came to my lectures. I am especially grateful for the huge Muslim response in the Northeast of the United States and also in the Chicago area. Perhaps my reader is also a Muslim, but did not read my last three volumes about the prophecies on Time of the End events found written in the books of Daniel and Revelation. Reader, there is a conspiracy on this planet to unite the inhabitants of this world into a New World Order of which this writer is totally against. **The New World Order (the Enlightenment Movement) is nothing less than a repeat of the same principles which the great rebel Nimrod used to incite the inhabitants of his day against God who preserved the ark of Noah and its eight inhabitants.**

However, this writer is very much aware of how the Muslim community, as a whole, **is violently against the New World Order and sees it as a threat to Islam**. Maybe this is why I have had so many Muslims reading my last books. In Volume One, *Beware It's Coming – The Antichrist 666*, I took my readers through a Biblical and historical study of the origins of Baal worship and its doctrines which were adopted by the Roman Catholic Church and the Protestants. In Volume Two, *The New Age Movement and The Illuminati 666*, we studied the documented 221-year history of the secret society of the Illuminati which some have stated never existed. However, the above book follows the footprints of the Illuminati from Bavaria to the United States with documented history. With documented proof, Volume Two shows not only the rise and evolution of the Illuminati, but how, indeed, the threat of Communism/Socialism, the New Age Movement, and the New World Order all derived from the secret society of the Illuminati founded on May 1, 1776, in Ingolstadt, Germany, by Professor Adam Weishaupt.

Volume Three, *The Real Truth about UFO's and The New World Order Connection*, takes the reader through a documented journey showing how the Greek philosopher Plato is not only the New Age and New World Order advocates' greatest prophet, but he is also a great prophet of democracy. I show the claim of what ancient peoples on **both sides of the Flood** believed about **ancient astronauts** visiting this planet to help establish a supernatural society of people on the island continent of **Atlantis**. New Agers teach their children that these **ancient astronauts** were the **ancient gods** of the **Egyptians, Persians, Greeks, and the Toltec, Mayan, and Aztec peoples**. Today, learned occultists teach that these **ancient gods**, like **Hermes, Ra, Osiris, Isis, Ishtar, Zeus, Apollo, Diana, Quetzalcoatl, Kulkulcán**, etc., etc., are the **UFOs** that have been sighted in our skies. In the same book, by using the Bible I show that these ancient astronauts are Lucifer and his fallen angels. However, I was shocked again by Mormon scholars when this writer found out by reading *The God Makers* on pages 196 and 197 that the Mormons are teaching their members that Jesus visited the American Indians and that the pagan Toltec and Aztec god Quetzalcoatl was really Jesus!

Reader, a confederacy is, indeed, developing against the God of Abraham and it was foretold both by Daniel the prophet and the apostle John, the penman of the book of Revelation. Both of these servants of the Most High God of Israel foretold that the headquarters of this universal conspiracy in the **Time of the End** would eventually move itself "between the seas in the glorious holy mountain" **in the Land of Israel**. With documented proof and with the Holy Scriptures, I point out to the delight of Muslims, perhaps, how Zionism is not only a hybrid or pseudo-Jewish faith, but how there is absolutely **no promise** in Scripture that the God of Abraham would ever again in this present world **re-establish** the Jews as a State in Israel. The Jews who were/are behind the Zionist Movement were/are mainly white European and Russian Jews (Ashkenazi), not the original Hebrew **(Sephardic)** Jews. Volume Three points out from prophecy (Daniel 11:45) how **Lucifer** was not only to use the Land of Israel in our time to further his grand design, but how he will personate Christ Jesus (1 John 2:18) as these things develop. It shall be Satan, not Jesus, who is predicted in Daniel 11:45 to set up the headquarters (tabernacles) of his confederacy in Israel. For 6,000 years, Satan has been conditioning the inhabitants of this world to be fooled into accepting him as Christ and his kingdom as the Kingdom of God. To help us see how Satan's final deceptions are developing, let's look again at the religion of Islam.

First of all, I am not a Muslim, nor was I ever. However, I am quite knowledgeable of Islam's doctrines and how **Islam is the youngest of all the world religions. I am very aware that it is also the fastest growing religion today in the world with its 1.1 billion members.** My Muslim reader, I know the Koran (Qur'ãn) rejects Jesus as the Son of God,[41] but I also know how Jesus through His apostle John foretold the rise and evolution of Islam in the book of Revelation. I will humbly map this out for you, as well as what Islam is prophesied to do shortly. However, I am very much aware of how learned Orthodox Muslims believe that Jesus was a true prophet of God and how He was from a line of prophets starting with Adam, Noah, Abraham, Aaron, and Moses, and how you believe that Muhammad (after Jesus) was the last of the prophets. I am aware of the fact that Muslims obey the dietary laws written out by Moses, which Roman Catholics and Protestants ignore. I am aware of the high moral standards of Islam's law and how true Muslims do not drink, gamble, steal, or charge usury among their members. I know that true Muslim women are dressed in modest apparel of which the God of Abraham told Moses to write in the Old Testament and also

[41]***The Meaning of The Holy Qur'ãn*, 'Ali, Surah 5:71–76, pp. 271, 272.**

the apostle Paul in the New Testament in 1 Timothy. This writer is also very much aware of how Orthodox Muslims are not hypocrites of their faith and look with disgust and abhorrence at Jews and Christians (Roman Catholics and Protestants) who claim to be of the faith of Abraham while they eat the blood of animals and feast on the flesh of hogs, crabs, and lobsters which are forbidden not only in the Qur'ãn in Surah 2:173, but also in the Bible in Leviticus 17:10–14 and Leviticus, Chapter 11; Deuteronomy, Chapter 14; and Acts 15:20, 29. I know how **Orthodox Muslims cringe when they see Jews and Christians, who are dressed in lewd apparel with painted faces and decked with jewelry, speaking God's name in vain, drinking beer or whiskey with cigarettes dangling from their mouths, sitting in front of slot machines or the card tables gambling, or on the dance floors making lewd sexual gestures at each other.** This writer can understand why Shiite Muslims metaphorically call the United States "**the great Satan**" for many degraded Americans, especially citizens of the Hollywood and Music Industry, have, indeed, become the mouthpiece of the Dragon in the world today. There has, indeed, been a great falling away from Biblical principles and a great departure from the God of Abraham by those who call themselves Jews and Christians in the United States. This writer understands how American (Western) influence has also corrupted the morals of the youth in Islamic countries via the medium of Hollywood and the Music Industry, who, by the way, are indeed the mouthpieces of the New World Order. We shall also see that this is true shortly.

However, my Muslim reader, are you aware that there are Christians who are not cross worshippers, as you call Roman Catholics, but who obey the dietary laws given by the God of Abraham to Moses? Are you aware that not only do these Christians obey what God said can be eaten and what of the unclean cannot; but, my Muslim brother or sister, there are Christians who have come back to the original diet given to Adam and Eve. We are vegetarians. Believe it or not, there are Christians who do not feast on hogs, crabs, lobsters, or on any other unclean foods. There are Christians throughout this world who **do not** dress in lewd apparel, paint their faces like Jezebel or the Pharoah, wear jewelry, drink alcohol or smoke cigarettes, gamble, steal, participate in sports, or sit in movie theaters beholding from Hollywood's heros every abomination known to mankind. My Muslim reader, there are still Christians today who also have denounced this world as evil and are patiently looking forward to the restoration of this world by God Himself! God has promised us that He will create a new heaven and a new earth (See Isaiah 66:22; Revelation 21:1), and that every race will live in harmony with each other. The God of Abraham told Abraham that because of him all nations shall be blessed (See Genesis 22:18), and that God's coming house of prayer "**shall be called an house of prayer for all people**." Isaiah 56:7. There will be no more religious confusion because it is written that God Himself would live in the midst of them!

"And I saw a new heaven and a new earth: for the first heaven and the first earth were passed away; and there was no more sea. And I John saw the holy city, new Jerusalem, coming down from God out of heaven, prepared as a bride adorned for her husband.

"And I heard a great voice out of heaven saying, Behold, the tabernacle of God is with men, and he will dwell with them, and they shall be his people, and God himself shall be with them, and be their God. And God shall wipe away all tears from their eyes; and there shall be no more death, neither sorrow, nor crying, neither shall there be any more pain: for the former things are passed away.

"And he that sat upon the throne said, Behold, I make all things new. And he said unto me, Write: for these words are true and faithful. And he said unto me, It is done. I am **Alpha and Omega**, the beginning and the end. I will give unto him that is athirst of the fountain of the water of life freely.

"He that overcometh shall inherit all things; and I will be his God, and he shall be my son. But the **fearful**, and **unbelieving**, and the **abominable**, and **murderers**, and **whoremongers**, and **sorcerers,** and **idolaters**, and all **liars**, shall have their part in the lake which burneth with fire and brimstone: which is the second death." Revelation 21:1–8.

Before we look into the prophecies concerning the Islamic community and what they will surely do shortly to those who do not have the **Seal of God in their foreheads**, we need to see the promises which were given to Abraham and his two sons, Ishmael and Isaac.

We will again study more into the secret order of Sufism and what they teach and what Sufism developed into in the 19th and 20th centuries as we continue.

Jews, Christians, and Muslims, as a whole, have lost sight of this very important truth. While all of the above religions claim to be of the faith of Abraham and claim to be the only True Faith, it should be remembered by all of the above that the famous Hebrew named Abraham **was neither** a Jew **NOR** a Christian **NOR** a Muslim when God pronounced His blessings on him. None of these religions were in history in his day when God said, "And I will bless them that bless thee, and curse him that curseth thee: and **in thee shall ALL families of the earth be blessed**." Genesis 12:3.

My Muslim reader, I have studied the history of the origins of the Arab people, the life of Muhammad, and the development of Islam and its two main divisions for some time now. I have read in the Scriptures how the God of Abraham pronounced a blessing on both Ishmael and Isaac and how both Ishmael and Isaac buried Abraham, but I am also aware of the fact that Muslims are divided because of the many interpretations of Islamic Law found in the Qur'ãn. I know that the Sufi says the Bible has been corrupted by the Jews. I have learned how you are taught that it was Ishmael, not Isaac, who Abraham was going to sacrifice and how Jesus was not crucified but just taken to Heaven. However, I have spent some time studying the Koran, comparing it with what was told to Moses in Arabia while he stood on Mt. Horeb (Sinai) as he received God's Word. This writer has proved for himself that the Holy Scriptures, which were given to Moses, the prophets that followed him, and the apostles in the New Testament, were, indeed, inspired by the God of Abraham who used these holy men to communicate His will to men. True, there were a few discrepancies in translation of words from the Hebrew and the Greek, but not in doctrine. The contradictions which are, indeed, found among Jews and Christians have been brought about by false interpretations of the Scriptures, not by the Scriptures themselves. I have also found this to be true among the Sufi shaykhs and even in their own interpretation of the Koran. Are there not multitudes of different interpretations of Islamic Law which have divided the Muslim community into different hate factions today? Reader, this is the same problem among Catholics and Protestants. Erring human beings have put their trust in man instead of God. Jesus Christ, however, said through **John in Revelation 12:9 that it has always been the seven-headed Dragon that has caused so much religious confusion for he has deceived the whole world, and that includes Jews, Christians, and Muslims**.

Let's now take a brief historical look into how the Arab community began. Do not the Arabs trace their lineage to Abraham and Ishmael and to Abraham and Keturah? (See Genesis, Chapters 23 and 25.) Do not Arabs today contend that a true Arab is one who comes through the lineage of Abraham and Keturah instead of Abraham and Hagar because Hagar was an Egyptian and not a Hebrew as was Abraham? Was not the son of Hagar Ishmael, who had a son named Nebajoth whose descendants became known as the Nabatheans? Was it not the Nabatheans who founded Nabataea and lived in Edom and what is now Jordan?[42] Was it not the Nabatheans who, like the Jews, apostatized and turned from the worship of God to worship the sun, moon, and the stars? **Was not the Kaaba, the sacred shrine in Mecca, used by the pagan Arabs to worship pagan gods centuries before Muhammad was born?**[43] My Muslim reader, are you aware of the origin of that five-pointed star ★(pentagram) which Muslims adopted, as well as the Freemasons, and which Muslims claim represents the five pillars of Islam? Do you understand the origin of the symbol of the crescent moon used in the flags of Turkey and other Islamic countries? My Muslim reader, are you aware of the origin of the name ***Allah*** in that it was never used by Jews or Christians to denote the name of God before the birth of Muhammad, but was used to denote the **moon-god** which was the **chief deity** of the pagan Nabatheans in Arabia and Canaan? We will see the historical facts about the statements above and a lot more about the origins of the doctrines of Islam as we continue.

There is hardly any mystical teaching found in these last days among the Hindus, Buddhists, Roman Catholics, Protestants, Muslims, or even

[42]***The Encyclopedia Americana*, Vol. 19, 1991, p. 707.**

[43]***The Koran with Parallel Arabic Text*, translated by Dawood, p. ix.**

the North, Central, and South American Indians which does not have its counterpart in the "**Secret Doctrine**" (hidden teachings) of the ancient Chaldeans of Babylonia. Let's again take a brief look at the origins of how the worship of the Chaldean and Semitic gods developed and then where the name ***Allah*** originated. The Holy Scriptures in Genesis 10:21–25 and 1 Chronicles 1:17–19 state that the Elamite peoples (descendants of Shem) are also from the same lineage of Heber (Eber). The word ***Hebrew*** derived out of the name ***Heber***, the great grandson of Shem. It means "***belonging to Eber***."[44] Abraham was a Hebrew. (See Genesis 14:13.)

During the early Post-Flood Era, it was Elam and his Semitic descendants who originally founded the Land of the Persian Gulf area that borders Arabia, which later became known as the Land of Shinar. Moses, who was also from the Semitic race, wrote in Genesis 10:6–12 and 11:2 that it was Nimrod, the son of Cush (Kush) who was the son of Ham (Noah's son), and his companions who, "as they journeyed **FROM THE EAST**" (Genesis 11:2) or from the Hindu Kush area (India), established the first cities of Shinar.

My Muslim reader, it is interesting to note that the name ***Cushan*** was the former name of Ethiopia. (Habakkuk 3:7 – see marginal reference.) When the Israelites apostatized and refused to obey Him, God used a pagan, Mesopotamian king to punish the Israelites for their idolatry. This Chaldean king was named **Chushan-rishathaim**. (See Judges 3:8, 10.) **His name means "*man of Cush; he of the twofold crime*."**[45] The Cushites, after entering Mesopotamia, continued their migration from India and settled in Egypt and other parts of Africa. Egypt is called the Land of Ham. (See Psalm 105:23, 27.)

It is also interesting to note how Kush, (also known as Hermes or Nebo) who was the first prophet of mysticism on this side of the Flood, was honored by the Japanese Buddhist mystics who named their school of mysticism after Nimrod's father; they called it ***Kusha***. It was introduced into Japan from China in A.D. 658 by two Japanese monks named Chitsu and Chitatsu who learned their

[44]***Young's Analytical Concordance to the Bible*, Young, pp. 287, 473.**

[45]***Nelson's Illustrated Encyclopedia of Bible Facts*, ed. Packer/Tenney/White, Jr., p. 628.**

metaphysical teachings from the traditions of an Indian, Buddhist sage named Vasubandhu.[46] It is also eye-opening to learn that **one of the four Buddhas was Kushinagara**, and this name was also the name of a town where Buddha was said to have died.[47] It should also be noted that Gautama Buddha was also a Cushite and a Hindu.

However, it was the Cushites (descendants of Cush) of Nimrod's day who established the first learning center of the ancient world. These disciples of Cush and Nimrod established two well-known cultures and dialects of the Hamitic language and also two separate identities. These Cushites from India became known as the Chaldeans and the Sumerians. The land of the Chaldeans was Babylonia, and a nation called Sumer had a capital by the name of **Ur**. The city of Ur is where a well-known Hebrew was living at that time, and this Hebrew was a descendant of the Elamites, who had lived there a few centuries before the arrival of the Cushites. His name was Abram (Abraham). Abraham's father was Terah, and it was from the Sumerian capital city of Ur that God told Abraham to leave. Abraham was the youngest son of Terah, and he was born 1996 B.C. and died at the age of 175 in 1821 B.C.[48] Moses, writing under the inspiration of the Holy Spirit, plainly records in Genesis 11:31 that Sumer's capital city Ur was of the Chaldeans (Cushites) which many scholars have lost sight of. The Sumerians and their religion have often been mistaken as being Semitic. It is very necessary to briefly study the documented history of both divisions of the Chaldeans living at Babylon and Sumer because their culture and religion had, indeed, spread not only into all of the Near East, but into Arabia and other parts of the West as well.

According to *Young's Analytical Concordance to the Bible*, Chaldea was the southern portion of Babylonia.[49] The Chaldeans were proved to be a Cushite race by their language, which closely resembles the Galla or ancient language of Ethiopia. Ethiopia was anciently known as "**the land of Cush**."[50]

[46]*A Dictionary of Comparative Religion*, ed. Brandon, p. 403.
[47]*Ibid.*, ed. Brandon, p. 403.
[48]*Young's Analytical Concordance to the Bible*, Young, pp. 8, 9.
[49]*Ibid.*, Young, pp. 152, 153.
[50]*Ibid.*, Young, p. 308.

It was the Chaldeans who are credited, both in the ancient and modern worlds, for being the inventors of the religion and sciences of astrology, which, as we saw earlier, was also known as Chaldean wisdom. In the Sumerian pantheon of the gods of astrology, the pagan god Enlil was regarded by them as the divine ruler of this world. The Sumerian priests altered the record of the Flood, which had been handed down verbally from the patriarch Noah, and attributed the Deluge to **Enlil** instead of to **Elohim**, the God of Abraham. Surely the reader has discovered how many stories of the gods of mythology have their counterparts in the records of the Torah, which are the first five books of Moses. According to this myth, not only did Enlil cause the Flood, but the priests of Sumer said that it was **Enlil**, the son of **Anu** the sky-god, who was the fatherly progenitor to whom the creation of the sun, moon, vegetation, and implements essential to human control of the earth was ascribed. The myth goes on to state that Enlil, to the Sumerians, held the tablets by which the fates of all people were settled.

My Christian reader, is this not also a counterfeit of the prophecy of the Promised One first proclaimed to Adam and how the Father in Heaven has placed the fate of mankind into the hands of His only begotten Son, who is the Son of God and the Creator of all things? (See John 1:1–3, 14; Ephesians 3:9)

The Chaldeans, who became mortal enemies of the Israelites as their history developed, like other pagan nations were accustomed to naming their kings, towns, cities, and capitals after their chief deities and also to renaming conquered nations, towns, and cities after their favorite gods. King Nebuchadnezzar was a Chaldean (Ezra 5:12) and his name in Chaldean means "***may Nabu (Nebo) guard my boundary stones***."[51] Nebuchadnezzar, after bringing the captive Hebrews to Babylon for a period that would last 70 years as foretold by the prophet Jeremiah in Jeremiah 25:1–12, changed the name of the Hebrew prophet Daniel, which means "***God is judge***," to ***Balat-usu-usur***, which translated from Chaldean to Hebrew is ***Belteshazzar***. The name ***Belteshazzar*** means "***Protect his life!***"[52]

[51]*Nelson's Illustrated Encyclopedia of Bible Facts*, ed. Packer/Tenney/White, Jr., p. 671.

[52]*Ibid.*, ed. Packer/Tenney/White, Jr., p. 624.

Listed next are the pagan names given to Daniel's three companions and their meanings:

Shadrach – "*servant of [the god] Sin*"[53]

Abed-nego – "*servant of Nebo; servant of Ishtar*"[54]

Meshach – "*the shadow of the prince; who is this?*"[55]

However, like the names of Zoroaster and Zarathushtra, who the Greeks mistakenly pointed to as being the sixth century B.C. Iranian prophet, scholars on both sides of the Atlantic mistakenly attributed the names Baal and Bel as being the same god. However, Isaiah, the Hebrew prophet of Elohim, shows in his book in Isaiah 46:1 that Bel is a synonym for Nebo.

"Bel boweth down, Nebo stoopeth, their idols were upon the beasts, and upon the cattle: your carriages were heavy loaden; they are a burden to the weary beast." Isaiah 46:1.

This prophecy against Nebo is really against Satan who was disguising himself as the god Nebo, who the king of Babylon worshipped. Nebuchadnezzar was allowed to destroy Jerusalem because of Israel's idolatry. Our Lord used pagans to punish the Hebrews for practicing paganism. This king of Babylon, says Daniel 1:2, also carried the sacred vessels of the house of God into the Land of Shinar to the house of his god. However, Isaiah prophesied years earlier that the sacred vessels of Nebo at Babylon would **also** be carried away at Babylon's coming destruction. Again,my Muslim brother or sister, are you aware that the Quranic term for a prophet is **Nabi**? Shortly, we will also find the origin of the name **Allah** which Muslims **mistakenly** use for **God**. However, it should also be noted that Nebuchadnezzar turned away from mysticism and worshipped the Most High God of Abraham (Daniel 4:34-37). It was an Ethiopian (Cushite) eunuch who Philip was told to visit while he stood in his chariot reading the Scriptures; he became one of the first Black Christians. (See Acts, Chapter Eight.)

The fulfillment of Isaiah 46:1 about the god-prophet Nebo (Nabu) began after the death of Nebuchadnezzar. The last king of Babylon

[53]*Nelson's Illustrated Encyclopedia of Bible Facts*, ed. Packer/Tenney/White, Jr., p. 680.

[54]*Ibid.*, ed. Packer/Tenney/White, Jr., p. 612.

[55]*Ibid.*, ed. Packer/Tenney/White, Jr., p. 668.

was **Nabonidus, the father of Belshazzar**. He fled to northern Arabia in exile after the priests of Marduk rebelled in Babylon because of Nabonidus' making the moon-god Sin, who was earlier believed to be the father of Shamash the sun-god, the chief god at Babylon.[56] Nebo was believed to be the son of Marduk,[57] who the pagan Romans later worshipped as Mars. However, the priests of the worship of Marduk had earlier bumped out Sin and Shamash as the favorite gods in Babylon. Nabonidus, however, said he received a vision from his moon-god Sin to **reinstate** his favorite god's worship. Marduk had in the past been a **lesser** god under the Babylonian pantheon. Now, here are some very astonishing facts about the **origin** of the god Allah and some signs of Islam which Muslims in the past were determined to make the whole world submit to.

The **moon-god Sin** is also known in mythology as **Nanna** and was depicted in Chaldean art as an enthroned and bearded figure wearing tiara and surmounted by a **crescent moon** in the shape of a boat. His chief culture centre was the Sumerian city of Ur, and he was regarded by the Chaldeans as "**lord of the month**" who maintained justice at night. **Sin, the moon-god,** was not only believed to have been the father of the sun-god **Shamash** in this version of Babylonian mysticism, but **Sin was the father of Ishtar**,[58] the powerful goddess of sex and war who was **Ashtoreth** to the apostate Hebrews, **Diana** to the Ephesians, and **Isis** in Egyptian mysticism. Her symbol originally was the stellar **(eight-pointed)** star which was called **Sirius** in the Old World. The Roman Catholics have adopted this stellar star to symbolize their virgin and to this day call **Mary the Queen of Heaven!** This was originally the title of Ishtar or Ashtoreth (Ashtaroth). (See Judges 2:13; Jeremiah 44:17–19.) On page 28 of *Beware It's Coming – The Antichrist 666*, I show a Chaldean seal from the British Museum showing Ishtar with a bow and arrows in her hand and her eight-pointed star (Sirius) hovering over her head.

This above information may have brought disbelief and maybe a

[56]***Beware It's Coming – The Antichrist 666*, Sutton, p. 121.**

[57]***World Religions From Ancient History to the Present*, ed. Parrinder, p. 116.**

[58]***A Dictionary of Comparative Religion*, ed. Brandon, p. 580.**

chuckle or two among the Muslim readers for I am aware of the Islamic Law and also of the Second Commandment in Exodus 20:4, 5 which forbids Muslims and those of the Judeo-Christian faith to worship other gods or saints and the making or bowing down to idols (graven images) which Roman Catholics ignore and fill their churches with. However, my Muslim reader, are you aware that the five-pointed star in your flag which you use to symbolize the **five pillars of Islam (faith, prayer, charity, fasting, and pilgrimage)** in pagan philosophy originally symbolized the"**Son of the Morning**" (Lucifer) of whom the **pagan Arabs worshipped as Athtar**?[59] **I have discovered that this symbol of the morning and evening star baffles even the astrologers about its origin.** The plaited pentagram has also been used as a **protective sign** among occultists against evil powers and can be seen drawn on the doors of barns. **Witches use this star to invoke their spirit guides or to cast their spells. To the pagan Greeks, the morning star was called Phosphorus or Heosphorus, and translated into Latin the name *Phosphorus* becomes *Lucifer*.**[60] This **occult star** used to invoke Satan can also be seen in the American flag as well because it was the Freemasons who borrowed much from Sufism and who designed the American flag. **The five-pointed star (Venus) is often personified in poetry as the star which announces the approach of Aurora, the dawn.**[61] **Lucifer in ancient mythology has been symbolized by this morning star and is known poetically as the "SON OF THE MORNING" according to Isaiah the prophet.**[62] Again, reader, please keep in mind that Lucifer is not only the "Son of the Morning" in Bible prophecy, but he is also the cosmic **seven-headed Dragon**, which the ancient Chaldeans used to symbolize the religion, the sciences, and the signs of astrology.

Another pagan sign of astrology, which Roman Catholics borrowed from mysticism and which the Muslims adopted after they conquered the Byzantine Empire and destroyed Constantinople in

[59]*Mythology of All Races*, Vol. 5, ed. MacCulloch, p. 4.

[60]*The Dictionary of Classical Mythology*, Grimal, translated by Maxwell-Hyslop, p. 371.

[61]*Ibid.*, Grimal, translated by Maxwell-Hyslop, p. 371.

[62]Isaiah 14:12.

A.D. 1453, was the **crescent**. The symbol of the crescent has always been one of the symbols to invoke Sin, IL, or a female moon-goddess known as the Queen of Heaven, whom the Roman Catholics today call the Virgin Mary. **Although a Sufi may urge that the crescent was used by pagan Arabs before the establishment of the Roman Catholic Church, nevertheless, the crescent placed in a position as a boat was used to honor the Chaldean moon-god Sin and symbolized his heavenly vehicle as he traveled across the Cosmos.** We will see more of this in a moment. However, the Muslim Sufis changed the position of the crescent into the waning moon, which symbolized the morning crescent. This symbol of the moon-god Sin was the symbol of the Ottoman Empire whose history and deeds were foretold by the apostle John in Revelation, Chapter Nine. The combination of the waning moon and the pentagram as the symbol of the Muslim faith developed in recent history.[63]

As already discussed, another astonishing thing I learned as I studied Islam was its attitude towards Jesus. In *The Meaning of The Holy Qur'ãn*, it states that those who believe that Jesus is the Son of God "**Allah's curse be on them**."[64] However, before the birth of Muhammad, the apostle John wrote under the inspiration of God:

"Who is a liar but he that denieth that Jesus is the Christ? **HE IS ANTICHRIST, THAT DENIETH THE FATHER AND THE SON.** Whosoever denieth the Son, the same hath not the Father: [but] he that acknowledgeth the Son hath the Father also." 1 John 2:22, 23.

Most Protestant Christians are not aware that the Koran (Qur'ãn) openly denies that Jesus of Nazareth was the Son of God and demands that there is no god but God (Allah) and Muhammad is the messenger of God.[65] (Emphasis mine.) **We have reached the point in our historical study about the origin of Islam in which a serious in-depth look at the origin of the god Allah is very much needed so the reader may know why the Qur'ãn rejects the Deity of Christ and Jesus Christ as the Saviour of the world. It should be remembered by Bible-believing Christians that the great Dragon**

[63]*Dictionary of Symbols*, Liungman, pp. 263, 264.

[64]*The Meaning of The Holy Qur'ãn*, 'Ali, Surah 9:30, p. 446.

[65]*The Muslim Almanac*, ed. Nanji, p. 12.

"deceiveth the whole world" (Revelation 12:9) and "Who is a liar but he that denieth that Jesus is the Christ? He is **ANTI-CHRIST**, that **DENIETH** the Father and the Son." (Emphasis mine.) 1 John 2:22.

As pointed out, the **eldest son of Ishmael (Nebajoth)** had descendants living in Arabia, Lebanon, and in what is now known as the country Jordan who were called the **Nabataeans**. According to the *Encyclopedia of Gods* and *The Oxford English Dictionary*, **the name *Allah* derived from the name *Ilãh*.[66] *IL*, as pointed out earlier, was one of the old chief gods of astrology in northern Canaan. The ancient astrological god *IL***, according to the *Encyclopedia of Gods*, was worshipped as the creator god not only in Canaan, but also in Lebanon and the Syrian coastal regions. His worship can be traced back to **2000 B.C.** His name appears on a stele found at **Ras Shamra** (ancient Ugarit). However, it should be notedthat the moon-god was called Hubal to the Meccans of Arabia.

Non-believing mythologists often confuse the god *IL* with being the origin of the Hebrew God (*EL*), but nothing could be further from the truth. The name *IL*, however, was a counterfeit god Satan camouflaged himself as to confuse ancient peoples from worshipping ELOHIM.

The name ***Ilãh*** derived from the name ***IL***. It means "***the god***." Reader, it is a historical fact that the god ***IL*** was the supreme god of the Nabataeans living in Canaan, who were the descendants of Ishmael. ***IL* is the equivalent to the Babylonian moon-god Sin,**[67] after which a wilderness named "**Sin**" that borders southern Arabia is named. (See Exodus 16:1; Numbers 33:11–12) The creator god ***IL*** or ***Ilãh*** is **TRANSLATED IN ARABIC AS ALLAH**. The word ***al*** in Arabic means "***the***;" hence, the name ***al-ilãh*** means "***the god***," as does ***ALLAH***.[68] Allah was **originally** an ancient moon-god.

It is said by Muslim scholars that it was **Hubal** (not Allah) who was the moon-god to the Meccans, which is true, and that

[66]***Encyclopedia of Gods*, Jordan, p. 11; *The Oxford English Dictionary*, Vol. 1, p. 228.**

[67]***Mythology of All Races*, Vol. 5, ed. MacCulloch, pp. 5–7.**

[68]***The Oxford English Dictionary*, Vol. 1, p. 228.**

Muhammad pulled down his image at the Kaaba and used it as a doorstep.[69] However, to the Arabs living in northern Canaan in Lebanon, **Allah** was the moon-god, not **Hubal**. Nevertheless, the god Allah was one of the gods of the pagan pantheon who, like Sin, lost his position to another god, which in this case was Hubal. Like King Nabonidus of Babylon who was determined to **reinstate** the moon-god Sin over Marduk (who bumped him out of his rightful position), so did Muhammad **reinstate Allah** in Mecca as the **chief god**. The name ***Allah***, which was the moon-god to the Arabs in northern Canaan, **was not ever** used as the name of God in the Old Testament. If Islam is as it claims to be (which is just an extension of the Judeo-Christian faith), why are there no Hebrew names found in Islamic literature addressing Him as God? Abraham was a Hebrew and so was Moses and Jesus. Muslims claim that God has 100 names of which 99 names are revealed. Out of all the **99 names**, the reader will not come across the names that the Hebrew prophets, starting with Moses, called God in the Koran. However, it is a historical fact that the name **IL** or **al-ilãh (the god**), which is **Allah** in Arabic, was, indeed, the **moon-god** to Arabs living in Canaan, Lebanon, and Syria. My Muslim reader, Satan disguised himself as Allah, the astrological moon-god, centuries before the birth of Muhammad.

This is very shocking to learn, as it was for me as well. However, the above information is written in history, and there is even more historical proof that **Allah is not Elohim,** but is actually Satan who fooled the pagan Arabs to bow and worship him as the moon-god.

According to *Mythology of All Races*, there were many astrological names that the ancient, pagan Arabians used in their worship of the sun, moon, and stars as well.[70] In southern Arabia, the descendants of Ishmael and their brethren had three other principal deities that also date back centuries before Muhammad was born. In one tradition, the pagan Arabs living in Arabia named their unholy trinity as **Shamshu**, **'Athtar, and Shahar**. Sometimes, in the evolution of Arab pagan traditions in southern Arabia, the sun-god was a female deity while other traditions had him as a male deity named Manaf.

[69]***The Concise Encyclopedia of Islam*, Glassé, p. 160.**

[70]***Mythology of All Races*, Vol. 5, ed. MacCulloch, pp. 4, 5.**

However, **'Athtar (Lucifer) was the morning star Venus**, whose symbol (★) today appears on the Islamic flag, as well as on the American flag, while **Shahar** was another name of the moon-god rather than Hubal, Sin, or IL. There is plenty of evidence that the old Chaldean moon-god Sin was, indeed, also worshipped in other traditions in the Arabian peninsula.[71]

Here are some more astonishing facts of how Islam is a blend of Chaldean and Western mysticism. **Sin**, the moon-god (the father of Shamash, the sun-god) is symbolized in Mesopotamian mythology by the new moon and perceived as a **bull** whose horns are the **crescent of the moon**.[72] Ironically enough, while Muslims use the **WANING MORNING CRESCENT WITH THE PENTAGRAM (☪)** which symbolizes Islam, today this same horizontal moon sign of Sin signifies the **ARABIC LEAGUE**, a union of Islamic states.[73]

As pointed out, Nabonidus (Nabunidus), the last king of Babylon (555–538 B.C.), fled to Teima in Arabia, which was north of El-Ola, when he tried to reinstate the worship of **Sin, the moon-god, again at Babylon**. There have been found in the southern area of Arabia inscriptions which record **Nabonidus' flight to Arabia**,[74] and it is certain that the Babylonians with their chief god Sin had influenced his worship among both the Arabians and the Canaanites living in their southern borders long before the days of Nabonidus.

Another earlier Mesopotamian king who identified with the god Sin was the evil King Sennacherib. This Assyrian king killed his own brother to usurp the throne. **Sennacherib's name means "*Sin has substituted for my brother.*"**[75] He was the most feared king of Hezekiah's day who not only blasphemed the God of Abraham, Isaac, and Jacob, but planned to overthrow Jerusalem. However, the angel of the Lord smote 185,000 men of his army, and this king of Assyrian

[71]***Larousse Encyclopedia of Archaeology*, ed. Charles-Picard, p. 279.**

[72]***Encyclopedia of Gods*, Jordan, pp. 236, 237.**

[73]***Dictionary of Symbols*, Liungman, p. 226.**

[74]***Mythology of All Races*, Vol. 5, ed. MacCulloch, p. 5.**

[75]***Nelson's Illustrated Encyclopedia of Bible Facts*, ed. Packer/Tenney/White, Jr., p. 679.**

mysticism was forced to retreat back to Nineveh where he met death by the hands of his own two sons. (See 2 Kings, Chapters 18 and 19.) His palace was uncovered by British archaeologists at Nineveh, the old capital of Assyria,[76] which the Cushite Nimrod built centuries before. (See Genesis 10:10, 11.)

As the reader may recall, it was the "**wilderness of Sin**" which the mighty prophet Moses led the children of Israel across after they crossed on dry land through the Red Sea. **It was from the Arabian Mt. Sinai that the Great I AM met Moses.** Has the reader ever wondered why **Mt. Sinai** was also called **Mt. Horeb** as well? Amazingly enough, the pagan name ***Sinai*** derived from **Babylon's old moon-god Sin,**[77] as did the name for the **wilderness of Sin** which in Biblical times was located in southern Canaan. This mountain of God was properly called by Moses Mt. Horeb (Choreb). (See Exodus 3:1; 17:6; 33:6 and Psalm 106:19)

As ***IL,*** the old creator god, was to the Nabataeans, so was Sin to the Arabs in Arabia. As we are seeing, his worship is alive and well today. It is a well-known fact that before the founder of Islam was born, the center of ancient idolatry in Arabia was in Mecca. The moon-god's most religious center of worship was **"the Kaaba," a shrine in Mecca which was sacred to the pagan Arabs centuries before the birth of Muhammad**.

The Kaaba is at the center of the Islamic faith. When Muslims pray five times to Allah, they pray towards the Kaaba from all the different parts of the world in which they live. Among the five pillars of Islam, Muslims from all over the world are required to make at least one pilgrimage to the Kaaba in their lifetime.

Muslim traditions claim that this shrine in Mecca had originally been built by Adam, was later destroyed by the Flood, and was then rebuilt again by Abraham (Ibrahim). During the apostasy of the Ishmaelites, the Kaaba was the most sacred center of the pagan Arab's worship. Pagan Arabs before the birth of Muhammad made pilgrimages to this shrine in Mecca as do Muslims today. **The Kaaba housed a pantheon of 360 gods of which Hubal, the**

[76]***The Cambridge Illustrated History of Archaeology*, ed. Bahn, pp. 104, 105.**
[77]***Mythology of All Races*, Vol. 5, ed. MacCulloch, pp. 5, 6.**

moon-god, was the most honored among the pagan Arabs at Mecca in Muhammad's earlier days.[78] However, again, my Muslim reader, at the head of the pantheon of gods at the Kaaba was Allah, who had lost his rightful place among the other idols.[79] There is today overwhelming evidence that Allah was **originally** a pagan Arab deity and not the God of Abraham. There is a definite **pattern** and **parallel** seen here between Nabonidus, the king of Babylon, and that of Muhammad. As Nabonidus had a dream from his god Sin to reinstate his worship in Babylon, so did Muhammad receive a revelation to exalt Allah as the only true god. Muhammad simply **cleansed** the Kaaba of **other idols** and **reinstated Allah as the only god**. As any Muslim knows, Muhammad was rejected by Meccans for 12 years for making Allah the only god. Wars were fought over this in which Muhammad finally became victorious.

It should also be noted here that before his revelations, which the Muslims say were given by the angel Gabriel, Muhammad was **neither** a Jew nor a Christian. He was also a **pagan Arab** whose tribe (the Quraysh) were like the Levites in a sense, for they were chosen as the **keepers of the Kaaba** and its sacred things in Mecca. It was in A.D. 630 that Muhammad was said to have cleansed the Kaaba of all the pagan gods except for **one, Allah (the god)**, whom Muslims have **misinterpreted** as being the God of Abraham. My Muslim reader, this truth can be easily verified by looking into your own historical books.

It is also a historical fact that the apostatizing Ishmaelites and their Arabian brethren left the worship of the True God of Abraham mainly for the worship of the ancient Chaldean gods which were introduced and adopted by them as they traded with their neighbors.

As established from the Koran (Qur'ãn), the Kaaba at Mecca was used not only to worship this god Allah (Sin), but also a number of female deities who they regarded as the daughters of Allah. Among these goddesses were **Al-Lãt, Al-'Uzzã, and Manãt** who, to these pagan Arabs, represented the **Sun, Venus, and Fortune**.[80] It was indeed Muhammad, however, who turned the erring Arabians from

[78]***The Concise Encyclopedia of Islam*, Glassé, p. 179.**

[79]***The Koran With Parallel Arabic Text*, translated by Dawood, p. ix.**

[80]***Ibid.*, translated by Dawood, p. ix.**

polytheism to monotheism, as did another mystical prophet, centuries before, named Zarathushtra (the Persian prophet) with his claim that Ahura Mazda was the only God and that he was his prophet.

In the beginning, Muhammad, who claimed to be the **last prophet** of the God of Abraham and that Islam **was not a new religion but just an extension of the Judeo-Christian faith**, had his followers face towards Jerusalem when they prayed. However, after the Jews and Christians rejected the worship of Allah and Muhammad as a prophet of God, he commanded his Muslim followers to pray towards the Kaaba. As I write, fanatical Muslim extremists and their leaders, like Osama bin Laden, have united with numerous Egyptian, Algerian, Palestinian, Filipino, and Jordanian terrorist groups who bin Laden has trained in his camps[81] to murder in the name of Allah in an effort to rid Muslim lands of Western influence and to make Islam a universal religion. In John 8:44, Jesus said the **Devil was "a murderer from the beginning,"** and his **attributes** are clearly seen in this astrological god named Allah whose **spirit moves** his followers with **no remorse** to **murder or maim** those who do not obey Islam's god. Osama bin Laden, in his great ignorance, thinks he is following the dictates of the God of Abraham when he exhorts Muslims to kill Americans anywhere in the world.[82]

According to *Newsweek*, March 1, 1999, Osama bin Laden, who has a price on his head for his involvement with the bombing of the American embassies in Nairobi and Dar es Salaam back in August of 1998, is now the **most-wanted man** in the world. Bin Laden's murderous character of the real god he worships and is guided by was also demonstrated back in the 80s. In 1984, bin Laden, who is a Saudi millionaire, contributed to a Muslim organization which posed themselves to the world as a worldwide Islamic charitable network who even had offices in Detroit and Brooklyn. They were known as the Maktab al-Khidamat, who were raising money to help the Afghans in their struggle against the Russians. It turns out that this same charitable Islamic organization was used in Brooklyn by the blind Sheikh Omar Abdel Rahman to bomb the World Trade Center in 1993.[83]

[81]***Time*, August 24, 1998, p. 51.**

[82]***Newsweek*, August 24, 1998, p. 30.**

[83]***Newsweek*, March 1, 1999, p. 40, 42.**

CHAPTER V

THE PROPHECY OF THE RISE OF THE STAR OF ISLAM

"And the fifth angel sounded, and I saw a **STAR FALL FROM HEAVEN** unto the earth: and to him was given the **key** of the **bottomless pit**. And he opened the **bottomless pit**; and there arose a smoke out of the pit, as the smoke of a great furnace; and the sun and the air were darkened by reason of the smoke of the pit. And there came out of the smoke **locusts** upon the earth: and unto them was given power, as the scorpions of the earth have power.

"And it was commanded them that they **should not** hurt the grass of the earth, neither any green thing, neither any tree; but only those men which have **NOT THE SEAL OF GOD IN THEIR FOREHEADS**. And to them it was given that they should not kill them, but that they should be tormented **FIVE MONTHS**: and their torment was as the torment of a scorpion, when he striketh a man. And in those days shall men seek death, and shall not find it; and shall desire to die, and death shall flee from them.

"And the **shapes of the locusts** were like unto horses prepared unto battle; and on their heads were as it were crowns like gold, and their faces were as the faces of men. And they had hair as the hair of women, and their teeth were as the teeth of lions. And they had breastplates, as it were breastplates of iron; and the sound of their wings was as the sound of chariots of many horses running to battle. And they had tails like unto scorpions, and there were stings in their tails: and their power was to hurt men **FIVE MONTHS**.

"**And they had a KING over them,** which is the **ANGEL** of the **bottomless pit**, whose name in the Hebrew tongue is **Abaddon, but in the Greek tongue hath his name Apollyon. One WOE is past; and, behold, there come TWO WOES more hereafter**."

Revelation 9:1–12.

A HISTORICAL OUTLINE of the FIRST WOE of ISLAM while under the RULE of the ARABS (SARACENS)

A.D. 570 Muhammad was born. He is symbolized in Muslim poetry as a Star.

A.D. 608 The Kaaba is rebuilt. Muhammad places black stone sacred to Muslims in it. Muhammad claims to have received a revelation in a cave while he was practicing meditation. Muhammad begins his mission to conquer the world for Allah.

A.D. 620 Muslims claim Muhammad was floated to Jerusalem from Mecca and then taken to the presence of Allah in one day. Dome of the Rock built in A.D. 691 at site.

A.D. 622 The Hijra. Muhammad flees with his disciples to Medina after struggling with opposing Meccans for 12 years. He narrowly escapes an assassination. Muslims start their lunar calendar on this date. First Muslim community established in Medina.

A.D. 624 Muhammad finally becomes victorious over Meccans and in six years the entire city of Mecca submits to the authority of Muhammad and his reforms. Pagan Arabs remove all the 360 gods at the Kaaba and accept the worship of Allah only. Muhammad changes the direction Muslims face while praying from Jerusalem to the Kaaba after being rejected by Jews and Christians. Muslims bring woe upon Jews and Christians in Arabia.

A.D. 628-29 Muhammad sends out invitations to Muqawqis of Egypt, Chosroes II of Persia, Heraclius of Byzantium, and other rulers inviting them to accept Islam and him as its prophet. Chosroes II dies and Siroes his successor sees the invitation and tears it up.

A.D. 632 Muhammad dies suddenly of fever. This begins a dispute over who is to be Muhammad's successor. Abu Bakr succeeds as caliph and begins wars on non-Muslims. Arabian Muslims bring woe upon apostate Christians and other non-Muslims.

A.D. 638 Muslims take the city Jerusalem away from the Roman Catholics, and it stays under the rule of Muslims until 1099 when the Crusaders take it back.

A.D. 661 Ali, Muhammad's cousin and fourth caliph, is assassinated by a Kharijite Muslim, and Muawiya claims to be the true caliph and his order of Islam becomes known as the Umayyads. Within 100 years, Muslims conquer Mediterranean countries.

A.D. 750 A Muslim named al-Arba stirs up Islam against the Umayyad's apostasy, and al-Arba and his followers, the Abbasids, rule Islam's conquered lands. Those who refused to become Muslims, if they survived the sword, had to pay a tax to the Muslim leaders if they wanted to live and continue to live in the conquered land of Islam. When the Abbasids came to power, they again moved the capital of Islam to Baghdad. The Abbasids became content with the huge tax revenue they received from non-Muslims and lost interest in continuing the Jihad to make the whole world submit to Islam. After securing their power, the Abbasids began to settle down in the areas already captured by earlier Saracens and intermarried with the Persian captives. They became interested in promoting business, education, and the arts. Baghdad became the center of world trade. The Abbasids adopted Persian customs and lived a luxurious lifestyle. The Abbasid dynasty lasted some 500 years, but the borders of Islam remained the same. The Abbasids were the last Arab rulers. The Muslim Arabs began to divide and break up into four divisions because of sultans collecting taxes for their own personal use. Muslims regain control of Jerusalem in A.D. 1187.

A.D. 1258 The Mongolian Hulagu Khan invades the capital of Islam, overthrows the last Arab dynasty, and establishes the Mongol il-Khanid dynasty in Persia. After sacking Baghdad, the Mongols move their capital to Tabriz.

"One woe is past; and, behold, there come two woes more hereafter." Revelation 9:12.

CHAPTER V

This chapter is focusing on the prophecies about the founder of Islam, its Star, and his followers who were symbolized in Bible prophecy as **200 million desert locusts which swarmed out of Arabia and terrorized the Persian Zoroastrians, Greek Orthodox Catholics, Hindus, and Buddhists**. Revelation 9:1–11 scans Islam's **first period** from A.D. 570 to A.D. 1258 as seen on the chart. With a prophetic look, Revelation 9:12–21 scans the **second period of Islamic history** which was under its most powerful rule in history and was known as the Ottoman Empire. **There is also a chart showing this period of Muslim history and conquest near the end of this chapter.**

As the God of Abraham punished the Israelites for practicing mysticism by using heathen nations like Assyria and Babylon, so did this same **God use Islam** to be a scourge to those who willingly ignored or did not obey the **Gospel of Jesus Christ**.

The book of Revelation says that there have been people of this world who have **willingly** and **unwittingly** worshipped the Dragon (See Revelation 13:4) because "**that old serpent, called the Devil, and Satan, which deceiveth the whole world:** he was cast out into the earth, and his angels were cast out with him." Revelation 12:9. In Revelation 12:12, Jesus tells the rest of the angels who remained loyal to Him, "Therefore, rejoice, ye heavens, and ye that dwell in them," but He says to the people of this world, **"WOE TO THE INHABITERS OF THE EARTH AND OF THE SEA! for the devil is come down unto you, having great wrath, because he knoweth that he hath but a short time."**

Before we look at the amazing prophecies about Islam and what it is predicted to do in our day, let's go back again and take another look at the rebellion of Lucifer against God. As pointed out, this planet has been Lucifer's strategic battlefield to continue his battle with Elohim for 6,000 years. He lost his place in Heaven for trying to usurp the authority of Him "**who dwelleth between the cherubims**." What Lucifer attempted to do in the Heavenly courts among the angels is what he is now attempting, behind the scenes, to accomplish among all of the human race today. Lucifer a.k.a. Satan is now trying to completely usurp the worship of the True God on this planet among humans by using human beings.

The Son of God said in Luke 10:18, "I beheld Satan as lightning fall from heaven." Our Messiah has symbolized this struggle between Him and Lucifer in the book of Revelation as a great cosmic or spiritual war. Here, again, is how Satan is pictured in the book of Revelation.

"And there appeared another wonder in heaven; and behold a **GREAT RED DRAGON, HAVING SEVEN HEADS AND TEN HORNS, AND SEVEN CROWNS UPON HIS HEADS**. And his tail drew the third part of the stars of heaven, and did cast them to the earth: and the dragon stood before the woman which was ready to be delivered, for to devour her child as soon as it was born." Revelation 12:3, 4.

In Revelation 12:13, Jesus through His apostle points out to us that "when the dragon saw that he was cast unto the earth, he persecuted the woman which brought forth the man child." The woman who the Dragon is attacking symbolizes **Jesus' true people** not only from the past ages, but also those today who shall have gotten the **victory** over the Dragon, and over his beast, and over his image, and over his mark, and over the number of his name (**666**). (See Revelation 15:2.)

In Bible prophecy, there are "**TWO WOMEN**" symbolizing the people of this planet; again, this signifies not only human beings in past ages, but also people in our very day. Christ's people are in Revelation, Chapter 12. In Revelation 14:4 and 2 Corinthians 11:2, His true followers are called virgins who are in contrast with the other woman found in Revelation, Chapters 17 and 18. This woman is **the Dragon's people**, and she is the **Mother of Harlots** and abominations of the earth. This Mother of Harlots has "**a golden cup in her**

hand full of abominations and filthiness of her fornication." Revelation 17:4. In verse two of Chapter 17, this Mother of Harlots has "committed fornication, and the inhabitants of the earth have been made **drunk (intoxicated) with the wine of her fornication**." This Mother of Harlots is also called, as we have already seen, **MYSTERY**, which is **MYSTICISM** and its various branches with its origin being with the Babylonian Chaldeans. This is why they are called in Revelation 17:5 "**MYSTERY, BABYLON THE GREAT, THE MOTHER OF HARLOTS AND ABOMINATIONS OF THE EARTH**" for all systems of mysticism originated at Babylon.

Jesus symbolizes His true followers as a **virgin** because they do not have the secret doctrines or mystical practices of mysticism in their worship of God which astrology, Hinduism, Buddhism, Zoroastrianism, the various branches of the pseudo-Judeo-Christian faiths, and Islam, as well, have and are centered around. When the ancient Israelites blended the various systems of mysticism from the nations around them into the worship of Elohim, our Lord in Ezekiel, Chapter 16, called them **harlots** in the past; and so is it today with those who are claiming to be Christ's people but practice and promote the doctrines of these modern Chaldeans of spiritual Babylon.

It says in Revelation 12:4 that the dragon drew with his tail the third part of the stars of heaven. Again, Lucifer's name means "***day star***," and he is also known as the "***light bearer***," the shining one or the **illuminated one**. Jesus symbolized the one third of the fallen angels who united with Satan as **stars** as well. Here, again, we see how one must be a diligent student of the Holy Scriptures because Jesus in Revelation 22:16 says, **"I am the root and the offspring of David, AND THE BRIGHT AND MORNING STAR."** The King of kings and Lord of lords was not referring to the morning star seen at dawn in the Eastern sky which the pagan goddess Venus was named after, as well as Athtar who the pagan Arabs worshipped in their ignorance or Baal, the day star (the sun), who in reality was Lucifer. This Day Star and Morning Star are used metaphorically in prophecy to depict spiritual light shining in spiritual darkness. Jesus was referring to the **inward spiritual light** one receives while he makes God's Word a lamp unto his feet and Christ as his hope.

"We have also a more **sure word of prophecy**; whereunto ye do well that ye take heed, as unto a **light that shineth in a dark place**, until the day dawn, **AND THE DAY STAR ARISE IN YOUR HEARTS**." 2 Peter 1:19.

John, the apostle of Jesus Christ, while wrapped in vision, wrote the book of Revelation. As he wrote while moved by the Holy Spirit, he saw a **STAR** fall from Heaven to the earth. This was not a meteor or a real falling star, for the book of Revelation is written in symbolic language. Let's take another look at Revelation 9:1, 2:

"And the fifth angel sounded, and I saw a **STAR** fall from heaven unto the earth: and **TO HIM WAS GIVEN THE KEY OF THE BOTTOMLESS PIT. And HE OPENED THE BOTTOMLESS PIT;** and there arose a smoke out of the pit, as the smoke of a great furnace; and the **SUN AND THE AIR WERE DARKENED BY REASON OF THE SMOKE OF THE PIT**."

My Muslim reader, are you aware that **the Koran (Qur'ãn) in Surah 53 symbolically refers to Muhammad as a declining or falling star?** Among the Muslims, Muhammad is also affectionately called a **compatriot** in the Koran. In *The Koran With Parallel Arabic Text*, we read: "By the **DECLINING STAR,** your **compatriot** is not in error, nor is he deceived!"[1] (Emphasis mine.) Muhammad, the declining star of Islam as he is called in the Koran, Surah 53:1, was born into an aristocratic family declining in wealth around A.D. 570 and was later orphaned.[2]

The history of Muhammad was as a "**declining star**," but, according to the Muslims, he arose again as the "**morning star**." As established, the five-pointed star (★) was a symbol of Athtar (Lucifer) of the pagan Arabs before the birth of Muhammad. Revelation 9:1 says that "to him (the declining star) was given the **KEY** of the **BOTTOMLESS PIT**." The "bottomless pit" is also where the red dragon-like beast comes out of, and this red beast is uplifting the Mother of Harlots to the world in Revelation 11:7; 17:3, 7–13. In Revelation 17:3, 7, 8, 13, 14, we read:

[1]***The Koran With Parallel Arabic Text*, translated by Dawood, Surah 53:1, p. 525.**

[2]***The World's Religions*, Clarke, p. 88.**

"So he carried me away in the spirit into the wilderness: and I saw a woman sit upon a scarlet coloured beast, full of names of blasphemy, having seven heads and ten horns.... And the angel said unto me, Wherefore didst thou marvel? I will tell thee the mystery of the woman, and of the beast that carrieth her, which hath the seven heads and ten horns.

"The beast that thou sawest was, and is not; and **SHALL ASCEND OUT OF THE BOTTOMLESS PIT, AND GO INTO PERDITION:** and they that dwell on the earth shall wonder, whose names were not written in the **book of life** from the foundation of the world, when they behold the **beast that was, and is not, and yet is**....

"**These have one mind**, and shall give their power and strength unto the beast. These shall make war with the Lamb, and the Lamb shall overcome them: for he is Lord of lords, and King of kings: and they that are with him are **called**, and **chosen**, and **faithful**."

As Revelation, Chapter Nine, shows, this is a terrible persecuting power which has also killed those loyal to Jesus. An in-depth study of the **Beast from the Bottomless Pit** is diligently examined in Volume Two of this series of Time of the End prophecies. The Beast from the **BOTTOMLESS PIT SYMBOLIZES** the various **POLITICAL** powers of **SPIRITUALISM** (mysticism) which Satan has worked through, while the woman (Babylon the Great) it is carrying symbolizes the various **RELIGIOUS** powers. Both derived from the secret doctrines promoted by the Chaldeans of Babylon.

The BOTTOMLESS PIT, out of which both the LOCUSTS and this BEAST come from, suggests to us that this is symbolizing the abode of Satan himself, for this fallen angel is the king of the bottomless pit (Revelation 9:11), not "the Star" who is given the KEY. As the names *Abaddon* and *Apollyon* mean *"Destroyer,"* so does the word *"Devil."*[3] This falling star of Revelation 9:1 who is given the **key to the bottomless pit** is amazingly, however, given as a symbol for Muhammad in the Islamic Koran. In Arabic, **Al-Najm** is expressed as **"*The Star*" meaning Muhammad**. In another version of the Koran, *The Holy Koran*, we read these eye-opening words:

"The word *Star*, which gives its name to this chapter, occurs

[3]***Young's Analytical Concordance to the Bible*, Young, p. 252.**

in the first verse. The last chapter deals with the success of the faithful and the destruction of their enemies and this speaks of the eminence to which the Holy Prophet would rise. The first section states that the Prophet does not err, and WOULD RISE TO THE HIGHEST EMINENCE TO WHICH MAN CAN RISE."[4] (Emphasis mine.)

Although it is really **Lucifer who is the king or angel of the Bottomless Pit**, he has, however, from ancient times always had a human being **representing him AS HIS VISIBLE HEAD over the various branches of his Babylon the Great**. We can clearly see that this is true in Isaiah 14:4–22 and Ezekiel 28:1–19. Both Hebrew prophets address the king of Babylon and the king of Tyre as if they were Satan themselves. Reader, please examine Isaiah, Chapter 14, and Ezekiel, Chapter 28. Here we see how Satan's headquarters were at Babylon first; and, then, when the Medo-Persians came and took over Babylon, Satan moved his seat to Tyre. Later, Satan moved his seat to Pergamos (Revelation 2:12, 13) which was under Greek dominance and then eventually to pagan Rome (Revelation 17:9), the city of seven mountains. All of these nations practiced mysticism, and all had rulers claiming to be gods. As we saw earlier, **mystical kings often claimed to be the vicar of their god or his incarnation**.

There are only **two** vicars of Allah in Muslim history, so far, who united the Muslims in an **UMMA (one united government)**. The first, of course, was Muhammad when he was alive. After his death, the Muslim community broke up into squabbling, hate factions who even warred against each other for supremacy. Although the Abbasid dynasty was the ruling faction of Islam for some 500 years, they were never able to unite the Muslims into one faith under one government. The Abbasids were the last Arab rulers which ended the **first period** of Muslim Arab dominance. The **second period** shifted to the **Asian Mongols** who had a "**KING OVER THEM**" by the name of **Osman I**. It was this king, **vicar of Allah**, who united once again all Muslims into an **UMMA (united government)** which became the **Ottoman Empire**. After Osman's death, his Ottoman

[4]***The Holy Koran*, translated by 'Ali, Surah 53:1, p. 1000.**

Empire, which continued for over 541 years, remained united under one government until corruption among its succeeding sultans began to weaken it. In the middle 1800s, the Ottoman Empire became known as the "**old sick man of Turkey**." Egypt became its worst enemy and was challenging its power to dominate. **On August 11, 1840,** the sultan of Turkey placed his government under the protection of a Christian alliance of Europe. **This was the mile marker in history** that not only ended this once holy terror to Roman Catholicism, but also the Bible prophecies of the Ottoman's **five months of terror and its hour, day, month, and year seen in Revelation 9:5, 10, 15**. We will study these time prophecies shortly.

There are two more beasts in Revelation, Chapter 13. They are the **BEAST** from the **SEA** (Revelation 13:1–10) and the **BEAST** from the **EARTH** (Revelation 13:11–17). An in-depth study about the **three beasts** is also diligently explored in Volumes One, Two, and Five of this series on ancient prophecies foretelling the **Time of the End**.

In the book of Daniel, Chapter Seven, a **KEY** will be found for Bible-believing Christians to open the mystery of what a Beast represents in Bible prophecy. A Beast in Bible prophecy is not a giant computer in Brussels, Belgium, as some have interpreted, but it is a symbol of a nation or kingdom as Daniel 7:17, 23, 24 clearly says. The angel Gabriel told Daniel that the "**four beasts**" which he saw in vision symbolized **"four kingdoms," which history says were Babylon, Persia, Greece, and Rome.**

As there are "two women" symbolizing the people of Christ (Revelation, Chapter 12) and the people of Lucifer (Revelation, Chapters 17 and 18), so are there given **TWO KEYS** which open the doors to understand the **Mystery of Godliness** (1 Timothy 3:16) and the **Mystery of Iniquity** (2 Thessalonians 2:7). It was the Hebrews in the Old Testament to whom God through Moses and the prophets gave His sacred oracles to be distributed throughout the world and, if obeyed, would lead its disciples to be restored with favor to the Father. These sacred oracles (the Holy Scriptures) pointed to the Lamb of God who taketh away the sins of the world. However, those who kept charge of this plan of salvation locked up these sacred oracles to themselves. Jesus told the lawyers and the religious leaders of the Jews of that day the following:

"Woe unto you, lawyers! for ye have taken away the **KEY OF KNOWLEDGE**: ye entered not in yourselves, and them that were entering in ye hindered.

"And as he said these things unto them, the scribes and the Pharisees began to urge him vehemently, and to provoke him to speak of many things: Laying wait for him, and seeking to catch something out of his mouth, that they might accuse him." Luke 11:52–54.

One very important truth a diligent student in the Holy Scriptures must know and believe is that "**the just shall live by faith**," "but without **faith** it is impossible to please him; for he that cometh to God must believe that he is, and that he is a **rewarder** of them that diligently seek him." Romans 1:17; Hebrews 11:6.

Those who by faith in God's Word believe in what is written and that what is written shall all come to pass, Jesus tells the following: "Unto you it is given to know the **MYSTERIES OF THE KINGDOM OF GOD:** but to others in parables; **that seeing they might not see, and hearing they might not understand**." "For the preaching of the cross is to them that perish foolishness; **but unto us** which are saved it is the power of God. For it is written, I will destroy the wisdom of the wise, and will bring to nothing the understanding of the prudent." Luke 8:10; 1 Corinthians 1:18, 19.

Just what is this Mystery of Godliness? The apostle Paul answers this question in 1 Timothy 3:16:

"And without controversy great is the mystery of godliness: **God was manifest in the flesh**, justified in the Spirit, seen of angels, preached unto the Gentiles, believed on in the world, received up into glory."

The apostle Paul, who at first rejected the Gospel of Christ, here now declares that Jesus is "God manifest in the flesh," and the apostle, writing under the inspiration of the Holy Spirit, says:

"Wherefore I give you to understand, that no man speaking by the Spirit of God calleth Jesus accursed: AND THAT NO MAN CAN SAY THAT JESUS IS THE LORD, BUT BY THE HOLY GHOST." 1 Corinthians 12:3.

When Adonai appeared to Moses at Mt. Horeb, Moses asked the Lord God what he should reply when the Israelites would ask him what God's name was. God told Moses, "**I AM THAT I AM**: and he said, Thus shalt thou say unto the children of Israel, **I AM** hath sent me unto you." Exodus 3:14. About 1900 years later, Jesus said in John 8:58, "Verily, verily, I say unto you, Before Abraham was, **I AM**." Jesus Christ was accused of blasphemy and was ignorantly crucified for this statement.

King David compared Adonai to a Heavenly shepherd. David, writing under the inspiration of the Holy Spirit, said, "The Lord is my **shepherd**; I shall not want. He maketh me to lie down in green pastures: he leadeth me beside the still waters." Psalm 23:1, 2. Jesus said, "**I AM THE GOOD SHEPHERD**: the good shepherd giveth his life for the sheep. I am the good shepherd, and know my sheep, and am known of mine. My sheep **HEAR MY VOICE**, and I know them, and **they follow me**." John 10:11, 14, 27.

Isaiah, the Hebrew prophet, foretold the **Mystery of Godliness**' appearance in this evil world and something else this child would be called in the near future. "For unto us a **child is born**, unto us a **son** is given: and the government shall be upon his shoulder: and his name shall be called **Wonderful, Counsellor, THE MIGHTY GOD, The everlasting Father, The Prince of Peace**." Isaiah 9:6. This Holy Child was to be born of a virgin and would become a living sacrifice for our sins.

"Therefore the Lord himself shall give you a **sign**; Behold, a **virgin shall conceive, and bear a son, and shall call his name Immanuel**."

"He was oppressed, and he was afflicted, yet he opened not his mouth: he is brought as a lamb to the slaughter, and as a sheep before her shearers is dumb, so he openeth not his mouth. He was taken from prison and from judgment: and who shall declare his generation? for he was cut off out of the land of the living: for the transgression of my people was he stricken.

"And he made his grave with the wicked, and with the rich in his death; because **he had done no violence, neither was any deceit in his mouth**. Yet it pleased the Lord to bruise him; he hath put him to grief: when thou shalt make his soul an offering for sin, he shall see his seed, he shall prolong his days, and the pleasure of the Lord shall prosper in his hand." Isaiah 7:14; 53:7–10.

The sure Word of prophecy foretold not only Christ's crucifixion, but also His resurrection. "For thou wilt not leave my soul in hell; neither wilt thou suffer thine Holy One to see corruption." Psalm 16:10. This was a prophecy about Christ written by the King-Prophet David. In the New Testament, which is a record of Christ Jesus' life and words, Jesus said in Revelation 1:18: **"I am he that liveth, and was dead; and, behold, I am alive for evermore, Amen; and have the keys of hell and of death." In John 11:25, Jesus said: "I am the resurrection, and the life: he that believeth in me, though he were dead, yet shall he live."** The apostle Paul, speaking about this power of Christ, says in 1 Corinthians 15:51–55: "Behold, I shew you a mystery; We shall not all sleep, but we shall all be changed, In a moment, in the twinkling of an eye, at the last trump: for the trumpet shall sound, and **the dead shall be raised incorruptible**, and we shall be changed. For this corruptible must put on incorruption, and this mortal must put on immortality.

"So when this corruptible shall have put on incorruption, and this mortal shall have put on immortality, then shall be brought to pass the saying that is written, Death is swallowed up in victory. O death, where is thy sting? O grave, where is thy victory?"

Just as there is a Mystery of Godliness promoting Christ as the Saviour of the world, so has Satan's Mystery of Iniquity, Babylon the Great, sought to counterfeit every point of the plan of salvation which is written in the Holy Scriptures.

In the Old Testament in Malachi 4:2, the Messiah was also called the **Sun of Righteousness. Jesus says, "I am the light of the world: he that followeth me shall not walk in darkness, but shall have the light of life." John 8:12.** Another force in nature that symbolizes the Godhead is the air or wind. When speaking to His disciples about how the Holy Spirit works upon the heart of mankind, Jesus taught the following: "The wind bloweth where it listeth, and thou hearest the sound thereof, but canst not tell whence it cometh, and whither it goeth: so is every one that is born of the Spirit." John 3:8.

However, again the power of the "**prince of darkness**" was to foul the air and cover the rays of the "**Sun of Righteousness**" through this power in Revelation, Chapter Nine. In verse one, we saw how the star was given the ***key*** **to the bottomless pit**. The key given to this **declining star** was an opportunity for Muhammad to **unlock** the **hidden secrets of mysticism** and to spread this knowledge which also rejects the Deity of Christ.

"**And he (the Star) opened the bottomless pit**; and there arose a **smoke** out of the pit, as the smoke of a great furnace; **AND THE SUN AND THE AIR WERE DARKENED BY REASON OF THE SMOKE OF THE PIT**." Revelation 9:2. (Emphasis mine.)

When this "declining star" opened the bottomless pit, a smoke arose and the sun (Sun of Righteousness) and the air (Holy Spirit) were darkened (obscured). The Star of Islam, Muhammad, was, indeed, the founder of a new religion which somewhat **blocked the full rays of the "Sun of Righteousness"** to penetrate the hearts of the people of the Mediterranean coastal regions who had first embraced Islam. The Koran rejects Jesus as the Son of the Living God and teaches its believers to do the same. The Muslims claim that Muhammad **practiced meditation** (yoga) and while he was in a **trance**, the angel Gabriel appeared to him in a cave and gave the Koran to him in its entirety. Muhammad **could not read or write** so this message **was delivered into his soul**,[5] and he later verbally delivered it to his Companions.

Ironically enough, the book of Revelation was written near the very area where the Muslim's Ottoman Empire would later give birth. John, the apostle of Jesus Christ, was banished for his faith by Rome to the lonely island of Patmos just off the coast of a country which is known today as Turkey. It was on this lonely island, about 64 years after the death and resurrection of Jesus, that John was visited by our Lord. John said:

"I was in the Spirit on the Lord's day, and heard behind me a great voice, as of a trumpet, Saying, **I am Alpha and Omega, the first and the last**: and, What thou seest, write in a book, and send it unto the seven churches which are in Asia; unto Ephesus, and unto Smyrna, and unto Pergamos, and unto Thyatira, and unto Sardis, and unto Philadelphia, and unto Laodicea.

"And I turned to see the voice that spake with me. And being turned, I saw seven golden candlesticks; And in the midst of the seven

[5]***The Concise Encyclopedia of Islam*, Glassé, p. 243.**

candlesticks one like unto the Son of man, clothed with a garment down to the foot, and girt about the paps with a golden girdle.

"**His head and his hairs were white like wool, as white as snow**; and his eyes were as a flame of fire; And his feet like unto fine brass, as if they burned in a furnace; and his voice as the sound of many waters. And he had in his right hand seven stars: and out of his mouth went a sharp two-edged sword: and his countenance was as the sun shineth in his strength.

"And when I saw him, I fell at his feet as dead. And he laid his right hand upon me, saying unto me, Fear not; I am the first and the last: I am he that liveth, and was dead; and, behold, **I am alive for evermore, Amen; and have the KEYS of hell and of death**.

"Write the things which thou hast seen, and the things which are, and the things which shall be hereafter; The mystery of the seven stars which thou sawest in my right hand, and the seven golden candlesticks. The seven stars are the angels of the seven churches: and the seven candlesticks which thou sawest are the seven churches." Revelation 1:10–20.

In verse 20, our Lord revealed that a "**star**" in Bible prophecy represents an **angel**, and an angel is a "**messenger**."[6]

It is a very well-known fact in Islam that the Koran calls Allah's prophet (Muhammad) his messenger and the last of the line of prophets to come. Just as the Mystery of Godliness has always had His angels (messengers) down through the ages promoting the coming Kingdom of Christ, so has Satan had his "angels" (messengers) hiding or blocking and counteracting the Gospel of Jesus Christ.

"But if our gospel be hid, it is hid to them that are lost: In whom the god of this world hath **BLINDED THE MINDS OF THEM** which believe not, lest the light of the glorious gospel of Christ, who is the image of God, should shine unto them." 2 Corinthians 4:3, 4.

As the **prince of darkness** used human beings **to unlock** his own secret wisdom from below (symbolized in prophecy as the **bottomless pit**), so has the "**Light of the world**" given His messengers a **key** to **unlock** wisdom that comes from **above.**

To the diligent seeker of Christian knowledge comes the promise:

[6]***Young's Analytical Concordance to the Bible*, Young, p. 37.**

"For I will give you a mouth and wisdom, which all your adversaries shall not be able to gainsay nor resist." Luke 21:15. However, a record of how Satan can work among us as he did when Jesus walked this earth is found in Matthew, Chapter Four. Satan can appear to humans in many different forms. Jesus Himself was approached by this great pretender and deceiver. **Satan came to Jesus as a messenger from Heaven misquoting Scripture, but, to counteract Satan, Jesus used the Holy Scriptures and overcame him.** As the record shows, the Prince of Peace defeated Lucifer in a war in Heaven and then again at the cross. Satan and all who unite themselves willingly or unwittingly under his black banner will eventually be overcome by God's people as well. This will be done through nonviolent means (without military force) for it is against the principles of Heaven to use force to make people worship God.

Christ Jesus, our Leader and Captain of the Host of the angels of Heaven, told Peter after severing off a man's ear with his sword, **"Put up again thy sword into his place: for all they that take the sword shall perish with the sword." Matthew 26:52. "He that leadeth into captivity shall go into captivity: he that killeth with the sword must be killed with the sword. Here is the patience and the faith of the saints." Revelation 13:10.**

Jesus told Pilate when He was taken by force to appear before him, "**My kingdom is not of this world: if my kingdom were of this world, THEN WOULD MY SERVANTS FIGHT, THAT I SHOULD NOT BE DELIVERED TO THE JEWS:** but now is my kingdom not from hence." John 18:36. In Revelation 12:11, it tells us how we shall overcome Satan. **"And they overcame him by the blood of the Lamb, and by the word of their testimony; and they loved not their lives unto the death."**

However, this is actually the **opposite** of how this **Star** of Islam, Muhammad, began his career as a messenger for Allah. Muslims, from the time of Muhammad to this very day, have used **violence and force to spread Islam**. Was this not also the tactic of Islam's rival, the Roman Catholic Church? The Koran, which was supposedly dictated to Muhammad by the angel Gabriel, tells Muslims to use violence against those who are against Allah and his Star (messenger). In the Qur'ãn, this god Allah says the following:

"God will bring to nothing the deeds of those who disbelieve and debar others from His path. As for the faithful who do good works and believe in what is revealed to Muhammad – which is the Truth from their Lord – He will forgive them their sins and ennoble their state. This, because the unbelievers follow falsehood, while the faithful follow the truth from their Lord. Thus God lays down for mankind their rules of conduct.

"When you meet the unbelievers in the battlefield **STRIKE OFF THEIR HEADS** and, when you have laid them low, bind your captives firmly. Then grant them their freedom or take ransom from them, until War shall lay down her burdens."[7] (Emphasis mine.)

One of Muhammad's first politically-sanctioned murder victims was a female poet with a vulgar mouth. She circulated mocking lyrics about Islam's founder, and for it she met certain death. Her name was Asama bint Marwan.[8] Today, it is a **capital offense** in Islamic lands against anyone who dares to question the authority of the prophet of Islam or even renounce Islam as an impostor or leave the religion, as it was with Salman Rushdie.

It is important that the reader has some knowledge of the history of the wars **(jihad)** which Muslims waged against the Jews, the Persians (Zoroastrianism), the Byzantine Empire (the Greek Orthodox), which is now modern Turkey, and the Hindus and the Buddhists so that you can understand **THE FIVE MONTH'S PROPHECY** in Revelation 9:5, 10 and the prophetic time period of **"THE HOUR, AND A DAY, AND A MONTH, AND A YEAR, FOR TO SLAY THE THIRD PART OF MEN"** in verse 15. If the reader will, again, carefully read Chapter Nine of the book of Revelation, he shall discover that there are "**TWO DIVISIONS**" or **TWO WAVES** to come from this prophecy. The first prophecy about Islam from verse one to verse 12, specifically in verses five and ten, includes the **five prophetic months**. These items mentioned in the first 12 verses are all sounded by the fifth angel, and these prophetic utterances are called the **FIRST "WOE"** which will be

[7]***The Koran With Parallel Arabic Text*, translated by Dawood, Surah 47:1–4, p. 506.**

[8]***God Has Ninety-Nine Names*, Miller, p. 92.**

followed by "**TWO WOES MORE**" upon the people of this planet during the **SECOND DIVISION OR WAVE** foretold in Revelation 9:12. Notice again the following in verse 11 of Chapter Nine.

"And they had a **KING over them**, which is the **ANGEL of the BOTTOMLESS PIT**, whose name in the Hebrew tongue is **Abaddon**, but in the Greek tongue hath his name **Apollyon**."

It states that they had a "**king**" over them which is the angel of the bottomless pit. There are three key words here that need to be investigated under a magnifying glass. They are ***king***, ***angel***, **and *bottomless pit***. Jesus through His apostle said that this king in the Hebrew language was called **Abaddon**, but in the Greek tongue hath his name **Apollyon**. As we saw, **this cannot mean Muhammad for he is symbolized as this king's star and was given "the key of the bottomless pit."** (See Revelation 9:1.) It plainly states in verse 11 that this **KING** is also the **ANGEL** of the **bottomless pit. This king is that old serpent, the Devil, who is the fallen angel and was worshipped in Greek mythology as Apollo, the sun-god and the son of Zeus. In Hindu mysticism**, this destroyer is worshipped as **Shiva**; and to the ancient Toltecs and Aztecs, this part-evil and part-good god was **Quetzalcoatl**, whose name means "***bird serpent***." This bird serpent was **Kulkulcán** to the Mayan Indians of southern Mexico and Guatamala. This was nothing less than the worship of "that old serpent, called the Devil, and Satan, which deceiveth the whole world." Revelation 12:9. **The angel of the bottomless pit was worshipped all over the world but was camouflaged as the various astrological gods. The bottomless pit symbolizes Satan's abode at Babylon from which he first sent out his counterfeit religion which is symbolized by Jesus as Babylon the Great, the Mother of Harlots in Revelation 17:5.** From the days of Cush and Nimrod, the Dragon has used human beings involved in mysticism (Spiritualism) to make war on Christ and His people who have shunned its spiritually intoxicating wine. However, the reader must keep in mind that Satan is using human beings to destroy human beings, and that down through the ages he has always used a human being to be the visible head of his power. The Devil is a destroyer and so are those who he is controlling. **Jesus symbolically**

called Satan a thief, for this Destroyer has robbed God of the worship that should have been given to Him alone. This religion Satan invented to direct humans away from God is, indeed, mysticism.

As pointed out to the reader, this **symbolic woman** (Revelation, Chapters 17 and 18), who expresses the character of Jezebel, has begotten daughters for she is a mother. Her family of daughters who identify with her title **Mystery** were the Hindu Cushites, her first-born who became known in Babel (Babylon) as the Chaldeans. Later, another daughter, Zoroastrianism, was born, along with two other daughters named Buddhism and Confucianism, and all of their children follow closely behind. Next, after the death of the apostles Peter and Paul at Rome, Satan mated mysticism with Christianity and begot a hybrid child named the Roman Catholic Church whose fusion of mystical knowledge with Christianity, which is symbolized as the "**wine of her fornication**" (false doctrines), has been adopted and passed on from generation to generation by Protestant denominations. We will see that all this is true when we study what the **Seal of God is that Christians had better identify with**.

Again, it is worthy of notice to show that this **Babylon the Great** is riding on a ***RED*** **beast** with seven heads and ten horns **(the Beast from the Bottomless Pit)**. See Revelation 17:3, 8–14. As we have seen, the **ANGEL** (king) of the **BOTTOMLESS PIT** gave his **STAR** pupil (Muhammad) a **KEY** that unlocked all the mysteries the Devil (Abaddon a.k.a. Apollyon) has to offer in the secret doctrines of mysticism. **Muhammad** became the **number-one apostle of Allah (IL, the moon-god)** for Islam, the youngest child of mysticism, was to grow up and become not only the most knowledgeable teacher of mysticism (Spiritualism), but the **orders of Sufism would be where the ORACLES OF THE OCCULT WOULD BE KEPT AND SAFEGUARDED BY ITS MOST LEARNED SHAYKS (MASTERS)**. This Morning Star of Islam received a **KEY** which let out the most intoxicating bellows of the **black smoke of black magic** which would darken the rays of the **Sun of Righteousness** "lest the light of the glorious gospel of Christ, who is the image of God, should shine unto them." 2 Corinthians 4:4. This Star of Islam would also acquire a host of its most violent defenders in their day. In history, Muhammad's first followers became known as the **Arabian Saracens**. In Revelation 9:3, 4, they are symbolized as part of the first of the **TWO SEPARATE WAVES OF PLAGUES OF LOCUSTS WHICH WERE TO COME UPON THE PEOPLES FROM SPAIN TO INDIA**.

"And there came out of the smoke **locusts upon the earth**: and unto them was given power, as the scorpions of the earth have power. And it was commanded them that they should not hurt the grass of the earth, neither any green thing, neither any tree; but only those men **WHICH HAVE NOT THE SEAL OF GOD IN THEIR FOREHEADS**." Revelation 9:3, 4.

It is very interesting to note that locusts are a type of grasshopper, and they come in "**two forms**:" the **SOLITARY PHASE** and the **GREGARIOUS PHASE. Solitary locusts like to act alone while gregarious locusts like to travel in large swarms.** Locusts have the ability to change to **solitary** or **gregarious** modes depending on the size of their population.[9] These two types of **locusts also develop two different shapes and colors**. It is also interesting to learn in history that the **Muslims** were both **SOLITARY** and **GREGARIOUS destroyers** when their first wave swarmed out of Arabia under **ARAB power** and then again later as an **ASIAN power (Ottomans)**.

After the death of Muhammad, **Arab Muslim invaders** acted in a ***solitary*** way; they were not united under one banner. However, the **Asian Muslims** were ***gregarious*** in the way they destroyed nations **for Osman I united the Muslims under one central government**. Africa's most devastating plague species is the **desert locust *Shistocerca gregaria***. Densities of this locust may attain in the region of **200 million locusts per square mile.**[10] **The desert locust (*Shistocerca gregaria*)** occurs over a great part of north and central Africa, Iran, Bangladesh, and India, extending to Turkey and even southern Europe.[11] Locusts are also able to survive without feeding for considerable periods, subsisting on stored fats which supply more energy than other food.[12]

[9]*Insect Attack*, Lampton, pp. 29, 30.

[10]*Grasshoppers and Mantids of The World*, Preston-Mafham, p. 177.

[11]*Insects of The World*, Wootton, p. 164.

[12]*Ibid.*, Wootton, p. 166.

The book of Revelation symbolizes Arab Muslims as locusts because Arabia is also plagued from time to time by these desert locusts. They were a **fitting symbol** for these expert Arabian horsemen with their talents for using the point of the sword. With the promise from Allah that their sins would be forgiven them if they died in battle for their Lord, **Arab Muslims swarmed out of Arabia like plagues of locusts into Egypt, the Persian Empire, and Byzantium. The Arabs fought these nations with fanatical valor and within a hundred years took over their lands.** As stated previously, it is incredible that real locusts could number **200 million per square mile in a swarm**. In Revelation 9:16, we read: "And the number of the army of the horsemen were two hundred thousand thousand." **Two hundred thousand thousand equals 200 million horsemen. Swarms of migrating locusts are sometimes so large they shut out the sunlight.**

Another fact in history which identifies the armies of Islam as being the locusts of Revelation, Chapter Nine, is Abu Bakr's command to his Muslim warriors before they were sent out to conquer non-Muslims. In Revelation 9:4, it was prophesied that this first wave of **DESTROYING LOCUSTS** (Muslims) would be commanded to "**not hurt the grass of the earth, neither any green thing, neither any tree**." In Edward Gibbon's *The Decline and Fall of the Roman Empire*, the following words are quoted from Muhammad's first successor, Abu Bakr:

"When you fight the battles of the Lord, acquit yourselves like men, without turning your backs; but let not your victory be stained with the blood of women or children. **Destroy no palm trees, nor burn any fields of corn. Cut down no fruit trees, nor do any mischief to cattle, only such as you kill to eat.** When you make any covenant, or article, stand to it, and be as good as your word. As you go on, you will find some religious persons who live retired in monasteries, and propose to themselves to serve God that way; let them alone, and neither kill them nor destroy their monasteries: and **you will find another sort of people that belong to the synagogue of Satan, who have shaven crowns; be sure you cleave their skulls, and give them no quarter till they either turn Mahometans or pay 'tribute.'** "[13]

[13]***The Prophecies of Daniel and The Revelation*, Smith, p. 498.**

In verses seven through ten, Arab Muslims (depicted as locusts) have crowns like gold, faces as the faces of men, hair of women, teeth as the teeth of lions, breastplates of iron, and tails like scorpions with stings in their tails. In the early days of Muhammad, **the Arabian Saracens (Muslims) wore turbans like unto a coronet**. The ancient Arabs were distinguished by the miters which they wore. Their countenances showed firmness of mind, and they had a custom of wearing long hair. However, there was nothing effeminate in their demeanor for they were pictured in Bible prophecy as having teeth (swords) as the teeth of lions to devour. Their breastplates of iron (cuirass) were used by Muhammad and his followers when they fought against the Koreish of Mecca, who rejected him, in A.D. 624.[14] What is the usual color of iron? It is black. It is also interesting to learn that the original color of the banner Muhammad used and also the velvet drape that covers the Kaaba at Mecca is black.[15]

From the time of Muhammad to our present day, Islam has promoted its religion by using the point of the sword. As we have seen, the Koran encourages Muslims to kill those who oppose them and even promises if a Muslim dies in battle for his religion, he (his immortal soul) will go to Heaven. Maybe now the reader will understand why Muslim fanatics in Israel have strapped explosives on themselves and triggered them to go off in a marketplace or a crowded area to kill not only Jews, but also themselves.

Remember the **fatwa** (death warrant), which was put in force by the Iranian government, issued against a United Kingdom novelist named Salman Rushdie back in 1989? **Recently, it was in the news how former singer/song writer Cat Stevens is refuting media speculation suggesting that royalties from Boyzone's number-one single, *Father and Son* (which Stevens wrote), are indirectly supporting the death sentence on Rushdie.** Salman Rushdie wrote a novel entitled ***The Satanic Verses*** in which he criticizes Muhammad and Islam. **Cat Stevens, who converted to Islam, changed his name to Yusuf Islam.** According to ***Billboard*** magazine, there was a widespread boycott in the U.S. of anything

[14]*The Prophecies of Daniel and The Revelation*, Smith, p. 501.
[15]*The Sufis*, Shah, pp. 368, 369.

from which Cat Stevens would gain because of this incident. Cat Stevens' reply was "this seems to directly contradict the sacred First Amendment."[16]

Learned Bible-believing Christians are finally opening their **sleepy eyes** and are becoming seriously concerned with the threat of the New World Order and the New Age Movement as their diabolical plans are coming out more and more in the light. However, Christians are still in the dark about the threat of Islam and its revolutionary plans. Christians of the 20th century have forgotten about or are just plain ignorant of what Muslims throughout history did to Christians who would not give up their faith in Jesus as the Son of God and as the Saviour of the world. However, the hostage takeover in Lebanon, the suicide bombings by Muslim terrorists and the killings of American Marines in Lebanon, the bombings of PAN AM 103 and the World Trade Center, the teachings of Louis Farrakhan, the threat of Qaddafi and Saddam Hussein, the Gulf War, and Osama bin Laden and the bombings of American Embassies in Africa have shaken minds about the threat of Islam.

According to the magazine *Essence*, 90% of the American-born converts to Islam are Black and have left the Christian faith.[17] Now, as I am writing, Muslim nations are refusing to cooperate with U.S. officials to pressure Saddam Hussein into destroying his arsenal of chemical weapons and the Hindus of India and the Muslims of Pakistan are flexing their nuclear muscles at not only each other, but the whole world. Back in March of 1993, *Life* magazine had a lengthy article about how **fundalmentalist Muslims** of the Old World have an **abhorrence of the West** and, like Bible-believing Christians, see this New World Order scheme as a threat to them. However, unlike Bible-believing Christians, **Shiite Muslim fundalmentalist mullahs** (who are militant clergyman) are arming themselves for a possible conflict. **Often, however, the conflict is not between Islam and the West but between more secular Muslims within the Islamic faith itself.** From Algeria to Egypt and Jordan and elsewhere

[16]*Billboard*, February 24, 1996, p. 43.
[17]*Essence*, November 1995, p. 108.

in the Muslim world, the Shiite fundamentalist version of Islam has brought **new fears** among the Muslim's population.[18]

In *The Los Angeles Times*, it states: "**In Algeria, Islam's Holy Month Is Killing Season.**"[19] This article records how the holiest month of the Muslim faith, which is known as the **Ramadan**, was ushered in by a **bloody massacre** of more than 300 Muslims by Islamic extremists who amazingly said, "**they get closer to God when they carry out these terrorist acts**." The above article also points out that the **only aim** of the Muslim terrorist is to have a state based on Islamic Law, and they will use "**any means**" to achieve their purpose. "**Democracy**," says Djamil Benrabah, a human rights activist, "**contradicts the plans and aims of these people**." However, Pakistanis have been killing Pakistanis on the basis of race in the most brutal manner possible for years in the Sind province, and political messages are carved into the buttocks of ethnic opponents. Kurds have been gassed and bombed in Iraq and attacked in Turkey by fellow Muslims for decades. The newspapers have recorded how many well-known Muslim leaders, like Malcolm X and/or heads of their governments, have met a violent death. They have been shot **(Anwar Sadat)**, or hanged **(Zulfikar Ali Bhutto of Pakistan)**, and blown up in the air **(Zia ul-Haq, also of Pakistan)**. There have been massacres by an Islamic State on innocent Muslim citizens by their army or police in Syria, Bangladesh, Iraq, and in Iran.[20] The God of Abraham warned in Hosea 4:6, **"My people are destroyed for LACK OF KNOWLEDGE: because thou has rejected knowledge, I will also reject thee."**

It has been my observation that just as Christians ignore the writings of the Koran and the teachings of its prophet, so do Muslims ignore the Old and New Testament's admonitions from Jesus and His disciples. As with all who connect themselves with mysticism, the Muslims **do not believe in the literal truth of the Holy Scriptures**. They think the Scriptures have been **corrupted** by the Jews and the Catholic priests and that they have a secret

[18]*Life*, March 1993, p. 58.

[19]*The Los Angeles Times,* January 1, 1998, p. A–11.

[20]*Utne Reader*, March/April 1994, p. 83.

mystical hidden meaning. This belief is one of the tools **Black Muslims** use to lure **Black Christians** into Islam. **The Koran, which was supposedly dictated by the angel Gabriel, denounces the Jew for corrupting the Scriptures and the Christian for worshipping Jesus as the Son of God.**[21]

However, heated debates over the interpretation of these writings of the ***Companions*** about the prophet Muhammad and who was to be his successor arose in the first decades of Islam. **These heated debates led to violence and caused this once-unified community of Arabian Saracen Muslims to divide into divisions, which were the Sunnis, the Shia a.k.a. Shiites, and a smaller sect known as the Khawarij.**[22]

It is because of rejecting the **Holy Scriptures** and the many various interpretations by Muslim clergy that Muslims have since the death of Muhammad killed each other. This became a contradiction of Islam for it was supposedly established by Allah's prophet Muhammad to unite all religions as **one**. Before the kingdom of Abdulaziz, which was established in 1932, the sect of the Shia were considered by the Sunni Muslims in Saudi Arabia to be the lowest class of Muslims and were treated by the Sunni worse than a slave.[23] Islam's whole history has been written in blood. From the founding of Islam by Muhammad unto this present day, untold masses of human lives have been destroyed and have gone down into untimely graves because of the religion of Islam. History says not only were Zoroastrians, Hindus, Buddhists, Jews, and Christians opposed to the claims of Islam, but the Muslims themselves were as well.

Like the desert locusts it was symbolized as in prophecy, today modern Islam has again developed primarily into two mainstreams. These two mainstreams of Islam, as we have seen, are known as the **Sunnis** and the **Shiites**. The Muslim Order known as Sufism actually does not identify with any particular Muslim sect. They operate like the tribe of the Levites did in ancient Israel. They have received huge sums of money from all sects of Islam to help maintain and

[21]***The Meaning of The Holy Qur'ãn*, 'Ali, Surah 9:30, p. 446.**

[22]***The Muslim Almanac*, ed. Nanji, pp. 161–172.**

[23]***National Geographic Magazine*, September 1980, p. 298.**

promote Islam's mysticism among all Muslims. However, the Sunnis and the Shiites, like the Roman Catholics and the Protestants, have been violently opposed to each other's claim over who was to be the head of their religious movement.

As the Bible-believing Protestants have most violently opposed the claim of the Papacy, which is that the pope of Rome was given the exalted position to sit at the head of all religious bodies as God's Vicar on earth, so have the Muslims had this problem among themselves. Very few American Christians understand this and are not aware of the differences between Muslims, and, likewise, the Muslims are not aware of the differences between Christians in the New World. **However, there is hope for the Muslim people for the God of Abraham said that in the end there would be a people from all the families of the world who will be united under His banner.**

For years I had a false image of all Muslims, just as Muslims have also had a false image of all Americans. To my surprise after studying Islam, I discovered that although Muslims have been deceived and confused about the Deity of Christ, some **Orthodox Muslims love Jesus and the morality and the goodness He brought to the world**. Although they have been taught that Jesus is not the Son of God and are worshipping God ignorantly, like Roman Catholics and most Protestants, **some Muslims have a high sense of morality among their true followers** and, as we have seen, **have adopted and obey what the God of Abraham told Moses about dress, about not eating blood, about not committing fornication, about not eating pork, and about not bowing down to graven images.**

Reader, some **Muslims believe that Jesus was a true prophet of God** and claim their religion to be just an extension of Christianity, but they believe that **Christians and Jews have apostatized** and are giving a **false image of Jesus**.

However, Muslims, as well, need to take a long hard look at their own history and see what kind of image they have projected to the non-Muslim community. Not only are Muslims known in history for winning converts to Islam **by using the point of the sword**, but also for how they have **slaughtered each other**. It is important that the Bible-believing Christian has some knowledge about the dangerous **split** in Islam between the Sunnis and the Shia (Shiites) for this will enable the reader to understand more of what is behind the **Islamic terrorists** and their attacks on American citizens which we have shockingly witnessed on our news programs.

According to the interpretation of the written traditions in the Koran, Muhammad was the ***Seal of the Prophets***[24] or the last of the prophets from Adam to Jesus. Hence, Muslims believe that the founder of Islam could not be succeeded by another prophet. The sudden death of Muhammad in A.D. 632, as we have examined, left the once-unified Muslims in a chaotic and rivaling state. It was because of the disunion of Islam, which at that time had split into different warring groups or factions, that a successor **(Caliph)** to Muhammad was first invented to try to ensure a unity in Islam. **The Caliph is a title equivalent to the pope of Rome to the Catholics, for he was both the temporal and the spiritual head of Islam.**[25]

However, at this time, a division developed among Muslims over just who was worthy to be the **Caliph** to succeed Muhammad. The Sunnis, considered to be the **orthodox branch** of Islam, appointed Abu Bakr, who was afterwards succeeded by Umar, Uthman, and then Ali, brother-in-law and cousin of Muhammad. Violent opposition in Islam arose, at this time, over these first four caliphs, and each one of them died a violent death. **There are Muslims who believe that it should have been Ali (the fourth Caliph), not Abu Bakr, to have been the first Caliph because Ali was a relative of Muhammad. This sect of Muslims also believes that only those who are related to Muhammad have the right to rule Islam. This argument has still divided Muslims into sometimes warring factions.** Those Muslims who oppose the Sunnis are called Shia (Shiites), and they broke away and divided also into rivaling divisions. The following is a brief diagram showing the different Caliphs and also the different sects of the Muslims:

[24]***The Muslim Almanac*, ed. Nanji, p. 163.**

[25]***Ibid.*, ed. Nanji, p. 163.**

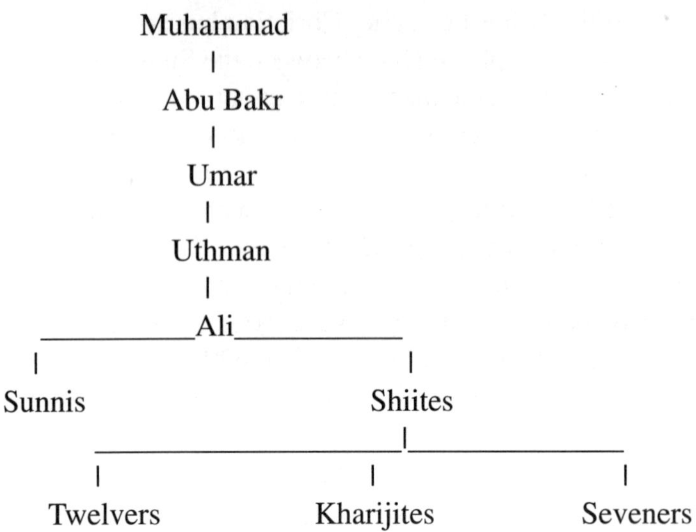

There are more Sunni Muslims than Shiites, and Shiites make up about ten percent of Islam. Iran, who constantly calls Americans "**the Great Satan**," is ruled by the Shiites. They also live in Iraq and Pakistan and have adopted and mingled Hinduism within their beliefs. In Lahore, Pakistan, Muslim shrines have replaced the ancient temples, but many of the Hindu rites survive.[26] Indonesia is the largest Islamic country in the world; it has 170 million Muslims. However, its faithful have also borrowed rites from their Hindu and Buddhist ancestors. They worship the forces of nature and their ancestors, along with Allah.[27]

However, the Shiites claim to be the true followers of Islam because of their bloodline from Muhammad to his cousin Ali. Shiites believe that only rulers who are direct descendants of Ali are considered to be infallible and have the right to be what they call an Imam.[28] **The Shiites have a deep-seated hatred towards Americans and accuse the Sunni Muslims of apostasy and the Westernization of Islam. Today, the Muslims are in a *SOLITARY* state. They again have NO CENTRAL GOVERNMENT**

[26]***National Geographic Magazine*, July 1972, p. 23.**

[27]***Life*, March 1993, p. 64.**

[28]***The World's Religions*, Clarke, p. 91.**

or a king over them. However, they have the belief that there is coming someone who shall unite them once again.

The Shiites invented a belief that through their order of Islam would come a **line of Imams (deliverers)** who will help restore Islam back to its original state as it was in the days of Muhammad. Shiites preach that "**Twelve Imams**" would come through them in succession, **and the last will be al-Mahdi (messiah) who will conquer all religions and make Islam a universal state.** They believe he will appear at the end of time over the span of a few years. Muslims believe their messiah will appear to restore righteousness briefly before the end of the world. Some believe he will come before the Antichrist appears and before the Second Coming of Jesus Christ.[29] However, among the Muslim divisions there is found much confusion about who this al-Mahdi really is. Muslims, because of their rejection of the Holy Scriptures, are being led by this "**Angel of the Bottomless Pit**" to not only be used again as his destroying locusts, but are being conditioned to accept Satan when he appears as Christ shortly.

According to Matthew Gordon, who wrote the book *Ayatollah Khomeini*, Khomeini belonged to the largest of the Shia (Shiite) sects called the Twelver Shia.[30] According to Gordon, **the Eleventh Imam is Hasan al-'Askari**, who had a son born in 869 named Muhammad al-Mahdi. This Muhammad is considered to be the **Twelfth Imam**, which is where the group derived its name, "Twelver," or ***Ithna Ashariya*** in Arabic.[31] The Twelfth Imam, who was the basis for many legends and stories of miracles, is thought to have gone into a small cave under a mosque in Samarra, Iraq, never to be seen again. This is why he is called the Hidden Imam by the Twelver Shia. It is believed that this Imam remains in seclusion.[32]

The ***Mahdi*** (The One Led By God), this messiah of Islam, according to the Twelvers, will be the leader of a powerful army and completely annihilate all the forces of evil in the world, including corrupt and oppressive governments. **The Twelver Shia**

[29]***The Concise Encyclopedia of Islam*, Glassé, pp. 246, 247.**

[30]***Ayatollah Khomeini*, Gordon, p. 39.**

[31]***Ibid.*, Gordon, p. 40.**

[32]***Ibid.*, Gordon, p. 40.**

believe that a thousand-year period of justice and peace will come on this earth before the coming of the Judgment Day.[33] In other traditions found in the Hadith, however, it proclaims that there is **no Mahdi but Jesus, the son of Mary**.[34] Even though there are different interpetations about who the **Madhi** will be, **the belief of the coming of a Madhi is found among both the Sunni and the Shiite Muslims**.[35]

Keeping in mind the prophecies from Jesus and His disciples about false christs and false prophets which would arise from His day and also how the Antichrist (Satan) himself will come to **PERSONATE JESUS** (1 John 2:18), let's again take a closer look again at the warnings about how to detect the Antichrist.

"Little children, it is the last time: and as ye have heard that **ANTICHRIST SHALL COME**, even now are there many antichrists; whereby we know that it is the last time." 1 John 2:18. The word ***antichrist*** means "***instead of Christ***." This, in Scripture, applies to anybody or any institution that tries to take the place of Christ. Today, there is not just one Antichrist, for the apostle John said, **"There are many antichrists."** However, as pointed out in the last three volumes of this series on **Time of the End** events, the last false christ will be Satan himself. He will personate Jesus as he looks now in Revelation 1:13–16. Bible-believers may detect this Arch Deceiver and Destroyer by just remembering the promise of 1 Thessalonians 4:16, 17 which reads:

"For the Lord himself shall descend from heaven with a shout, with the voice of the archangel, and with the trump of God: and the dead in Christ shall rise first: Then we which are alive and remain shall be caught up together with them in the clouds, to **MEET THE LORD IN THE AIR**: and so shall we ever be with the Lord."

Reader, we should always keep in mind that when Jesus of Nazareth comes the second time, He will **not** walk this earth; we will meet Him in the **air**. Here is another important truth. **THE THOUSAND-YEAR REIGN OF CHRIST OF REVELATION 20:6 WILL NOT BE ON THIS EARTH, BUT IN HEAVEN.**

[33]***Ayatollah Khomeini*, Gordon, p. 41.**

[34]***The Concise Encyclopedia of Islam*, Glassé, p. 247.**

[35]***Ibid.*, Glassé, p. 247.**

Revelation 9:12, which is prophesying about the Islamic part in this controversy between Christ and Lucifer, says the following: **"ONE WOE IS PAST; and, behold, there come TWO WOES MORE hereafter."** Jesus predicted that there would be "**THREE WOES**" which this power symbolized as **locusts** would inflict on those **who have not the Seal of God in their foreheads**. The **first woe** was during the **time of the Arabs when they ruled the Muslims**. However, they were ***solitary*** in their efforts and were not united. The **second woe** came when they had a **king** over them who was visibly representing **Abaddon or Apollyon, the Destroyer**. Again, the history of Islam has **two waves** in which Islam was **likened to plagues of locusts**. The **first woe** caused by the Arab Muslims was from the years **A.D. 610 to A.D. 1258**. In A.D. 1258, **the Mongols overthrew the power of the Arab dispensation of Islam. Between the years A.D. 1258 and A.D. 1299, there was a shift in Islamic power.** For 41 years, a transformation of the destroying power of Islam took on a new mode. The **second woe** on the Old World by the people of Islam **began in the year A.D. 1299** by the **ASIAN Muslims a.k.a. the Ottoman Empire**, and it was foretold in Scripture that this **scourge** upon papal Christians and other non-Muslims **would continue until August 11, 1840**.

As locusts have the ability to **change their appearance** and also their demeanor from ***solitary*** to ***gregarious***, so did the **swarms of Muslims who first flew out of Arabia later change their demeanor.** This began to happen when **Genghis (Jenghiz) Khan (1162?–1227)** made his debut. The Buddhists, who centuries earlier had been smitten by the plague of these invading locusts out of Arabia, later **became like a strong East wind in the 13th century** that swept the Muslims away. This blast of wind hit the Abbassids, the ruling dynasty of the Arabs, in Baghdad, which was the capital of the Muslim forces in A.D. 1258. This East wind was the Mongols who were originally from the Siberian forest and had developed an area which became known as Mongolia. **The Mongols were a branch of the Semitic race, as are the North, Central, and South American Indians.** Besides their physical features, another fact that links the Mongols to the New World Natives, both anciently and presently, is their religion. It was the same as the American Native religion is today. Mongols were **shamanists** who saw God as a **Great Spirit** whose presence is active in nature. Another word that can describe their beliefs is **pantheism**. They worshipped the forces of nature as gods, as do the Hopi and Navajo Native Indian religions today. However, long before the arrival of the invading Muslims to central Asia, the Mongols had adopted some teachings of Buddhism and its sect called Taoism.

Like Islam, the Mongols had among them a mystic who claimed to have been visited by a heavenly visitor while he was practicing enchantment (meditation) in a cave; his name was Temujin. He claimed to have seen a vision or a dream of a Buddhist Bodhisattva who appeared to him and told him that he had been chosen to restore the earth to the primordial condition it had known before which civilization had hidden. According to the legend, he awoke from his dream and found in his hand a ring that confirmed his mission. ***Temujin***, which means "***blacksmith***," assumed a power name. He called himself **"Jenghiz Khan" which means "*Oceanic*" or universal ruler. This is the same title of the Dalai Lama.** The word ***lama*** is of Mongol origin and **it means "*Oceanic*."**[36] This has been the traditional title of the Tibetan head of state and its religion since the Mongol Altai Khan in the 16th century. As pointed out in the first chapter, the Dalai Lamas are revered as the reincarnation of the Avalokiteshvara, who is regarded as a savior to Buddhists. Presently, there have been 14 Dalai Lamas.

The Mongols conquered China and had their sights, as Islam does, on ruling the whole world. After a Muslim Khwarazmian governor massacred 100 Mongol envoys who they called spies, the Mongols began invading the Muslim realm. Jenghiz Khan died in 1227, but his empire was divided among his grandson and three sons who continued a Khan dynasty. **It was Hulagu Khan who invaded the Muslim Abbasid Empire, sacked Baghdad, and took Damascus, thus ending the Arab domination of Islam in the year A.D. 1258.**

From the time Muhammad received his first revelation while practicing meditation in a cave in A.D. 610 and was told by his visitor, who claimed to be Gabriel, to make Islam universal **unto** the year A.D. 1258, the Arab Muslims had brought much pain upon the third part

[36]***The Concise Encyclopedia of Islam*, Glassé, pp. 273, 274.**

of Christianity, which was the Eastern Roman Catholics, and also upon their rivals who were the Jews, the Zoroastrians, Hindus, and Buddhists. However, **"ONE WOE IS PAST; AND, BEHOLD, THERE COME TWO WOES MORE HEREAFTER." Revelation 9:12.**

In Revelation 9:7, it tells us that these destroying locusts from the bottomless pit "were like unto horses," and in verse 17 these locusts, which were like unto horses, changed their demeanor as desert locusts do. In verses 17 and 18, we read:

"And thus I saw the horses in the vision, and them that sat on them, having breastplates of fire, and of jacinth, and brimstone: and the heads of the horses were as the heads of lions; and out of their mouths issued fire and smoke and brimstone. By these three was the third part of men killed, by the fire, and by the smoke, and by the brimstone, which issued out of their mouths."

The above prophecy symbolizes how the Muslims not only changed their ethnic attire, but how they engaged in warfare. The Saracens (Arabs) used their Arabian horses and their swordmanship to scourge and overthrow the Persians and the Eastern Roman Catholics. However, it should be remembered that after the Arabs lost their founder, they were never united under one central government or had an accepted king over all of them. Prophecy predicted that all this was to change when the **Destroyer** turned to the Mongolians to continue Islam's conquest. Amazingly, the Mongolian hordes began to wear the garb of Islam after being its most strongest rival and conqueror. Between A.D. 1258 and A.D. 1299, 41 years of strife continued between the Arabs and the Mongols, whose armies were much more superior. However, **by 1299 an Asian by the name of Osman I had converted to Islam and called his band of Muslims *Turks*, which is where ancient Anatolia gets its modern name of Turkey.**

Osman I became sultan and resumed the effort to make Islam the universal religion which had been discontinued by the overthrow of the Abbasid dynasty. In A.D. 1299, Osman I attacked Nicomedia, the capital of Bithynia, on July 27 of that year. It was **Osman I,** sometimes known as **Othman** or **Atman to the Greeks**, who was the **first to unite the Muslims since Muhammad** into an **UMMA (under one central government)** with one leader at its head. Here, we can see with 100% accuracy how Revelation, Chapter Nine, foretold the scourge of Islam upon apostate papal Christians and the Zoroastrians in this region of the Mediterranean.

For 150 years, the Ottomans (Turks) fought against the Byzantines (Eastern Holy Roman Empire), the third division of Christianity. Osman and his successors had reduced the borders of the Byzantine Empire to what remained just inside the walls of Constantinople. All this took place under the first five prophetic months or 150 years of the Ottomans (1299–1449).

In 1449, Constantine IX asked permission from the sultan at that time to take the throne at Constantinople, thus showing his voluntary submission to the Turks. However, Constantine did not know that he was soon to become the last Eastern emperor. The Ottomans, up to the year 1449, were never able to conquer the last stronghold of the Byzantines, but for two years Constantinople remained untouched under Constantine IX until another sultan emerged.

In 1451, Mehmet II became the Ottoman sultan. His ambition was not only to capture Constantinople, the last stronghold of the Byzantine Empire, but he saw himself like another Muhammad and assumed the name of Muhammad II. Osman I and his succeeding sultans were never able to conquer with their swords the walls of Constantinople. However, Muhammad II had at his disposal the canon and the musket, which had been recently introduced, to help his army penetrate its walls. These destroying **locusts (Turks)**, who had the appearance of **horses with fire and brimstone issuing out from their mouths** and with **breastplates of fire and jacinth (blue)** instead of **iron,** were a **fitting description** by the apostle who wrote these words in the first century as he viewed this strange scene. The **Turks** would ride to **one side of their horses shooting from under the necks of their horses** which would appear at a distance (to a man who never saw gunpowder) that these **bursts of fire and smoke** appeared as **coming from the horses' mouths**.

The colors of the **Turkish uniforms** these Asian Muslim warriors wore were **red, blue, and yellow**, which were symbolized in prophecy as **the color of their breastplates; fire means red, the color jacinth or hyacinth is blue, and the brimstone is yellow.**[37]

[37]***The Prophecies of Daniel and The Revelation*, Smith, p. 509; Revelation 9**:17.

Constantinople, which had been the capital of the Eastern Roman Empire, became the center of the Ottoman Empire until its fall which began in the year A.D. 1840.

From the time of Islam's birth, the mystics of this international religion (the Sufis) have been its secretive guiding light. Sufism admits to borrowing paradigms (ideas) and concepts from the pagan Hindus and the Greeks and that the philosophies of Plato and Aristotle were integrated into Islam.[38] As established earlier, the **Sufis developed into the most learned teachers of Oriental mysticism on earth, and they established occult schools to be used as recruiting stations to convert the world to Islam.** According to Shah's *The Sufis* on page 286, Sufi schools have attracted large numbers of students who never became Muslims. They sought to learn their mystical knowledge, not join their religion. As we continue to study about Sufism in the 20th century, the reader shall see that this is the same thing today. Sufi orders developed in the sixth through the 12th centuries A.D.[39]

As pointed out earlier, **the Rosicrucians, whose real name is the Illuminati, claim that their founder brought his knowledge of mysticism from Arabia, Fez, and Egypt and can be traced to the Qadiri Sufi Order**.[40] Long before Freudian or Jungian ideas (teachings from Carl Jung, the New Age prophet) emerged among New Age and New World Order advocates in the 18th and 19th centuries, Sufi masters from Spanish and Persian schools had already been teaching their students about psychological states, theories of psychology, and psychotherapeutic remedies.[41] The Sufi shaykhs were teaching their students that man originally arose out of the sea long before Darwin set sail on the H.M.S. Beagle.

This above information about Sufism was astonishing to me at first, but what was even more astonishing to me was when I learned who it was that trained the troops for the army to fight for Allah! Before the name ***Sufi*** was used to describe Islam's mystics, they were known as a "**Dervish**," and eventually they united themselves into

[38]*The Concise Encyclopedia of Islam*, Glassé, pp. 375, 376.

[39]*A Dictionary of Comparative Religion*, ed. Brandon, p. 594.

[40]*The Way of the Sufi*, Shah, p. 41.

[41]*Ibid.*, Shah, pp. 36–38.

four major orders. These Sufi orders were located in four strategic areas in the Old World to promote their mystical practices and the spread of Islam. They are listed below:

1. Chishti Order
2. Qadiri Order
3. Suhrawardi Order
4. Naqshbandi Order[42]

It was astonishing to learn that the Sufi ***Madrasa*** (theological colleges), who preach from their mouths a doctrine of love today, were also ancient "**boot camps**" to train elite Muslim troops to kill for Allah. **The Sufi schools also became like the Secret Service or the CIA of Islam.** The schools of Sufism are where the **Janissaries received their military training. The Janissaries were the Green Beret of the Muslim troops and struck the apostate Roman Catholics of the Old World with woes as swift and as painful as a serpent strikes.** "For their power is in their mouth, and in their tails: for their tails were like unto serpents, and had heads, and with them they do hurt." Revelation 9:19. **Amazingly enough, the Janissaries were originally Christian-captured boys who were taken from their conquered parents and made personal slaves to the sultans.**

The Janissaries were not allowed to marry or to own property, but were given over to the Sufi masters to be taught by them and to be converted as Muslims so they could be trained to fight for Allah. They not only became the sultan's personal slaves, but also his elite soldiers.[43] It was the Janissaries who finally gained access to the city of Constantinople in **A.D. 1453, and this led to the overthrow of Catholic Emperor Constantine IX of the Byzantine Empire**.

The Ottoman Sultan Mehmet II, who also took the title of Muhammad II, promised his Muslim warriors all the riches of Constantinople and its women if they would conquer it. After the Muslims conquered Constantinople, the blood of its citizens stained the waters known as the Golden Horn, and the Church of Theodosia's altar tables were used to rape young women and boys.[44]

[42]*The Sufis*, Shah, pp. 284, 285, 288.

[43]*The Rise of Islam*, Child, p. 50.

[44]*The Ottomans*, Wheatcroft, pp. 20–22.

It was **Josiah Litch**, a 19th-century Millerite preacher who lived during the fall of the Ottoman Empire, who discovered the time prophecies of Revelation 9:5, 10, 15. Litch accurately predicted the fall of the Ottoman Empire on August 11, 1840, before it happened. Ellen G. White, who was also living during this fulfillment of Bible prophecy, points out the following about Josiah Litch in her multimillion bestseller, *The Great Controversy*, on pages 334 and 335:

"In the year 1840 another remarkable fulfillment of prophecy excited widespread interest. **Two years before**, Josiah Litch, one of the leading ministers preaching the second advent, published an exposition of Revelation 9, predicting the fall of the Ottoman Empire. According to his calculations, this power was to be overthrown 'in A.D. 1840, sometime in the month of August;' and **only a few days previous to its accomplishment he wrote**: 'Allowing the first period, 150 years, to have been exactly fulfilled before Deacozes ascended the throne by permission of the Turks, and that the 391 years, fifteen days, commenced at the close of the first period, it will end on **the 11th of August, 1840, when the Ottoman power in Constantinople may be expected to be broken. And this, I believe, will be found to be the case**.'

"At the very time specified, Turkey, through her ambassadors, accepted the protection of the allied powers of Europe, and thus placed herself under the control of Christian nations. The event exactly fulfilled the prediction."

Reader, although the threat of Islam's determination to force the whole world into their version of a **one-world government** under their god Allah was checked for some 150 years since 1840, **this is by no means the end of this threat from these destroyers symbolized in Revelation, Chapter Nine, as plagues of locusts which arose from the bottomless pit**. If the reader will turn to Revelation, Chapter 11, he will discover that the **SECOND WOE is still continuing in Bible prophecy** and it is, indeed, unveiling itself to us today. **This second woe continues until the probation of mankind ceases.** In verse seven, we see something else ascending from the **bottomless pit** besides locusts; it is a **BEAST** who makes war on God's **TWO WITNESSES**. We will begin to study this prophecy in the next chapter.

Below is a breakdown of the prophecies of Revelation 9:5, 10, 15:

FIVE MONTHS

(30 days in a Jewish month)

30 days in one month

X5 months

150 prophetic years

(A year in Bible prophecy represents 360 days or 360 years.)

(See Numbers 14:34; Ezekiel 4:6.)

HOUR, DAY, MONTH, YEAR

1 hour = 1/24 of a day **OR** 360 ÷ 24 = 15 days

1 day = 1 prophetic year

1 month = 30 prophetic years

1 year = 360 prophetic days (years)

TOTAL = 391 years + 15 days

TOTAL YEARS THE OTTOMAN EMPIRE WOULD SCOURGE THE OLD WORLD

A.D. 1299 **5 months** 1449 **hour, day, month, year** August 11, 1840

150 years **391 years + 15 days**

Reader, the motive behind the ethnic cleansing atrocities inflicted on the Muslims of Kosovo by Slobodan Milosevic's Serb forces of Yugoslavia today traces back to the days of the Ottoman Empire (1299–1919). By 1389, the conquering Asian Muslims (Turks) extended their borders by the point of the sword into the Balkans whose citizens had mainly been adherents of the Greek Orthodox Church and its Byzantine Empire. In 1453, Muhammad II made Constantinople, which was the capital of the Byzantine Empire, the capital of Islam, and in 1521 the Muslims captured Belgrade. From 1912–13, Greece, Bulgaria, and Serbia warred with the Ottoman Empire to regain the Balkans. The Balkan Wars spilled over into WWI and the Ottoman Empire, who had lost its military might by 1840, disappeared by 1919. At the end of WWII, the Balkans had become slaves to the Communists. Today, the Serb forces, who are the remnants of the old Byzantine Empire, are again fighting to win back their territory which was lost during the Turk's murderous campaigns to force Islam throughout SE Europe.

The Star of Islam

A HISTORICAL OUTLINE of the SECOND WOE of ISLAM while under the RULE of the TURKS (ASIANS)

A.D. 1258 The Arab Abbasids were overthrown by invading Mongol-Tartar armies. This ends the first woe on Greek Orthodox Christians and Persians by Arab Muslims. The second woe begins with Osman. It was Osman a.k.a. Othman who again reunited the Muslims under one banner. The Muslims were divided into rivaling factions since the death of Muhammad in A.D. 632. Osman, who settled in Arabia, united all the Muslims under one government. This government became known as the Ottoman Empire. These ruling Asian Muslims became known as the Turks.

A.D. 1299 Osman's first attack against the non-Muslim community was aimed at the Eastern Holy Roman Empire in Nicomaedia in Anatolia (present-day Turkey). These Asian Turks fought almost a perpetual war during this 150-year period, reducing the Byzantine Empire of the Greeks to the shoreline of their fortress city named after Emperor Constantine I . In 1449, Emperor Constantine IX becomes the last emperor of Byzantine.

A.D. 1449 The Arabs tried to take Constantinople during its Muslim rule but never succeeded. After the death of Osman, he was succeeded by a series of warlike sultans who continued to extend the borders of Islam. In 1451, Muhammad II becomes sultan and begins plans to destroy Constantinople, the last Byzantine stronghold. The Muslim Turks had an elite army known as the Janissaries. The Janissaries were the Green Berets of the Muslim army. Under the Arab rule, Saracens invaded their neighbor's land by using their most able Arabian horses and their swords. However, the Turks became more sophisticated. The Turks were unsuccessful in their first siege of Constantinople in 1391. However, 52 years later under Muhammad II, they would use the canon to break down the walls of Constantinople which before were impregnable to their early Saracen brethren.

A.D. 1453 In 1453, Muhammad II launched his attack on the Greek Christian city which lasted six weeks. During the destruction of Constantinople, there was a terrible slaughter of its citizens, whose idols of the Virgin Mary and the crosses which they clung to were also destroyed. After Muhammad II had secured the survivors, whose children were raped by these barbarians, Muhammad II made them slaves. Constantinople, which was the capital of the Greek Orthodox religion, became the headquarters of the Muslim faith. Muhammad II renamed the city Istanbul. After the fall of the Greeks at Constantinople, this city which was renamed Istanbul became the center of the Muslim world. United under one government, the Ottoman Empire was the biggest and deadliest Muslim Empire against the non-Muslim community. It became the scourge of apostate Christians and Jews who also blended Spiritualism with the worship of God. After Constantinople, Muhammad II conquered Athens and the Greek peninsula, Albania, and Bosnia. The Ottoman Empire continued to push its borders after the fall of the Byzantine Empire under other sultans, especially Suleiman when he became sultan in 1520. Suleiman captured Belgrade in 1521, Rhodes in 1522, and then the whole of the north coast of Africa. He was also a terror to Europe as his borders of Islam were reaching Vienna near his death in 1566.

A.D. 1840 The Ottoman Empire reached its zenith under Suleiman, and it began to decline after his death. A succession of incompetent sultans followed, and the Ottoman Empire by 1840 placed itself under the protection of a Christian alliance. At this time, the Muslim scourge was put on hold.

CHAPTER VI

SUFISM
AND THE BIRTH OF THE
HIPPIE COUNTERCULTURAL MOVEMENT

"These have one mind, and shall give their power and strength unto the beast. These shall make war with the Lamb, and the Lamb shall overcome them: for he is Lord of lords, and King of kings: and they that are with him are called, and chosen, and faithful."

Revelation 17:13, 14.

CHAPTER VI

This chapter is a continued study of the **SECOND** and **THIRD WOES** which the book of Revelation prophesied would come forth upon the peoples of the whole world who have embraced precepts of Spiritualism (mysticism) in the past, present, and also in the future. In the last chapter, we saw the prophecies which revealed how Satan (symbolized as **THE ANGEL OR KING OF THE BOTTOMLESS PIT**) would be allowed to send **his destroyers (the Muslims)**, who are symbolized as **two waves** of **SOLITARY** and **GREGARIOUS destroying locusts** swarming out of the **BOTTOMLESS PIT**, to punish the Old World inhabitants for their apostasy from this planet's True God.

Between A.D. 610 and A.D. 1258, it was the **ARAB MUSLIMS** who delivered the **FIRST WOE** upon the idolatrous Catholic Christians of the Byzantine Empire, the Jews, the Zoroastrians of the Persian Empire, the Hindus, and the Buddhists. History records that this terrible plague of death and destruction was delivered by the **Arabian Saracens** who, within the first 100 years of their history, extended their borders from Spain to India. As we saw in the last chapter, they were symbolized in Revelation, Chapter Nine, as a plague of **200 million SOLITARY desert locusts** who had swarmed out of Arabia into their regions.

The **SECOND WOE** or the **SECOND WAVE** of the **GREGARIOUS LOCUST PLAGUE** commenced on the Old World inhabitants in the **year A.D. 1299** when the power of Islam had **shifted to the Asians (Turks)** under the leadership of **Osman I**. It was the Turkish Sultan Osman who had reunited the Muslims under **one Islamic government**, which was known as **the Ottoman Empire**. This unity had not happened since Muhammad, its founder, had been alive. The Turkish Ottoman Empire was allowed to **BEGIN TO DELIVER THE SECOND WOE UPON THOSE WHO IGNORED OR OBEYED NOT THE GOSPEL OF OUR LORD JESUS CHRIST.** The scourge on the inhabitants of the Old World by the waves of invading **Turkish Muslims** brought **even more** carnage and enslavement than that of the **Arabian Saracen Muslims**. The Ottoman Empire's efforts to make the whole world Islamic by waging wars on the non-Muslim community **started in A.D. 1299** and **ended on August 11, 1840**, as it was foretold in Revelation 9:5, 10, 15. However, we are still living under the time of the **SIXTH ANGEL** and the **SECOND WOE**, and this **SECOND WOE** did not stop at the fall of the Ottoman Empire.

About 64 years before the fall of the Ottoman Empire, Satan, symbolized as the **ANGEL** (king) of the **BOTTOMLESS PIT** (Revelation 9:11), raised up **ANOTHER POWER** symbolized in prophecy as a "**BEAST**." This "**BEAST**," like the "**LOCUSTS**," would come forth from **THE BOTTOMLESS PIT** (Revelation 11:7; 17:3, 7–14), which is representing the **abode of Satan himself**. It is here in **Bible prophecy** that our **Lord Jesus lifts this spiritual veil** for us so we can detect just who are these principalities, powers, and the rulers of the darkness of this world, which are working through spiritual wickedness in **HIGH PLACES** to overthrow Him and His people. (See Ephesians 6:12.)

Again, it is very important for the reader to understand more about how the **Order of Freemasonry** is, indeed, a **child of Sufism (Islamic mysticism)** in order to see how **Islamic mysticism, Freemasonry, the Illuminati, the Theosophical Society, and the New Age and the New World Order conspiracies** tie in with the prophecy about the "**Beast from the Bottomless Pit**" of Revelation 11:7 for **ALL OF THE ABOVE ARE AGENCIES OF SPIRITUALISM. Freemasonry and the secret society of the Illuminati are just a continuation of Sufism, which is Islamic mysticism.** It is here in history that the **French Revolutionists** appear. **The RED SCOURGE of SOCIALISM/COMMUNISM**, which is foretold to bring even **MORE WOE** on the **WHOLE WORLD**, derived from this same era. In Revelation 11:1–14, we read:

"And there was given me a reed like unto a rod: and the angel stood, saying, Rise, and measure the temple of God, and the altar, and them that worship therein. But the court which is without the temple leave out, and measure it not; for it is given unto the Gentiles: and the holy city shall they tread under foot **FORTY AND TWO MONTHS**.

"And I will give power unto my **two witnesses**, and they shall prophesy a **THOUSAND TWO HUNDRED AND THREESCORE DAYS**, clothed in sackcloth. These are the two olive trees, and the two candlesticks standing before the God of the earth.

"And if any man will hurt them, fire proceedeth out of their mouth, and devoureth their enemies: and if any man will hurt them, he must in this manner be killed. These have power to shut heaven, that it rain not in the days of their prophecy: and have power over waters to turn them to blood, and to smite the earth with all plagues, as often as they will.

"And when they shall have finished their testimony, **THE BEAST THAT ASCENDETH OUT OF THE BOTTOMLESS PIT** shall make war against them, and shall overcome them, and kill them. And their dead bodies shall lie in the street of the great city, which **SPIRITUALLY IS CALLED SODOM AND EGYPT**, where also our Lord was crucified.

"And they of the people and kindreds and tongues and nations shall see their dead bodies three days and an half, and shall not suffer their dead bodies to be put in graves. And they that dwell upon the earth shall rejoice over them, and make merry, and shall send gifts one to another; because these two prophets tormented them that dwelt on the earth.

"And after three days and an half the Spirit of life from God entered into them, and they stood upon their feet; and great fear fell upon them which saw them. And they heard a great voice from heaven saying unto them, Come up hither. And they ascended up to heaven in a cloud; and their enemies beheld them.

"And the same hour was there a great earthquake, and the tenth part of the city fell, and in the earthquake were slain of men seven thousand: and the remnant were affrighted, and gave glory to the God of heaven. The **SECOND WOE** is past; and, behold, the **THIRD WOE** cometh quickly."

Ancient Prophecies About Mysticism

A comprehensive study of the **BEAST FROM THE BOTTOMLESS PIT** is found in **Volume Two**. This beast was identified as being a symbol of the **partly religious** and **partly political powers** of the people of **Spiritualism (mysticism)** which the **Dragon** used to war against **Christ and His people** from the **Tower of Babel** of the **Old World** to the **Tower of Babel** now set up in the **New World**, which is the **United Nations**. Here is a brief outline which shows what powers this terrible Beast from the Bottomless Pit left in history from Nimrod's day to our day. Babel, Babylon, Persia, Greece, pagan Rome, Islam, Sufism, Freemasonry, the Illuminati (French Revolutionists), the New World Order, Socialism/Communism, the Theosophical Society, the Federal Council of Churches, the World Council of Churches, the Council on Foreign Relations, the Wainwright House, the United Nations, the Club of Rome, and the World Trade Organization are just a few of the agencies which were set up by people who had occult connections. All of these organizations, **save Islam**, were studied thoroughly in Volumes Two and Three. **This volume, however, is focusing on how Islam ties in with Bible prophecy.**

As pointed out in Volumes One, Two, and Three, the book of Revelation foretold the rising of **THREE DIFFERENT BEASTS**, which are the **Beast from the Bottomless Pit** (Revelation 11:7; 17:3, 7–14), **the Beast from the Sea** (Revelation 13:1–10), and **the Beast from the Earth** (Revelation 13:11–17). **The Beast from the Sea** is the prophecy revealing the rise and the evolution of the Roman Catholic Church and its enslavement in the Old World which began in A.D. 538 and continued for **FORTY-TWO MONTHS**, which in Bible prophecy is symbolizing **1,260 years**. This terrible, religious dictatorship of the popes was stopped in 1798 by the power which is symbolized as the **Beast from the Bottomless Pit**. This beast is symbolizing the people of Spiritualism (**not** the Papacy) who overthrew the Papacy in the third quarter of the 18th century. They were the **French Revolutionists (the Freemasons a.k.a. the Jacobins)** who, as we saw earlier, were the people who belonged to the secret society of the **Illuminati,** which, by the way, is a **child of Islamic mysticism (Sufism). Please also keep in mind that the "MYSTIC SHRINE" of FREEMASONRY derived out of "ISLAMIC MYSTICISM"** that **Sufism** borrowed from **Plato** and that the **ANGEL (KING)** and the **BEAST** of Revelation 11:7 came out of the "**BOTTOMLESS PIT**."

The Beast from the Earth, who speaks as a **Dragon** (Revelation 13:11) and causes the whole world to unite again with the Papacy **(the Beast from the Sea)**, is, unfortunately, the United States of America who arose in history while the Roman Church was being scourged and overthrown by the Illuminati **between** the years of **1776** and **1798**. As we shall see, although Islam is still one of the biggest threats to those who believe that **Jesus Christ is the Son of God**, nevertheless, Bible prophecy warns that it will be the **pope of Rome** (**the head of the Beast from the Sea** – Revelation 13:1–10) who shall emerge out of this religious confusion (Babylon the Great) and become the head of this New World Order scheme at the time foretold. This will be accomplished through the Papacy's financial, religious, and political ties with the United States. Did not the United States government exalt John Paul II and use tax money from American Protestant citizens to bring the Roman Catholic pope to America?

Let's go back now in history to find more of the origins of **Sufism** and how it spread to America, and let's also study some more **incredible Bible prophecies** which foretold the rise of **Muhammad** and **Islam,** their **Freemasonry/Illuminati** connection, and the **THREE WOES** they would deliver upon **apostate Christians** and the **non-Muslim community**. Let's also look at more historical facts of how the secret societies of **SUFISM (Islamic mysticism)** are not only the **EASTERN FATHER OF FREEMASONRY** and the **Illuminati**, but how the "**Hippie Countercultural Movement**" and the **"Flower Children" of the 60s were fathered by a Sufi master and musician!**

I pointed out in Volume Two of this series that the real name of the international secret society of the Rosicrucians is the Illuminati. For those who have not read Volume Two, I will again quote from their own words. Here from their book, *Rosicrucian Questions and Answers with Complete History*, is their claim: "**I, BROTHER OF THE ILLUMINATI, WITH POWER DECREED, DO DECLARE THIS MANIFESTO**."[1] (Emphasis mine.)

[1]***Rosicrucian Questions and Answers with Complete History*, Lewis, p. 25.**

Keeping this in mind about the Rosicrucians in Europe and America, let's now see some similarities between Sufism and other mystical religions and their crosslinks on both sides of the Atlantic.

The earlier Sufis were also known as a "dervish," and one of the first Sufi dervishes to settle in India was Hujwiri who died in 1063.[2] He is considered among the secret order of Sufism to be one of the most learned Sufi masters. During the conquest of Islam, Muslim invaders of India and "**wandering dervishes**" upon entering the land made a point of paying homage at his shrine. However, the Sufi Master al-Hallaj is looked upon among the Sufis as one of their faithful martyrs. He was put to death by Islamic leaders for blasphemy. It is forbidden under Islamic Law to worship human beings and saints, however, **Muslims often wander beyond the borders of their own Law. Today, Muhammad and his Sufi masters are as revered among some Muslims as Christ is among Christians.**

As the wizard Zoroaster (Zarathushtra) taught his disciples to unite themselves into a "**mystical union**" with only one god (Ahura Mazda), so did the Sufi Master al-Hallaj promote a uniting of the soul into a **"mystical marriage" with Allah**. This pantheistic doctrine, however, offended the Orthodox Sunni Muslims. The Persian Sufi Master al-Hallaj (while in an ecstatic trance) was executed in Baghdad for stating, "I am God," which was blasphemy to the Sunni Muslims for Islam teaches "There is no god but God (Allah), and Muhammad is His Messenger (Prophet)."[3] (Emphasis mine.)

I was also astonished to learn that the chessboard and its war game of "Chess" are an invention of Sufism. The black and white (Yin Yang) alternation of light and dark, which symbolizes the struggle between good and evil, was seen displayed on the floors of dervish meeting places,[4] as well as in Masonic Lodges today.[5] Not one out of a thousand Protestant Christians has ever heard of the Sufis; however, among learned and modern, New Age occultists, Sufi schools are the Yale, the Harvard, or the

[2]***The Sufis*, Shah, p. 287.**
[3]***The World's Religions*, Clarke, p. 86.**
[4]***The Sufis*, Shah, p. 289.**
[5]***The Masonic Report*, McQuaig/Shaw, p. 49.**

West Point of mysticism. The late **Dag Hammarskjöld, who was instrumental in establishing the "United Nations Meditation Room," was a student of Sufism.**[6]

The word ***Sufism*** derived from the word ***suf*** which means ***wool*** and was originally applied to those in Islam who dressed in the simple woolen garment which Sufis wore.[7] The Sufis, whose ministry began with Muhammad in the seventh century of our Christian Era, borrowed their dress and their ideas for establishing schools from Roman Catholic monks who had previously clad themselves in coarse woolen garb as a sign of penitence and renunciation of worldly vanities.

The most famous Sufi master was **Jalal ud-din Rumi** (1207–73), who founded the ***whirling dervishes***.[8] Like mystics of other religions, the **Sufi dervishes** desire a **"mystical union"** with their chief deity. This goal is believed to be achieved through certain practices, similar to those of the Buddhists, such as **renunciation of the world, abstinence, poverty, meditation (yoga), *sama*, and the *dhikr***. The ***sama*** is the practice of intense and ecstatic listening and meditation to the accompaniment of Sufi music.[9] **The *dhikr* is a meditation practice involving the rhythmical repetitions (chants) of religious phrases invoking the 99 names of God.**[10] While the Sufi repetitiously sings out the names for his god, wild ecstatic music by drums is sounding as he whirls himself into a ritual dance simulating the rotation of the planets around the sun. This wild display of chanting and dancing to the beat of their drums is done in hopes that the **Sufi will be induced into a trance so he may gain union with his deity**.[11] Reader, please keep this in mind later when we study the origin of the wild and ecstatic Pentecostal, rock, Christian contemporary, and rap music today.

However, in the Scriptures we can find a warning about using repetitious chants or mantras with a rosary as the Hindus, Buddhists,

[6]***The Way of the Sufi*, Shah, p. 20.**

[7]***The Encyclopedia of Religion*, Vol. 14, ed. Eliade, p. 104.**

[8]***The Rise of Islam*, Child, p. 29.**

[9]***Tales from the Land of the Sufis*, Bayat/Jamnia, p. 175.**

[10]***World Religions*, Bowker, p. 162.**

[11]***The World's Religions*, Clarke, p. 98.**

Roman Catholics, followers of Muhammad, and even New Agers use in their worship services. Jesus taught to **never use repetitious chants** to invoke the God of Abraham, Isaac, and Jacob.

"But when ye pray, **USE NOT VAIN REPETITIONS, AS THE HEATHEN DO**: for they think that they shall be heard for their much speaking. Be not ye therefore like unto them: for your Father knoweth what things ye have need of, before ye ask him." Matthew 6:7, 8.

As the God of Abraham set up schools of the prophets to teach the oracles of God and to promote them, so did the Sufi Muslims establish secret schools to teach and promote doctrines that derived from Spiritualism. This may explain why Hollywood has always displayed Arab nations in their cartoons or motion picture fantasies as mystical lands full of jinnis and mystics flying through the air on magic carpets.

Like Hinduism and Buddhism, Islam believes in supernatural beings who inhabit the earth and assume various forms and exercise talismanic power. Although Islam believes in just one God and in the past warred with Roman Catholics who bowed down to idols; nevertheless, I have discovered that the Muslim faith is like that of the New Ager and is saturated with doctrines of a metaphysical kind as well. According to Mojdeh Bayat and Mohammad Ali Jamnia who were born in Tehran and are initiates of the Nimatullahi Sufi Order and who are the authors of the book, *Tales from the Land of the Sufis*, it is stated in the Glossary of their book that the majority of Sufi Orders trace their lineage back to Ali who was Muhammad's cousin.[12] **The above authors go on to state how MUHAMMAD taught ALI himself how to traverse the stages of the spiritual path to become a PERFECT HUMAN BEING.** Here, again, the reader can see the similarities between Buddhism's mystical teachings and that of Islam. As we saw earlier, the mystic Gautama Buddha claimed to have reached perfection as well. However, Gautama called this mystical experience ***Nirvana***. In the book of Revelation, which is a "**revelation**" from our Lord Jesus Christ, we are told why our God has punished in the past and will punish in the future those who ignore the Gospel and continue to accept doctrines that derived from Spiritualism.

[12]*Tales from the Land of the Sufis*, Shah, p. 173.

"And the rest of the men which were not killed by these plagues **yet repented not** of the works of their hands, **THAT THEY SHOULD NOT WORSHIP DEVILS**, and idols of gold, and silver, and brass, and stone, and of wood: which neither can see, nor hear, nor walk: **Neither repented they** of their **murders**, nor of their **sorceries**, nor of their **fornication**, nor of their **thefts**." Revelation 9:20, 21.

Nevertheless, a teaching found in Islam, which is similar with that of the Buddhists, has linked them with **SUPERNATURAL BEINGS (DEVILS)**. The Sufi masters teach their students about invisible beings who have hoofed feet and goatlike faces and who are endowed with magical powers. In the Holy Scriptures, they are called "**satyrs**." (See Isaiah 13:21.) They are equivalent to what are called **genies** or **elves**, which some Christians ignorantly teach their little ones are Santa's helpers. In Roman mythology and in the Latin language, the word "***genie***" derived from the word "***genius***" which means "***guardian spirit***."[13] The Sufi masters call these supernatural beings "**JINNS**" and, ironically enough, openly admit that the **jinn** is a **demon**, but go on to teach that there are **good demons** and **bad demons**. Some believe that some jinns also seek God, and Sufi masters have had **JINNS** as their disciples.[14]

As pointed out earlier, Mormons and witches invoke demons in order to control them by first engaging in special Temple Ceremonies to protect themselves from harm as they dangerously try to use demonic powers. Again, I would like to remind the reader of the warning from the apostle Paul to the Gentiles. "Now the Spirit speaketh expressly, that in the **latter times** some shall depart from the faith, **GIVING HEED TO SEDUCING SPIRITS**, and **doctrines of devils**." 1 Timothy 4:1.

Nevertheless, according to *The Muslim Almanac*, Muslims not only believe in the concept of the ***jinni*** **(jinn)**, but also in the ***pari*** **(fairy)**.[15] The ***paris*** are regarded by Muslims as **helpers and protectors** of their communities. **The Hopi Indians of northeastern Arizona** call their protecting spirits "**kachinas**" and believe that their

[13]*The American Heritage Dictionary*, Based on the New Second College Edition, 1983, p. 293.

[14]*Tales from the Land of the Sufis*, Bayat/Jamnia, p. 174.

[15]*The Muslim Almanac*, ed. Nanji, pp. 374, 375.

eternal survival depends on them. **They participate in ceremonies and a cycle of dances to invoke them**[16] and make unto themselves dolls to honor and impersonate them. Hopi Indians perform religious rites in hope that the "**kachina**" will **possess them with their power**.[17] Today, the **Tibetan Buddhists** call these pagan deities "**dakinis and mahakalas**" and, like the Hopi Indians, wear masks to represent their deities during their ceremonies and special religious occasions.[18]

To invoke their ***paris***, Muslims offer them ***sofreh*** (votive meals) to solicit their protection and aid. Like in most beliefs of Eastern religions, as well as in the beliefs of the Native American Indians, the ancient Toltecs, and the Mayan Indians of Central America, the followers of Muhammad believe in good spirits and bad spirits. These **bad paris** are widely known in the mountains of **Hindu Kush**, a mountain range named after the founder of India who was **Kush (the Biblical Cush – Genesis, Chapter Ten), the father of Nimrod**. They are said to have caused psychic abductions, possession, debilitating illnesses, and even death. As the Indians from America have their shamans (medicine men) to ward off evil spirits, so do the Muslims have the ***Pir*** (Sufi masters).[19] As the Muslim has his Pir to help him learn Islamic mysticism, so does the Ashkenazi Jew have his Cabalist to teach the Jewish version of mysticism of which Plato, the Sufis, and the Freemasons have borrowed heavily from as well.

Of all the Masonic writers in their evolution, none stands out among Freemasons in America as the most recognized authority of their dogma more than their past Grand High Priest and Sovereign Grand Commander of the Southern Jurisdiction of the United States, **Albert Pike**. In his book, *Morals and Dogma*, which this writer has in his possession, Albert Pike states the following: "All truly dogmatic religions have issued from the **KABALAH** and return to it: everything scientific and grand in the religious dreams

[16]*The Mystical Year*, Time-Life Books, p. 64.

[17]*Ibid.*, Time-Life Books, p. 64.

[18]*The New York Times*, November 3, 1997, p. E2.

[19]*The Muslim Almanac*, ed. Nanji, p. 227.

of all the **ILLUMINATI**, Jacob Boehme, Swedenborg, **Saint-Martin**, and others, is **BORROWED FROM THE KABALAH; ALL THE MASONIC ASSOCIATIONS OWE TO IT THEIR SECRETS AND THEIR SYMBOLS.**"[20] (Emphasis mine.) Albert Pike, by the way, was made the head of the Illuminati in the United States by Giuseppe Mazzini (the successor of Weishaupt) after Adam Weishaupt died in 1830. All this can be seen on the documented pages of Volume Two of this series. However, in Latin America, it was another fellow Freemason who continued this New World Order conspiracy against Christianity there. This Mason was none other than Simón Bolívar who continued his version of this **occult, world revolution** among gullible Latin Americans who think, even today, that this revolutionary was a great hero. Simón Bolívar and the history of his revolutionary plans in South America are all revealed on the documented pages of Volume Three of this series.

BOTH SUFISM and FREEMASONRY could be considered as JEWISH THEOSOPHY or MYSTICISM BECAUSE BOTH BORROWED FROM THE KABBALAH, as did the GREEK PHILOSOPHERS as well. According to *The Oxford Illustrated Encyclopedia of Peoples and Cultures*, the **Kabbalah is Jewish mysticism**[21] and is **based** upon **astrology** and the study of occult interpretation of the Old Testament and other texts which define the spiritual and symbolic value of numbers and letters.

As established earlier, the Kabbalah (Cabala) has been made popular among those who follow their idols of the entertainment field. Another lengthy article which promotes the Kabbalah and was written by David Van Biema is found in *Time* magazine, the November 24, 1997, issue. **Van Biema states on pages 92–93 in the above magazine how Madonna threw a Kabbalah cocktail party to help spread its teachings and how Roseanne, Elizabeth Taylor, and Barbra Streisand are all students of the Kabbalah.** Van Biema goes on to promote the Hardoon's Kabbalah Learning Center that attracts many of the stars to Jewish mysticism (occultism).

[20]***Morals and Dogma*, Pike, p. 744.**

[21]***The Oxford Illustrated Encyclopedia of Peoples and Cultures*, ed. Hoggart, Vol. 7, p. 175.**

Again, the origin of the Kabbalah can be traced to the wizard Zoroaster whose religion of Zoroastrianism was the official religion of the Persians during the time Nehemiah led the captive Israelites back to Jerusalem from Babylon. All Western **New Age ENLIGHTENMENT Movements**, Freemasonry, the Illuminati, Sufism, Theosophy, and even the religious dreams of Plato's Utopian Society (Marxism) have their **roots** in the philosophies of the ancient **Kabbalah**. However, to the delight of Jewish Socialists, **Islam also stresses communal living and the sharing of wealth.**"[22] The lie of reincarnation, occult numerology, the practice of sorcery (magic), and the use of charms and amulets to invoke demons are all written on the pages of the Kabbalah. Those who practice these things are, according to Deuteronomy, Chapter 18, not only repeating the sins of the Canaanites, but are an abomination unto the Lord.

"There shall not be found among you any one that maketh his son or his daughter to pass through the fire, or that useth DIVINATION, or an OBSERVER OF TIMES, or an ENCHANTER, or a WITCH, Or a CHARMER, or a CONSULTER WITH FAMILIAR SPIRITS, or a WIZARD, or a NECROMANCER. FOR ALL THAT DO THESE THINGS ARE AN ABOMINATION UNTO THE LORD: and because of these abominations the Lord thy God doth drive them out from before thee." Deuteronomy 18:10–12.

Reader, as we continue, it shall be very clear that Sufism (Islamic mysticism), Freemasonry, the Illuminati, and Jewish Theosophy all promote the precepts of what the ancient Canaanites were guilty of, however, in just under another form and, unfortunately, in the name of the God of Abraham. Although these above movements have worked separately to spread their own versions of Spiritualism and have their own separate ideas about uniting the world today into a mystical union; nevertheless, the origin of their crafts came from the same stall. The Hindu Cushites, who migrated to Mesopotamia and later became known as the Chaldeans, are the father of Spiritualism, and their brethren, who founded the Egyptian mysteries, are the mother. They are the spiritual parents of all Oriental mysticism of which the West borrowed. Spiritualism's first **political power** (the

[22]***Utne Reader*, March/April 1994, p. 87.**

Beast from the Bottomless Pit) was formed at Babel under Nimrod. It was from Babel that other religions and mystical, political movements (under the guidance of this planet's invisible Prime Minister) sprang forth to war against the True God and His people.

Maybe the following information about Freemasonry will help the Southern Baptist, who has defended Freemasonry, understand more of what many of his members are involved in. In *Webb's Monitor of Freemasonry*, we will read as follows: **"So broad is the religion of Masonry, and so carefully are all sectarian tenents excluded from the system, that the Christian, the Jew, and the Mohammedan, in their numberless sects and divisions, may, and do harmoniously combine in its moral and intellectual work with the Buddhist, the Parsee, the Confusian, and the worship of Deity under every form."**[23]

As we have seen, Freemasonry, like Islamic mysticism, is another mystical order and for centuries has been involved in promoting a "**mystical union**" of **ALL** nations and religions under one banner. Every major religion in the world is represented under the roofs of their Masonic Lodges. A Christian who believes in the Bible may be surprised to learn that one out of twelve men today in the United States is a member of Freemasonry. Most of our congressmen and senators are Freemasons, as were the founding fathers and presidents of the United States. Although Sufism and Freemasonry owe their doctrines to the ancient Kabbalah, the Jewish book of magic, it should be understood, however, that today Islam and Freemasonry are **two separate revolutions**. Although Islam and Freemasonry both derived out of the philosophies of Oriental mysticism, which can be traced back to the Kabbalah and then to the Chaldeans, it is very important to understand that Freemasonry for over two hundred years has been promoting the New World Order **commune** to which **Muslims as a whole are violently opposed**. In the eyes of a Muslim, the New World Order is a threat and is looked upon as Western imperialism. While New World Order and New Age advocates are busy trying to unite all mystical orders on both sides of the Atlantic into a mystical union

[23]*Webb's Monitor of Freemasonry*, Morris, p. 280, quoted from *The Masonic Report*, McQuaig/Shaw, p. 5.

of all religions and governments under the auspices of Freemasonry and the United Nations, in which Zionism has played a major part, the Muslims, on the other hand, are determined that their Islamic revolution will make the inhabitants of this planet submit to Allah only. Like Freemasonry, Islam is a mixture of all religions, as well, but accepts only Allah as this world's true god and Muhammad as its prophet.

It should be understood that the Muslims hate the **degraded lifestyles** of the **American** and **British people** which are constantly displayed in a most disgusting way by the finest of **Hollywood** and the **Music Industry**. Fanatical Muslim fundamentalists, like the New Agers and the New World Order advocates, have within their movements secret societies like the "**MUSLIM BROTHERHOOD**" and the"**EGYPTIAN ISLAMIC JIHAD**" who are working to overthrow the New Agers and the New World Order advocates. **Muslim leaders** who are **uniting** with **Western** thought are considered **apostates** and **enemies of Allah**; such was the case of the **Shah of Iran** and **Anwar Sadat** who, by the way, was murdered by his own Muslim guards.

While the Muslims are stirring themselves up against the advocates of Zionism and the New World Order conspirators, so are white supremacist factions within the United States doing the same. White supremacists today look with the same eyes as Hitler did toward the Jewish people. They think that this whole Illuminati/Communist/CFR conspiracy is solely Jewish, and neo-Nazi groups are trying to stir up another American Revolution to overthrow the CFR/U.S. government because of this erroneous belief. A complete, documented study about the secret society of the Council on Foreign Relations (CFR) is found in Volume Two of this series. A complete study on the origin of Zionism and its connection with the Illuminati/Communist/United Nations conspiracy is examined in Volume Three.

While Satan is creating huge divisions between the people of Spiritualism and white supremacist dissenters, yet there is still another powerful and determined foe which is flexing his political and religious muscles against all of the above. Jesus warned that this power would receive a deadly wound but would later recover and regain its power during the Time of the End. Jesus warned that the leader of this power would be branded with the number 666. In Revelation 13:18, we read:

"Here is wisdom. Let him that hath understanding count the number of the beast: for it is the number of a man; and his number is Six hundred threescore and six."

This religious threat to Bible-believing Christians is coming from the Vatican. Like the Muslims, the Roman Church also used the point of the sword to force the inhabitants of the Old World to obey its religious dictates and, like the people of Spiritualism, has its own ideas for a New World Order commune today. This power, the Roman Catholic Church, is symbolized as the Beast from the Sea (Revelation 13:1–10) and its **Vicarius Filii Dei** (Vicar of the Son of God) or **pope** who sits as its head has been branded with the number 666. It is also very eye-opening to learn that the title "**John Paul II**" will add to this number of doom, as well, if the reader will spell his title, **Iõannes Paulus Secundo, in Latin**.

Below are the official title of the pope and John Paul II's name in Latin and the computation of their names using Roman numerals:

V I C A R I U S F I L I I D E I[24]

5, 1, 100, 1, 5, 1, 50, 1, 1, 500, 1 = 666

I Õ A N N E S P A U L U S S E C U N D O

1, 5, 50, 5, 100, 5, 500 = 666

However, this writer does not think John Paul II will be the pope who shall become the head of the New World Order because of his age and health; John Paul II is in the autumn of his years. It will be to our interest to watch and see who this next pope shall be. The Papacy and its clergy have, indeed, revolutionary plans to regain the power which it lost in 1798 to the French Illuminati a.k.a. the Jacobin Clubs. To see how serious these plans are, just read the book, *The Keys of This Blood*, written by the Jesuit professor, Malachi Martin.

During the third quarter of the 18th century, this period was also known as **the Enlightenment or the Age of Reason Era** and was promoted by Jefferson, Franklin, and Paine, who were actually the apostles of the New World Order. The above men used their influence in politics to forbid by legislation the worship of God and His Son in France. The **French Revolutionists** not only warred against the tyrannical reign of the Roman Catholic Church,

[24]***Our Sunday Visitor*, November 15, 1914.**

but also the entire Christian faith. These 18th-century **Illuminists** and antichrists (popularized by Masons) caused the French citizens to burn their Bibles in the streets by using their **religion of Deism** (Enlightenment) as a tool to overthrow Christianity. The people of France were **de-Christianized** by these **Jacobin** conspirators, as multitudes of Americans today have been as well. However, these French Revolutionists later turned their guns on each other and were thrown into one of mankind's most terrible eras of terror. It was called the **REIGN OF TERROR**, which will be repeated and experienced again today by those who do not know God or obey the Gospel of our Lord Jesus Christ.

The other religious radicals today who are helping to stir up another coming Reign of Terror are the American Protestant right wingers a.k.a. fundalmentalists who are symbolized in prophecy as the Beast from the Earth (Rev.13:11–17) and who, like the Roman Church (the Beast from the Sea), are in the name of Jesus Christ trying to force their religious beliefs by using the power of the State. Although they are violently opposed to the New Age and the New World Order plans presently, it will be the apostate Protestants of the United States who will reinstate the power of the pope whose "**DEADLY WOUND WAS HEALED**." The Papacy received this deadly wound from the French Revolutionists (Freemasons) in 1798. After the Papacy's power is regained, the Bible predicts that "**ALL THE WORLD WONDERED AFTER THE BEAST (the Papacy)**." Revelation 13:3.

The God of Abraham, Isaac, and Jacob punished the Israelites by using heathen, pagan nations as His instruments to destroy their cities and them, as well, after they continually refused to obey Him. The Muslims, likewise, became the scourge of the Catholic Greek Orthodox Church people and its capital city of Constantinople, which is now Istanbul, because of their continued refusal to obey God's commandments. **When the Muslim invaders attacked the Greek Byzantine Empire, their graven images of Jesus and the saints and their rosaries and crosses, which they clung to, served as NO PROTECTION FROM EVIL AND DEATH WHICH WAS COMING UPON THEM AS THEY WERE TAUGHT TO BELIEVE. This, too, will be the fate of those in our day who cling to the precepts of mysticism and continue to ignore the Holy Scriptures. This will also**

be the destiny of those who do not turn away from their sins and idolatry and who have not the Seal of the Living God in their foreheads.

In A.D. 538 about 32 years before the birth of Muhammad, papal Christianity had already proclaimed that their pope of Rome was the only Vicar of God, and the Papacy went on to begin to call itself "**the Corrector of Heretics**." Those who refused to recognize the authority of the Holy Roman Catholic Church or its pope began to feel the terrible persecuting power of the Destroyer as he used papists to punish by the point of the sword those who would not submit themselves to the Vicar of Christ, whose seat was located where there are seven mountains. Like Islam and Mormonism, the Papacy was and is a theocracy.

In the meantime, Muhammad in the year A.D. 610 began to preach to the pagan Arabs in Mecca about worshipping Allah and submitting only to him. At this time, the Arabs, like the Roman Catholics, were bowing themselves down in front of graven images, as well, only their graven images had the faces of the gods of astrology (which are the sun, moon, and the stars), instead of Jesus, Mary, and Peter.

Muhammad preached against worshipping graven images which he and his parents were accustomed to when they were living. However, he was rejected at first by the pagan Meccans but became successful in his mission, as we saw, **by the use of the point of the sword**. As Islam extended to the borders of China, many Buddhists of central Asia were turned from praying to the graven image of Buddha to Allah, who had been worshipped as the moon-god among pagan Arabs.

Again, Satan (that old serpent, called the Devil) actually has only **one religion** which he has successfully used to deceive the human race over and over again. This religion is **astrology** from which all the esoteric sciences of Spiritualism derived. **The only difference between the ancient Eastern religions and the mysticism of Islam is really only their outward exterior.**

The similarities between Buddhism and Islam, which had been veiled for centuries, however, became very apparent when the six major religions of the world met together for the first time ever at the **World's Parliament of Religions held in Chicago in the fall of 1893**. Alexander Russell Webb, who had been a strenuous advocate of promoting Buddhism through the **Theosophical Society**, suddenly converted to Islam and was also one of the delegates of this first Interfaith Congress. Not only was Webb's presence at this same congress a most uncomfortable and controversial experience among theosophists, but it was also eye-opening to the 19th- century New Agers. Henry S. Olcott (1830–1907), a convinced Buddhist and co-founder of the Theosophical Society, saw Webb at this Interfaith Congress. **When Olcott asked Webb as to the reason for his sudden change of allegiance to Islam, Webb simply told him that although he had become a Muslim he had not ceased to be an ardent theosophist because Islam, as he understood it, was distinctly in accord with Theosophy.**[25]

Reader, as pointed out before, Sufism is the highest form of mysticism (Illuminism a.k.a. Enlightenment) on the earth today, not only in the Old World, but now in the New World. It is very important to see more of the evolution of Sufism in America and what it has developed into today. We have already seen the 1995 *Publisher's Weekly* announcement to bookstores urging them to make room on their shelves for Sufi books. However, Sufism began to become known in the U.S. in 1910 and became the foundation for the Hippie Countercultural Movement.

Although Madame Blavatsky, the New Age prophetess and co-founder of the revolutionary Theosophical Society, borrowed from the Sufis, it was **Buddhism which she used** in her effort to make New Age Spiritualism (mysticism) a universal religion, **not Sufism**. However, the New Age Movement's explosion of Eastern Spiritualism in the 70s and 80s did not come overnight upon the people of the United States nor only by the writings of other well-known New Age writers such as the ancient Greek writer Plato, Adam Weishaupt, Benjamin Franklin, Thomas Jefferson, Thomas Paine, Albert Pike, H. P. Blavatsky, Annie Besant, Alice Ann Bailey, David Vaughn, David Spangler, Marilyn Ferguson, or Shirley MacLaine. **Much of the New Age phenomena and the "Hippie Movement" owe their ideas and mystical revolution to a relatively unknown Muslim revolutionary and Sufi master named Hazrat Inayat Khan (1881–1927). Sufism was actually first introduced in America by this same Muslim Sufi master during the first decade of the 20th century.**

[25]***The Extraordinary Life & Influence of Helena Blavatsky, Founder of the Modern Theosophical Movement*, Cranston, p. 426.**

Hazrat Khan was born in India into a family of Muslim musicians of which he was himself. Khan founded a secret society in the U.S. called the **Sufi Order in the West**. According to the *New Age Encyclopedia*, Khan had been initiated into Sufism at age 24 and had received a mission from his sheikh to bring Sufism to the West. His mission was to unite the East and the West in the religion of **love** and **wisdom** so that doctrinal bias would be replaced by the power of **mysticism.**[26]

Bible-believing Christians need to remember that **Sufi masters are known for their talents in poetry and music. Khan made his way by performing as a musician and by lecturing.**[27] Khan was known as Pir-o-Murshid (teacher) of the secret society of the **Muslim Chishti Order of Sufism in India**. Khan lectured at Columbia University, toured the United States, and met his first initiate, Ada Martin, whom he named Rabia.[28] Rabia Martin, a Kabbalist, also became Khan's first teacher (murshid) of Sufism in the West. She established the first Lodge of Sufism in America in Fairfax, a small village near San Francisco, and she called it '**Kaaba Allah**.'[29]

Although there were, indeed, many non-Muslims who studied Islamic mysticism (Illuminism) in the secret schools of Sufism, nevertheless, the initiate had to be a **male** and a **Muslim** to be a **Sufi teacher** in the Old World. However, after Hazrat Khan's arrival in America, this secretive Sufi master in 1910 founded a secret society of Sufism which **did not require** his members to become Muslims and would accept women as Sufi teachers. Besides Rabia Martin, Khan appointed **three other women as Sufi teachers**. They were Lucy Goodenough, Saintsbury Green, and Mevrouw Egeling.[30]

Hazrat Inayat Khan started a form of Sufism in the U.S. which was completely **INDEPENDENT OF ISLAM** and which also had, like the revolutionary **Theosophical Society**, women teachers. However, instead of using **Buddhism** as a vehicle to unite the **East** and the

[26]*New Age Encyclopedia*, Melton, pp. 441, 442.

[27]*The Illustrated Encyclopedia of Active New Religions, Sects, and Cults*, Beit-Hallahmi, p. 279.

[28]*New Age Encyclopedia*, Melton, p. 442.

[29]*The Book of Enlightened Masters*, Rawlinson, p. 398.

[30]*Ibid.*, Rawlinson, p. 21.

West into a mystical union and universal brotherhood with the author of Spiritualism, Khan used Islamic Illuminism (mysticism). To begin to recruit soldiers into his mystical and countercultural, nonviolent cause, this Muslim musician set up a secret society in the San Francisco area preaching love and peace. Soon Hazrat Khan began to attract both young men and women to him because of his messages of love and because of his musical talents and his mystical power and knowledge.

It was between the years 1910–1923 that Khan preached his eloquent messages of love and wisdom to the students in the Berkeley and San Francisco areas where he fathered "spiritual" FLOWER CHILDREN of which developed into the New Age Hippie Movement. Keeping in mind that Sufism includes invoking supernatural beings named **jinns (genies)**, one such follower was Samuel Lewis who, like Khan's first disciple and teacher, Rabia Martin, was a Jewish Kabbalist. It was actually Rabia Martin who brought Samuel Lewis, who later became a **Hippie Guru**, into their newly-formed **Sufi Order in the West**. Samuel Lewis was born in San Francisco in 1896 into a wealthy, Jewish family. His mother was a **Rothschild**, and his father was **vice-president of the Levi Strauss jeans company**.[31]

Lewis had already believed that the religions of mysticism differed outwardly but were esoterically identical. He was a convinced Spiritualist and, like the beliefs of the Theosophical Society, believed in a **spiritual hierarchy** of ascended masters. After joining Rabia Martin at her 'Kaaba Allah' near San Francisco, Lewis claimed to have met the "immortal Sufi master" named "**KHIDR**," whom the Muslims believe is an "immortal Jew" who they claim appeared to Moses and taught him. This supernatural being **(the "KHIDR" a.k.a. Khwaja Khizr) is, as we saw earlier, mentioned in the Koran**. There are confused interpretations among the learned Sufi masters of just who this **KHIDR** is. Some have said he is Elijah, but those who believe the Holy Scriptures know that the **DRAGON DECEIVETH THE WHOLE WORLD (Revelation 12:9)**. One thing is for sure; the Scriptures show that it is **God (Jesus) "who ONLY hath IMMORTALITY,** dwelling in the light which no man can approach unto; whom no man hath

[31]***The Book of Enlightened Masters*, Rawlinson, p. 396.**

seen, nor can see: to whom be honour and power everlasting. Amen." 1 Timothy 6:16. "Neither is there salvation in any other: **FOR THERE IS NONE OTHER NAME UNDER HEAVEN GIVEN AMONG MEN, WHEREBY WE MUST BE SAVED**." Acts 4:12.

Nevertheless, not only did Samuel Lewis go on to become one of the most well-known teachers (murshids) of the Sufi Order in the West, but he also is said to have had the Hindu destroying-god Shiva, Buddha, Zoroaster, Moses, Muhammad, and Jesus Himself appear to him.[32]

Like his Ṣufi Master Hazrat Khan, Lewis preached the power of Islamic Illuminism mingled with love and peace to gullible, young students in the San Francisco area and, like so many today of the New Age Movement, they were fooled "because they received not love of the truth, that they might be saved. And for this cause God shall send them **STRONG DELUSION, THAT THEY SHOULD BELIEVE A LIE: That they all might be damned who believed not the truth, but had pleasure in unrighteousness**." 2 Thessalonians 2:10–12.

Samuel Lewis was, according to the Bible, a **necromancer**, as was Zoroaster, Buddha, Muhammad, and Joseph Smith, the founder of the Mormon Church. **The Sufi Order in the West** became a school of **necromancy**. Amazingly, because of its musical emphasis, this Sufi Order continued to gain more and more followers until it expanded worldwide. In 1967 while the Fifth Dimension was announcing "This is the dawning of the '**Age of Aquarius**' " to the "**Flower Children**" and the Beatles were promoting an explosion of **psychedelic experiences** through their album, *Sgt. Pepper's Lonely Hearts Club Band*, during the "**Hippie Era**," Samuel Lewis claimed in the same year (1967) to have been told by God that he was to be the spiritual teacher for the Hippies. He began to collect a hundred followers.[33]

In the meantime, Hazrat Khan's son, Vilayat Inayat Khan, founded another branch of Sufism in upstate New York after his father's death in 1927. Following in his father's footsteps, Pir Vilayat Inayat Khan, who was born in 1916, founded the **ABODE OF THE MESSAGE which was located just north of what was to become a historical event for the New Age Hippie**. In an old picture found

[32]*The Book of Enlightened Masters*, Rawlinson, p. 398.

[33]*Ibid.*, Rawlinson, p. 402.

on page 280 of *The Illustrated Encyclopedia of Active New Religions, Sects, and Cults*, it shows Pir Vilayat Inayat Khan surrounded by college-aged disciples as he walked the streets preaching love, peace, and Islamic mysticism (Illuminism).

The Khans and Lewis can be credited for being the granddaddies of the **"Flower Children" and grandfathers of the "Hippie Movement." Again, Vilayat Khan's ABODE OF THE MESSAGE is located north of the very area in New York where the Hippie Aquarian Arts Festival a.k.a. Woodstock took place among the "Flower Children" of 1969.** We will be examining more about what was really behind the famous Woodstock Music and Arts Festival shortly.

The original name of Hazrat Khan's mystical, revolutionary school which he founded in San Francisco in 1910, however, is still known today in America as the **Sufi Order in the West**.[34] The Sufi Order in the West also combines **Hindu and Islamic mysticism with occult practices** such as meditation, recitation, rhythmic chanting, and dancing **mingled with Christian, Buddhist, and yoga traditions**.[35] Today, the Sufi Order in the West has branched out worldwide; it is calling itself the **International Sufi Movement**. They are busy spreading the unity of God by uniting all religions through preaching love and wisdom, thus hoping to end the bias of faiths and all hatred caused by distinctions and differences. They are in an effort to establish a "**Universal Brotherhood**."[36] However, at the death of Hazrat Khan in 1927, the Sufi Movement split into two mainstreams among its American and European disciples until Hazrat Khan's son, Pir Vilayat Inayat Khan (b. 1916), took over the Sufi Movement as its international leader in 1957. Under his leadership, the Sufis have become associated with the "**holistic health movement**."[37]

[34]***The Illustrated Encyclopedia of Active New Religions, Sects, and Cults*, Beit-Hallahmi, p. 279; *The Book of Enlightened Masters*, Rawlinson, p. 21.**

[35]***The Illustrated Encyclopedia of Active New Religions, Sects, and Cults*, Beit-Hallahmi, p. 279.**

[36]***Encyclopedia of Associations: International Organizations*, ed. Eldridge, 1993, p. 1405.**

[37]***New Age Encyclopedia*, Melton, p. 442.**

Sufism and the Hippie Countercultural Movement

It is alarming, indeed, for Bible-believing Christians to become aware of how this once-Protestant Christian country, since the turn of the 20th century, has been overrun by the philosophies of Hinduism, Buddhism, and Kabbalism. Sufism (like Hinduism, Buddhism, and Kabbalism) teaches its students that they have within them hidden, latent powers of which they must become awakened to and, as we saw before, this doctrine and belief is known among occultists as Self-Realization. The name ***Swami Paramahansa Yogananda*** stands out in New Age history as the most influential Hindu leader in America who promoted this false belief about the divinity within you. The actor Dennis Weaver, who is famous for his roles in the TV series *Gunsmoke* and *McCloud*, is a long-time follower of the late Yogananda, this New Age guru.[38]

The International Sufi Movement claims to not only awaken the student seeking their guidance to their own divinity, but makes the claim, like all occult secret societies, that they have the secret of all religion and the power of mysticism. This international school of Sufism operates also as an esoteric school for meditation and spiritual development.[39] However, as shown before in Deuteronomy 18:10–14, this form of spiritual development and mystical knowledge is forbidden by the God of Abraham, the Father of the Hebrew Jews, and will make the practitioner vulnerable to receive false christs.

Nevertheless, several Celtic, Ashkenazi Jews were attracted to Khan's Sufi Order in the West at its founding. As we saw, Hazrat Khan's first convert was a Jewish Kabbalist named Rabia Martin who brought in another Jewish Kabbalist named Samuel Lewis into her order. They met in a bookstore in San Francisco and after learning of their mutual Kabbalistic interest, they developed a friendship which would last over 20 years until Rabia Martin met a false christ named **Meher Baba**. Martin eventually handed over her Sufi disciples which she accumulated to this **wizard**.[40] Meher Baba's followers asserted that he was the **Avatar (God incarnate) of the Age**, the last in this epoch which

[38]***New Age Encyclopedia*, Melton, p. 95.**

[39]***Encyclopedia of Associations: International Organizations*, ed. Eldridge, 1993, p. 1405.**

[40]***The Book of Enlightened Masters*, Rawlinson, p. 22.**

included Zoroaster, Krishna, Rama, Buddha, Jesus, and Muhammad. Many stories of miracles and of contacts with ancient, holy men and women are told about his early years.[41] Meher Baba, whose name means "**Compassionate Father**," chose to call his brand of Sufism "**Sufism Reoriented**" after receiving disciples from Rabia Martin.

Several offshoots of Khan's original Sufi Order in the West and his son Vilayat's **ABODE OF THE MESSAGE**, as well as Meher Baba's Sufism Reoriented, have sprung up such as Baba Lovers, Friends of Meher Baba, the Society for Avatar Meher Baba in New York City, and the Baba League.[42]

Keeping in mind that Jesus foretold false christs and teachers would appear and that a universal religious and political confederacy against Him and His Bible-believing people would develop in these last days, it is most important that we are aware of how this is coming to pass. Like Zoroaster, Muhammad, the Papacy, Adam Weishaupt, and Joseph Smith, Hazrat Khan also hoped to establish his own version of a **mystical commune** of all the inhabitants throughout the known world.

When Hazrat Inayat Khan founded this new form of Sufism in San Francisco, he gathered a few disciples and after appointing the learned Kabbalist and Jewish woman named Rabia Martin as the *murshida* of the Sufi Order in the West, Khan left San Francisco with a few disciples to start more of these non-Muslim secret societies of Sufism in Europe. His first stop was in Britain where he married an American and laid the foundation of a Sufi Order there.[43] This American woman who **Hazrat Khan married was the niece of fellow Spiritualist Mary Baker Eddy, the founder of Christian Science.**[44] This Sufi Order in England was founded in 1914 by Khan, but in German-speaking countries this secret society of Sufism became known as the Zenith Institute as well.[45] Now, it's time to see how the

[41]*The Illustrated Encyclopedia of Active New Religions, Sects, and Cults*, Beit-Hallahmi, 1993, p. 183.

[42]*Ibid.*, Beit-Hallahmi, 1993, p. 183.

[43]*The Book of Enlightened Masters*, Rawlinson, p. 40.

[44]*The Joy of Sects*, Occhiogrosso, p. 449.

[45]*The Illustrated Encyclopedia of Active New Religions, Sects, and Cults*, Beit-Hallahmi, 1993, p. 279.

historical crosslinks between the New Age Movement and Islamic Illuminism developed. Another disciple of Hazrat Khan was Sheena Govan who met one of Hazrat Khan's disciples, Dorothy Maclean, in Toronto, Canada. **Dorothy Maclean was an active member of Khan's Sufi Order in the West.** However, Sheena Govan, ironically enough, was the daughter of the founder of the Evangelical Faith Mission established in the late19th century. Sheena married a fellow occultist named Peter Caddy. After becoming a disciple of Khan's brand of Sufism, Govan also wanted to branch out and develop her own following. However, Peter Caddy and Sheena Govan divorced, and Peter married Eileen Combe who, strangely enough, at the same time became one of Sheena's Sufi students. **In 1965, Peter Caddy, Eileen Caddy, and Dorothy Maclean from the Sufi Order in the West together founded another Sufi school called the Findhorn Community in northern Scotland.** The Findhorn Community developed into the most sought-after New Age center outside the United States. According to the *New Age Encyclopedia*, **Findhorn was seen as embodying the New Age ideas about the belief of receiving a spiritual transformation, and New Age leaders, especially in the United States, have looked to the Findhorn Community for guidance.**[46]

However, this is not all Findhorn became famous for. New Age Spiritualists are very vulnerable to Satan's delusions because they remain willingly ignorant of the Holy Scriptures. The Holy Scripture's warnings about devils a.k.a. fallen angels **personating heathen deities** are unnoticed by the unbelieving and, because of this, they can be seduced by the power of these devils into obeying them instead of God. Amazingly enough, the Findhorn Community also teaches how to invoke heathen deities. Eileen Caddy claimed that she had been chosen to be a **channeler** (medium). As pointed out earlier, Sufi masters believe in supernatural beings called "**jinns**." In **Hinduism**, they are called "**devas**" and the Mother Goddess is simply called a "**devi**,"[47] but in the Bible they are called "**DEVILS WORKING MIRACLES**." (See Revelation 16:14.)

[46]***New Age Encyclopedia*, Melton, p. 171.**

[47]***The Joy of Sects*, Occhiogrosso, p. 77.**

Eileen Caddy, one of the **founders of Findhorn**, claimed to channel **devas** which she was fooled into believing were **VEGETABLE DEITIES**. Soon afterwards, Dorothy Maclean, who came from the **Sufi Order in the West** and became a member of the staff at Findhorn, is also said to have channeled and made contact with these nature spirits **(kachinas)** who are commonly known among New Agers as **devas**. Like the North American Native religions, which are shamanism, the Findhorn Community in their early history became famous for their abilities to communicate with spirits and for the vegetable gardens they grew with the help of their **devas**. It is claimed by the Findhorn Community that their nature spirits (devas) were associated with various plant, species, or landscape features. The first **deva** Dorothy Maclean claimed to have invoked was said to have been a **pea deva**. Maclean was told by her **pea deva** that their garden would succeed as they co-operated with the **devas** by seeking their advice and gaining their permission to rearrange the landscape. It is said that Findhorn's garden became known throughout the neighborhood and the New Age community and attracted visitors. One of these visitors was a Spiritualist named Robert Ogilvie Crombie who invoked the **god PAN**,[48] who is not only **the god of nature** to the **pagans**, but is also **the god of music**. We will see more about **Pan** when we study the history of rock music.

By 1967, the garden at Findhorn became so famous for its crops that it was viewed by New Agers as miraculous and paranormal because of the abundance of vegetables it produced in the region's poor soil. The small Sufi group at Findhorn began to reach out to other New Age Enlightenment groups and began to receive members and in 1972, they formed the **Findhorn Foundation**. In 1970, another Spiritualist by the name of David Spangler, who wrote a booklet entitled *The Christ Spirit and the New Age* (1967), had also joined Findhorn. Spangler, before he joined the Findhorn Community, became known to the Findhorn Community because of his booklet, so he took the lead in developing the Findhorn Foundation's educational program.

Eileen Caddy and David Spangler continued to receive communications from their **devas** about love and truth and began to publish their messages, and in 1976 they published an expanded

[48]*New Age Encyclopedia*, Melton, p. 172.

version entitled *Revelation: The Birth of a New Age.* **According to *The New Age Encyclopedia*, this book written by Caddy and Spangler not only became the manifesto for the Findhorn Community, but one of the most cogent statements of the goals and ideals of the entire New Age Movement.**[49] Spangler told his readers that the New Age Movement derived from the operation of a variety of forces, including technology, astrology, and spirituality. He went on to state that astrologically the planet Earth was moving into a new cycle known as the **Age of Aquarius**, and the spiritual forces which were leading the inhabitants of this planet into this New Age were coming from a spiritual hierarchy known as the Great White Brotherhood. Spangler stated that at the top of this **Great White Brotherhood is the Solar Logos, the ruling force for this solar system.**

Another Kabbalist, besides Rabia Martin and Samuel Lewis, who stands out in history in this evolution of the New Age Enlightenment is **Gershom Scholem**. He is considered among the Ashkenazi Jews as the most learned scholar of the Kabbalah. Ironically enough, Scholem was a professor of mysticism and the Kabbalah at Jerusalem. It should be noted here that the **Hasidic Jewish community** is very open about their involvement in Spiritualism. According to the Jewish *Encyclopaedia Judaica*, it has been the **Hasidic branch** of Judaism that has been mainly involved in magic and witchcraft.[50] The Kabbalah itself is the handbook of Jewish mysticism.

In 1974, Gershom Scholem published a book about the Kabbalah entitled *Kabbalah.* Scholem was hailed by the *St. Louis Post-Dispatch* as "**the greatest living authority on Kabbalah**." The *Library Journal* said of Scholem's work: "**concise and dependable information on practically any aspect of Kabbalism**." The *Kansas City Star* said of Scholem's *Kabbalah*: "The clearest possible exposition and interpretation of a subject that will never cease to fascinate."

Reader, just what is the Kabbalah? It is nothing less than **ancient Hinduism** and **Buddhism** wrapped in **Jewish apparel**. **The Kabbalah** is also the handbook for **a sorcerer, a Satanist,** and **a witch**. Before the destruction of Jerusalem in A.D. 70, the teachings

[49]***The New Age Encyclopedia*, Melton, p. 173.**

[50]***Encyclopaedia Judaica*, Vol. 11, 1972, pp. 703–715.**

of the Kabbalah had long been cloaked in obscurity and known only by a select few. **Its basic doctrine is rooted and grounded in transmigration of the soul and yoga, as are the beliefs of the Buddhist and the Hindu, for many of the Kabbalah's mystical practices were borrowed from Hinduism via Zoroaster.** Gershom Scholem openly preached to his students that Platonic and Gnostic doctrines **are interwoven in the same beliefs as that of the Kabbalah**.[51] The Hindu and Buddhist doctrine of transmigration of the soul a.k.a. reincarnation or rebirth is known among Ashkenazi Jewry as ***Gilgul***.[52] **It is here that we can find the number-one deception of the 60s, 70s, 80s, and the 1990s which is today helping Hindus, Buddhists, Jews, Muslims, apostate Christians, and those who follow the philosophies of Confucius to find common ground in which to unite themselves under one banner.**

However, the **number-one deception** which both **Plato** and **New World Order advocates** are determined to spread politically is **forced international Socialism a.k.a. world communal living.** Today, the doctrines of **reincarnation** and **Socialism (Marxism)** are spreading like wild fire even among Christians. The Spiritualism found among the Hollywood crowd and this New World Order scheme is as popular as the magical kingdom of Walt Disney. The **public library shelves** are lined with this **New Age Socialism** and new immortality deception. As we have seen, New Age celebrities, without blinking an eye, have publicly blurted out and comically announced how they have lived many past lives. Some have even made a lot of money because of it. Knowledge about karma and reincarnation is considered among New Age Buddhists as the path to Enlightenment.

The term ***Illuminati*** means ***enlightened ones*** in Latin. Among 18th-century European and Russian revolutionists and humanist philosophers, this **enlightenment** was known as the **Age of Reason or the Age of Enlightenment**. Followers of Buddha who are seeking **enlightenment** are called a **Bodhisattva** among the Hindus and the Buddhists. This so-called illuminism of the mind among New Agers is a spiritual awakening to the belief that man is a god. However,

[51]*Kabbalah*, Scholem, p. 47.

[52]*Ibid.*, Scholem, p. 344.

according to Buddhists, the seeker of enlightenment must go through a process of the law of karma and reincarnation by living past lives in other bodies of humans or animals. Many Christians have become aware of these false teachings of the New Age Movement, however, they fail to see how our Jewish brethren who are of the flesh are not only up to their eyes in Spiritualism, but Plato's and Marx's communal message as well.

Fritz A. Rothschild, who is the Chairman of the Jewish Philosophy Department at the **Jewish Theological Seminary of America** in New York, compiled the writings of five of the most learned scholars of Ashkenazi Jewry into a book entitled *Jewish Perspectives on Christianity*. On pages 92 and 93 of this book, Rothschild, whose mother Bella Rothschild was murdered by the Nazis at Auschwitz, points out that **Plato is the founder of every system of state omnipotence and of all hierarchy**. **Plato wrote that the state alone should decide everything for its citizens, that absolute power must be given to the state, and that there must not be left to the individual any right of what is his own.** Rothschild also points out on the above pages that every secular, ecclesiastical, and every ideological dictatorship, even up to the Bolshevism of our own days, derived its teachings from Plato's ideas. Karl Marx, who was born into an Ashkenazi family, also derived his Socialist ideas from Plato. Astonishingly enough, Rothschild freely admits **"THUS JEWISH LIFE LIVES IN UNIVERSAL SOCIALISM."**[53] We will come back and study the history of the spread of Plato's Socialist ideas by Jews and New Age Christians as we continue, but let's investigate, again, from Jewish sources the origin of **Gilgul** (reincarnation) which is found in the Ashkenazi Jewish beliefs.

Vicki Mackenzie, an international bestselling New Age writer, was astonished to learn that **Hasidic Jews** also for centuries shared New Age beliefs about reincarnation. In her book entitled *Reborn in the West – The Reincarnation Masters* on pages 103–115, Mackenzie tells her story about how she became aware that Hasidic Jews believed in reincarnation through a book written by a Hasidic rabbi named Yonassan Gershom. The name of his book is *Beyond The Ashes – Cases of Reincarnation from the Holocaust*. **This Hasidic**

[53]***Jewish Perspectives on Christianity*, ed. Rothschild, p. 93.**

rabbi claimed in his book to have come in contact with Jews who had died in the Holocaust but have been reincarnated (*Gilgul*) into Gentile bodies.

Mackenzie says on page 104 of her above book that she had personally interviewed Rabbi Gershom, and he had freely told her that **Hasidic Jews certainly believe in reincarnation and that he himself was a rabbi's son in another life who had been shot in a village in Eastern Europe. Gershom said that many members of the Hasidic community deliberately have large families in order to give bodies to the souls who died in the Holocaust. Gershom went on to tell this astonished New Age writer that Isaac Luria, the Jewish rabbi and mystic of the 16th century, and Baal Shem Tov, the founder of Hasidic Jewry, both believed in the occult doctrine of transmigration of the soul a.k.a. reincarnation.**

Mackenzie, as she writes in her books, centers around how both children and adults in the United States are being taught that they are the reincarnation of some ancient lama (guru) chosen by the Buddhas to guide others on this so-called path (dharma) of enlightenment. Buddhists also believe that at death the mind (soul) of the person separates from the body and transmigrates into another body. **The Buddhist's goal is to reach perfection by conquering bad karmas in which they lived in past lives.**

The Buddhas are those who have supposedly **reached perfection** by paying back and conquering all bad deeds they have committed in their past lives. This **freedom from karma** is known as Nirvana. Those who have reached Nirvana have reached full Buddhahood. The founder of Buddhism, Gautama Buddha, taught his followers that he had reached Nirvana while meditating under a Bodhi tree. The term "***Bodhi***" signifies ***enlightenment*** and ***wisdom*** among Buddhists, and a teacher of Buddhism is called a ***Bodhisattva***. Hence, Buddhists believe that ancient Bodhisattva's souls transmigrate into bodies of the living to continue to teach others the path of Enlightenment. **Hollywood's Steven Seagal claims to be the reincarnation of a 15th-century lama.**[54] However, the most honored Bodhisattva today is the **14th Dalai Lama who claims to be the reincarnation**

[54]*Time*, October 13, 1997, p. 74.

of the bodhisattva ("buddha to be") known as Avalokiteshvara, the embodiment of compassion.[55] The Dalai Lama is considered among multitudes of adherents of New Age Spiritualism as its messiah. New Agers address him as "His Holiness." In his book, *The Path to Enlightenment*, there is a glossary in which the term ***Buddha*** is defined. It states Buddha "***means one who is purified of the obscurations to liberation and omniscience; one who has expanded his or her mind to encompass all excellences and knowledges.***"[56]

There are many voices being heard today from the gurus of Spiritualism who are preaching their version of a Path of Enlightenment and/or salvation. We will be looking at who they are and how the most famous Hollywood and Music Industry stars have made them popular worldwide. However, reader, we are warned from the Holy Scriptures, "Beware lest any man spoil you through **philosophy** and **vain deceit**, after the **tradition of men**, after the **rudiments of the world**, and not after Christ." Colossians 2:8.

About 1900 years before Christ, the God of Abraham revealed **His plan of salvation** in written form through Moses. The Hebrews were the depositories of the oracles of God. In the Old Covenant, a temporary system was set up to bring a sinner back into favor with His Maker. It was written in the Torah, which are the first five books of Moses. The Sacrificial Law, which required sinners to kill animals in symbolic ceremonies for atonement of their sins, was within the Torah. The blood of these animals was sacred and was pointing to another sacrifice which was yet to come. David, under the inspiration of the Holy Spirit, wrote of what the coming Messiah and Deliverer would do for His people. "Sacrifice and offering thou didst not desire; mine ears hast thou opened: burnt offering and sin offering hast thou not required. **Then said I, Lo, I come:** in the volume of the book it is written of me." Psalm 40:6, 7. **Jesus, who was sinless, gave His body as a sacrifice for the sins of the world.** He was the **real Lamb of God** to which the ancient Jewish Passover was pointing.

"For God so loved the world that he **gave his only begotten Son**, that whosoever believeth in him **should not perish**, but have

[55]***The World's Religions*, Clarke, p. 148.**

[56]***The Path to Enlightenment*, ed. Mullin, p. 223.**

everlasting life. For God sent not his Son into the world to condemn the world; but that the world through him might be saved. He that believeth on him is not condemned: but he that believeth not is condemned already, because he hath not believed in the name of the only begotten Son of God.

"And this is the condemnation, that **light** is come into the world, and **men loved darkness rather than light, because their deeds were evil**. For every one that doeth evil hateth the light, neither cometh to the light, lest his deeds should be reproved. **But he that doeth truth cometh to the light, that his deeds may be made manifest, that they are wrought in God." John 3:16–21.**

Jesus is the Saviour of the world; however, the apostle John warned, "**Beloved, believe not every spirit, but try the spirits** whether they are of God: because many **false prophets** are gone out into the world. Hereby know ye the Spirit of God: Every spirit that confesseth that Jesus Christ is come in the flesh is of God:

"And every spirit that confesseth not that Jesus Christ is come in the flesh is not of God: and this is that **spirit of antichrist**, whereof ye have heard that it should come; and even now already is it in the world." 1 John 4:1–3.

The apostle John warned of a **SPIRIT OF ANTICHRIST** which would come into the world. The word "***antichrist***" means "***instead of Christ***." "Jesus saith unto him, **I am the way, the truth, and the life: no man cometh unto the Father, BUT BY ME**." John 14:6. However, the Unitarian Universalist Church, like Buddhists, not only rejects that Jesus is the only Saviour of the world, but it also rejects His Divinity. Unitarians, although they have a seemingly Christian storefront, are in truth nothing less than a New Age center determined to unite all religions into a one-world religion (as their Sufi brethren are promoting). Although the Unitarians are often believed to be a Christian denomination, nevertheless, it would not take a learned Bible-believing Christian very long after visiting their churches to find out that they promote yoga and other mystical practices of mysticism.

New Agers believe that ancient astronauts (UFOs) came from the Cosmos and taught the Atlanteans the secrets of the universe in which they learned to harness the energy found in the quartz crystal.

Modern shamans say the antediluvians used this power from the crystal to develop flying machines and to power their ships before the Flood. The Atlanteans had also developed a highly advanced Utopian society a.k.a. **Golden Age** with a Utopian form of government which was divided into **TEN KINGDOMS**. In Greek mysticism, the god who founded Atlantis was Poseidon, and he had ten sons named Teitans (Titans) who divided Atlantis into **TEN KINGDOMS**. Reader, while reading the pages of this volume, please keep in mind Daniel's prophecy about Megiddo Valley in Israel and how both the books of Daniel and Revelation warn of a future confederacy of all **religions** and **nations** which shall emerge in our day having "**TEN DIVISIONS**." (See Daniel, Chapter Two, and Revelation, Chapter 17.)

According to the myth about Atlantis, it was a paradise in which its citizens had enjoyed a long Golden Age and had developed a communal (Socialist) form of government. However, as time went on, the Atlanteans misused this crystal knowledge which was supposedly a gift from their gods. They began to use this advanced knowledge to war with neighboring nations. The Atlanteans (Titans) warred also with the Olympian gods as they supposedly attacked Athens. Zeus destroyed the continent of Atlantis because of it, and only a remnant of the Atlanteans survived from the two races who supposedly lived on the continent of Atlantis. These two races were the Aryans and the Toltecs. According to New Age beliefs, the Aryans who survived the destruction of Atlantis first fled to the north while the Toltecs fled to Egypt. New Age shamans preach that the Egyptians were descendants of the Atlanteans (Toltecs) who later migrated to the Americas. This explains, they say, how the Mayans, Incas, and the Aztec Indians had knowledge about how to not only build pyramids, but why many of their signs and symbols like the swastika, the cross (†), and the zodiac were common knowledge among them.

It is historically true that the gods whom the ancient pagans worshipped on both sides of the Atlantic were, indeed, just a recollection of gods from one area in the Old World. As pointed out in more detailed documentation in my last volume, the ancient Toltecs and Aryans did have a part in promoting their versions of this religion of the worship of the sun, moon, and the stars throughout the known world. However, they originally came from Mesopotamia, not Atlantis. The Toltecs learned to build their pyramids from the Nimrodites, not from the Atlanteans.

As pointed out earlier, I have discovered while studying this New Age conspiracy that their most honored prophets from Plato to our present day have, indeed, promoted the re-establishment of the Golden Age of Atlantis before the turn of the next century. Today, the New World Order and the New Age Enlightenment Movement without a doubt have crosslinks and are trying to unite the whole world under Plato's Atlantean plan, which is to re-establish the Golden Age of Atlantis. However, today they are trying to unite all of this planet's religions and nations together under the roof of the United Nations. This plan to re-establish a New Atlantean global community during the next millennium was thoroughly studied in the documented pages of my last volume entitled *The Real Truth about UFO's and The New World Order Connection.*

However, again, just to show to the reader how, indeed, the entertainment field has been the biggest herald to help condition the minds of the people of this world to accept this New Age and New World Order plan, I want to tell my readers what my wife and I saw while we visited "**Sin City**" a.k.a. Las Vegas. Las Vegas is Sodom and Gomorrah re-established to those who follow Jesus and His teachings. It is not only a very disgusting place, but also a very dangerous place. Nevertheless, Las Vegas is one of the most sought-after and fastest growing cities now in the world. However, I have not seen a worse place on earth which lures people away from the God of Abraham to bow before Baal (Lucifer a.k.a. Satan) more than Las Vegas. I used to think New York and Hollywood were the worst cities until we visited Las Vegas during the winter of 1998. Here, witchcraft is freely promoted in the form of entertainment, and overindulgence is a way of life; here, the heathen gods of the occult are magnified and openly displayed before the eyes of their visitors. Las Vegas is a place where Egyptian and Eastern mysticism mingles with Western mysticism and where sex, perversion, gambling, and the drunkenness of Sodom and Gomorrah are socially accepted.

Las Vegas has a tour magazine entitled *What's On In Las Vegas*. It places ads for the Casino hotels and nightclubs by displaying who is performing live on their stages. In the November 18/December 1, 1997, issue, ***Caesar's Palace*** placed a full-page ad in an effort to draw people to come and view their magical world. This ad reads as follows:

"Let your imagination run wild exploring our mysterious halls, tunnels and chambers. Have a drink at our haunted bar. ENJOY GREAT DINING, ENTERTAINMENT, WIZARDS, FIREBALLS AND SORCERY. And just keep telling yourself it's only an illusion. Yeah, right. But at least you won't have a headache in the morning."[57] [sic]

In Exodus 20:3–4, **God warns His people that they are not to have other gods or graven images among them. However, at *Caesar's Palace*, the Roman gods are proudly displayed everywhere.** In one section of the hotel, you will find a shopping mall with a garden in the center. At every hour at the center of the mall, **a blast of music suddenly announces the appearance of the god Atlas**, who suddenly rises up from the garden floor. **Graven images of the god Atlas of Atlantis** and his two children become alive before astonished eyes as these statues begin to talk and move like humans. Fire and water spray out, along with a crystal which emerges from the ground in front of them. Crystal power is believed to have been given by **"ancient astronauts" to the Atlanteans**, but they misused it; and, because of it, Zeus destroyed Atlantis by earthquakes. All of this is portrayed during this free performance. My wife and I saw this performance of these mechanical and computerized lifelike graven images as we spied out the land. **We saw onlookers walk away from this pagan-influenced performance with glazed looks on their faces.**

A full-page display ad, which invites visitors to come to the *Monte Carlo Resort and Casino* to see Master Magician Lance Burton, is on page 87 of *What's On In Las Vegas*. If the reader remembers, it was the magicians of Egypt who Satan used to **counterfeit** some of the miracles which Moses did by the power of God. Today, Satan has

[57]***What's On In Las Vegas*, November 18/December 1, 1997, p. 61.**

human beings who are enslaved to him as were the Israelites to the Egyptians's Pharoah, who fought against the God of Abraham in the days of Moses. Down the street of what is called **the Strip**, there is the ***Luxor Casino and Hotel,* displaying and exalting Rameses II and Isis, Horus, and Osiris, the demoniac gods of Egypt**. Part of the *Luxor Casino and Hotel* complex is in the shape of an Egyptian pyramid with the appearance of a crystal capstone which throws a bright light at night. In addition to the crystal-like capstone, bolts of white light during nighttime hours shoot upward and downward along the four edges of the pyramid-shaped casino as onlookers, who are already dazzled by how the *Luxor Casino's* architects captured and reproduced ancient Egypt's pagan culture, look on in amazement.

Christians who have united themselves with the God of Abraham and are studied in the Holy Scriptures will unmistakenly see in the coming chapters of this volume how, indeed, it has been Hollywood (since its early days) and the Music Industry which the Dragon has been using to promote not only every immoral act known to mankind, but also Islamic and New Age mysticism and this proposed New World Order commune. When Moses came down from the presence of God after receiving the Ten Commandments, he witnessed the rebellion, dancing, drinking, sexual perversion, and idolatry of many of the Israelites as they were playing the top ten songs of their day. As Moses asked in his day, **"Who is on the Lord's side?"** when he came down from the Mountain of God, so is this same God saying today that Bible-believing Christians should separate themselves from **THE MIXED MULTITUDE TODAY** who are recycling the same sins of the ancient Israelites who rebelled against God in the days of old.

"WHEREFORE COME OUT FROM AMONG THEM, AND BE YE SEPARATE, SAITH THE LORD, AND TOUCH NOT THE UNCLEAN THING; AND I WILL RECEIVE YOU, AND WILL BE A FATHER UNTO YOU, AND YE SHALL BE MY SONS AND DAUGHTERS, SAITH THE LORD ALMIGHTY." 2 Corinthians 6:17, 18.

CHAPTER VII

ANCIENT PROPHECIES ABOUT HOLLYWOOD AND THE MUSIC INDUSTRY

"And a mighty angel took up a stone like a great millstone, and cast it into the sea, saying, Thus with violence shall that great city Babylon be thrown down, and shall be found no more at all.

"And the voice of harpers, and musicians, and of pipers, and trumpeters, shall be heard no more at all in thee; and no craftsman, of whatsoever craft he be, shall be found any more in thee; and the sound of a millstone shall be heard no more at all in thee."

Revelation 18:21, 22.

CHAPTER VII

To begin this prophetic and historical study which vividly unveils Lucifer's stealthy and strategic warfare against God's remnant people and which reveals how Lucifer (Satan) has used the entertainment field to bring human beings under his banner, we must first go to the ancient Bible prophecy of Ezekiel 28:12–19. In Ezekiel's prophecy, which was written centuries before the Son of God became "God manifest in the flesh" (1 Timothy 3:16), the ancient Hebrew prophet outlines Lucifer's rebellion in Heaven and the reward which shall come to him shortly.

"Son of man, take up a lamentation upon the king of Tyrus, and say unto him, Thus saith the Lord God; Thou sealest up the sum, full of wisdom, and perfect in beauty. **Thou hast been in Eden the garden of God**; every precious stone was thy covering, the sardius, topaz, and the diamond, the beryl, the onyx, and the jasper, the sapphire, the emerald, and the carbuncle, and gold: the workmanship of thy **TABRETS** and of thy **PIPES** was prepared in thee in the day that thou wast created.

"**Thou art the anointed cherub that covereth**; and I have set thee so: thou wast upon the holy mountain of God; thou hast walked up and down in the midst of the stones of fire. Thou wast perfect in thy ways from the day that thou wast created, till iniquity was found in thee. **By the multitude of thy merchandise they have filled the midst of thee with violence**, and thou hast sinned: therefore I will cast thee as profane out of the mountain of God: and **I will destroy thee**, O covering cherub, from the midst of the stones of fire.

"**Thine heart was lifted up because of thy beauty, thou hast corrupted thy wisdom by reason of thy brightness:** I will cast thee to the ground, I will lay thee before kings, that they may behold thee.

Thou hast defiled thy sanctuaries by the multitude of thine iniquities, by the iniquity of thy traffic; therefore will I bring forth a fire from the midst of thee, it shall devour thee, and **I wll bring thee to ashes upon the earth in the sight of all them that behold thee**. All they that know thee among the people shall be astonished at thee: **thou shalt be a terror, and never shalt thou be any more**." Ezekiel 28:12–19.

As established, the book of Revelation symbolizes Lucifer as a **red, seven-headed Dragon**. This red, seven-headed Dragon represents not only Lucifer, but also his rival religious system of astrology. Down through the many centuries, Satan has used **astrology** to not only counterfeit and counteract the worship of the Godhead, but also to overthrow the worship of the Father, His Son, and His Holy Spirit. This conflict of the ages between Christ and Lucifer is vividly portrayed in Jewish prophecy in Revelation, Chapter 12. **The seven heads on the Dragon represent astrology's "seven chief gods" in which Lucifer has hidden the worship of himself. The horned-god "Pan" is often at the top of the ancient pantheon of gods in Old World mythology.** As pointed out in *The New Age Movement and The Illuminati 666* book, Pan is not only the personification of nature, but also of music and revelry.[1] It should be remembered by the reader that **Lucifer was the "Master Musician"** in Heaven before his fall. He used his talent for music and poetry as a weapon to deceive one third of the angels in Heaven into following him instead of Christ. Hence, this same tactic, as we shall see, has proved to have been a very effective weapon of Lucifer's among human beings as well. Reader, who has more influence on the worldly-minded human beings in helping them choose how they will dress and act than the heros of the entertainment field? It would be very eye-opening, indeed, for the Bible-believing Christian to read in the May 11, 1998, issue of *People Weekly* on page 17 and see the statement expressing that many "**showbiz folk**" are today "preferring Buddhism, Scientology, and the New Age teachings of such gurus as Deepak Chopra and Marianne Williamson." The article goes on to state how rock and movie idols have crossed over to embrace the New Age Movement. It freely states that Michael Jackson left the faith of the

[1]*Man, Myth & Magic*, Vol. 14, ed. Cavendish, 1995, pp. 1972, 1973.

Jehovah's Witnesses in 1987 and is now a New Ager and has become friends with Deepak Chopra. It also states that Lisa Marie Presley, Jackson's former wife, has embraced the New Age religious beliefs of former Catholic John Travolta, which is (as we saw earlier) Scientology. This same article points out that the movie idol Tom Cruise has been a New Ager by embracing Scientology and can be quoted that he intended to become a priest. He entered a Franciscan seminary at age 14, but quickly abandoned the idea because he loved women too much to give them up. This article went on to say Madonna, ironically enough, claims to be a Catholic while, at the same time, she is a Kabbalist. Another Kabbalist is Courtney Love, who was formerly a Buddhist and who set up an altar in her home for the ashes of her late husband Kurt Cobain. Goldie Hawn is also mentioned as having embraced Buddhism as a path to life, as well as Richard Gere. According to this article in *People Weekly*, Olivia Newton-John has announced to her fans that she is also a New Ager and a follower of Deepak Chopra. It is interesting to note, however, that Charlton Heston, who played Moses in the movie, *The Ten Commandments*, and who is not a New Ager but is the newly-elected president for the National Rifle Association, is mentioned in the same above article in *People Weekly*. He reminds his fans that he is not Moses and has no religious credentials. However, it was announced in May 1998 on the news program of the *Today Show* that Charlton has publicly challenged celebrity New Agers such as Barbra Streisand to a debate about national gun laws which New Agers are determined to enforce. Streisand, however, has stated that she does not want to enter into a debate with Heston.

A lengthy article written by Ann Powers about the singer/actress Madonna and her deep connection with Spiritualism via Kabbalism and yoga can be found in ***The New York Times***. Madonna is now claiming to have a new religious experience and her new album, "Ray Of Light," is her testament of how she is shedding her kinky sex image. Madonna says, "**I'm slowly revealing who I am**."[2]

Let's again look at the incredible parallels of the worship of the gods and goddesses, which were in reality Lucifer and his fallen

[2]*The New York Times*, March 1, 1998, p. 34.

angels, and how the entertainment field is recreating the same scenes again that happened to the apostate Israelites whose deeds were not only recorded in Heaven, but were also recorded by Moses at Mt. Horeb.

There are two pagan gods Lucifer disguised himself as in antiquity who the ignorant of Scripture have exalted and worshipped because of their musical talents, and they are "**Pan**" **and** "**Osiris**." First, let's continue to see how the Dragon, "that old serpent, called the Devil, and Satan," was worshipped via the worship of Pan, the god of nature and music. It is not by chance that the Arcadian god Pan is pictured in pagan arts as a **PIPER** having two horns on his head with cloven feet. It is not by coincidence that we use the occult word "***pantheism***" to define the belief occultists have that "God and nature are one." Like the word "***pantheon***," which describes a temple dedicated to all gods, the words "***pantheism***" and "***pandemonium***" derived out of the name ***Pan***. The word "***Pan***" simply means "***all***," and in Greek mythology, this shepherd-god evolved into a figure of all-encompassing nature.[3]

Pan, who was **part man** and **part goat**, was very ugly. He was the god of the woods and enjoyed arousing terror in people in lonely places.[4] He would appear suddenly with his frightful facial expressions causing people to "***panic***." This is also the origin of the word "***pantomime***." **It means a play or some kind of entertainment using facial gestures. Pan is worshipped as Baphomet today.**

Pan was also a shepherd in Greek mythology. He often played his **seven-piped flute** while watching over flocks; hence, the origin of the history behind the **seven-piped Pan flute and Pan as the Piper**. Pan fashioned his simple pipes from a bed of reeds. This Pan flute is also known as the **syrinx**.[5] However, the lovely music that Lucifer was able to play was originally given as a gift from the Almighty God.

"The workmanship of thy **TABRETS** and of thy **PIPES was prepared in thee in the day that thou wast created**. Thou art the anointed cherub that covereth; and I have set thee so." Ezekiel 28:13, 14.

Lucifer, the Master Musician before his fall, pleased God and

[3]***Dictionary of Symbolism*, Biedermann, p. 253.**

[4]***Man, Myth & Magic*, Vol. 14, ed. Cavendish, 1995, pp. 1972, 1973.**

[5]***Dictionary of Symbolism*, Biedermann, pp. 252, 253.**

the unfallen Heavenly beings with his beautiful music. This ability to entertain the Heavenly host with music which directed its listeners to sing praises to our God gained Lucifer much appreciation and influence among the Heavenly beings. The Scriptures are silent about when Lucifer was created and how long he stayed loyal to the Godhead, but Lucifer's rebellion against our Heavenly Father did not come suddenly.

"Thou wast perfect in thy ways from the day that thou wast created, till iniquity was found in thee. Thine heart was lifted up **BECAUSE OF THY BEAUTY, thou hast corrupted thy wisdom by reason of thy brightness: I will cast thee to the ground, I will lay thee before kings, that they may behold thee**." Ezekiel 28:15, 17.

Lucifer's name means "***DAY STAR***" **or** "***LIGHT GIVER***."[6] What is the day star? It is the sun! Satan, whose name means "***destroyer***" or "***accuser***," was worshipped as the sun-god by the ignorant of God's Word from every kindred, tongue, and nation. This fiendishly-cruel tyrant and enemy of both Christ and mankind camouflaged himself as Baal, Zeus, Jupiter, Osiris, Adonis, Apollo, Brahma, Shiva, Krishna, Kulkulcán, Quetzalcoatl, Pan, Titan, etc. Revelation 9:11 says, "Whose name in the Hebrew tongue is **Abaddon, but in the Greek tongue hath his name Apollyon**." As we saw, these two names mean "***destroyer***." It is very shocking, indeed, to read how Jehovah's Witnesses, of whom I have studied and disagreed with since 1970, say in their book, *Revelation: Its Grand Climax at Hand!*, that this king of the bottomless pit (Abaddon or Apollyon) and these people symbolized as locusts represent the leader of the Jehovah's Witnesses and its church members![7]

Pan, both in Arcadian and Grecian mythology, is pictured as part man and part goat. These apparitions of **Satan or his demons appear as devas or jinns among the Sufis**. Among the **ancient Israelites**, they were pictured with **pointed ears, horns, and legs like a goat** and are known as **satyrs, according to Scripture**.[8] They also

[6]*The Interpreter's Bible*, Vol. 5, ed. Buttrick/Bowie/Scherer, p. 261.

[7]*Revelation: Its Grand Climax at Hand!*, Watchtower Bible and Tract Society of New York, pp. 142–153.

[8]Isaiah 13:21; 34:14.

appear as **elves** or **fairies**. Are not New Agers and the Hollywood crowd trying to condition the world to believe that aliens from other galaxies are coming to the earth? **Are not these apparitions of UFOs appearing on the Big Screen and television as elves?** A complete study about Atlantis (which is the central theme of the New Age Movement), UFOs, and the New World Order and its connection is all exposed in Volume Three in this series of Time of the End prophecies.

Pan, the **god of music** who is at the **head of the pantheon of gods** in many pagan traditions, is also worshipped among Satanists in just another form. This goat-like demon was/is known as the **Baphomet**[9] among Satanists and other occultists from times of antiquity to this present day. Reader, keep in mind that Lucifer's talent for playing the drums and the flute is recorded in the Scriptures. In pagan religions, the drum is a sacred instrument. The drum projects a primordial sound, divine truth, revelation, and the thunder of the gods. To the African, the drum has magical power, and to the Buddhist, it means the voice of the Law, joyous tidings, and the drum of the immortal in the darkness of the world. To the Hindu, the drum is attributed to Siva (Shiva) and Kali who are worshipped among the Hindus as the **"Destroyers." The drum, cymbals, and tambourine were all used in ecstatic dancing and to incite sexual orgies.**[10]

To show some more **parallels** between the "**show biz folks**" and how the doctrines of Illuminism and the idealogies of Marxism have crosslinks and are being promoted through the Motion Picture and/or the Music Industries, let's begin to take a look at a very popular movie that was made before *Star Wars* was released. Keeping in mind that Satan and/or his angels have been worshipped in the form of **elves** or what the Muslims called **jinns**, how did the movie, *Close Encounters of the Third Kind* (produced by Steven Spielberg in 1977), portray the aliens when they first contacted man? **They used music!** What did they look like? **They were elves.**

According to a *A Biographical Dictionary of Film*, "***Close Encounters*** is as close to a **mystical experience** as a major film has come..."[11]

[9]*Man, Myth & Magic*, Vol. 2, ed. Cavendish, 1995, p. 195.

[10]*An Illustrated Encyclopaedia of Traditional Symbols*, Cooper, pp. 56, 57.

[11]*A Biographical Dictionary of Film*, Thomson, p. 708.

Spielberg (the Jewish, Hollywood producer, director, and long-time pal and sometimes collaborator of George Lucas)[12] went on to produce movies which vividly portrayed doctrines from the Kabbalah on the Big Screen. These movies included ***Raiders of the Lost Ark*** and ***Indiana Jones and the Temple of Doom***, starring the New Age hero, Harrison Ford. In George Lucas' ***Star Wars***, did not Lucas exalt Spiritualism's (Illuminism's) power called "**THE FORCE**" a.k.a. Solar Logos and did he not show his young movie fans that Luke Skywalker's **pointed-eared elf mentor was a shaman**? Remember Peter Pan with his pointed ears and Tinker Bell, the fairy, with her wand in her hand displaying the powerful pentagram star of magic? All of these ideas were borrowed from the philosophies of ancient mythology in which Satan's worship was camouflaged and wrapped.

"The workmanship of THY TABRETS and of THY PIPES was prepared in thee in the day that thou wast created."

"THINE HEART was lifted up because of THY BEAUTY, thou hast corrupted thy wisdom by reason of THY BRIGHTNESS." Ezekiel 28:13, 17.

God says that Lucifer's problem was over his self-image and his love of himself. Can we see this same image portrayed by these lewd and proud people of the entertainment field?

Reader, the influence of music in some form is almost universal among all peoples, from the savage to the most civilized. Music and those who have been musicians, like Lucifer among the angels, have always had a powerful influence on both primitive and modern man as well. However, please keep in mind that it was God who invented music, not Lucifer. Just as Lucifer has had his musicians, so has the Father. However, it was Lucifer who perverted music to what it has become today.

According to *A New Standard Bible Dictionary*, it states the following: "It is likely that among the Hebrews, as among other peoples of antiquity, musicians as a class were somewhat definitely recognized. 'Singing men and singing women' are named as helpers at festivities (II S. 19:35; cf Ec. 2:8) and perhaps as professional mourners (Ec. 12:5; Mt. 9:23).

[12]***65 Years of the Oscar*, Osborne, p. 310.**

"Their institution is attributed to David, under the advice of Gad and Nathan (II Ch. 29:25, etc.) and they are said to have been divided into Kohathites, Asaphites, and Merarites (I Ch. 6:31–48)…. They also served on occasion with the army (II Ch. 20:21–22, 28)."[13]

Our Lord who created the heavens and the earth is really the Father of music. He gave it to the Heavenly inhabitants to bring them joy and happiness. Lucifer was once, indeed, the master conductor of music among the Heavenly host. **However, it was Christ who created Lucifer.**

Just as Lucifer had a powerful influence among the angelic host because of his musical talents, the same has been true for poets and musicians for nearly 6,000 years. **As our Father has inspired his poets and musicians, so has the Evil One.** Shortly, the reader will see why our **Lord Jesus Christ pronounced a curse on the popular music of this world**. (See Revelation 18:21, 22.)

Babylon the Great of Revelation, Chapter 17, represents the history of the people of the world whose minds have been intoxicated with the philosophies of Spiritualism, which have come to us down through the ages from the religion of astrology. As there is wisdom from above, so is there wisdom from below. As there are children of the Light, so are there children of the prince of darkness.

"Spiritually speaking," France can be called "Sodom and Egypt" because of the perversion and atheism (humanism) the revolutionaries launched against Jesus during the 18th century. The French Revolution, which was a monstrous attack on Christianity, was not only brought about by the Illuminati who infiltrated King Louis XVI's government under the auspices of Freemasonry, **but it was also brought about by the influences that the popular musicians, poets, actors, and actresses of the stage of that day had among the French citizens.** Pan a.k.a Lucifer, the god of music, used the entertainers of that day to program the young French students to turn violently against Christ and His people. Two of the most noted antichrists of that day, besides Voltaire, were a stand-up comic or clown and a female dancer. The famous comedian was known as **"Monvel;" he was the George Burns**

[13]*A New Standard Bible Dictionary*, ed. Jacobus, 1936, p. 599.

of his day. Monvel was not only a famous comedian of the third quarter of the 18th century in France, but he was also a **priest of Illuminism**[14] who was promoting among his fans hate propaganda against God and the violent overthrow of Christianity.

Another entertainer of that time who certainly could be considered an antichrist, **for there are "many antichrists"** (1 John 2:18), was a famous dancer and actress of the opera. Like Monvel, she did her best to use her popularity among her fans to promote hate propaganda against God and His Son Jesus Christ. **She was the Shirley MacLaine of her day** and, like MacLaine, looked upon herself as a goddess. This 18th-century, New Age feminist claimed that she was comparable to the Greek Goddess of Wisdom (Athena) who during the time of the French Revolution was being exalted as the "**Goddess of Reason**."

As we journey through history, there are many, many milestones which track Satan's achievements since the French Revolution in his effort to overthrow the worship of Christ. I would like to remind the reader that it was from the secret society of the **French Jacobins** that the atheistic or humanistic **red** scourge of Marxism derived which teaches today that the State should decide everything for its citizens. However, Jesus taught us to keep Church and State separate!

It is also very eye-opening, indeed, to learn how ancient mankind was switched from worshipping the True God to worshipping Pan, Osiris, or some goddess by the use of music, astrology, and lust.

In Revelation 13:4, it says the following of the people who represent spiritual Babylon the Great: **"And they worshipped the dragon which gave power unto the beast."**

It is interesting to know how Lucifer (the Dragon) was not only worshipped as the various gods and goddesses of astrology throughout the ancient world, but also as a god of music. We have already seen how Lucifer was worshipped as Pan with his symbol being the seven-piped Pan flute. We will again look at how today the people of this world are following the influences of Pan later on in Chapter Eight, but let's take a look now at a very popular god of music named **Osiris** and see how his influences are with us today.

[14]***The Prophecies of Daniel and The Revelation*, Smith, 1944, pp. 284, 285.**

It is also to our interest to see how the Israelites unwittingly and ignorantly exalted Lucifer at Mt. Horeb when they made a **golden calf**. This golden calf represented the Egyptian **sun-god Osiris, which in reality was Lucifer** (the day star). In the Egyptian myth about Osiris, the husband of **Isis**, it says that his brother Typhon became envious of him and killed him. After being slain by Typhon, Osiris' **soul transmigrated into a bull named Apis which became a symbol of divinity**. Hence, Osiris was symbolized in Egyptian mysticism as a young **bull or calf**.[15] This is the origin of where the Israelites got the idea of worshipping the golden calf along with its wild, ecstatic music which led them into sexual perversion.

Before the death of Osiris, the Egyptian myth says that the Black god Osiris and his wife Isis descended from the Cosmos to the earth to bestow gifts and blessings on its inhabitants. It was Isis who showed humans the use of wheat and barley, and it was Osiris who made the instruments of agriculture and taught men the use of them, as well as how to harness the ox to the plough. Osiris then gave men laws, the institution of marriage, a civil organization, and taught them how to worship gods. After bringing civilization to the Nile Valley, Osiris assembled a host with which he went to bestow his blessings upon the rest of the world. This Egyptian myth goes on to state that **Osiris conquered the nations of the world everywhere, not with weapons, but only with music and eloquence.**[16]

Today, this invisible Foe and Master Musician is using and repeating the same tactics which he used in the French Revolution to plunge unsuspecting human beings again into complete anarchy, however, this time worldwide! No? If the reader is still a skeptic of Bible prophecy, maybe after we journey through the history of **Hollywood's and the Music Industry's connection with both mysticism and Marxism** in the coming chapters of this volume perhaps you, too, will come to the realization that the **Dragon, "that old serpent, called the Devil, and Satan," has, indeed, "DECEIVETH THE WHOLE WORLD."** Revelation 12:9.

Before the rise of Marxism, Adam Weishaupt, the founder of the

[15]***The Two Babylons*, Hislop, p. 45.**

[16]***The Age of Fable*, Bulfinch, pp. 292, 293.**

Illuminati on May 1, 1776, and a pervert himself, did, indeed, use humanism (atheism) a.k.a. **the Religion of Reason** and the heros of the entertainment field and intellectuals of that day to help poison the minds of young, French citizens against Christianity. According to *Harper's Encyclopedia of Mystical & Paranormal Experience*, the term ***Illuminati*** was first used in Europe in the 15th century. It was a name given to the **adepts** of occultism, specifically to those who were quite learned or who possessed "**light**" from direct communication with a higher source. It was associated with occult sects and secret combinations, including the **Rosicrucians**, the **Freemasons**, the **Martinists**, the **Templars**, the **Ordo Templi Orientis** (O.T.O.), and with **Helena P. Blavatsky**, **Franz Hartmann, and Rudolf Steiner of the Theosophical Society**.[17]

Illuminism of the 18th century was antimonarchal, and it was denounced by the Bavarian government as politically dangerous. As we saw earlier, there was at the same time, however, another secret society of the Illuminati besides Adam Weishaupt's in the 18th century who was doing their best to make Spiritualism the universal religion in the world. This order of the Illuminati was founded by Louis-Claude de Saint-Martin (1743–1803), a French mystic. These orders of the Illuminati had connected with them other well-known **occult revolutionary** figures such as Goethe, Cagliostro, and Franz Anton Mesmer.[18]

As pointed out in Volumes Two and Three, the slogan for this occult Enlightenment Movement of the18th century was called ***Novus Ordo Seclorum***. Franklin and Jefferson, who were expert astrologers, used this motto to promote the American Revolution. As admitted by learned doctors of Spiritualism, politically this occult slogan means "***New World Order for the Ages***" and religiously it means the "***Age of Aquarius***."

Today, we have 20th-century successors to these conspirators who are continuing this occult attack on Christianity as I write. As Osiris set out to conquer the world by the use of music and eloquence, so have these *red* revolutionaries from both camps of the Communist and Socialist parties done the same. While the

[17]*Harper's Encyclopedia of Mystical & Paranormal Experience*, Guiley, pp. 280, 281.

[18]*Ibid.*, Guiley, pp. 280, 281.

Jacobin Clubs in France were advocating a violent overthrow of Christianity from the *left* in the 18th century, there were other socialists on the ***right*** at that time **who were using nonviolent means to achieve the Utopian goal**. Like the comedian Monvel and the self-proclaimed "Goddess of Reason" of the French Revolution, there have been entertainers just like them who are bent on conquering or overthrowing Christianity in the United States while, at the same time, they are claiming to be great religious and social reformers.

As we shall see over and over again as we continue, **mysticism today is a mixed bag of deceptions**. However, all are moving in the same direction and are being united under the same banner except **Muslim Fundamentalists** who are looking at the licentious and proud characters of Hollywood and the Music Industry with loathing. Reader, keep in mind the **THREE WOES** God said shall come upon the people of this world who do not repent of their sins and have not the **SEAL OF THE LIVING GOD IN THEIR FOREHEADS**. Again, Islam and its 1.1 billion disciples are violently opposed to the New World Order, however, let's continue to see documented evidence of how Hollywood and the Music Industry are, indeed, playing their parts in this last great drama between Christ Jesus and Satan. Daniel 12:1 said that this coming event in the history of mankind would be "**A TIME OF TROUBLE, SUCH AS NEVER WAS** since there was a nation even to that same time: **and at that time THY PEOPLE SHALL BE DELIVERED, every one that shall be found written in the book**."

In Volume Two entitled *The New Age Movement and The Illuminati 666*, I pointed out with documented proof that the ***red*** scourges of Communism (the sister of Socialism) and Socialism were both born in the same stall. In Volume Three entitled ***The Real Truth about UFO's and The New World Order Connection***, it was brought out how Plato was not only the great prophet of the New Age and New World Order schemes, but also of the "**Atlantean Plan**" which is central to modern, Western occult thinking today. Among these occult/Marxist conspirators, Plato is actually considered to be the father of the ideologies of Adam Weishaupt and Karl Marx. Communism **derived** out of the **Enlightenment Movement** of the French Revolution a.k.a. **Illuminism**, which developed into Communism after Marx published ***The Communist Manifesto*** in 1848.

Next to Plato and Marx, one of the most exalted heros of the Marxist ***red*** revolution who helped the **Socialist Dream** continue into the 19th century was from the entertainment field; his name was **George Bernard Shaw**. History records that George Bernard Shaw used his influence as a famous entertainer and writer to help convince young minds to join the **Marxist revolution**.

It was in the years of the1880s that the Socialist and propagandist George Bernard Shaw launched his efforts to overthrow Christianity. In *The Encyclopedia of World Biography*, the following is found about this antichrist:

"In 1882 Shaw's **CONVERSION TO SOCIALISM** began when he heard Henry George, the American author of *Progress and Poverty*, address a London meeting. George's message 'changed the whole current of my life.' **His reading of Karl Marx's *Das Kapital* in the same year 'made a man of me.'** For 27 years Shaw served on the **Fabian Society's** executive committee."[19]

George Bernard Shaw began his efforts to preach the gospel of the New World Order Socialist overthrow in the 1880s and died in 1950 as a great humanitarian reformer in the minds of most gullible Americans.

However, before the death of this noted entertainer and before Joseph McCarthy tried to expose Communism in high places within the United States government, **Congressman Pernell Thomas of New Jersey in the fall of 1947 exposed to the House Committee on Un-American Activities that Communists had infiltrated the Motion-Picture Industry**.

Here from the Congressional Record – House, 10770, November 24, 1947, are the words of Congressman Thomas addressing the House in Washington, D.C.:

"I would like to say to the House this eight-point program included an investigation of Fascist organizations wherever they might be found. It included an investigation of COMMUNISM IN OUR OWN GOVERNMENT. It included an investigation of COMMUNISM IN THE LABOR UNIONS. It included an investigation of COMMUNISM IN OUR ATOMIC-ENERGY PLANTS.

[19]*The Encyclopedia of World Biography*, Vol. 10, 1973, p. 25.

It included an investigation of COMMUNISM IN OUR EDUCATIONAL INSTITUTIONS. It likewise, as I have just stated, included an investigation in the MOTION-PICTURE INDUSTRY." (Emphasis mine.)

Congressman Thomas goes on to say: "**During the first week of the hearing here in Washington, we subpoenaed before us some of the most prominent producers, directors, writers, and actors in Hollywood. They all gave testimony as to the extent of Communist influences there.** During the second week we subpoenaed before us those who had been accused of being Communists or having engaged in Communist activities. They were subpoenaed because our investigation had disclosed that they were Communists or had long records of Communist affiliation and activities. Most of these later witnesses were writers–writers who receive $100,000 to $150,000 a year–and who have written the scripts for hundreds of movies which you have seen from time to time. Others were directors and producers. Most of them were members of the **Screen Writers Guild–a guild which the evidence and testimony indicated was under the influence of the Communists within it.**"

As a result of these Congressional hearings at Washington in 1947, over 300 top movie stars and prominent writers and directors, known as the infamous "**Hollywood Ten**," were exposed. **When the question, "Are you now or have you ever been a member of the Communist Party,"** was given to these ten Hollywood writers and directors, they first tried to deny it by refusing to answer this straightforward question. They all received brief jail terms for contempt. They were:

"1. Ring Lardner, Jr.
2. Edward Dmytryk
3. Robert Adrian Scott
4. Lester Cole
5. Dalton Trumbo
6. John Howard Lawson
7. Albert Maltz
8. Alvah Bessie
9. Samuel Ornitz
10. Herbert Biberman" [20]

Nevertheless, some of these ***red*** revolutionaries were again allowed to return to the Big Screen and TV Screen to continue to send pro-Marxist and anti-American messages through the scripts which

[20]***National Review*, October 27, 1989, p. 42.**

they wrote later. It was Ring Lardner, Jr. who wrote the script for *M*A*S*H** (1970), a satire about the Korean War with the Communists, that made the United States Army medical field and its leaders look like Curly, Larry, and Moe. The above blacklist of the Hollywood Ten itself received some sympathy when New Ager Barbra Streisand starred in and sang the theme for the movie, *The Way We Were* (1973). This movie was about a sympathetic Communist married to a liberal screenwriter.[21]

National Review had a story entitled "The Hollywood Ten: The Real Blacklist" by Joseph Farah. Mr. Farah is a syndicated columnist and editor of *Between the Lines*, a publication monitoring political abuses by the media and in Hollywood. He writes the following on page 42 in the *National Review*:

"In 1947, a group of prominent writers and directors known as the Hollywood 10, all members or former members of the Communist Party, refused to answer the questions of a congressional committee investigating the Party's activities in Hollywood. Each of the ten served brief jail terms for contempt.

"Forty-two years later, Hollywood's treatment of the two surviving members of that group is a study in contrasts. Ring Lardner, Jr. continues to write and is widely celebrated in the film community, a hero who wears his status as a noncooperative witness like a badge of honor. Edward Dmytryk, on the other hand, is a pariah, shunned by many of his former colleagues; he now makes a living teaching his craft to university students."

Farah goes on to point out: "The hypocrisy within the industry was never more evident than last spring when the Writers Guild of America presented Lardner with a special lifetime-achievement award for 'personal integrity;' the speeches and proclamations made it clear that he was being hailed for his refusal to answer one straightforward question from the House Committee on Un-American Activities: 'Are you now or have you ever been a member of the Communist Party?'"[22]

Once the reader realizes that Communism and international Socialism are brothers and sisters and that one is violent and one

[21]*Encyclopedia of the American Left*, Buhle/Buhle/Georgakas, p. 329.
[22]*National Review*, October 27, 1989, p. 42.

works nonviolently attacking the mind instead of the body, it is very easy to see how the degraded lifestyle of most Americans has nearly brought this country to national ruin.

As J. Edgar Hoover tried to warn years before the Congressional hearings took place in 1947, this Marxist, world revolutionary movement infiltrated Hollywood years ago in the 30s. **"Hollywood," says Farah, "because of its wealth and influence, was one of the prime targets for subversion."[23]**

In the Congressional Record for the year 1947 on page 2691 (as I pointed out in *The New Age Movement and The Illuminati 666*), it was shown that Communism did, indeed, infiltrate Hollywood. **"The American Communists launched a furtive attack on Hollywood in 1935 by the issuance of a directive calling for a concentration in Hollywood."[24]**

The Congressional Record for the year 1947 goes on to say on page 2691:

"In movie circles, Communists developed an effective defense a few years ago in meeting criticism. They would counter with the question, **'After all, what is the matter with Communism?'** It was effective because many persons did not possess adequate knowledge of the subject to give an intelligent answer."[25]

In a response to this exposure, Hollywood moguls have made a documentary trying to cover up this truth by accusing former FBI Director J. Edgar Hoover of being a homosexual of which, ironically enough, some of Hollywood's most famous citizens have been.

In my many years of research and investigation, I was astonished to discover how Marxism today is divided into many different divisions. Not only have these world revolutionaries been using the Movie Industry to promote the degradation of America to help it fall, but they have been corrupting the minds of the youth to turn against the established authority and its morality which was once based on the Christian religion. **Marxism is a poisonous *red* fog which has nearly engulfed the whole world today and is undetected by even those**

[23]*National Review*, October 27, 1989, p. 43.

[24]*The New Age Movement and The Illuminati 666*, Sutton, p. 223.

[25]*Ibid.*, Sutton, p. 223.

who oppose it. In Volume Five, the reader will learn that Marxism was not only embraced by many in the entertainment field, but the reader may be shocked to learn that there are Humanist Marxists, Catholic Marxists, Protestant Marxists, New Age Marxists, and Jewish Marxists.

Today, the cause of Marxism has been cosmetically changed to now appear to have the face of a nonviolent, kind, peace-loving, environment-conscious, Socialist movement. Instead of using force, these Socialist conspirators are using lawyers and politicians to legislate this Socialist Dream. How? They are controlling what people do in the United States through the permit and license gimmick. Just try to go into the wilderness areas of the United States to camp. We can't even get firewood today in many places in this country without first registering at the Ranger Station for a permit. Do you want to build an addition onto your house or dig a septic system? What have the lawyers and politicians legislated you must do first?

Back in 1947 and even before the Joseph McCarthy era, there were loyal Americans trying to expose Marxism/Communism in Hollywood and in our government in Washington. In the late 1940s and 1950s, the queen of television was Lucille Ball of the *I Love Lucy Show*. Even today, very few know that Lucille Ball was a member of the Communist Party. In the magazine, *The Nation*, an editorial was written about Lucy on the cover page of the May 22, 1989, issue. It is entitled, "Postcript on Lucy." This article reads:

"Everybody, as we were reminded by profuse and effusive obituaries, loved Lucy. She was zany, she was wacky, 'the first lady of CBS.' But everybody hated Communists, and Lucy–according to her September 4, 1953, testimony before the House Committee on Un-American Activities–had registered to vote as a member of the Communist Party in 1936."

This article goes on to say:

"She named no names and went back to work on Monday. Lucy told HUAC she had registered as a Communist only to make her granddad, a lifelong socialist, happy. Was Lucy putting the committee on or kowtowing to it? Which mattered more to CBS, harboring a Red or being in the black? One can't find the answer in such mainstream media as *The New York Times*, *The Washington Post*, *Time*, or

Newsweek, since none of their obits mentioned the HUAC encounter. That's at least consistent with their failure to report on the blacklist in the first place."

While actors and actresses who were members of the American Communist Party were made into great heros as they played roles in movies which promoted fornication, murder, robbery, war, and hate, the Roman Church hierarchy also saw an opportunity to promote their cause. In the 40s and 50s, many movies were produced to exalt the Roman Catholic Church. The Papacy quickly grasped the power of influence of both the Movie Industry and television. War, gangster, and orphanage movies provided a perfect setting for the Roman Catholic priest to be portrayed by Pat O'Brien, Bing Crosby, James Cagney, or Spencer Tracy as the great hero of mankind. Loretta Young also helped wipe away the dark past of the Papacy from American minds while this popular actress played the humble nun.

The Mormon Church, as well, quickly learned how to promote their cause and gain sympathy for their religious movement by producing movies about Brigham Young, which are sprinkled with romance and adventure and show some history of how Young led the exodus of Mormons from Nauvoo, Illinois, to the Salt Lake. As early as 1913, when the Motion-Picture Industry was in its early stages, the leaders of the Mormon Church began to use the Big Screen to promote Joseph Smith's plan for the Kingdom of God and his plan to subordinate all the nations of the world under his secret priesthood of the Order of Melchizedek. The Mormons, like so many other Christian denominations, are not above using pop music and worldly attractions to lure unbelievers into their fold. Donnie and Marie Osmond are their champions of the entertainment field.

Just outside of St. George, Utah, the Mormons during the summer put on an Outdoor Musical Drama called *Utah!* in an area known as Tuacahn, a Heritage Arts complex built near the cliffs of Snow Canyon State Park. **Here with their cast of almost 100**, the Mormons use music, special effects, dancing, and drama to not only gain sympathy for their version of the promotion of the Kingdom of God, but also to win new converts to Mormonism.

Volume Five will expose even more facts about the rise and evolution of the Illuminati/Marxist conspiracy and will also show on its documented pages how it was foretold in Bible prophecy. We will investigate into even more subtle mind-controlling and brainwashing tactics which were used to prepare the minds of the inhabitants of this world to accept Marxism, which derived out of the Enlightenment Movement of the 18th century. Marxism or Socialism is from the abode of Satan himself; it is his cement to paste together all Kabbalists, all New Agers, all businessmen, all politicians, all Catholics, and all Protestants who are ignorant of the Scriptures and who do not obey the Gospel of Jesus Christ. Satan may be able to succeed in bringing every scheme he has invented to lure multitudes away from taking Christ's side, but the Scriptures foretold: **"That at the name of Jesus every knee should bow, of things in heaven, and things in earth, and things under the earth; And that every tongue should confess that Jesus Christ is Lord, to the glory of God the Father." Philippians 2:10, 11.**

In the early 60s, occult, ***red*** revolutionaries especially began to promote the sins of "Sodom and Egypt" through their songs. Around the world in 1966, this "**Platonic plan**" of the occult to take this world for Lucifer was heard by New Age musicians and poets in symbolic language found in the lyrics of a popular rock song. The name of the rock song is "*Aquarius*." Here are the lyrics of the popular song which is still heralding in the New Age Enlightenment Movement today:

"When the moon is in the seventh house – And Jupiter aligns with Mars – Then peace will guide the planets – And love will steer the stars – This is the dawning of the AGE OF AQUARIUS – The Age of Aquarius – Harmony and understanding – Sympathy and trust abounding – No more falsehoods or derisions – Golden living dreams of visions – Mystic crystal revelation – And the mind's true liberation."

As pointed out to the reader, the religion of astrology is that religion of "Babylon the Great," which in the book of Revelation symbolizes all the people of the world who do not obey and believe the Gospel of Jesus Christ. However, today, New Agers who unwittingly are royal citizens of spiritual Babylon the Great think that the "**people of the book**" (the Bible) are the most ignorant and gullible people on earth. They think Bible-believing Christians have absolutely no idea what New Agers are up to as they work in the high places of the political and religious world to bring about their plan to re-establish the **Golden Age of Atlantis**. Reader, the central theme of their New Age message lies in this popular song, "*Aquarius*." **New Agers teach and believe that this world is to go through seven different ages with the last age being the "*Age of Aquarius*" to which "*Novus Ordo Seclorum*" in Latin is symbolically or astrologically pointing. Many in their ranks think that this "*Age of Aquarius*" a.k.a. Golden Age of Atlantis has now already begun.**

Nevertheless, very soon from the **"Northeast" area of the United States (where the New Age Movement gave birth) there is coming such a revival of Christianity which has not been seen since the days of Jesus and His apostles!** There shall come forth a message from Jesus through His loyal followers who shall expose not only the false claims of Socialism and mysticism, but also the truth about the "**Righteousness of Christ**" which has been cleverly hidden by Satan through his wizards whom he has used to lay the foundations of other world religions. **This loud cry of the "Third Angel" of Revelation, Chapter 14, combined with the message of the Angel of Revelation, Chapter 18,** shall be heard loud and clear from the mouths and pens of humble instruments of Jesus who shall cause these powerful wizards of the New Age Movement to rage and tremble with astonishment as they watch those who have been deceived by their witchcrafts and mystical philosophies leave their ranks and **join hands with those who "keep the commandments of God, and have the testimony of Jesus Christ (spirit of prophecy)."** (See Revelation 12:17; 19:10.) We shall study this prophecy and wonderful promise from Jesus in Volume Five.

In Revelation 18:21, 22, Jesus warns His people about the musicians of Babylon the Great and what shall become of them, their music, and their influence.

"And a mighty angel took up a stone like a great millstone, and cast it into the sea, saying, Thus with violence shall that great city Babylon be thrown down, and shall be found no more at all.

"And the voice of harpers, and musicians, and of pipers, and trumpeters, shall be heard no more at all in thee; and no craftsman, of whatsoever craft he be, shall be found any more in thee; and the sound of a millstone shall be heard no more at all in thee." Revelation 18: 21, 22.

However, to be able to expose Babylon the Great's abominations which they have committed against the Holy One of both literal and spiritual Israel, we must, of course, understand just what Babylon the Great actually is. Babylon the Great, spiritually speaking, is being built by laborers whose mortar is a mixture of Spiritualism and mysticism. These laborers are busily building a spiritual city to corral the world under one roof, shutting the True God of this world out! It should not be so shocking to the reader that so many well-known names in history shall appear in the books on earth and in Heaven as laborers and promoters of this Utopian Platonic commune if the reader will keep in mind that Jesus through His apostle John warned us that it would be "**THE GREAT MEN OF THE EARTH**" (Revelation 18:23) who the Dragon would use to war against Him and His people.

Adam Weishaupt, the founder of the secret society of the Illuminati, died in 1830 and a man named **Giuseppe Mazzini**, an Italian revolutionary, took over the leadership of the Illuminati. Mazzini wanted to update Weishaupt's plan for the 19th-century man; he did so by using Karl Marx, who once embraced Satanism, to rewrite it. As the reader knows, this became *The Communist Manifesto*. A more thorough study of this fact is found on the documented pages of Volume Two.

Reader, the world has been duped into believing that the Communist threat was put to death by Mikhail Gorbachev at Berlin in 1989, but we will see that this threat has not died; it just put on another mask. **Socialism has a violent and a nonviolent side.** Humanists, like Marx, Lenin, Trotsky, Stalin, Mao Zedong,Castro, "Che" Guevara, and other despots of the Communist parties, used military force in an effort to bring about their version of this plan of Plato and Weishaupt to re-establish the Golden or Utopian Age of Atlantis. After Adam Weishaupt, Benjamin Franklin, Thomas Jefferson, Thomas Paine, Simón Bolívar, Giuseppe Mazzini, Karl Marx, and Albert Pike passed on, Lenin, Trotsky, Stalin, Mao Zedong, Castro, "Che" Guevara, and other Latin Americans continued the violent side of this occult, world revolution. At the same time, Illuminists such as H.P. Blavatsky, Annie Besant, Mohandas (Mahatma) Gandhi, George Bernard Shaw, H.G. Wells, Sidney Webb, George Orwell, Hazrat Khan, Aleister Crowley, and Alice Bailey promoted a **nonviolent religious approach** to establish a New World Order. All of the above names were Socialists, but were from two mainstreams. In the late 19th and 20th centuries, these nonviolent, New Age and ***red*** Socialist conspirators used secret societies such as the Marxist **Fabian Society, the Theosophical Society, and the O.T.O. TO SECRETLY CONTINUE PLATO'S AND ADAM WEISHAUPT'S ATLANTEAN/ILLUMINATI PLAN. They used their pen and voice and/or used staged protests to war against unsuspecting Christians.** The historical proof of these things is recorded in Volumes Two and Three of this series of books on the prophecies from Daniel and the Revelation. However, we will again briefly study about the Fabian Society and the Theosophical Society when we look into George Bernard Shaw's and Mahatma Gandhi's connection shortly.

Among the New Age Hindus, this secret warfare to conquer their rivals, such as Christianity, by the use of nonviolent means is known as **Satyagraha.**[26] We will also investigate this Hindu technique of overcoming their enemies by the use of Satyagraha, which is nonviolent resistance, when we investigate the promotion of this Socialist Dream through the use of **folk music**.

Leninism/Marxism is a deadly scourge and often the people who are involved in it are not aware of what they are fighting for, because the Dragon "**DECEIVETH THE WHOLE WORLD**." Revelation 12:9. However, Communists know how they can use the Music and Movie Industries as a weapon to **produce culture shocks among the youth to help break down a nation's stability**. Let's look again a little at music and Lucifer's connection, and then let's turn again and look at those who have been closet Socialists and occultists and have used their influences to promote this New Age or New World Order scheme.

Music that is uplifting and soothing will help relieve a troubled heart. However, music that is devilish has not only led people into idolatry and into a degraded lifestyle, but also to commit suicide or murder. Music has also been used to send messages to its listeners. Music is spiritual. This is why we had better be careful of what kind of music we allow to enter the memory bank of our brains.

"For where your treasure is, there will your heart be also." Matthew 6:21.

[26]***The Joy of Sects*, Occhiogrosso, pp. 64, 65.**

Among the primitive peoples found throughout Babylon (the world), **music has often been linked with the spirit world through fertility rites, human sacrifices, orgies, voodoo, ritual magic, invoking gods or Satan, or summoning evil spirits**. As pointed out, the Scriptures point out that Lucifer at one time was the great Master Musician in Heaven. Ezekiel 28:13 portrays the talent Lucifer had of playing the **tabrets and pipes**. The tabret or timbrel is **a percussion instrument** and, in Biblical times, it was a small, bowl-shaped drum, perhaps a tambourine. **Sacred drums** were ever present among the Canaanites who practiced voodoo and during the practice of their fertility rites. The drums were not only to summon evil spirits, but were also used to help drown out the screams of victims who were used for human sacrifices.

Our Lord warned our ancient brethren, the Israelites, not to mingle with the people of Canaan or to adopt their culture! However, as Bible history sadly reveals, they **"were mingled among the heathen, and learned their works. And they served their idols: which were a snare unto them. Yea, they sacrificed their sons and their daughters UNTO DEVILS, And shed innocent blood, even the blood of their sons and of their daughters, whom they sacrificed unto the idols of Canaan: and the land was polluted with blood." Psalm 106:35–38.**

Voodoo drums were used to not only drown out the cries of human sacrificial victims, but were also used to stir its listeners into a state of wild excitement. What can be seen today during rock concerts and at the Mardi Gras?

In *Man, Myth & Magic*, Volume 5, we read:

The use of 'sacred' drums for magical ceremonies and as an aid for the pagan priest, magician, or shaman to put himself into a trance-like state are found all over the primitive world. The drum in the form of a tambourine has been used as the chief instrument in the practice of divination. Among the Africans, a slave was sometimes killed on a drum in hopes that his spirit would inhabit it. Among the Tibetans, there can be found drums made from human skulls.[27]

When Moses came down from the mount after receiving the two

[27]***Man, Myth & Magic*, Vol. 5, ed. Cavendish, 1995, pp. 663, 664.**

tables of stone on which were written the Ten Commandments, he met Joshua on his way. As they were nearing the camp of the Israelites, they heard strange sounds coming from the Israelite camp.

"And when Joshua heard the noise of the people as they shouted, he said unto Moses, There is a noise of war in the camp. And he said, It is not the voice of them that shout for mastery, neither is it the voice of them that cry for being overcome: but the noise of them that sing do I hear." Exodus 32:17, 18.

Moses was well aquainted with heathen drums and music, mysticism, and revelry, for he grew up in the midst of it while living among those of the Pharoah's court.

Among the ancient Babylonians and Egyptians, a young bull symbolized strength and divinity. When Moses saw the ancient Israelites holding an ancient Music and Arts Fair, he also "**saw the calf, and the dancing**" and **"saw that the people were naked." Exodus 32:19, 25. Lewd dancing and music brought the Israelites into idolatry.** The Scriptures also record that it was the **TEMPLE MUSICIANS** of Moses' day who stirred up a rebellion later among the Israelites against him. (See Numbers, Chapter 16.)

The historical records of the Bible are filled with examples for us today. What would have been the result if Moses and Joshua had lived in the summer of 1969, and they came upon the camp of nearly one-half million young people who were listening to their favorite musicians banging on their drums and strumming their guitars with some dressed in funny clothes or no clothes at all and with some dancing, clapping their hands, drinking beer, smoking pot, shouting and singing, or openly engaging in sexual intercourse on a 600-acre dairy farm in **Woodstock, New York**?

According to *And The Beat Goes On*, the **Woodstock Music and Arts Fair was hailed as the start of the millennium.**[28] Woodstock a.k.a. the Aquarian Arts Festival of 1969 is the symbol of what Plato, the prophet of Spiritualism, said would appear some day; to New Agers, **"Woodstock Nation" is a symbol of what the whole earth is to be like during what they call the coming Golden Age or Aquarian Age.** Charles Boeckman, writing positively and favorably

[28]***And The Beat Goes On*, Boeckman, p. 214.**

about the events which occurred at Woodstock, states the following in his above book on page 214:

"No one who was there will ever forget it. Nothing that has happened in recent times can quite compare with it. This is what the world should be like. This was what all the great religious leaders and prophets had in mind: a world filled with love and concern for one another. A banishment of prejudice, hatred, violence."

A world filled with love, free of prejudice, hatred, and violence Jesus promises will become a reality on the other side of the millennium. However, as pointed out before, there will never be peace on this side of the millennium until Satan, his angels, and those who placed themselves on Satan's side are destroyed in the lake of fire.

While the New Age musicians sing peace and harmony among mankind from one side of their mouth, **sex, drugs, and Spiritualism** come from the other side. A religion that gives its followers license to practice idolatry, take drugs, and commit fornication is not what one religious leader had in mind. Jesus Christ, speaking of His coming kingdom, taught:

"He that overcometh shall inherit all things; and I will be his God, and he shall be my son. But the fearful, and unbelieving, and the abominable, and murderers, and whoremongers, and sorcerers, and idolaters, and all liars, shall have their part in the lake which burneth with fire and brimstone: which is the second death." Revelation 21:7, 8.

Amazingly, to the natural man Woodstock is looked upon as a great model of how mankind should live."But the **natural man** receiveth not the things of the **Spirit of God**: for they are foolishness unto him: neither can he know them, because they are **spiritually discerned**." 1 Corinthians 2:14.

In the book, *The Story of Rock*, we read:

"The weekend celebration assembled a majority of the year's most popular groups and offered rock to crowds estimated as high as half a million people. The event became known as 'Woodstock' and the young people who were there in fact or in spirit became '**Woodstock Nation**.' It was a spectacular statement of what young people had claimed throughout the sixties: that they possessed their own culture, a world filled with music, drugs, and love, most of which were free.

During a three-day period, the dream materialized. Against a background of music–**by the Jimi Hendrix Experience, Blood, Sweat, and Tears, the Jefferson Airplane, Janis Joplin, Joan Baez, Arlo Guthrie, and Ravi Shankar,** among others–rock fans roamed the pastures of the Catskills, sharing food and water, bathing in the nude, and, most important for the event's public image, shunning violence of any kind. **Woodstock was a model of rock's communal message."**[29]

Two musicians who both came from families who were known members of the American Communist Party helped to spread **Woodstock's Communist (communal) messages**. They were Country Joe McDonald who was named by his parents after Joseph Stalin, whose nickname was also "**Country Joe**,"[30] and Arlo Guthrie, the son of the Communist folk singer, Woody Guthrie.

It was actually Joni Mitchell, however, who wrote the song "*Woodstock*," but she never attended the music festival. She watched it on television. Mitchell, at that time, gave an unknown rock band a copy of the tape of the song and Crosby, Stills, and Nash recorded "***Woodstock***" immediately. This song made Crosby, Stills, and Nash instant rock stars and a household name within the New Age Hippie Countercultural Movement.

The 1969 Woodstock Music and Arts Fair was not only a model for Plato's New Atlantis, but it was also hailed to be the model for all future rock concerts to come and was looked upon as the start of the new millennium or the **Age of Aquarius**. However, just four months later, it became not a harbinger of peace and love, but of violence and murder.

Four months after Woodstock 1969 in Altamont, California, another free rock concert for thousands of fans was held. Charles Boeckman, again in his book, records what happened. On page 215 of his book, *And The Beat Goes On*, we read the following:

"**A band of Hell's Angels**, hired for $500 worth of beer to maintain order, ran amuck, beating the crowd back with weighted pool cues. When the band played, it turned the crowd on to greater frenzy. **Mick Jagger** stopped the music repeatedly, begging the crowd to calm down, threatening to leave. But he played again

[29]***The Story of Rock*, Belz, p. 210.**

[30]***Life*, August 1994, p. 40.**

and the ugly scene like the tail-end of an LSD nightmare ground to a bloody finish as the Hell's Angel bunch knifed and stomped to death a black man who was brandishing a gun. The glory that had been Woodstock was short-lived. The innocence of the whole movement died at Altamont."

Besides this, "two fans are killed when a Plymouth convertible runs through the crowd. Another fan, under the influence of drugs, falls into an irrigation channel and drowns."[31] We will see more about what the Rolling Stones have been up to after the reader understands who Aleister Crowley was in history.

From the summer of 1969 to our present day, we have seen what wild excitement and trouble these poets and musicians who bang on their drums and strum on their electric guitars have instigated. As these head banglers pump the minds of their listeners with songs promoting Marxism, anarchy, Spiritualism, drugs, sex, perversion, violence, and revolution, the crowd is put into a frenzy. What could happen to those who continue to attend such devilish attractions is expressed in the words of the rock group, Motley Crue, who were interviewed in *People Weekly*:

"We go on tour and get broken bones, diseases, the crowd leaves bloody. It's more like going to war."[32]

What about the musical ***Hair***? Those of us who grew up with rock music since the 50s know that one of the biggest attacks launched against Christ and His righteousness in the 60s was this occult revolutionary musical of perversion. Songs that openly launched sodomy and drugs were heard, along with the New Ager's national anthem, "*Aquarius*."

The national anthem of the **Krishna consciousness movement**, which exalts the pagan messiah of Hinduism, is heard on the *Hair* album as well, along with another song called "*Hashish*," which promotes other drugs such as cocaine, alcohol, opium, and LSD. This musical actually set the stage for the Beatles and the Rolling Stones to also try to uproot Christian morality among the young student population. In the third quarter of the 18th century, these same tactics were used by the French Revolutionists to overthrow papal Christianity

[31]***The Rolling Stones Chronicle: The First Thirty Years*, Bonanno, 1990, p. 97.**

[32]***People Weekly*, January 22, 1990, pp. 90, 91.**

and to lead them into anarchy. It is most important that the reader has some knowledge and understanding of what took place in France and what led to the French Revolution because these scenes are surely being repeated today!

As the reader has probably noticed, I have repetitiously referred back to the Illuminati of Bavaria as the source of our investigation into this New World Order scheme. I am purposely doing this for the benefit of my reader. This worldwide, **occult, revolutionary conspiracy**, which was first launched by the Illuminati in the 18th century, is so broad that it is very difficult for first-time readers to grasp all of what has been written about it, so I would like to back up a little and review.

Again, let's briefly study into the Illuminati's history. The Illuminati of Bavaria, Germany, was founded on May Day, 1776, by an apostle of Lucifer named Adam Weishaupt. He planned a Socialist, world revolution which was **based in Plato's fabrication of re-establishing the Utopian government of Atlantis**. One of the ways Weishaupt planned to overthrow all governments and all religions was by getting control of the great centers of education and replacing the teachings of Christianity with a "**Religion of Reason**," which became known as **Deism**. It was from Deism or humanism that Communism derived after Karl Marx rewrote Weishaupt's plan for a New World Order. The reader needs to remember that **Marx was a Socialist, and Communism's goal is to force international Socialism**, which the leaders of the New Age Enlightenment Movement teach as well.

Both Socialism and Communism developed from the pagan philosophies of the Greek philosopher Plato. This can be easily confirmed by just scanning the pages of Plato's *The Republic*. The pagan prophet drew his ideas of a Socialist form of world government after the pattern (which he either fabricated or was inspired by Lucifer a.k.a. Satan) of the government of Atlantis.

Plato tried to sell his **Utopian/Atlantean plan** to a ruler of Syracuse, in what is now Sicily, but failed. Then, late in life, the pagan prophet of Spiritualism composed two more dialogues which picked up where *The Republic* had left off. These two dialogues became known as ***Timaeus*** and ***Critias***, and were **written around 355 B.C.** Plato wrote how the lost continent of Atlantis was established by the god Poseidon who had five sets of twin sons; the first-born child was Atlas, **for whom the continent and the surrounding ocean were named**. It was said by Plato that Poseidon divided Atlantis into **ten parts**, granting Atlas the biggest and the best portion and making him sovereign over his brothers, who were made rulers over the remaining provinces.[33]

The New World Order scheme with its **TEN DIVISIONS**, which was studied thoroughly in Volume Three, is based in Plato's Utopian/Atlantean plan. The people of the New Age and the New World Order Movements want to re-establish the government of Atlantis. However, little do these New Age conspirators know that their scheme to unite the world into a world confederacy with **ten divisions**, which is patterned after the government of Atlantis, was foretold well over two thousand years ago by this world's real Creator (Christ Jesus). The Hebrew prophet Daniel foretold an attempt to establish a world kingdom which would have ten divisions. This world kingdom was symbolized as the feet of the image which King Nebuchadnezzar had seen in a dream and also as the **ten horns** on the **Beast from the Bottomless Pit** which the apostle John later viewed in vision. Daniel prophesied:

"And whereas thou sawest the **feet and toes**, part of potters' clay, and part of iron, **the kingdom shall be divided**; but there shall be in it of the strength of the iron, forasmuch as thou sawest the iron mixed wth miry clay. And as the toes of the feet were part of iron, and part of clay, so the kingdom shall be partly strong, and partly broken.

"And whereas thou sawest iron mixed wth miry clay, they shall mingle themselves with the seed of men: **but they shall not cleave one to another, even as iron is not mixed with clay.**

"And in the days of these kings shall the God of heaven set up a kingdom, which shall never be destroyed: and the kingdom shall not be left to other people, but it shall break in pieces and consume all these kingdoms, and it shall stand for ever.

"Forasmuch as thou sawest that the stone was cut out of the mountain without hands, and that it brake in pieces the iron, the brass, the clay, the silver, and the gold; the great God hath made

[33]***Mysteries of the Unknown: Mystic Places*, Time-Life Books, pp. 15, 16.**

known to the king what shall come to pass hereafter; and **the dream is certain, and the interpretation thereof sure**." Daniel 2:41–45.

As pointed out, the apostle John prophesied about the **Angel** (king) and the **locusts** of the **BOTTOMLESS PIT** (Revelation 9:3–11). This, as we saw, is symbolizing Satan and his number-one power, which is **Spiritualism**. Sufism (Islamic mysticism), as we have seen, developed into the most powerful and secretive orders of all of Spiritualism's various divisions. Both Freemasonry and the Illuminati are children of Sufism. The Freemasons with their Muslim Order of the Mystic Shrine proves the fact that they are just a continuation of this form of mysticism. Jesus told us through John, His penman, that **another power** besides the **locusts** would come forth out of the **Bottomless Pit**. It is called the **"Beast" from the Bottomless Pit**. A beast in prophecy symbolizes a "**political power**" as in Daniel 7:17, 24, but it is not a giant computer or the Devil himself as it has been often falsely interpreted. The "**RED**" Beast from the Bottomless Pit is carrying the **Mother of Harlots** in Revelation, Chapter 17. **The red Beast from the Bottomless Pit is the political power of Spiritualism, which in the third quarter of the 18th century made war on Jesus Christ and the Holy Scriptures.** History says this political power, which is symbolized as the ***red*** Beast from the Bottomless Pit, was the **Freemasons** a.k.a. the Enlightenment Movement, who were **cells of the Illuminati** and who caused the French Revolution. It is here that the New World Order and the New Age Movement began, and it is here that the origin of Marxism can be traced.

However, Socialism and Communism did develop into slightly different ideologies. While Communism became a totalitarian dictatorship led by brutal tyrants, other Socialists, however, looked at Leninism/Stalinism and Maoism as apostasy from true Socialism. There was a split in Socialism as there was a split in Christianity and Islam. **It should be understood by the reader that the people of Spiritualism are advocating Socialism/Marxism as well.** There are those who have advocated force to bring about Plato's plan to establish a Utopian worldwide government, while others have been busy using nonviolent means to reach the Socialists' goal. If the reader will observe in Revelation, Chapter 12, the seven-headed **red** Dragon, which is symbolizing the religion of astrology and its author, has **ten horns** as well. In the astrological religion of Egypt, Osiris the sun-god, who conquered the world by using music and eloquence, also divided the world into **TEN KINGDOMS**.[34]

Keeping in mind again that the Holy Scriptures say that these ancient and modern gods of astrology are actually the **Angel from the Bottomless Pit and his other fallen angels**, it is not too difficult to see how Satan planned his last great effort to take complete control of this world by patterning this New Age and New World Order after the myths about his chief gods and their abodes in Atlantis and Egypt. In Revelation, Chapter 17, the apostle John saw in vision that this **Beast from the Bottomless Pit, which is symbolizing the world-wide political powers of Spiritualism,** also has **ten divisions**. In Revelation 17:12–14, we read the following:

"And the **ten horns** which thou sawest are **ten kings**, which have received no kingdom as yet; but receive power as kings **one hour** with the beast. These have one mind, and shall give their power and strength unto the beast. These shall make war with the Lamb, and the Lamb shall overcome them: for he is Lord of lords, and King of kings: and they that are with him are called, and chosen, and faithful."

Spiritualism is, however, divided into two mainstreams which are known as **white magic** and **black magic today**. Since the French Revolution, there have been multitudes who have been secretly working behind the scenes to bring about **Plato's "Atlantean Plan,"** which was studied thoroughly in Volume Three of this series. **An effort to unite Eastern mysticism with Western mysticism (while capturing, at the same time, unsuspecting and ignorant, young Christians who do not know their Bibles) lies at the heart of this Atlantean Plan.** Although it appears that occultists, Socialists, and Communists throughout history have had separate ideas in what they were trying to achieve, originally they all came from the same stall and have definitely had crosslinks!

The most brilliant stars among the people of white magic and the New Age who promoted this scheme from Adam Weishaupt's Illuminati to the time Karl Marx made his debut until the middle of the 20th century include the following: Giuseppe Mazzini, Albert Pike,

[34]***Dictionary of Pagan Religions*, Wedeck & Baskin, p. 322.**

Helena P. Blavatsky, Annie Besant, Franz Hartmann, Rudolf Steiner, Hazrat Khan, Mahatma Gandhi, John D. Rockefeller, Jr., Carl Jung, Edgar Cayce, Alice Bailey, and Eleanor Roosevelt. Among New Agers today, these people are considered to be the great 19th and early 20th-century heros for their cause. In black magic or Satanism, it is Aleister Crowley, Anton LaVey, Michael Aquino, Timothy Leary, the Beatles, the Rolling Stones, the Who, Ozzy Osbourne, Kiss, AC/DC, and the rock group Led Zeppelin who can, as we shall see, be credited with being among the first among the black magic disciples to promote what is known as "**death-rock music**" among the student population of America.

There is, however, yet another front or branch of this Socialist/occult world revolution, as we have seen, coming from the humanistic or atheistic standpoint. Their prophets are Plato, Hegel, the Jacobins of France, Karl Marx, Horace Greeley, George Bernard Shaw, H.G. Wells, Helen Keller, Antonio Gramsci, Harry F. Ward, Lenin, Trotsky, Stalin, "Che" Guevara, Castro, Mao Zedong, Theodor Herzl, and David Ben-Gurion. There are others, but the above are some of the most brillant stars who are considered to be among the first to help the "humanistic" side of this Socialistic, hegemonic conspiracy.

This New Age plan to unite all religions and all governments by the year 2000 also saw its beginnings in the French Revolution. It was continued by Karl Marx on the left, and later in the 19th century it was promoted by New Age Socialists on the right who were calling themselves the **Theosophical Society**. This dangerous occult and revolutionary secret society of white magic was co-founded by a witch named Helena P. Blavatsky. The Theosophical Society adopted the nonviolent approach to force international Socialism upon the world. Blavatsky continued promoting this revolutionary plan, however, from more of a religious slant. Unlike the Communists, these New Age Socialist revolutionaries used their voice and pen rather than their swords and guns to promote their ideas for **social change**. Blavatsky continued to promote this world revolution to overthrow all governments and all religions in the name of Buddhism. While promoting Plato's Socialist Dream, this 19th-century pythonist did her best to spread the lie of **"Metempsychosis," which is just another term for reincarnation or transmigration of the soul**. She also promoted the belief in Bodhisattvas a.k.a. Mahatmas a.k.a. Ascended Masters and their supposed Great White Brotherhood. Blavatsky was among the first in the West to teach yoga (meditation) and channeling. Although today it is looked upon by Spiritualists as being primitive, the Theosophical Society can be considered to be the Mother of most orders of New Age Spiritualism in the West while Freemasonry is the Father.

To gain recruits and to unite Eastern Illuminism with Western Spiritualism, Blavatsky (the New Age prophetess) co-founded the Theosophical Society to not only be a school that would teach the sciences of white magic, but would also train missionaries to spread this same plan. **Blavatsky was succeeded by Annie Besant who moved the international headquarters of the Theosophical Society to India.** It was the New Age prophet Mahatma Gandhi and the Socialist/prophetess Annie Besant who can be credited for not only overthrowing the worship of Jesus in India, but the British government as well. After Besant and Gandhi went to await their reward, another rising star of Spiritualism branched out to carry out this occult-based, ***red* revolutionary scheme**. Her name was Alice Ann Bailey. She, too, got her start by being a member of Blavatsky's Theosophical Society and, today, her writings are among the most sought-after among New Agers. However, most in the Christian community have never heard of her, but this is not the case with Gandhi. **Today, multitudes of Bible-believing Christians are confused about Gandhi; he was not a Christian. Gandhi was a Hindu Marxist, and he was a member of the Theosophical Society, as was Thomas Edison and Abner Doubleday, the inventor of baseball.[35]** A more in-depth study about Blavatsky, Besant, and Gandhi and what part they played in this occult/Socialist world revolution is written on the documented pages of Volume Three of this series.

However, again, from a humanistic and/or an atheistic slant, these same world revolutionary plans of Plato and Marx were continued by the well-known, science-fiction writer H.G. Wells and by an entertainer, critic, writer, and antichrist named George Bernard Shaw who, along with Annie Besant and Sidney Webb, ran the infamous

[35]*Encyclopedic Handbook of Cults In America*, Melton, p. 87.

secret combination in England known as the **Fabian Society**. After the death of Karl Marx and to help attract the humanists and the atheists into this world revolution, the writings of George Bernard Shaw, Eric Blair a.k.a. George Orwell, and H.G. Wells served the Socialists' cause immensely and continued to prosper these world revolutionary plans from the late 1800s through the 1940s and 1950s. Shaw, Wells, and Orwell were all at one time members of the infamous **Fabian Society** which greatly helped to secure Communism in Russia.

Jesus told us in Revelation 18:23 that the Dragon (Satan) would use "**THE GREAT MEN OF THE EARTH**" or, in other words, the **"most famous" people of the world to further his cause**. While the famous writers of the entertainment field (Shaw, Wells, and Orwell) were doing what they could to promote the Socialist Dream, **Helen Keller (1880–1967)**, as shocking as it may sound, was doing the same. Helen Keller, who died in 1967 at the age of 87, unfortunately was also drawn into this **occult-based, Marxist conspiracy** and was a very close comrade of George Bernard Shaw. Most Americans know about the disease that left her deaf, blind, and mute and how she remarkably overcame her disabilities with the help of Anne Sullivan. Keller appeared in vaudeville and in motion pictures and wrote books about the triumphs over her disabilities and campaigned for other handicapped people which made her very famous. Helen Keller's **extraordinary feats** led Mark Twain to characterize her as "the greatest woman since Joan of Arc." *Good Housekeeping* included her in its selection of "America's Twelve Greatest Women."[36] Nevertheless, this remarkable woman, who was an inspiration to millions all over the world, placed herself under the ***red*** banner of Socialism. **Today, not many Americans know that the director of the FBI, J. Edgar Hoover, maintained a detailed investigative file on Helen Keller's Socialist activities. Hoover knew she was a radical, left-wing Socialist and carefully monitored and recorded her movements.[37] This occult revolutionary** had crosslinks with both the Fabian Society and the Theosophical Society and used her influence (like Shaw, Wells, and Orwell) to promote the **Socialist Dream** to the unsuspecting American public.

[36]***Encyclopedia of the American Left*, Buhle/Buhle/Georgakas, p. 397.**
[37]***Ibid.*, Buhle/Buhle/Georgakas, p. 397.**

However, before the death of Helen Keller in 1967, a new brand of **occult/Socialist revolutionaries arose** and continued these plans for a New Age and a New World Order. We have seen a few of the most well-known prophets of Socialism from among those of white magic and humanism who helped promote this world revolution. Now, let's look again at those among black magic. We must travel back to the year 1875 to trace the origin of the world revolutionary plans of those who are considered to be the people of black magic. This was not only the date that the notorious Theosophical Society was founded, but it was also the birthdate of the first 20th-century pope of Satanism. His name was **Aleister Crowley**.

Aleister Crowley (1875–1947) was another **occult revolutionary and culture shocker**. He was also the **Simon Magus** of the 20th century. Crowley was born in Warwickshire, England, in the year the infamous Helena Blavatsky co-founded the Theosophical Society.[38] This prophet of black magic is viewed among the people of Spiritualism as one of the most celebrated magicians, sorcerers, and occult writers. Crowley, through the secret combination of the Golden Dawn from which he was expelled, taught how to set up magic circles, how to consecrate talismans, and taught and practiced ceremonial magic. He was violently against Christianity and sought to uproot any trace of the name of Jesus Christ.

Crowley, like H.P. Blavatsky and Annie Besant, saw himself as a great religious leader of a new religion and an usher of a new era or aeon of which he said would last 2,000 years.[39] Crowley was a necromancer and often invoked a spirit named **Aiwass** which he believed was worshipped in ancient Sumer of Babylonia as **Shaitan (Sheitan)**, the same **devil-god** known in ancient Eygpt as **Set**.[40] However, unlike Blavatsky and Besant, Crowley proclaimed to his Satanist followers that he was the **Antichrist** which Revelation, Chapter 13, warned about and he founded a new Order, the **Argenteum Astrum**, in which he promoted that he was the **Lord of the New Aeon**.[41]

[38]*Encyclopedia of the Unexplained*, ed. Cavendish, 1974, p. 70.

[39]*Man, Myth & Magic*, Vol. 2, ed. Cavendish, 1983, p. 559.

[40]*Encyclopedia of the Unexplained*, ed. Cavendish, 1974, p. 71.

[41]*Dictionary of Mysticism and The Occult*, Drury, p. 52.

Again, like H.P. Blavatsky and Annie Besant, Crowley claimed to have communicated with a **higher power**, or so-called ascended masters of the **Great White Brotherhood**[42] **a.k.a. UFOs** who are believed to be the ancient gods of the Babylonians, Egyptians, Greeks, Romans, etc. and who are coming to revisit this planet again. Aleister Crowley claimed to be an **adept of the Illuminati** and worked to overthrow the morals and the power of Christianity through a secret society to which he belonged called "**Ordo Templi Orientis**" (**O.T.O.**). This same secret society was co-founded by the infamous H.P. Blavatsky along with Karl Keller in 1902.[43] As pointed out in Volume Two, *The New Age Movement and The Illuminati 666*, **in the 60s this secret society (O.T.O.) had a Lodge operating under the name of "The Process Church of the Final Judgment" of which Charles Manson became a member.**[44]

Reader, to understand where all this religious and political confusion is coming from, please remember that both occultists and humanists are divided in their beliefs; they are, indeed, a mixed bag. **Occultists are divided into systems of white magic and black magic. Crowley was a prophet of black magic while Blavatsky, Besant, and Bailey were writing to those in white magic.** At the same time, Shaw, Besant, Wells, Orwell, and Keller from the Fabian Society were writing to capture humanists (atheists) and intellectual minds into joining this ***red*** revolution. **It is extremely necessary that the reader becomes aware of what these scribes of modern witchcraft and humanism promoted so that he may learn what the British *red* revolutionaries (the Beatles and the Rolling Stones rock bands) did to the American student population in the 60s and 70s.**

As H.P. Blavatsky and Alice Ann Bailey of Theosophy were two of the most sought-after writers of white magic, Aleister Crowley was and is today one of the most sought-after scribes of black magic. **Aleister Crowley, like Blavatsky and Bailey, claimed to have received information from his spirit guide as**

[42]*Encyclopedia of the Unexplained*, ed. Cavendish, p. 70.

[43]*Man, Myth & Magic*, Vol. 2. ed. Cavendish, p. 561.

[44]*The New Age Movement and The Illuminati 666*, Sutton, pp. 120–123.

he wrote about the coming New Age. As already pointed out, this spirit guide or ascended master's name, according to Crowley, was Aiwass.[45] Aiwass was nothing less than the Devil or a demon posing as an ancient dead person from the past who dictated to Crowley through his wife Rose to write his infamous book, *The Book of the Law*, which became the main theme for the rest of his books.[46] Crowley's infamous slogan, **"Do what thou wilt shall be the whole of the Law,"**[47] (which has inspired multitudes to commit every evil under the sun) is found in this book.

What is so amazing about this self-proclaimed antichrist is that **Aleister Crowley once embraced the Christian faith and was raised in a strict Plymouth Brethren Christian home**. He initially took up interests that were appropriate for an enterprising young man. He even studied at Cambridge to prepare himself academically.

However, Crowley's Christian education began to come to a halt when he met a **Buddhist monk named Alan (Allan) Bennett (1872–1923) in 1898. Bennett played an important part in establishing Buddhism, not only in the West, but in Britain and Ireland as well.** Bennett was at one time a member of the ***Order of the Golden Dawn***, as was Crowley. Bennett was ordained as a **Buddhist monk in 1902** and took the name **Ananda Metteya**. He had a strong influence on the founding of the ***Buddhist Society of Great Britain and Ireland*** in 1907.[48]

It was Alan Bennett who first introduced Crowley to ritual magic[49] and, soon afterwards, he departed from the faith, "giving heed to seducing spirits, and doctrines of devils." 1 Timothy 4:1. It was because of first being introduced to Buddhism that Aleister Crowley went on to become one of the worst sorcerers and enemies of Jesus and His people. Crowley's revolutionary and evil influences are still warring against us today through his writings.

[45]***Man, Myth & Magic*, Vol. 2, ed. Cavendish, 1983, p. 559.**

[46]***Dictionary of Mysticism and The Occult*, Drury, p. 52.**

[47]***Man, Myth & Magic*, Vol. 2, ed. Cavendish, 1983, p. 559.**

[48]***Man, Myth & Magic*, Vol. 3, ed. Cavendish, 1995, p. 302.**

[49]***Dictionary of Mysticism and The Occult*, Drury, p. 51.**

Back in 1994, the November 28 issue of *Newsweek* on pages 52–59 revealed a lengthy study about the **huge fascination which American citizens have today with mysticism and the occult**. In a *Newsweek* poll, a majority of Americans (58%) say they feel the need to experience spiritual growth, and one third of all adults, according to *Newsweek*, report having had a **mystical or religious experience**. *Newsweek* went on to report that 20% of Americans claimed to have had a revelation from God in the last year and that 13% have seen or sensed the presence of an angel. They point out how the occult has become fashionable even among the young rock idols, such as the **Beastie Boys who rap for Buddha**. They point out how Angel Records since March of 1994 has sold 2.8 million copies of the **CD *Chant* by the Benedictine monks of Santo Domingo de Silos**.

The magazine goes on to talk about occultists who take their clients to visit occult, sacred sites in the world. One such travel agency, calling itself Deja Vu Tours, is based in Berkeley, California, and, says *Newsweek*, specializes in "**spiritual adventure**" travel. It boasts that its clients have "seen the sun rise at Stonehenge, visited the '**Room of the Spirits**' at the **Dalai Lama's Monastery**, participated in rituals led by a shaman at Machu Picchu, sung a greeting to the **Kumari, the Living Goddess of Nepal**, and received baptisms in the Jordan River."[50] Bostwick, the founder of Deja Vu Tours, told *Newsweek* that her clients claim **to sense that they have lived before and want to stand in the sacred places of their past.** Another occult tour guide and fellow traveler is the **well-known channeler and American mystic, Kevin Ryerson,** who guides his clients to **Egypt** in an effort to cause his clients to **receive a mystical experience among the ancient pyramids**.

Besides Richard Gere and Harrison Ford and his wife, the Dalai Lama has recruited a host of celebrities in an effort to help him win back his throne from the Chinese. Adam Yauch of the Beastie Boys, who says he **"raps" for Buddha**, and Erin Potts in 1994 co-founded the Milarepa Fund which was named for an 11th-century

[50]*Newsweek*, November 28, 1994, p. 54.

Tibetan Buddhist saint. They have started annual Tibetan Freedom Rock Concerts of which the first two raised $1.5 million.[51] This money was used to help restore the Dalai Lama to his exalted position as the reincarnation of what Tibetan Buddhists believe is the **Avalokiteshvara** in Tibet, which we saw earlier, is a **savior** to those who are on their pathway to **enlightenment (Buddhahood)**. The word "Lama" means "**Oceanic**" or, as we also saw earlier, "**UNIVERSAL RULER**," and the Dalai Lama's rival, **THE POPE**, has other plans.

As pointed out, the prophets and apostles of the Holy Scriptures prophesied that both men and women in these last days would unite themselves with demons by connecting themselves with the religion of the Dragon, which today is a very visible symbol in the Orient.

"And I saw **three unclean spirits** like frogs come out of the mouth of the **DRAGON**, and out of the mouth of the **BEAST**, and out of the mouth of the **FALSE PROPHET**. For they are the **SPIRITS OF DEVILS, working miracles**, which go forth unto the kings of the earth and of the whole world, **TO GATHER THEM** to the battle of that great day of God Almighty." Revelation 16:13, 14.

As discussed earlier, Aleister Crowley first united himself with **spirits of devils** when the Buddhist monk, Alan Bennett, introduced Crowley to **ritual magic**,[52] and soon he learned how to invoke a demon who fooled him into believing that he was the **Egyptian god Thoth,** who the pagan Egyptians worshipped as the **god of wisdom**.[53] As pointed out so many times before, the Holy Scriptures warn us that these ancient gods are **really demons, not gods**, as the ancient and modern pagans foolishly believe.

However, while at Cairo in March of 1904, Crowley and his wife Rose, who was of the **same persuasion**, were staying near the Boulak Museum where his wife led him to look at exhibit 666 in the museum. It was a graven image of **Horus** who was one of the gods among the **Egyptian unholy trinity**.

It was the exhibit of Horus which tallied with the number 666 that

[51]***USA Today*, June 12–14, 1998, p. 7E.**

[52]***Dictionary of Mysticism and The Occult*, Drury, p. 51.**

[53]***Ibid.*, Drury, p. 51.**

first led **Crowley to imagine that he was the Antichrist**. When he was small and when he misbehaved, his mother would compare him to the **wild beast** of Revelation 13:1–10, 18, so he subsequently came to believe that he was chosen to be the Antichrist. I wrote more about this in *The New Age Movement and The Illuminati 666* book.

***The Book of the Law*, Crowley's book which multitudes of young people have raced to the public libraries to read, contains these words:**

"With my Hawk's head [i.e., Horus] I peck at the eyes of Jesus.... I flap my wings in the face of Mohammed."[54]

Crowley was certainly antichrist. However, he was just **one** of the antichrists that would appear in these last days, for "there are **many antichrists**," says 1 John 2:18. **However, THE Antichrist started his conflict with Jesus in Heaven; and before this conflict is over, Satan himself will personate Jesus Christ.**

It is interesting to note that another demon Crowley claimed to summon was **Beelzebub** of whom the Pharisees accused Jesus of casting out demons through. (See Mark 3:22–30.) **Beelzebub or Baalzebub was the chief Oriental name for Satan.**

Crowley the magician died in 1947, but his evil influences of the early 1900s did not. What Aleister Crowley contributed towards Satan's plan of the Aquarian Age conspiracy was enormous. This sorcerer's books on magic, art, fortunetelling, hallucinogenic drugs, sex, and music are ever popular today, and **his books helped inspire the early 60's poets and musicians who were of the same persuasion to bring his ideas of the New Age conspiracy and its religion to their fans. Aleister Crowley is the Father of this popular "DEATH-ROCK" music which we shall be investigating shortly.**

Crowley, who was addicted to hallucinogenic drugs, is to his disciples of Satanism as Moses and the patriarchs of God were to the Israelites. However, the reader must keep in mind this very important note about modern Spiritualism today. Modern Spiritualism is **divided into two mainstreams: white magic**, which is known today as **Wicca witchcraft** and **black magic**, which is pointing to those who are in **Satanism**. Wicca is a blend of traditions of pagan Celtic,

[54]***Dictionary of Mysticism and The Occult*, Drury, p. 52.**

Native American, and Eastern spirituality. Like Hinduism, Buddhism, Illuminism, and Islamic mysticism, their goal is to become one with divinity by attaining personal perfection through **meditation**. Like Mormonism, they believe in a Mother Goddess and are being led towards godhood. It is here that Roman Catholics can find common ground with those in Wicca witchcraft. The Roman Catholics in Latin American countries practice what is known as Santeria,[55] which is white magic found in African beliefs and is fused together with Catholicism. The Virgin Mary is the Roman Catholic's Mother Goddess.

Those who are disciples of Wicca or white magic generally do not believe that Satan exists, while Satanists believe Satan to be a principle. Those who are wrapped in the folds of Spiritualism fight over their theology and urge their own beliefs among themselves as Catholics and Protestants do. They have claims among them that their power of mysticism is more advanced than others. **The Sufi master of Islam exalts himself over all of the New Age prophets; he looks at New Age prophets as being very primitive and exaggerative about the power of their mystical claims.**

However, Aleister Crowley, a professed worshipper of Satan, publicly stated that he wanted to be Satan's right-hand man. Eventually, he learned himself that the gods he first began to worship were really Satan. As pointed out, because of his ignorance of the Holy Scriptures, Crowley thought he was chosen to be the Antichrist. As the occult revolutionary Alice Bailey mapped out a plan for those who follow her in white magic, so did the **occult revolutionary** Aleister Crowley map out a plan to take this world by the year 2000 A.D. for those in black magic.

It was Aleister Crowley who adopted the word "**magick**" to distinguish real magicians from those of the entertainment field who are just illusionists. It is interesting to note that the adherents of Sufism, which is Islamic mysticism, distinguish themselves from their pretenders and fakes by **wearing a small cloth patch on their clothing**. Albert Pike, past Sovereign Grand Commander of Freemasonry, is often seen with his Sufi cloth patch on his jackets as he posed for the camera.[56]

[55]***U.S. News & World Report*, January 26, 1998, p. 42.**

[56]***The New Age Magazine*, April 1986, p. 3.**

Let's now look at another band with a communal message which young Bible-believing Christians may be shocked to learn about. It is a historical fact that **Mick Jagger of the Rolling Stones rock band** was not only a disciple of the late Aleister Crowley who was the self-proclaimed Antichrist, but Jagger's interest about becoming a ***red*** **revolutionary was kindled at the school founded by the late Socialist, entertainer, and writer George Bernard Shaw, Annie Besant, and Sidney Webb**. The name of this school was the **London School of Economics, which was under the leadership of Sidney Webb**, and at this school Jagger learned from his comrades that the old, present order would be overthrown and replaced with **a new, "freer" society**. In January of 1969, the slogan for this London School of Economics was "**KILL THE BOURGEOISIE.**"[57]

Although Jagger is said to have disagreed with the doctrines of Marx and Lenin, the multimillionaire singer was of all things against capitalism and became a "**committed revolutionary**" who wanted to see society overthrown. **Jagger felt a revolution was coming, and he saw the Rolling Stones as the vanguard of a historical, bloody period of change.** During the Vietnam War, Mick Jagger led tens of thousands of his brainwashed, squealing fans to demonstrate their hatred of so-called American imperialism. To help kindle the flames of this occult-based, ***red*** **revolution**, Jagger wrote the song "*Street Fighting Man*" in which can be heard, "**NOW IS THE TIME FOR VIOLENT REVOLUTION**."[58] Jagger's kinky connection with the occult side of this Illuminati-inspired despotic plan is old news. Anyone who has ever listened to the radio has heard this antichrist's songs which glorify the Devil. As Aleister Crowley caught worldwide attention in the middle 1900s by claiming to be **THE ANTICHRIST, so did Jagger quickly learn that the promotion of Satanism in the Music Industry catches the rebellious, young minds of the student population who buy records.** During his rock concerts, sometimes Jagger would appear as Satan and/or the Antichrist. As I write, the Rolling Stones are still promoting through their music their mixed bag of Marxism, Spiritualism, revolution, and

[57]***The Legacy of John Lennon*, Noebel, p. 70.**

[58]***Ibid.*, Noebel, p. 71.**

anarchy, which are based in the writings of Marx and Crowley. We will see more of what the Rolling Stones were promoting through their music among the young, student population in the next chapter.

However, as the various branches of mysticism have their plans to unite their people under one banner, so does Jesus today and He promises:

"I WILL BUILD MY CHURCH; AND THE GATES OF HELL SHALL NOT PREVAIL AGAINST IT." Matthew 16:18.

It is necessary that the reader understands who Aleister Crowley was and what he taught and believed in order to understand where the so-called "**death-rock**" music and its culture, which have become so popular among the young and rebellious student population, derived.

Aleister Crowley naturally hated God and His Son and the morality that Jesus taught. As established, Crowley taught his disciples to "**DO WHAT THOU WILT**." His books are not only filled with the doctrines of metaphysics, but they promote free sex, homosexuality, and devil possession by opening oneself to be controlled by them through mind-expanding drugs, meditation (yoga), and idolatrous music.

Not only was this evil man a sorcerer, but he was also a fortuneteller. While on drugs, he wrote to his readers about the experiences he received and of the hallucinations that mind-expanding drugs would induce. Crowley, while on drugs, described his surroundings as if he was looking through a kaleidoscope seeing symmetrical designs. Here we can see where Crowley got his ideas for his abstract art in which he used forms or designs that had little or no connection with reality, but had hidden messages. This became known as psychedelic art. As pointed out in *The Real Truth about UFO's and The New World Order Connection* book and earlier in this volume, Hermes is worshipped among the people of the occult as the author of all occult sciences. Ironically enough, the symbols of the god of music, merchants, and bankers (who was known as Hermes) can clearly be seen drawn in this kind of abstract art in the mural found in the **United Nations Meditation Room**. Crowley designed his own tarot cards in this way; hence, the origin of the psychedelic art and culture among the "**Flower Children**" of the 60s which was promoted by the Beatles, the

Rolling Stones, Jimi Hendrix, etc. **Remember?** What about the drug-related song, "*Lucy in the Sky with Diamonds*," by the Beatles?

In this song, "***Lucy in the Sky with Diamonds***," John Lennon said, "I was visualizing *Alice in Wonderland*, an image of this female who would come and save me–a girl with **kaleidoscope eyes** who would be the real love of my life. Lucy turned out to be Yoko...."[59]

We will look at the Beatles and their enormous contributions to advance this **Spirit of Antichrist** and this **Marxist revolution of Lucifer's Aquarian conspiracy** in the next chapter, for the Beatles borrowed heavily from the writings of both Marx and Crowley. However, the following statement from the apostle John is for those who can hear what the Spirit is saying unto the churches:

"I have not written unto you because ye know not the truth, but because ye know it, and that no lie is of the truth. Who is a liar but he that denieth that Jesus is the Christ? He is **ANTICHRIST**, that denieth the Father and the Son." 1 John 2:21, 22.

As established, Aleister Crowley was a Satanist and hated the principles of righteousness which Jesus taught His disciples. Instead of turning away from sin and degradation, Crowley's gospel was promoting it. Crowley's New Age or the Age of Aquarius would see a society where its citizens could "**do what thou wilt**." This society was seen at **Woodstock** in the summer of 1969 where free love and free drugs were allowed and where Satan, the Master Musician, was unwittingly glorified through his poets and musicians.

One of Crowley's self-proclaimed successors of the black magic side of this New Age revolution was Timothy Leary. Leary on a *PBS* late-night television program admitted the statement below to his viewers:

"I've been an admirer of Aleister Crowley. I think that I am carrying out much of the work that he started over a hundred years ago, and the sixties themselves. You know Crowley said he was in favor of finding your own self, and, 'Do what thou wilt, shall be the whole of the law, under love'."

Timothy Leary, the former Harvard professor who was also known as a guru of LSD, was also a follower of Vedanta Hinduism. Leary

[59]***Imagine: John Lennon*, Solt/Egan, p. 145.**

was an associate of Richard Alpert, a Jew who converted to Hinduism, and after studying with a guru in India, Alpert returned to the United States and changed his name to Baba Ram Dass.[60] **Richard Alpert a.k.a. Baba Ram Dass went on to become one of the New Age Enlightenment Movement's loudest voices as it progressed during the 70s.**

A musician and Hindu guru of **kundalini yoga** named Sri Chinmoy came to the U.S. in 1964 and also attracted a number of well-known, professional jazz and rock musicians, including Larry Coryell, John McLaughlin, and **Carlos Santana.[61] As the reader may know, Carlos Santana was one of the heros from the Music Industry who promoted and appeared at the Woodstock 1969 Aquarian Arts Festival.**

I tried to point out in my book, *The New Age Movement and The Illuminati 666* which I published over a decade ago, that there is, indeed, a New Age revolution going on that Americans need to be aware of. However, when I published this I was met with much opposition and rejection. However, today, the New Age conspiracy is known by almost all Christians because these conspirators have come out of the closet and are revealing their plans openly!

As I tried to point out in 1983, this worldwide revolution is going on right now! This revolution has both a religious and a political side, and it is being fought not only by guns, bullets, bombs, and tanks. These revolutionaries are attacking Christians and worldlings alike socially, economically, politically, and religiously through their political contacts, their spiritual wickedness in high places, and through their gurus of the entertainment field!

Just as there is a Gospel of Jesus being preached to every kingdom, tongue, and nation, so is there a gospel of Satan being preached by some of these **rock'n'roll sorcerers** and actors. Just as Jesus foretold that a new heaven and a new earth is coming "wherein dwelleth righteousness," so are the Evil One's disciples prophesying that a new Utopian Age is coming in this present world where anything goes. Just as the Gospel of Jesus Christ is causing

[60]*The Joy of Sects*, Occhiogrosso, p. 67.
[61]*Ibid.*, Occhiogrosso, p. 67.

its hearers to repent and to "prepare to meet thy God," so is the gospel of this Aquarian Age preparing those who reject Jesus to unwittingly accept Satan when he personates Jesus Christ shortly.

Crowleyism promoted free sex. You shall discover that it is not by chance that we have seen so much pornography which has led warped minds to commit such atrocious acts such as rape, murder, and child molestation. **Ted Bundy, before he was put to death, said he was led to be a serial killer by first becoming an avid reader of pornography.** What has *Playboy* magazine contributed to mankind? The former associate editor of *Playboy* magazine from 1967–1971 was Robert Anton Wilson, who was also the author of *Cosmic Trigger: Final Secret of The Illuminati*. Wilson was also a disciple of Crowley and talked about Timothy Leary in his book and how he believed Leary came to fulfill what Aleister Crowley started.

As pointed out earlier, the deceptions of mysticism are of such a great variety that it is very difficult to put them all into chronological order. However, Spiritualism and Marxism are sister and brother, and this New Age and/or New World Order scheme, as we are seeing, has crosslinks. In the next chapter, we will see even more evidence of how the philosophies of Spiritualism (mysticism) and/or Marxism have, indeed, been promoted by Hollywood's and/or the Music Industry's most famous names.

CHAPTER VIII

HOW THE NEW AGE, OCCULT REVOLUTION WAS AND IS PROMOTED AMONG THE STUDENT POPULATION FROM THE 40S TO THE 90S AND HOW AMERICANS ARE BEING CONDITIONED TO ACCEPT SOCIALISM (COMMUNAL LIVING)

"But I have a few things against thee, because thou hast there them that hold the doctrine of Balaam, who taught Balac to cast a stumblingblock before the children of Israel, to eat things sacrificed unto idols, and to commit fornication.

"So hast thou also them that hold the doctrine of the Nicolaitans, which thing I hate. Repent; or else I will come unto thee quickly, and will fight against them with the sword of my mouth."

Revelation 2:14–16.

CHAPTER VIII

The apostle Paul predicted in 2 Thessalonians 2:3, 4 the following: "Let no man deceive you by any means: for that day shall not come, except there come **A FALLING AWAY FIRST**, and that man of sin be revealed, the son of perdition; Who opposeth and exalteth himself above all that is called God, or that is worshipped; so that he as God sitteth in the temple of God, shewing himself that he is God."

The apostle of Christ said that the **SECOND COMING OF JESUS** will not occur **UNTIL A FALLING AWAY COMES FIRST**. A falling away from what? Paul warns here that in our time mainstream Christians would fall into **a state of apostasy** from the Word of God. Again, the apostle warned: "Now the Spirit speaketh expressly, that in the **LATTER TIMES SOME SHALL DEPART FROM THE FAITH, GIVING HEED TO SEDUCING SPIRITS, AND DOCTINES OF DEVILS**." 1 Timothy 4:1. Let's turn now and follow the rise and evolution of rock'n'roll and how these heros of the entertainment field did, indeed, play a major part in causing multitudes of young Christians to apostatize from the **real** Jesus of the Bible.

Another **New Age hero**, who most American Christians have been ignorant of, was none other than the late Elvis Presley. Some Christians may even get mad at reading such a statement. Nevertheless, Presley is **still** today hailed by **worldly-minded Christians** as not only the King of rock'n'roll, but also one of the most listened-to gospel singers. Nevertheless, let's take a look at Elvis' career and how he did, indeed, connect himself with this world revolution of the New Age Movement.

Back in the middle 1700s in England, a woman by the name of

Ann Lee a.k.a. Mother Ann, like the Sufi, embraced the "**mystical experience**" of receiving visions by the use of wild, ecstatic dancing. In 1758, she joined a hybrid sect of Protestant Christianity which became known as the **Shakers, which was founded by James and Jane Wardley**. Ann Lee was an illiterate and uneducated blacksmith's daughter who tried to promote celibacy.[1] The Shakers included celibacy and Communism (the communal ownership of property) in their cardinal principles, and **considered themselves to be a rebirth of the original primitive pentecostal church of the Apostles.**[2] This heretical, English Protestant sect claimed to possess the Holy Spirit by whose presence and power they could perform many supernatural feats. Like the Sufis of Islamic mysticism, the Shakers would throw themselves into a **hypnotic trance** by swinging their arms forwards and backwards while whirling themselves into a **circle dance**. Dancing was central to the"**Shaking Quakers**" during which they would move their heads from side to side and twitch and jerk in odd and apparently uncontrolled ways.[3]

Ann Lee stayed with the Wardley's religious movement for 15 years. The Wardleys told their followers in England that **the Godhead was not three persons but four,**[4] **and that the Second Coming of Christ would be in the form of a woman**.[5] Later, Ann Lee would claim this female messiahship and emerged in England as a leader of the Shakers a.k.a. **Shaking Quakers** who were led to believe that Christ had returned to the earth in the person of Ann Lee. This false christ said she was going to usher in the long-predicted rule of Christ of which she erringly, like so many do today, taught that Jesus' 1000-year reign (the millennium) will be here on earth instead of in Heaven.

THE SHAKER'S MAIN MODE OF WORSHIP, HOWEVER, CONSISTED OF COMMUNAL DANCING OR FEET STAMPING AND CLAPPING, WHILE OTHERS DANCED AND SHOUTED AND/OR CHANTED AND CLAPPED TO HYMNS.

[1]***The Encyclopedia of Parapsychology and Psychical Research*, Berger, p. 276.**

[2]***Encyclopedia Americana*, Vol. 24, 1995, p. 651.**

[3]***The Encyclopedia of Parapsychology and Psychical Research*, Berger, p. 277.**

[4]***Man, Myth & Magic*, Vol. 9, ed. Cavendish, 1985, p. 2544.**

[5]***Encyclopedia Americana*, Vol. 24, 1995, p. 650.**

During this wild excitement, the Shakers would also be seen shaking or trembling as they were stamping or whirling themselves into a trance. This is where they received their name the Shakers.[6] It was during this excitement of their religious services that they were able to speak in tongues, predict forthcoming events, and heal the sick.[7] Like Joseph Smith, Ann Lee thought that her religion was the only true faith and all the other Christians were in apostasy. After being thrown in jail for disrupting an Anglican worship service by engaging in her wild, ecstatic dancing, speaking in tongues, and irreverent accusations about the Church of England during their services, Lee claimed to have been given a vision while in jail to go to America and spread her religion there. This she obeyed in 1774.[8]

Ann Lee brought her small band of disciples to the Northeast area of America to a wilderness settlement at Watervliet, New York. The Shaking Quakers continued their wild, religious fervor even after their female Christ proved herself to be a false christ by dying on them. Ann Lee's promise and prophecy of ushering the long-expected millennial Reign of Christ in this present world died with Mother Ann. However, the Shaking Quakers' practice of Spiritualism continued. During their whirling, shaking, and trembling while under a trance-like state, the Shakers claimed that the spirits of ancient Indians would come and knock on the door while a Shaker meeting was taking place **AND ASK FOR PERMISSION TO ENTER**. After receiving permission to enter, these spirits would then proceed to take possession of their bodies and they would speak in tongues of Indians. It was reported that the Shakers **after being possessed by these spirits would begin shouting and whooping and dancing Indian dances**.[9] This counterfeit power of what the first apostles received on the day of Pentecost (Acts, Chapter Two) is known both to the New Agers and Christians. This phenomenon is called **"GLOSSOLALIA," WHICH IS PRODUCED DURING STATES OF INTENSE RELIGIOUS EXCITEMENT**.[10]

[6]***Man, Myth & Magic*, Vol. 9, ed. Cavendish, 1985, p. 544.**

[7]***Encyclopedia Americana*, Vol. 24, 1995, p. 650.**

[8]***Ibid.*, Vol. 24, 1995, p. 650.**

[9]***The Spiritualists*, Brandon, p. 38.**

[10]***The New Encyclopaedia Britannica***, Micropaedia, Vol. 11, 1997, p. 842.

According to *Mormonism – Shadow or Reality?* on page 63, Martin Harris, who was one of the three original scribes who wrote down the Book of Mormon while Joseph Smith was supposedly divining it via his peepstone, later left Mormonism and joined the Shakers.

Let's look a little at the modern, Pentecostal movement. It is here that we can begin to trace the evolution of the "**wild, ecstatic excitement**" of the modern-day Pentecostal movements which began at the turn of the 20th century in the United States. The Shakers are, indeed, the forerunners of this wild, ecstatic excitement of Pentecostalism which is vividly seen in the Black and White churches. Musicians, who call themselves disciples and followers of the Meek and Lowly Jesus, have crossed over the line which had at one time separated the Holy from the profane to adopt hillbilly, rock, contemporary, and even rap music into Christianity and have blended them with the worship of Jesus.

Elvis Presley was one of the first gospel singers to cross over into pop music and sing songs which promoted sex and romance. Presley's family were Pentecostals and he grew up in this kind of a fanatical childhood. While attending the services of some Pentecostal Churches, this writer has seen this same wild, unholy bedlam of music and so-called dancing in the Spirit as they bounce around the church or stand trembling or shaking or wooing like a ghost and blurting out from their mouths jabber that supposedly gives evidence in Pentecostal ears that they have the gift of the Holy Spirit. One of the first Christian crusades I attended in Hawaii (while trying to understand who Jesus was) was the Full Gospel and Business Men Fellowship. It was at this Pentecostal gathering in 1971 that I had my first encounter of this wild spectacle mentioned above and, I must say, it was very frightening to me. What was even more frightening was when I was told by Pentecostals that "**if you don't speak in tongues, you don't have the Holy Spirit**." Even though I did not know the Bible back then and what it really taught about this subject, I still knew that what the Pentecostal Protestants asserted was as false as Baal worship. Jesus said, "By their fruits ye shall know them." The apostle Paul stated that when we have the Holy Spirit, it would produce fruit which is **"LOVE, JOY, PEACE, LONGSUFFERING, GENTLENESS, GOODNESS, FAITH, MEEKNESS, TEMPERANCE: against such there is no law. AND THEY THAT ARE**

CHRIST'S HAVE CRUCIFIED THE FLESH WITH THE AFFECTIONS AND LUSTS. If we live in the Spirit, let us also walk in the Spirit." Galatians 5:22–25. Reader, what kind of fruits or gifts of the Holy Spirit did Elvis display throughout his career? Was he a religious reformer who demonstrated the character of the **Sinless One of Israel** or was he an open rebel who led multitudes away from Him?

In 1954, Presley, while claiming to be a Christian, caused one of the first in a series of "**culture shocks**" which the student population experienced in America during the years before the Beatles made their debut ten years later. In the year 1954, Elvis Presley with his long sideburns recorded the song, "*That's All Right.*" **This song marked a turning point in not only the history of American popular music, but in the morality of Americans as well.** Elvis blended Black rhythm and blues with country and western music while he, at the same time, blended the images of James Dean, Marlon Brando, and Tony Curtis who were heros of his.[11] This sent high school girls screaming and fainting and boys trying to grow long sideburns.

Otis Blackwell, who was one of the most well-known, Black rhythm and blues songwriters of all time, was the author of Presley's "*Don't Be Cruel*" and "*All Shook Up.*"[12] Presley had 14 consecutive million-sellers, RCA claimed, simultaneously topping pop, country, and rhythm and blues charts. His lewd gestures and the sexual connotations in the lyrics of his songs became a test for the nation's moral fiber.

Ed Sullivan, who said he would never allow Elvis Presley on his television show, found himself signing Presley to a $50,000 contract in 1956. It was the *Ed Sullivan Show* that really caused Presley's career to take off, as did later the Beatles as well. Presley set the stage for other rock stars to be allowed to promote sexually-stimulating songs and lasciviousness on stage and on television. Ironically, Elvis' career as a pop singer started in a Christian Church. Speaking of the Pentecostal preachers he watched as they "cut up all over the place, jumping on the piano, moving every which way," Elvis said, "I guess I learned from them."[13]

[11]***The Rolling Stone Illustrated History of Rock & Roll*, ed. DeCurtis/Henke, p. 21.**
[12]***Ibid.*, ed. DeCurtis/Henke, p. 27.**
[13]***Ibid.*, ed. DeCurtis/Henke, p. 25.**

Rock singers like Jerry Lee Lewis, Little Richard, Pat Boone, Ray Charles, Sam Cooke, Dionne Warwick, and the "Queen of Soul Music," Aretha Franklin – **all got their start by first singing hymns about Jesus in their churches.**[14] Aretha Franklin, who sang in her father's Detroit Baptist Church, had made her first solo record at age 14. Franklin toured the gospel circuit until 1961 when she **crossed over** to sing songs about sex and romance,[15] as did Dionne Warwick, who ended up promoting Spiritualism as the hostess of **Psychic Friends Network, and La Toya Jackson, as well, from her own La Toya Jackson's Psychic Network**. Warwick is the cousin of Cissy Houston, who is the mother of Whitney Houston, who calls Aretha Franklin *Aunty Ree*.[16]

Whitney Houston, like Warwick and Franklin, got her singing career started by singing hymns about Christ. Houston made a solo debut at age 11 singing "*Guide Me, O Thou Great Jehovah*" in the Baptist Church. Then, like her famous relatives, she later **crossed over** and sang songs promoting sex and romance, like "*You Give Good Love*" or "*Saving All My Love For You*."[17] John Lennon, while performing with his amateur skiffle group, the Quarrymen, at a church picnic on July 6, 1957, met Paul McCartney and asked him to join his group. McCartney convinced Lennon to let George Harrison join too and in 1958 they changed their name to Johnny and the Moondogs.[18]

Keeping in mind that Spiritualism is divided into two camps, the King of rock'n'roll, Elvis Presley, cannot be branded as a man who promoted Satanism. However, he was, indeed, **a victim of New Age pantheism**. In the book, *The Rolling Stone Illustrated History of Rock & Roll*, it states the following:

"By 1968 Elvis had exhausted his audience, as well as himself, with movies that were no longer drawing, records that, devoid of even a semblance of commitment, were no longer selling. The Beatles, the Rolling Stones, and Dylan had eclipsed their onetime mentor....

[14]*The Penguin Encyclopedia of Popular Music*, ed. Clarke, pp. 478–480.

[15]*Ibid.*, ed. Clarke, p. 434.

[16]*Ibid.*, ed. Clarke, p. 566.

[17]*Ibid.*, ed. Clarke, p. 566.

[18]*The New Rolling Stone Encyclopedia of Rock & Roll*, ed. Romanowski/ George-Warren, p. 59.

"Elvis's final years were a grotesque parade of tabloid headlines (Elvis at 40–Paunchy, Depressed, and Living in Fear....) and disturbing personal revelations (*Elvis: What Happened?* written by renegade members of the Memphis Mafia and on the newsstands just days before his death, told a dark tale of drugs, **spiritualism, and paranoia**)."[19]

Larry Geller, a New Ager who was Elvis Presley's hair stylist, friend, and guru, also wrote about Elvis's involvement with Spiritualism and of his life and career. The name of his book is *If I Can Dream: Elvis' Own Story*.

Larry Geller first became a hair stylist for entertainers of the Hollywood scene in 1959. He said that as he was nearing the completion of his studies in cosmetology at age 19, he happened to walk past a hair salon on Fairfax Avenue in Hollywood. There on the front door of the salon, he spotted the pagan Egyptian symbol of life, the **ankh**. As he entered the salon, he met Jay Sebring, whose real name was Thomas Kummer.[20] Even though Larry Geller did not have any experience as a hair stylist at this time, he was hired immediately by Jay Sebring.

Soon the new salon grew and in a few months it had clients who included Frank Sinatra, Glen Campbell, Robert Wagner, Peter Sellers, George Peppard, George Hamilton, Robert Conrad, Henry Fonda, Cliff Robertson, Milton Berle, Steve McQueen, Steve Allen, Robert Vaughan, Tony Franciosa, Robert Culp, and many others. Geller said on page 18 of the above book that Jay Sebring's salon "was without question the hottest salon in Hollywood. We put in eighteen-hour days, and even the biggest stars would patiently wait their turns."

Meanwhile, Larry Geller said in August of 1960 he was driving on Route 66 to see the sacred mountains of the Hopi Indians in Arizona, and he suddenly "experienced something so powerful that the only thing I can compare it to is being struck by lightning. In a few moments there in the desert, I was reborn and experienced a remarkable awakening that changed the course of my life."[21]

[19]*The Rolling Stone Illustrated History of Rock & Roll*, ed. DeCurtis/Henke, pp. 32, 34.

[20]*If I Can Dream: Elvis' Own Story*, Geller, pp. 17.

[21]*Ibid.*, Geller, p. 18.

Soon Geller's quest for knowledge into Spiritualism led him into various New Age techniques and systems which brought him into yoga, Tai Chi, meditation, vegetarianism, the study of the Cabala, Taoism, Buddhism, Judaism, and Christianity.[22]

During this time, Jay Sebring's hair styling salon became a virtual Hollywood *Who's Who*, and Elvis Presley at that time in 1964 was living in the Los Angeles area. He sent for Larry Geller to come to his house in Bel Air to fix his hair. **While Geller was doing Elvis Presley's hair, he found out that Elvis was also seeking New Age mysticism.** They were surprised to hear each other's common interest in metaphysics because at that time talking about such things was not the thing to do.[23]

However, Elvis Presley now finally found someone of the same persuasion to talk to about metaphysics and asked Geller in 1964 to work for him full-time as his hair stylist. Geller accepted the position. This proved to be a lifesaver, perhaps, for Geller. About five years later, **Jay Sebring**, who Geller worked for, would meet some other disciples of metaphysical persuasion whose leader was also a musician. Charles Manson's disciples murdered Jay Sebring, along with Sharon Tate, a former lover of Jay's and wife of movie director Roman Polanski. It is also eye-opening to learn that before these horrible murders took place, Dennis Wilson of the Beach Boys also had a connection with Charles Manson a.k.a. Jesus Christ/Satan. Wilson paid Manson, who was also a song writer, $5000 for two songs that he had written. Wilson was a friend of Manson, who was even his houseguest sometime before the murders took place. Wilson had nothing to do with these murders. He had parted company with Manson and his family before the murders after being exploited by them of $100,000. After Manson's arrest, Wilson was subject to constant death threats from others of Manson's Family.[24]

In the meantime, Larry Geller (according to his book) became Elvis' best friend, confidant, and spiritual adviser. Geller introduced

[22]***If I Can Dream: Elvis' Own Story*, Geller, p. 19.**

[23]***Ibid.*, Geller, p. 23.**

[24]***The Marshall Cavendish Illustrated History of Popular Music*, Vol. 6, ed. Cavendish, p. 780.**

Elvis to a host of books on New Age mysticism and beliefs which he shows in the back of his book. With the books Geller introduced Elvis to and those Elvis gathered himself, Elvis had a private collection of books on the esoteric arts of New Age white magic that totaled to nearly 1,000. Among Elvis' library were books written by the infamous Russian magician, channeler, and sorceress, Helena Petrovna Blavatsky. Elvis had Blavatsky's *Isis Unveiled* and *The Secret Doctrine* along with Alice Bailey's books on how the New Agers would overthrow all governments and religions before the year 2000 A.D.

According to Larry Geller, the first book on metaphysics that Elvis read was *The Impersonal Life* by Joseph Benner who, like Blavatsky, claimed to communicate with this secret brotherhood of spirit guides from the Great White Brotherhood, as did Annie Besant, Alice Bailey, and Aleister Crowley. Benner claimed, like J.Z. Knight and Shirley MacLaine, that he was a channel to bring mankind a message to seek the knowledge that man has a higher self and that mankind is also a god, but must be awakened to his self-potential. This is known as Self-Realization.

Elvis was, indeed, a victim of this lie. New Age Spiritualism blends elements of Christianity but rejects Jesus as the Son of the Living God, and so did Elvis. **Elvis acquired his ideas of wearing high-collared shirts and jumpsuits from drawings of various so-called masters (teachers) of metaphysics he saw as he read these books.** However, according to Geller, Elvis never claimed to be a channeler, but did claim to be guided by the **Great White Brotherhood**.[25]

It appears that Elvis Presley was not involved with Aleister Crowley's black magic. Black magic hates all forms of Christian doctrine and teaches to do the very opposite. Those who practice black magic or Satanism often observe the ritual of the Black Mass which is acted out to mock the Roman Catholic Mass. Satanists ignorantly view Christianity as including only the Roman Catholic faith and fail to see how Bible-believing Christians also reject the proud claims of her popes. To mock the power of the Papacy, Satanists turn the pagan crucifix upside down, recite the Lord's prayer backwards, use filthy water instead of holy water, use a naked woman as an altar,

[25]*If I Can Dream: Elvis' Own Story*, Geller, pp. 138, 139.

wear black attire instead of white during their rituals, and shun everything to the right because Jesus is said to be seated at the right side of the Father. However, contemporary witchcraft and/or white magic accepts Jesus as a great teacher and sometimes his mother as a goddess, rather than Isis or Diana. Nevertheless, Wiccans, at the same time, **reject the divinity of Christ**. Like Sufism, modern witchcraft has developed into a mixed bag, and they can easily be confused from one to another. Contemporary witchcraft a.k.a. **WICCA** was founded by Gerald B. Gardner (1884–1964) who spent most of his years in southern Asia seeking a knowledge of magic. He became a Freemason and joined a Theosophical group calling itself the Fellowship of Crotona. Gardner used a Wiccan name of "Scire" under which he wrote and published a number of books. He took **Oriental and Western mysticism** and fused them together and created a new religion centered upon the worship of a **Mother Goddess and her consort, the horned-god Pan**. Gardner started a coven in which he began to initiate several of his converts and among them were **the Illuminist Sybil Leek, Alexander Sanders, and Raymond and Rosemary Buckland**.[26] During the 60s, however, Wicca split into several independent covens across the United States.

As we showed earlier, white magic teaches that diligent seekers of occult knowledge can reach Christ-consciousness and become a god. The goal of adherents of mysticism on both sides of the Atlantic is to become one with divinity by attaining personal perfection (godhood). This subtle lie that man can become a god was Satan's second lie to Eve. (See Genesis 3:5.) This doctrine can be found especially in Hinduism and Buddhism which we examined earlier.

Sadly enough, such was the confused belief of Elvis Presley when he suddenly died in 1977 at his Graceland, Tennessee, estate. According to Larry Geller, Elvis changed his mind about Jesus being the only begotten Son of the Father when he read a book called *The Initiation of the World* written by Vera Stanley Alder.[27] This book

[26]*Encyclopedic Handbook of Cults in America*, Melton, pp. 211–213.

[27]*If I Can Dream: Elvis' Own Story*, Geller, pp. 138, 139.

introduced Elvis to this so-called group of "**spiritual masters**" called the Great White Brotherhood, whose job it is to oversee human affairs.[28]

Like Blavatsky, Bailey, and other Christians who left the faith, giving heed to seducing spirits and doctrines of devils, **Elvis eventually believed that he was working under the aegis of these masters, including Jesus**. Larry Geller said on pages 138 and 139 of his book, *If I Can Dream: Elvis' Own Story*, that **Presley had a different conception of Jesus depicted by the Bible and modern Christianity**.

According to Brad and Sherry Steiger, who are noted New Age writers, Presley was deeply involved in New Age beliefs. **He believed in past-life experiences, UFOs, and he thought of himself as a star man who in another life was from the Blue Star Planet.**[29] According to Geller, Presley, like H.P. Blavatsky, believed in the Great White Brotherhood and, in his mind, his life was being directed divinely by this brotherhood of masters. Geller states in his book that **Elvis Presley TRULY FELT THAT HE WAS CHOSEN TO BE HERE NOW AS A MODERN-DAY SAVIOR, A CHRIST.**[30]

I was not only deeply shocked when I was made aware of this statement, but I was also deeply saddened for Elvis was once my hero when I was 12 years old. Like most Americans, back then I had no understanding about the subtleness of Spiritualism and how it has established itself especially among the rock'n'rollers. **Elvis even called his back-up band the *New Age Voice*, which was named after the magazine Larry Geller published.**

While Elvis promoted the philosophies of the New Age Movement or white magic, the Beatles promoted Spiritualism's dark side. Please keep in mind that Spiritualism is divided into two mainstreams: white magic and black magic or Wicca witchcraft and Satanism. In this volume, we will not only examine what the Beatles contributed to this mixed bag of the occult's Aquarian conspiracy and the promotion of Socialism, but we will also look

[28]***If I Can Dream: Elvis' Own Story*, Geller, p. 139.**

[29]***Hollywood and The Supernatural*, Steiger/Steiger, pp. 200, 201.**

[30]***If I Can Dream: Elvis' Own Story*, Geller, pp. 138, 139.**

into "**Shock Rockers**," such as Ozzy Osbourne, the Who, Alice Cooper, AC/DC, and Boy George and anarchists like Megadeth and Marilyn Manson, the Antichrist Superstar.

While Elvis was used by the Evil One to blend Christ Jesus into New Age thinking, so did the Master Musician especially use the British bands of the Beatles and the Rolling Stones to cause multitudes of gullible, young people to become anti-Christian and anti-American. Not only this, but the British rock band, the Beatles, like the British Socialist George Bernard Shaw, were ***red*** **revolutionaries** who were determined to bring down what Socialists term "**American imperialism**" and to destroy the influences and morals of Christianity. This war against Americans by these **British entertainers** was not to attack us physically, but spiritually. **This was to be done not by the use of military weapons, but by attacking the mind while they used their pens, guitars, drums, and their voices to demoralize the minds of the young, American student population.**

Pastor David A. Noebel, who is the author of *The Marxist Minstrels: A Handbook On Communist Subversion Of Music* and *The Legacy of John Lennon*, has taken painstaking time to compile and fully document his books. He quotes from rock star's own words and from the words spoken by Communist and Socialist leaders that there has been and is, indeed, a **hidden and subversive RED SOCIALIST REVOLUTION** being promoted among the most famous entertainers of the world in an effort to overthrow the power and influence of the United States and its **Christian** people. Today, not one in a thousand American Christian people realizes that the great hero of rock'n'roll, **"John Lennon," was a Marxist revolutionary**.

Like Elvis Presley, the Beatles caused a series of culture shocks and became an instant household word after their performance on the ***Ed Sullivan Show***. They were greeted by 5,000 gullible, squealing fans when they invaded this country on February 7, 1964, in New York. Like Babylon the Great, **the Beatles' rock band promoted a mixed bag of Marxism, drugs, sex, and Spiritualism**.

The Beatles' open attack on Jesus needs no introduction either. Their anti-American and anti-Christian song, "***Back in the USSR***," had many wondering where they were coming from. Most fans of the Beatles did not understand what they were doing to their minds back then, just as today most have not the slightest understanding. The fans just liked the emotional excitement their music put them into. Unsuspecting listeners paid little attention to the words from their songs which entered into the memory banks of their brains.

In the book, *The Beatles*, Lennon said, "**We turned out to be a Trojan horse. The 'Fab Four' moved right to the top and then sang about drugs and sex.**"[31] Like the 18th-century antichrist and revolutionary Voltaire who hated Jesus, John Lennon was just as determined to overthrow the power, influence, and morals of Christianity and its Author in this present world.

John Lennon also said, "**Christianity will go. It will vanish and shrink. I needn't argue about that, I'm right and will be proved right. We're more popular than Jesus Christ right now.**"[32]

The Beatles' pro-Communist propaganda was also revealed in their business interest which they called Apple Corps, Ltd., which was operated from a Chinese junk in the Hudson River in New York. McCartney called it "**a sort of Western Communism**."[33]

However, when John Lennon made this statement, "**We're more popular than Jesus Christ right now**," multitudes of young people turned against them. There were public bonfires of Beatles' records and propaganda nationwide in this country.

Elliot Mintz, who was a media consultant and friend of John Lennon, said:

"The statement about the Beatles being more popular than Jesus caused John tremendous pain. In many ways, I don't think John as a Beatle ever recovered from the impact. It represented to some degree the end of the love relationship between the Beatles and the Press."[34]

Because of the young people's ignorance of the Bible, the Beatles managed to survive this setback and continued to sing their drug-related songs, along with their revolutionary propaganda which was

[31]***The Beatles*, Stokes, p. 211.**

[32]***The New Rolling Stone Encyclopedia of Rock & Roll*, ed. Romanowski/George-Warren, p. 60.**

[33]***The Beatles*, Stokes, p. 214.**

[34]***Imagine: John Lennon*, Solt/Egan, p. 95.**

revealed through their music. The Beatles' "**RED**" colors were also seen in their song, "*Revolution*." Part of the lyrics say:

"You say you want a revolution – Well, you know – we all want to change the world.... But when you talk destruction, Don't you know that you can count me out...."

On paper this line said "you can count me out...," but as the Beatles actually sing it, you can hear the word "***IN***" after they say the word "***OUT***."

"You say you got a real solution – Well, you know – we'd all love to see the PLAN – You ask me for a contribution, Well, you know – WE'RE DOING WHAT WE CAN....You say you'll change a CONSTITUTION – WELL, YOU KNOW – WE ALL WANT TO CHANGE YOUR HEAD...."

History shows, indeed, that the Beatles, the Rolling Stones, Bob Dylan, Joan Baez, and Jane Fonda, like the leftist revolutionary "Che" Guevara in Latin America, were some of the most popular icons who led young minds to accept this **COMMUNAL** message and to stage violent protest marches in the 60s and 70s.

These violent eruptions, like that of Kent State, shocked citizens of both the Old World and the New World. Serious-minded Christians should be still alarmed about the Beatles' music and their recent resurrection and what the remaining comrades will be allowed to promote among our unsuspecting and gullible youth of today.

After John Lennon and the rest of the Beatles broke up, Yoko and John lived in New York and formed alliances with the American Left, including 1960's ***red*** **revolutionaries Jerry Rubin** and **Abbie Hoffman**. Rubin and anarchist Hoffman were close comrades with the Lennons in New York City.[35] Abbot (Abbie) Hoffman (1936–1989) was best known for his abilities to enrage the peace-loving "Flower Children" to turn violently against the government by staging violent street demonstrations, such as the one at the 1968 Chicago Democratic National Convention in which Bobby Seale and the Black Panthers[36] also became known as a violent revolutionary threat. Speaking about the "Flower Children" who projected

[35]***The Lives of John Lennon*****, Goldman, p. 520.**

[36]***Encyclopedia of the American Left*****, Buhle/Buhle/Georgakas, p. 325.**

a pacifist image, Hoffman can be quoted as saying: "I always held my flower in a clenched fist... I was determined to bring the hippie movement into a broader protest."[37]

In 1973, Hoffman was arrested for participating in the sale of cocaine to undercover agents, but he vanished in February 1974 and spent more than six years underground. However, he returned to public view in 1980 to face his cocaine charges, but spent less than a year in prison after pleading guilty to a lesser charge. After he was released from prison, he continued his anarchist plans and was arrested again with former President Jimmy Carter's daughter, Amy, for causing a disturbance while protesting against the CIA at the University of Massachusetts.[38] Hoffman was not only a very confused individual, but he also had manic-depressive cycles and committed suicide on April 12, 1989.

Like Hoffman, Yoko and John did their best to stir up their fans to overthrow the "powers that be" by world revolution. Yoko and John were at their revolutionary peak by 1980 when an unbalanced Christian named Mark David Chapman, thinking he was fighting for the cause of Jesus, assassinated John Lennon on December 8, 1980, outside their Dakota apartment building in New York while he and Yoko were returning home from a recording session. Chapman, a former Hippie and drug user, claimed that Jesus appeared to him in his room when he was about seventeen years old. Overnight, Chapman transformed himself because of this experience. He claimed to have been born again and for a year he went everywhere with his Bible trying to make converts. Chapman became a Pentecostal; he spoke in tongues and danced in the spirit. He was a favorite counselor at the YMCA camps and traveled to Beirut to do missionary work but was called back because of the trouble that broke out in Lebanon at that time. According to Albert Goldman in his bestselling book, *The Lives of John Lennon*, Chapman received his inspiration to assassinate Lennon by reading a book entitled *The Catcher in the Rye* by J.D. Salinger.[39] Chapman saw himself as the character in the same

[37]*Enyclopedia of the American Left*, Buhle/Buhle/Georgakas, p. 324.

[38]*Ibid.*, Buhle/Buhle/Georgakas, p. 325.

[39]*The Lives of John Lennon*, Goldman, pp. 808, 809.

book and acted out a similar part. Chapman wanted to receive instant fame, however, by killing the Antichrist which he thought was John Lennon. Lennon, ironically enough, lived in the very same apartment building where Roman Polanski, the husband of Sharon Tate (who was the slain victim of the Manson Family), filmed his horror movie, ***Rosemary's Baby***, earlier in 1967. This fictitious movie was centered around Satanism and how a woman gave birth to a child who was the incarnate of the Devil and who went on to become the Antichrist. Like some rock stars, Hollywood has learned how there is big money to be made by using the Bible warnings about the Antichrist of which they not only give a false interpretation, but can inspire copycats as we shall see.

Brethren, we are not to attack the antichrists by using force. "NOT BY MIGHT, NOR BY POWER, BUT BY MY SPIRIT, SAITH THE LORD OF HOSTS." Zechariah 4:6. Jesus taught, "HE THAT KILLETH WITH THE SWORD MUST BE KILLED WITH THE SWORD. HERE IS THE PATIENCE AND THE FAITH OF THE SAINTS." Revelation 13:10. However, Satan will use scheme after scheme in his effort to try to rid the earth of loyal followers of Jesus. Nevertheless, **the Holy Scriptures declare that we shall overcome Satan and those who choose him "BY THE BLOOD OF THE LAMB, AND BY THE WORD OF THEIR TESTIMONY; AND THEY LOVED NOT THEIR LIVES UNTO THE DEATH." Revelation 12:11.**

As pointed out so many times in this volume, Satan's plans for us in these last days are the same tactics he used to lead the 18th-century French citizens to not only turn away from Christianity, but to also turn against and kill each other in the **anarchy** which broke out at that time. It is important to understand that France was also engaged in a war with England when their revolution took place. It shall be revealed in this chapter that **20th-century Jacobins** (Socialists), like the 18th-century Jacobins, are today also trying to use their musical talents and influences among the young, American student population to not only overthrow Christianity, but the United States government as well. Less than 20 years before the Hippie Era and the anti-war demonstrations, a congressman tried to warn sleepy, American citizens about **Communist subversion** which had been growing in this country since the early 30s while our country was suffering from a great depression. Keeping this in mind, we shall first look into what both folk and rock music have done to the minds of the American people, and then we'll look at the documented pages of the **Congressional Record of the year 1947** and what it had to say about the entertainment field.

Going back to the Hippie Era of the 60s (which has now been resurrected in the 90s), let's again take another look at what the Beatles were up to in their heyday. George Harrison was deeply involved in New Age mysticism of the Hindu persuasion. According to the book, *Imagine: John Lennon*, it states that between the months of August 1967 and March 1968 George introduced the Beatles to the **Maharishi Mahesh Yogi** and to transcendental meditation.[40] Soon, George Harrison released his rock song, "***My Sweet Lord***," which promoted the worship of the Hindu gods.

The teaching of uniting Eastern mysticism with Western mysticism is found in *The Secret Doctrine* written by Helena P. Blavatsky, and Aleister Crowley borrowed many of his New Age ideas from Blavatsky. While the Beatles were trying to overthrow Christianity, they also were trying to replace it with Eastern religions which already had multitudes of brethren here in the West. The Beatles were selling the American youth a basket of assorted fruits from the Tree of Knowledge of Good and Evil during their years together. Drugs, Marxism, rebellion, revolution, lasciviousness, and New Age Hinduism were always promoted from their menu of assorted hits which made these revolutionaries very rich.

As in Eastern religions, the Indian medicine man or shaman claims to be able to communicate with the spirit world. The occult teach, as we have seen, that there are great ascended masters from the spirit world who were once men and are now communicating knowledge and passing on their talents. As pointed out, their headquarters in the spirit world is known to the psychics as the Great White Brotherhood. It is no doubt that the Beatles would also embrace this false doctrine.

According to the book, *Imagine: John Lennon*, which speaks positively about Yoko and John Lennon, we read:

[40]***Imagine: John Lennon*, Solt/Egan, p. 112.**

"While John was becoming a househusband, Yoko was becoming the family's financial manager. She achieved substantial success, often seeking counsel from psychics and numerologists."[41]

Here, again, I would like to remind the reader of the following. It was the revival of Spiritualism in the 1800s which sparked a huge interest in contacting the dead, and this drew the Russian witch H.P. Blavatsky to America at the age of 42. According to *Man, Myth & Magic*, the population of Americans in the 1800s was about 38 million.[42] This same encyclopedia of parapsychology said on the same page:

"No less than 18 million Americans, it has been calculated, among a population of over 38 million, attended Spiritualist seances and read Spiritualist papers."[43]

Helena P. Blavatsky promoted the **Atlantean Socialist Plan** in her book, *The Secret Doctrine*, (which Elvis Presley studied) which has a history of how all the sciences of the occult began. They all have their base in the false belief of "life after death" or the immortality of the soul. This belief opens the door for Satan's wonder-working power! Satan has personated dead loved ones or great musicians who have died in the presence of human beings. These spiritual manifestations which are summoned by witch doctors and psychics often appear as souls of great heros or ascended masters. Not only does this belief of the immortality of the soul open its believer to fall victim to Satan's miracle-working powers, but it will also open the door of the heart to demon possession through the practice of meditation.

In the book, *Encyclopedia of the Unexplained*, it shows how multitudes have unwittingly connected themselves with devils by learning how to communicate with the spirit world. Over and over again, Satan or one of his evil angels appear to practitioners of Spiritualism promising them supernatural power to perform supernatural miracles or to receive musical talents. This practice of receiving talents to write and play music or to become an accomplished artist is known in witchcraft as **MOTOR AUTOMATISM**. The above encyclopedia says:

[41]*Imagine: John Lennon*, Solt/Egan, p. 200.

[42]*Man, Myth & Magic*, Vol. 1, ed. Cavendish, 1983, p. 290.

[43]*Ibid.*, Vol. 1, ed. Cavendish, 1983, p. 290.

"An **automatism** is a type of behaviour in which there is limited consciousness. During automatic writing, for example, the writer does not consciously know what he is writing: this is described as 'dissociation,' which means that there is some temporary separation of the part of the personality engaged in the writing process from the normal state of the individual....

"The world of music has its cases of automatic responses to influences, at least of the unconscious mind, but giving the impression **THAT SOME DECEASED MUSICIAN IS BEHIND THE PRODUCT,** either in composing the music as it was written, or in guiding the hands on the instruments playing it. Few cases have been publicized, but one is currently well known in England; Mrs. Rosemary Brown believes that her hands are sometimes controlled at the piano by Frank Liszt, although Bach and Beethoven also help her to write the music they wish to communicate to her."[44]

However, reader, the Bible says, "**THE DEAD KNOW NOT ANYTHING**." Ecclesiastes 9:5. The deception of motor automatism is nothing new. This is not a 20th-century, occult phenomenon made popular by rock stars and movie stars, but it dates back to the Father of Lies. Again, Satan's first lie to Eve was "**ye shall not surely die**." Genesis 3:4. He channeled this message to Eve by using a serpent.

Deceased musicians do not use the hands and voices of the living to channel their music through those who claim these experiences. This is done by none other than Pan (who is Satan) and his fallen angels who often pose as Bach or Beethoven or some other well-known musician or hero. Again, this forbidden knowledge of how to communicate with the spirit world is called necromancy. (See Deuteronomy 18:11.)

Present-day mediums are known as channelers. As it is claimed that spirits of dead friends or relatives speak through mediums, so do musicians claim to be the reincarnation of some ancient, great musician or a channel (medium) for deceased spirits who use their bodies to send messages through their songs. As the psychic claims to be a channel for an ascended master of the **Great White Brotherhood**, so do these demons promise inspiration to occult musicians

[44]***Encyclopedia of the Unexplained*, ed. Cavendish, pp. 49, 50.**

to enable them to write music or to perform for those who want to become great rock stars. However, along with these gifts from the spirit world, there comes a demand to give themselves over to be controlled by them. One very popular couple known to all rock'n'rollers did this very thing.

When John and Yoko were violently against Jesus and His church, they fell for the sophistry of Spiritualism. Albert Goldman, who wrote the *New York Times* bestseller, *The Lives of John Lennon*, pointed out how Yoko paid a witch named Lena $60,000 to help her receive blessings and protection from Satan by signing a pact with the Devil.[45]

Popular magazines are filled with abominations committed by these so-called "idols" who, by their example, have helped cause our young to commit such sins against our Heavenly Father. It was Aleister Crowley who can be given credit for causing a revival of black magic within the Hippie communal movement of the 60s, but it was the Beatles and the Rolling Stones who were Crowley's biggest promoters. **The Beatles' album, *Sergeant Pepper's Lonely Hearts Club Band*, displays the heros from the entertainment field and other world celebrities. The face of Aleister Crowley is seen to the far left at the top, and to the far right on the second row appears the face of Karl Marx.**

Interestingly enough, the so-called Fab Three (Paul, George, and Ringo) hoped to have incited Beatlemania II "with a little help from their friends," says *Time* magazine.[46] A reproduction of the album cover of the Beatles' 1967 *Sgt. Pepper's Lonely Heart's Club Band* is displayed on pages 104 and 105 of this issue of *Time* magazine.

A head shot of John Lennon, who is dressed in a black beret and army-like jacket portraying the same image as his fallen comrade and Marxist hero, "Che" Guevara, is pictured at the bottom right among the flowers. Fellow travelers Bob Dylan, Marlon Brando, Yoko, Julian and Sean Lennon, Michael Jackson, George Martin, Patti Boyd, Linda McCartney, Mick Jagger, Elvis Presley, Jeff Lynne, Michael Eisner, and Bob Iger are also included as new head shots

[45]*The Lives of John Lennon*, Goldman, pp. 704, 705.

[46]*Time*, November 20, 1995, p. 104.

with Ringo Starr, Paul McCartney, and George Harrison in the corner. The boxing champ Sonny Liston, who appeared on the original 1967 album, has been replaced by Mike Tyson.

While the Beatles were singing "**DOING WHAT WE CAN**" to promote world revolution, drugs, sex, and Spiritualism to their fans along with hidden messages found in their songs, the Fonda family in Hollywood were busy doing what they could. Even though Jane Fonda publicly apologized for her anti-American demonstrations against the Vietnam War which led multitudes of young people to follow in her footsteps, she is still living with the aftermath of what she helped promote and which is still permeating today. The "**spirit of anarchy**" is continuing and seeking to sweep away all who are ignorant of the Holy Scriptures into its destruction. As the "**Reign of Terror**" in France was largely promoted and led by the entertainers, businessmen, and politicians in their day, so are the heros of the Big Screen, TV and the Music Industry, and the politicians today leading the world into spiritual and political confusion which shall, like 18th-century France, result in **ANARCHY**.

These same scenes of human destruction are about to have a repeat of which the "**Reign of Terror**" was also just a shadow. The rock culture of the 60s and the 70s helped produce such devils as Adolfo de Jesus Constanzo, who sacrificed humans and participated in occult practices to win satanic protection over his drug-smuggling operation from Mexico's Rio Grande Valley into the United States. Officers recovered 15 bodies from shallow graves with many of them showing evidence of mutilation and torture. These people lost their lives over the use of drugs and the practice of black magic.

Nevertheless, the editors of *Time-Life* books in Alexandria, Virginia, are also promoting Spiritualism today through the volumes they have published. Their series of books on Spiritualism are entitled *Mysteries of the Unknown*. A book entitled *Mysteries of the Unknown–Spirit Summonings* is found among these volumes about Spiritualism and its history. In this volume, a psychic artist named Luiz Antonio Gasparetto claims that spirits of dead artists have chosen him as the vehicle to carry on their postmortem work.

Gasparetto is a Brazillan psychotherapist. His mother is a medium (channeler) and when he was young, he experienced motor automatisms in the form of automatic paintings. Here from the book, *Mysteries of the Unknown–Spirit Summonings*, I quote the following:

"On a visit to England in 1978, Gasparetto rapidly produced twenty-one pictures while appearing on a television program. Some were done simultaneously, with one hand drawing normally and the other creating an upside-down painting. In the spring of 1988, Gasparetto gave a series of demonstrations of psychic painting in California. In a single fifteen-minute tour de force, he produced six paintings. They more or less resembled the works of Renoir, Manet, Toulouse-Lautrec, and Modigliani."[47]

The above book on the same page goes on to point out the following about Gasparetto:

"He works in the dark or with his eyes closed, his face contorted as he furiously assaults the canvas with bare hands or feet. He uses no brushes or other implements. He says he is fully conscious as he paints but feels removed from the creative effort. Still, he says, he can chat with the dead master during the collaboration, both telepathically and verbally."

Again, the Bible says, "**The dead know not anything**." Ecclesiastes 9:5.

"Whatsoever thy hand findeth to do, do it with thy might; for there is no work, nor device, nor knowledge, nor wisdom, in the grave, whither thou goest." Ecclesiastes 9:10.

Necromancy is a forbidden science from the deceptions of the master deceiver himself. Those who turn to these so-called psychics to learn how to connect themselves with the spirit world will disconnect themselves with God and be in danger of being controlled by **"the rulers of the darkness of this world," and by "spiritual wickedness in high places."** (See Ephesians 6:12.)

However, the history of the entertainment field is filled with pages about how celebrities during the "**Hippie Era**" have unwittingly or willingly sold their fate to the Devil. Another example of this is seen in the "death-rock" band known as the Rolling Stones, and a story about them is found in the *Rolling Stone*

[47]*Mysteries of the Unknown-Spirit Summonings*, Time-Life Books, p. 138.

magazine. It reads: "Watching the Stones rehearse in 1994 is like watching a tribe of religious mystics piece together a sacred text."[48] The title of their concert tour also expresses what they are still about; they called their tour "*Voodoo Lounge*."

Hazrat Khan, the Sufi master who came to the San Francisco and Berkeley areas in the early 1900s, is really the patriarch of the Hippie Era of the early 60s. His mixture of the philosophies of love, peace, mysticism, and Socialism led to the formation of the "**Flower Children**" of the early 1900s which continued to produce other generations after them. This movement became known as the "**Hippie Countercultural Movement**" which blossomed into creating an image of what Spiritualists hoped would come in the near future. As pointed out, the "**Woodstock Nation**" of 1969 with its communal message was to be a symbol of how the world can live in peace and harmony while they enjoyed freedom to engage in Spiritualism, unlawful sex, and drugs. While the "**Flower Children**" of the 60s promoted this festival of free love, four months later **Mick Jagger of the Rolling Stones promoted a "Festival of Hate,"** which history recorded in Altamont, California. Jagger sang a song that threw the intoxicated crowd into a wild frenzy and, as we saw earlier, people were killed. The name of this song is "***Sympathy for the Devil***." Here are the words this troubadour for Satan sang on the night when this unholy bedlam broke out:

"**Please allow me to introduce myself. I'm a man of wealth, I am a man of taste. Been around for a long long year.... Sold many a man's soul and fate. I was around when Jesus Christ... had his moment of doubt and pain. Made damn sure Pilate... washed his hands and sealed his fate.... Pleased to meet you Baby, hope you guess my name....**" [sic]

Other songs from this group which promoted a connection with the Devil were ***"Their Satanic Majesty's Request," "Goat's Head Soup,"* and*"Dancing with Mr. D."***

As established, the god Pan is worshipped as the god of music, drunkenness, and revelry in the circles of the occult. Another occult musician who demonstrated Pan's character was the late

[48]*Rolling Stone*, August 25, 1994, pp. 56, 57.

Jim Morrison of the Doors' cult rock band. Jim Morrison, who was up to his eyes in Spiritualism, lived in Venice, California. While he was living in Venice, California, and while he was jogging, **HE MET THE SPIRIT OF MUSIC... AN APPEARANCE OF THE DEVIL on a Venice canal. While being interviewed, Morrison said, "I saw a Satan or Satyr, moving beside me, 'a fleshly shadow of my secret mind.' "** (Emphasis mine.)

Jim Morrison helped switch young minds from the "Flower Power" of Hippie consciousness to the often frightening aspects of psychedelia and the self-destructiveness of the drug culture. He not only encouraged his fans to follow in his bizarre and anarchical performances on stage, but Morrison urged violent resistance to police repression. Rock credits alleged that the popular poet and his Doors' rock band were merely a "pop outfit" masquerading as leaders of youth revolution. This was confirmed in part when the 1969 album, *The Soft Parade*, and songs like "*The End*," "*Light My Fire*," and "*Riders of the Storm*"[49] were buzzing in the minds of young rock'n'rollers.

Ray Manzarek, who is still with the Doors' rock band, admitted the following on a nationally-televised interview about the late Jim Morrison: **"JIM MORRISON WAS A SHAMAN; HE WAS POSSESSED, MAN!"**

However, Jim Morrison is still very popular among the rock'n'rollers today. While my wife and I went to a health food store in Venice, California, in August of 1994 and planned to enjoy our vegetarian supper by the shore, we saw a huge painting of Jim Morrison on an apartment building while looking for a place to park. The artist showed Morrison in concert with his microphone in hand. However, the huge exalted painting of Morrison failed to show the other thing Morrison would usually have in his other hand which helped put the poet into an early grave. The painting shows Morrison with a youthful, healthy look, but the artist left out the bottle which he carried around with him as he sang from a drunken stupor.

Before the popular Jim Morrison died, he sang in one of his songs

[49]*The Harmony Illustrated Encyclopedia of Rock*, ed. Clifford, p. 48.

"**cancel my subscription to the resurrection**," and he went to his grave as a lost man. The poet's heart failed him while taking a bath. Today, Morrison's tomb has become a point of pilgrimage for latter-day Hippies.[50]

Tragically, it seems another has risen to taken Morrison's place. Eddie Vedder, who was voted by *Circus, America's Rock Magazine*, as the best vocalist, best songwriter, and most valuable player back in 1994,[51] appears to be walking on the same ground Morrison did. Eddie Vedder's band, Pearl Jam, was also voted as *Circus'* best rock band.

While Pearl Jam is worshipped by its young fans, *Circus, America's Rock Magazine*, said the following about Eddie Vedder:

"With all the success and glory, 'EV' (Eddie Vedder) appears to be at odds with the world. Angry, constantly brooding, feuding with his label and down on life in general, the 28-year-old former gas station attendant should take a long hard look at his personal situation. Despite his undeniable ability to create great music, some feel Eddie's antics are leading him inevitably towards self-destruction."[52]

Like Jim Morrison, Vedder goes into a shaman-like trance while performing. One way he writes songs is by "meditating" over a repetitive guitar riff.[53] Eddie Vedder, who is often compared to the spacey, poetic, and troubled Jim Morrison, joined the surviving Doors (Manzarek, Krieger, Densmore) at the Rock Hall of Fame.

The New Age preach that harmony, peace, and understanding will be seen in the Age of Aquarius. Another term which Spiritualists use to describe a blissful existence or a condition of agreeable activity is, as we have seen, "**NIRVANA**" of which the Hollywood guru Deepak Chopra today is its most heard and popular pied piper. As the reader may know, there is a very famous rock group who uses this Hindu mystical word "**Nirvana**" for the name of their band. They were the second most popular rock group as of the spring of 1994, and Kurt Cobain was its leader. Like Jim Morrison, Kurt Cobain, who was one of the great heros of the young people, couldn't stand himself.

[50]*The Harmony Illustrated Encyclopedia of Rock*, ed. Clifford, p. 48.

[51]*Circus, America's Rock Magazine*, February 28, 1994, p. 24.

[52]*Ibid.*, February 28, 1994, p. 82.

[53]*Ibid.*, February 28, 1994, p. 82.

His music and his fame hardly led him into a state of heavenly bliss, but instead led him into a state of mind where he took a shotgun to his head at his home in Seattle and tragically pulled the trigger. He was only 27 years old and went into an untimely grave as a lost soul.

The 1969 Woodstock Aquarian Festival had its silver anniversary of 25 years in August 1994. People of Spiritualism still point to this as a model of what the coming New Age shall be like. Back in 1969 while Jimi Hendrix performed a voodoo ritual by sacrificing his guitar with fire, Joe Cocker promoted the use of drugs in his popular song, "*I Get High With A Little Help From My Friends*."

Crosby, Stills, and Nash, like the Beatles, see themselves as world revolutionaries who are bent on promoting a society where anything goes. **Crosby** is known for his "**Hippie politicking**" and his jail sentence for **drug abuse**.[54] This Atlantean-type communal society, which calls itself the Age of Aquarius and allows free love, free sex, and free drugs, was seen at Woodstock, New York, on August 15–18 in 1969. **Woodstock was "Utopia" to those who know not God and obey not the Gospel of our Lord Jesus Christ.**

Life magazine, August 1994, promoted Woodstock 1969 as a festival of peace and love. Our sick society, which is so degraded by these heros of the Movie Industry and by these rock stars, cannot in their blindness see what is wrong. They cannot see why the human race is heading for anarchy and self-destruction instead of a state of Nirvana. Multitudes have gone down into untimely graves because of being led by Satan into drugs and free sex by these prophets and musicians of the New Age Enlightenment Movement who are prophesying their gospel of mystical Socialism from the lyrics of their songs.

While songs from these people of Spiritualism promote peace and love like in the song, "*Woodstock–We Got To Come Back To The Garden*," that Crosby, Stills, and Nash later recorded, the huge cult band, the Who, however, violently smashed their instruments in front of their astonished listeners at this Aquarian Music and Arts Festival. The Who rock band was formed in London the same year the Beatles invaded the United States in 1964. They are considered to be the godfathers of punk rock and were the first to integrate synthesizers.

[54]***The Penguin Encyclopedia of Popular Music*, ed. Clarke, pp. 302, 303.**

Keith Moon of the Who was known as the "madman of rock" because of his outrageous stunts – onstage and off – and because of his alcohol and drug addiction which put him into an early grave. They began to make inroads among the American Hippie culture in the U.S. when they released their song, *Happy Jack*.[55]

Daltrey portrayed the other darker side of this Aquarian conspiracy at Woodstock 1969. Roger Daltrey of the Who later said in *Life* magazine: "**I BELIEVED IN THE DREAM OF SOCIALISM**."[56] The Who were actually projecting in their act at Woodstock 1969 what was coming to replace the "**Flower Children image**" of the Hippie Era. Earlier in this interview with *Life* magazine and on the same page as above, Daltrey of the Who said, "We invented the word 'hype' in rock and roll. A rock opera? Smashing up the equipment? Pop art? Union Jack jackets? You name it, we did it."

Roger Daltrey's promotion of the "Socialist Communal Dream" had first been promoted centuries before the Aquarian Music and Arts Festival a.k.a. "Woodstock" took place in 1969. Woodstock Nation's founding fathers can be said to actually be Plato, Adam Weishaupt, Karl Marx, H.P. Blavatsky and her successors, George Bernard Shaw, H.G. Wells, Gandhi, Pastor Harry F. Ward, Helen Keller, and famous Socialist/Marxist, left-wing folk singers such as Woody Guthrie, the Weavers, Pete Seeger, Bob Dylan, Joan Baez, and, believe it or not, Dr. Martin Luther King, Jr. All of the ideologies of the leftist movement accumulated and were seen at the Woodstock Music and Arts Festival. The above names are considered to be some of the early left-wing heros who helped promote the "***Red* World Revolution**" through the use of subversive Christian-front organizations, labor unions, civil rights issues, and protest songs.

Left-wing folk singers like Woody Guthrie, a hobo of the Oklahoma dustbowl era, began to appear in the early and mid-30s singing anti-fascism songs as a cover, while at the same time he

[55]*The New Rolling Stone Encyclopedia of Rock & Roll*, ed. Romanowski/George-Warren, pp. 1072–1077.
[56]*Life*, August 1994, p. 42.

was promoting Communism. **Guthrie painted "This Machine Kills Fascists" on the body of his guitar.**[57] However, Woody Guthrie was identified under oath as having been a **member of the Communist Party,**[58] and his activities on behalf of international Communism were well-known in his day. Guthrie wrote for Communist papers such as the *Daily Worker* (NYC) and *People's World* on the West Coast.[59]

The ***red*** scourge of Communism, which actually derived out of the Enlightenment Movement of the 18th century a.k.a. Illuminism, had established itself by the 19th century as a German labor union known as the League of the Just. Karl Marx was a member and after the infamous *The Communist Manifesto* was published in 1848, the **League of the Just changed its name to the League of Communists.**[60]

It should be understood by the reader that both **Marx and Lenin used the labor unions as a vehicle and political stump** to spread the violent overthrow of all free nations and enslave them under the banner of Socialism. Woody Guthrie hopped onto the labor union band wagons (like he did freight cars as a hobo) as he traveled the U.S. to promote his version of the **Socialist Dream** to the poor working class. Guthrie wrote over 1,000 songs before his death in 1967 and some still serve as the folk movement's anthems. Some of them are "*Pastures Of Plenty*," "*This Land Is Your Land*," "*So Long, It's Been Good To Know You*," and "*Deportee*."

Woody Guthrie, the famous folk musician, helped inspire others like Pete Seeger, who was among the founders of the **Almanac Singers. This Socialist, left-wing folk group took their name from the *Farmer's Almanac*. Between the years of 1941 and 1942, the Almanac Singers sang for CIO union organizing campaigns and other radical political functions.** They performed by singing songs to the working class about life in the Depression as well as union songs. They were joined from time to time by fellow comrades such

[57]*Encyclopedia of the American Left*, Buhle/Buhle/Georgakas, p. 231.

[58]*The Marxist Minstrels: A Handbook on Communist Subversion of Music*, Noebel, p. 139.

[59]*The Penguin Encyclopedia of Popular Music*, ed. Clarke, p. 498; *The Marxist Minstrels: A Handbook on Communist Subversion of Music*, Noebel, p. 139.

[60]*Cyclopedia of World Authors*, Magill, pp. 724, 725.

as Burl Ives. The Almanac Singers' lifestyles reflected what they stood for. Their folk group consisted of about twelve singers and players who lived together in a loft commune near New York's Union Square. It was Pete Seeger and Lee Hays of this group who wrote the lyrics to the popular folk song, "*If I Had a Hammer.*"[61] Seeger also wrote "*Where Have All the Flowers Gone,*" "*We Shall Overcome,*" and "*Kisses Sweeter Than Wine.*" Seeger's popular civil rights anthem,"*We Shall Overcome,*" was made popular through the efforts of the **Highlander Folk School of Monteagle, Tennessee, with which Seeger and Dr. Martin Luther King, Jr. were associated for years**. The title of this song, **"*We Shall Overcome,*" became Fidel Castro's official revolutionary slogan.**[62] The Highlander Folk School was founded by Myles Horton in company with James Dombrowski, an identified Communist. Both Horton and Dombrowski were graduates of John D. Rockefeller, Jr.'s **Union Theological Seminary in Riverside, New York.**[63] Myles Horton (b. 1905) adopted the ideas of Marx and **Christian Socialism** and founded a Communist school to promote **"Christian Socialism" a.k.a. "the Social Gospel"** at Highlander Folk School in Monteagle, Tennessee. However, this Communist school was firebombed, seized by the State of Tennessee, and then sold.[64]

Reuters reported that Pete Seeger, who was a close associate of Martin Luther King, Jr., went to Moscow during the Vietnam War and sang a protest song there to students at its university.[65]

It was this same Pete Seeger who founded another folk group in 1948 called the "***Weavers***" who were at first more polished and less political than the ***Almanac Singers***. In 1950, Decca Records signed them to a contract in which they recorded two songs which

[61]***Encyclopedia of the American Left*, Buhle/Buhle/Georgakas, p. 231.**

[62]***The Marxist Minstrels: A Handbook on Communist Subversion of Music*, Noebel, p. 134.**

[63]***Ibid.*, Noebel, p. 175.**

[64]***Encyclopedia of the American Left*, Buhle/Buhle/Georgakas, p. 333.**

[65]***The Marxist Minstrels: A Handbook on Communist Subversion of Music*, Noebel, p. 135.**

made them very popular among the American people. The names of these songs were "***Goodnight Irene***" and "***On Top Of Old Smoky***."[66] It was Seeger's Weavers who were credited with causing a folk music revival during the 50s and 60s. However, after winning the hearts of the American people with their songs, they began to send more and more messages of left-wing propaganda through their music. The Weavers' strong left-wing political convictions became very noticeably expressed in not only their folk songs, but in their left-wing associations as well. This, however, began to open the eyes of some sleepy-eyed loyal Americans who became awakened and outraged to what they were up to. Their subversive Socialist-propaganda tactics against unsuspecting American people led both to the blacklisting and an FBI investigation. Political pressure forced the Weavers to disband in 1953 because they could not find a hall where they could perform. However, in 1955 they reappeared as a repentant and reformed people, but the Weavers never recovered from the deceptions which they had committed against the American people. In the film, *Wasn't That a Time* (1981), the Weavers' special reunion was chronicled in the movie.[67] However, Pete Seeger managed to continue the Weaver music in obscurity throughout the 50s.

After the popularity of the Weavers was brought to an abrupt halt and disappeared, another phase of the folk movement sprang when two students at Menio Park Business College, Bob Shane and Nick Reynolds, teamed up with Dave Guard to form the Kingston Trio. Their name was taken from Kingston, Jamaica, because the Kingston Trio adopted and reflected a calypso sound which was very popular in their day. The Kingston Trio recorded an old mountain ballad, "*Tom Dooley*," which they took to the top of the most popular songs of 1958. A student and an unknown musician at that time named Bob Dylan of Minneapolis began to adopt the musical style of the Kingston Trio until someone introduced Dylan to Woodie Guthrie's recordings and writings, and

[66]*The Marshall Cavendish Illustrated History of Popular Music*, Vol. 6, ed. Cavendish, p. 662.

[67]*Encyclopedia of the American Left*, Buhle/Buhle/Georgakas, p. 231.

this is where Bob Dylan's radical protest songs took root. Dylan became obsessed by Woody Guthrie's music, and Guthrie became Dylan's hero.[68]

It was Woody Guthrie who inspired both Pete Seeger and Bob Dylan to continue the **Socialist Communal Dream**. Guthrie's songs provided the main model for other fellow comrades, like Tom Paxton and Phil Ochs, who also invaded the college campuses with their radical left-wing propaganda through the use of their music. At the beginning of his musical career, Dylan imitated Guthrie not only in his style of singing, but in his dress as well. Like his hero, Dylan hopped on social issues of the day like the **Black civil rights movements, disarmament, and especially the Vietnam War as the vehicles to gain sympathy for his cause and to sell his records**. At that time, the music of Seeger and Dylan helped fuse together the gap between folk and pop music.

It was this same Bob Dylan who made his home in Woodstock, New York, who was the first to introduce the Beatles to marijuana. The Beatles and Dylan were close comrades at this time and helped influence each other's music.[69]

Multitudes of Americans have no understanding about the subtle tactics the Communists and Socialist conspirators have used to further their cause. **As the Bible teaches and promotes racial equality, so do the White, Black, Spanish, and Oriental Communist Party members.** The Communists and the New Age Marxists have been very successful in winning and pulling unsuspecting black and white Christians into this New Age and New World Order scheme by using social unrest about civil rights or by inciting opposition against American leaders who still oppose any form of a Communistic or Socialistic enslavement.

As established earlier, the Nation of Islam (Black Muslims) originally drew many of their members out of the 32° and the 33° African-American Freemasons of the Order of Prince Hall Freemasonry. Prince Hall Freemasonry has a women's auxiliary who

[68]*The Marshall Cavendish Illustrated History of Popular Music*, Vol. 6, ed. Cavendish, p. 662.

[69]*The Ultimate Beatles Encyclopedia*, Harry, pp. 210, 211.

are known as the **Order of the Golden Circle,** which was organized in 1886. The O.G.C. is supervised by a male, known as the Illustrious Deputy. The O.G.C. has supported national African-American civil rights organizations, including the N.A.A.C.P. and the United Urban League.[70]

Back in the October 1, 1996, issue of *USA Today*, the cover story was about the 60's and 70's popular civil rights advocate, Curtis Mayfield, who became famous for songs like "*Keep on Pushing*" and "*Move on Up*." This article, written by Steve Jones, tells of Curtis Mayfield's tragic accident which left him a quadriplegic. This article also goes on to tell that Mayfield's attitude towards pushing for civil rights has remained upbeat despite being unable to use his arms and legs. However, this article goes on to say that Curtis Mayfield is also pushing the New World Order Movement. He has even released a new album entitled ***NEW WORLD ORDER***, and *USA Today* announces, **"New album offers hope for 'New World Order.' "**

Leftist Joan Baez was another guitar-playing folk singer who jumped aboard the **Black civil rights issues** and the **Vietnam War protests** as vehicles to promote the **Socialist Dream**. Baez was heard by large audiences as she sang songs like "***We Shall Overcome***" written by leftist Pete Seeger. Baez became popular because of singing the protest songs of Guthrie, Seeger, and Dylan. Other well-known recording artists who sang the music of Seeger and Dylan were diverse artists such as the Byrds, Peter, Paul, and Mary, and, of course, Joan Baez herself who became Bob Dylan's lover and special comrade. Shocking as it may be for some to learn, nevertheless, **the civil rights leader Dr. Martin Luther King, Jr. was soft on Communism and was, indeed, a close associate of Pete Seeger at the Highlander Folk School at Monteagle, Tennessee, which was forced to be closed by the Tennessee State government when it was exposed as a Communist training center.**

As Bob Dylan's hero for civil rights was the Marxist Woody Guthrie, so was the New Age Marxist Mohandas Gandhi the hero of the late civil rights leader, Dr. Martin Luther King, Jr. Dr. King often

[70]***The International Encyclopedia of Secret Societies & Fraternal Orders*, Axelrod, p. 103.**

posed for a picture at his home while a picture of his fallen hero Gandhi was hanging from his wall. As pointed out earlier, Hindu Marxists, like Gandhi, use a technique to overcome their enemies by the use of a nonviolent resistance called **SATYAGRAHA**.[71] **Gandhi, who was a member of the New Age Theosophical Society, was successful in not only throwing out the British government from India by using Satyagraha, but also the worship of Jesus as the Son of God and Saviour of the world.** Gandhi made war against the British government by staging marches and protests and by practicing nonviolent civil disobedience demonstrations against British rule.[72] Among New Age Marxists, one who practices **Satyagraha**, like Gandhi, is known as a **satyagrahi** (male) or a **satyagrahini** (female). According to *The New Age Dictionary*, **Joan Baez is listed as a SATYAGRAHINI**.[73] In August of 1963, Martin Luther King, Jr. led a 200,000 people disarmament and civil rights march to Washington, and accompanying him were the following fellow comrades: satyagrahini Joan Baez who sang Pete Seeger's "*We Shall Overcome*," Bob Dylan who sang "*Pawn In Their Game*," and Peter, Paul, and Mary who sang one of Dylan's songs called "*Blowin' In The Wind*."[74] **Here, again, we see another parallel to the events that led to the SPIRIT OF ANTICHRIST seen in the French Revolution. Here, again, we can also find a parallel to the myth about the Egyptian god Osiris and how he conquered the whole world (not by using weapons of war, but by using music and eloquence).**

In the 60s while New Agers were promoting their "**Age of Aquarius**" scheme through their song "***Aquarius***," other Socialist/ Marxist musicians were doing what they could to block the American effort to stop the Communists from taking over Vietnam. Both Hollywood and the Music Industry had celebrities among their ranks who were busy in those days in an effort to make "anti-American" become a sociably-accepted thing and the latest fad to identify with

[71]*The World Book Encyclopedia*, Vol. 8, 1994, p. 25.

[72]*Ibid.*, Vol. 8, 1994, p. 25.

[73]*The New Age Dictionary*, Jack, p. 16.

[74]*The Marshall Cavendish Illustrated History of Popular Music*, Vol. 6, ed. Cavendish, p. 664.

among the Hippies. While brave, American soldiers in Vietnam were trying to stop the Communist aggression in that region of the world, they were at the same time receiving "**friendly fire**" in the form of **war protest songs** and **protest marches** which were stirred up by such comrades as Pope Paul VI, Dr. Martin Luther King, Jr., the World Council of Churches, folk and rock singers Bob Dylan, Joan Baez, the Beatles, and the Rolling Stones, and Hollywood's actress Jane Fonda.

Joan Baez, the New Age prophetess, became the queen of the campus circuit and a great hero as she sang to the gullible, American students anti-American protest songs which helped lead them into violence and campus unrest. While the Beatles were sending out messages such as **"Well, You Say You Want A Revolution,"** ***red*, revolutionary protest songs and protest marches were aimed** directly at the gullible, young "**Flower Children**" of California, (especially around the San Francisco and Berkeley areas) which the mystical musician and Sufi Master Hazrat Khan had helped to produce earlier. This Hippie Countercultural Movement became a weapon for the leftists. Jane Fonda and Joan Baez even went separately to join their comrades in Hanoi in an effort to halt the bombing of North Vietnam as the gullible and still confused American public looked on in amazement. During this same time while both Sufism and Hindu meditation were being introduced to American Hippies, the lyrics of many of the Beatles' songs especially promoted having a "**mystical experience**" by the use of drugs. Because of the chemical-induced mystical experiences of LSD, multitudes of young, Christian apostates who explored into the usages of the mind-expanding drugs were easily introduced into Hindu, Buddhist, Wiccan, and American Indian mysticism and the philosophies which promote white or black magic. According to *The Ultimate Beatles Encyclopedia*, the Beatles hired a diviner named Caleb to use **divination** via the **Tarot cards** to run their Apple Corps business dealings. The Beatles gave this diviner complete authority to authorize or approve their transactions.[75]

While George Harrison of the Beatles was the pied piper to help

[75]*The Ultimate Beatles Encyclopedia*, Harry, p. 129.

introduce Hinduism to young Americans and Timothy Leary was the prophet of LSD, it was the Ozzy Osbourne and the Led Zeppelin rock groups who helped introduce America's young people to Satanism.

We do not have to be a prophet to hear what the main message rock musicians today are piping into one's mind. Now since the 70s, many heavy metal music bands like Led Zeppelin, Alice Cooper, Kiss, AC/DC, along with Ozzy Osbourne (who are all still going strong today) have led many young people to follow in their footsteps. It is not difficult for a Bible-believing Christian to see the danger in listening to this kind of music known as "**death-rock music**;" however, today some of this same kind of music is pawned off to us as being Christian music. Even hard-core rap music has become acceptable among some Christian churches; it is, ironically enough, called **gospel rap** and is making lots of money for those who promote it.

Back in the November 28, 1994, issue of *Newsweek* magazine on pages 64 and 65, it had an lengthy article written by Michel Marriott about gospel rap music. Gospel rappers such as **T-Bone** and the **Gospel Gangstas** send thousands of **squealing teenagers**, who call themselves Christians, into the same kind of frenzy that the **Snoop Doggy Dogg** did during his concerts. According to this article in *Newsweek*, the "Gospel Gangstas" are a Los Angeles-based group of **former Bloods and Crips** who warn that Christians sometimes fall from grace. This **mingling of the Holy with the unholy** was witnessed by Moses at Mt. Horeb and, today, it has often led **Jesus' true sheep to be mingled with the Piper's (Pan's) goats**.

Like mainstream rap, this so-called "**gospel rap**" (according to this *Newsweek* article) finds much of its audience among White, suburban teens and young adults, though the performers tend to be inner-city Blacks and Hispanics.[76]

However, there are those today who have seen the error of their ways and have repented. My wife and I have witnessed teens and young adults who have received a true conversion from the world and have thrown their tapes with this kind of music in the fire to be burned. Nevertheless, there are also people today, perhaps in our own families, who will never repent or obey the call from Jesus to come

[76]***Newsweek*, November 28, 1994, p. 64.**

out of spiritual Babylon and leave its intoxicating music behind. Most will not, and Jesus Christ predicted, "**For many are called, but few are chosen**." Matthew 22:14.

"When the Son of man shall come in his glory, and all the holy angels with him, then shall he sit upon the throne of his glory: And before him shall be gathered all nations: **and he shall separate them one from another, as a shepherd divideth his sheep from the goats**:

"And he shall set the sheep on his right hand, but the goats on the left. Then shall the King say unto them on his right hand, Come, ye blessed of my Father, inherit the kingdom prepared for you from the foundation of the world." Matthew 25:31–34.

Before we close this volume, there are a couple of more things about the subtleness of **New Age Marxism** (which from the 30s has been bombarding the walls of Christendom) which we need to document in this volume. Fathers and mothers are wide awake now about how bad the violence has become among the young, student population. The cities have been made into virtual war zones because of the sale of drugs and by the gangs who compete for them. Parents are taking great precautions to protect the windows and the doors of their homes with security locks and bars or other security systems to keep out unwelcome intruders. However, multitudes never stop to think that they also need to protect their spiritual eyes and ears, which are the windows and doors of the heart, from Satan and his devils!

"Do not ye yet understand, that whatsoever entereth in at the mouth goeth into the belly, and is cast out into the draught? But those things which proceed out of the mouth come forth from the heart; and they defile the man. For out of the **HEART** proceed evil thoughts, murders, adulteries, fornications, thefts, false witness, blasphemies: These are the things which defile a man: but to eat with unwashen hands defileth not a man." Matthew 15:17-20

Jesus also taught us, "**For where your treasure is, there will your heart be also**." Luke 12:34. It is easy to see with born-again eyes where your children's heart really is by observing what is on their T-shirts and what is hanging on the walls of their bedrooms.

Revelation 12:17 says that this "***red* Dragon**" "**WENT TO MAKE WAR**" on God's people (not only physically, but spiritually as well). Satan, as you know, is attacking the **HEART** of man and is doing what he can to program it to be antichrist! Christ Jesus called Satan a thief and a robber. **This ancient Pied Piper (Pan) is, indeed, stealing away the hearts of both young and old from following the Good Shepherd and, as a result, Satan is robbing these human beings of receiving eternal life.** Let's again look at documented evidence of how the red Dragon has been promoting the spiritual side of his "***Red* Revolution**," especially through the Big Screen and via the Music Industry.

This writer now wants to point out how certain kinds of movies, music, television programs, and books have, indeed, a definite influence on the way people think. As pointed out in Volume Two, the Beatles can be credited with helping the Hippie and Yuppie movements think about exploring into Hinduism, permissive sex and drugs, and Marxism as the lyrics to their songs entered in through their ears and into their hearts. Not only did their songs influence multitudes to follow in their steps, but, as we have seen, the Beatles openly attacked Jesus. It is public knowledge that **John Lennon said, "Christianity will go"** and **"We're the Beatles; we're more popular than Jesus now."** Lennon's musical career led him into not only Spiritualism, but also into the Marxist revolution which was not detected by the vast majority of his gullible, American fans even to this present day. The reader may now understand that Communism is an atheistic approach in forcing international Socialism upon the whole world. After disavowing himself with Hindu mysticism, Lennon apparently ended up like Karl Marx (which was a humanist or an atheist) before he died. Like Mick Jagger, **John Lennon was, indeed, a Marxist revolutionary who did his best to de-Christianize the American, student population by bombarding their minds with the suggestions of sex, drugs, and world revolution as he sang his popular music. Lennon wrote many songs to promote this idea for a Socialist, world revolution.** Writing under the camouflage of being a Hippie "Flower Child" wrapped in peace and love, Lennon, (the pied piper from Britain, like Dylan, Baez, and Jagger) led his tens of thousands of squealing disciples to stage protests against the American soldiers. While singing lyrics like "***Give Peace a Chance***" or "***You don't know how lucky you are, boy...Back in the USSR***," Lennon demanded that America should remove their forces from Vietnam while saying nothing about the Communist armies.

The popular protest song, "*Give Peace a Chance*," Lennon wrote was actually a **declaration of war against the United States** as gullible and confused American students of that day parrotted his protest songs. This above song was about **America losing the war against Communism in Asia**, and his song, "*Working Class Hero*," was a **salute to his other Communist comrades in America** who were also stealthily working within America in an attempt **to bring it down into the dust**. Lennon himself was even amazed at the ignorance of the American people in that they could not see what he was up to. He had so camouflaged his image as a great prophet of peace and love that he had even went so far as to openly tell them what he really was. John Lennon told *Newsweek* magazine in the September 29, 1980, issue on page 77, **"when you stop and think, what the...was I doing fighting the American government."**[77]

The American people as a whole did not realize then, as well as now, that all of the revolutionary and protest songs, staged sit-ins, marches, rallies, and financial contributions to Socialist fronts of Lennon were, indeed, acts of war against the American people. One of Lennon's last ***red*** propagandistic and revolutionary songs before he was killed was the very popular song called "***Imagine***." Just to show again how the Piper will use his people to bring others under his banner, look closely at the Communistic views of Lennon's words in his song, "***Imagine***." This antichrist's words are as follows:

"Imagine there's **NO HEAVEN** – It's easy if you try – No hell below us – Above us only sky – Imagine all the people – Living for today – Imagine there's **NO COUNTRIES** – It isn't hard to do – Nothing to kill or die for – And **NO RELIGION** too – Imagine all the people – Living life in peace – You may say I'm a dreamer – But I'm not the only one – I hope someday you'll join us – **AND THE WORLD WILL LIVE AS ONE** – Imagine **NO POSSESSIONS** – I wonder if you can – No need for greed or hunger – A brotherhood of man – Imagine all the people – Sharing all the world – You may say I'm a dreamer – But I'm not the only one – I hope someday you'll join us – **And THE WORLD WILL LIVE AS ONE.**" (Emphasis mine.)

[77]***The Legacy of John Lennon*, Noebel, p. 73.**

The outright blasphemy spoken by Lennon against the Meek and Lowly Saviour of the world has not only been recorded by man, but by Him who dwelleth between the Cherubims. To help the Bible-believing Christian free himself from the "**Lennon spell**" that may have been cast on him by Lennon's music, listen to what this despot blasphemously said about the Lamb of God who taketh away the sins of the world. Lennon said, "Jesus is a garlic eating stinking little yellow greasy Fascist bastard Catholic."[78] [sic]

While the god of rock'n'roll music is conditioning his subjects to accept the philosophies of this New Age/Marxist communal message, at the same time, **the youth are being trained to be led into anarchy by listening to their favorite "death-rock" band**. The subversive folk music and the songs of peace and free love during the "**Flower Children**" Era of the 60s began to be replaced in the 70s by the morbid hard-rock or **death-rock music**, like that of the Rolling Stones, Ozzy Osbourne, Grateful Dead, Alice Cooper, AC/DC, Motley Crue, Megadeth, Slayer, Michael Jackson, Madonna, Guns and Roses, Pearl Jam, etc., etc., etc.

Let's take a moment to look at the group Megadeth. They, too, can be considered as revolutionaries and are open antichrists and, like their 18th-century brethren (the Jacobins) in France, they are using their musical influences to lead their fans into anarchy. This heavy metal band sings the song, "***Anarchy in the UK***," on one of their CD's entitled *Megadeth: So Far, So Good... So What!* My young readers, the lyrics are as follows:

"Right now **I AM AN ANTI-CHRIST**, and **I am an ANARCHIST**. Don't know what I want, but I know how to get it, I want to destroy, possibly? Cause **I WANT TO BE ANARCHY**. No dog's body. **Anarchy** for the U.K.

"It's coming sometime it maybe. I give a wrong time, stop a traffic light. Your future dream is a shopping spree. Cause **I WANT TO BE ANARCHY, IN THE CITY.**" [sic]

While this kind of music often has lyrics which promote violence, black or white magic, and fornication of every description, at the same time, some of these songs have often thrown their admirers

[78]***The Legacy of John Lennon*, Noebel, p. 73.**

into a wild frenzy with their music. Some of the more wild and ecstatic fans of these headbangers are led during their concerts to join into the practice of what is known as the circle dance and here open sadomasochism is encouraged. While some are "freaking out" with crowd surfing or stage diving, still others are dressed in their favorite **Goth attire with pierced eyebrows, noses, or lips and hurl themselves into the moshing pit where they are beaten, tortured, kicked, and often injured; some have even died**. Both crazed young men and women today jump into the moshing pit and place themselves at the mercy of a sadomasochist. This insane and kinky behavior, which is looked upon as "cool" to some, is known today as **moshing dancing**.

Who could the Master Musician possibly use more to spread his gospel of Spiritualism than the heros of the entertainment field? Who today has more influence on the young, rebellious teenager? Satan has switched the course of things among the young from being one of the "Flower Children" of the 60s who followed after love and peace to now becoming a "**Shock Rocker**" who follows after and becomes an **ANARCHIST** and/or an **ANTICHRIST**. Jesus told us what the people of this earth would devclop into just shortly before He comes back to rescue His people from Satan and those who have placed themselves on his side. Jesus said in Luke 17:26-30:

"**And as it was in the days of Noe**, so shall it be also in the days of the Son of man. They did eat, they drank, they married wives, they were given in marriage, until the day that Noe entered into the ark, and the flood came, and destroyed them all.

"**Likewise also as it was in the days of Lot**; they did eat, they drank, they bought, they sold, they planted, they builded; But the same day that Lot went out of Sodom it rained fire and brimstone from heaven, and destroyed them all. Even thus shall it be in the day when the Son of man is revealed."

Back on February 24, 1997, *Time* magazine announced Marilyn Manson's new album, ***ANTICHRIST SUPERSTAR***. This album is a takeoff of another blasphemous and sacrilegious song, "***Jesus Christ Superstar***," which misrepresented our Saviour and Lord. A photograph of Marilyn Manson and his other "Shock Rockers" who were dressed as Sodomites and looked as though they were possessed with devils is found in this issue of *Time* magazine.[79] I'm sure the reader has noticed how this **black attire** and **black lipstick** has become the latest craze among some of the wild and ecstatic youth of our day. Who would have ever dreamed that when Bill Haley and Elvis Presley began to make rock'n'roll (which was, indeed, a culture shock in their day) popular among young Americans of that day that it later would help lead the young and the rebellious in our day to become so degraded and conditioned in their minds so as to accept the characters of the Marilyn Manson band and their **industrial and/or death-rock music**.

Brian Warner, the leader of the band, and his fellow comrades have adopted the names of celebrity idols and serial killers for their act. Warner chose the names of the late sex queen Marilyn Monroe and the morbid serial killer and occult revolutionary, Charles Manson, to express the character he is projecting into the minds of his fans. His keyboardist calls himself Madonna Wayne Gacy and his bassist adopted the names of Twiggy and the Night Stalker of Los Angeles, Richard Ramirez. He calls himself Twiggy Ramirez. Marilyn Manson's band is not the first to bring to the youth this shock technique used among musicians of the Rock Era to help them sell their music. Ozzy Osbourne, Kiss, and Alice Cooper can take much of the credit for that. However, after the ***ANTICHRIST SUPERSTAR*** album was first released in November of 1996, it sold more than one million copies within four months. *Rolling Stone* magazine (in its January 1997 issue) exalted and proclaimed Marilyn Manson as the best new artist of 1996.

David E. Thigpen, who wrote an article about the Marilyn Manson band in *Time* magazine, fittingly entitled his article as "**Satan's Little Helpers**. The Marilyn Manson band brings death-rock to the mainstream. Are these guys really serious?"[80] Thigpen goes on to point out how Manson intentionally crafts his image to incite maximum shock. Both on and off stage he wears his black lipstick and mortician's white make-up which gives himself a deathly and freshly-exhumed look. According to Thigpen, Manson's most enthusiastic fans are known as the **Goths**, who are members of a popular, suburban youth cult drawn

[79]*Time*, February 24, 1997, p. 68.
[80]*Ibid.*, February 24, 1997, p. 68.

to **black attire** and death-rock music. This new fashion and culture is presenting itself on TV talk shows which are looking for anything to help boost their ratings and make them money.

Manson's sado-masochistic death-rock image is expressed as he, too, during his concerts throws himself down to squirm his bare chest on a carpet of broken glass. Amazingly, this self-proclaimed antichrist of the stage once attended a strict, Christian boarding school. However, while all of this is looked upon by the parents of some of these musicians and their fans as just an act or a passing fad, two Goths were arrested for murder just one month before *Time* magazine released this article about this ***ANTICHRIST SUPERSTAR*** album. A fan was asked what he liked the best about the Marilyn Manson band, and he answered that most rock stars take off the make-up when they go home, but "**with Manson it's real**."[81]

This constant **sowing of** Satanic influences via Hollywood, the Music Industry, violent TV programs, novels, magazines, computer games, and the Internet beginning in the late 50s has now **produced a crop** of murderous young people. Before the cowardly massacre of 12 defenseless students and one teacher in Littleton, Colorado, back in October 1997, Pearl, Mississippi, was to experience the new **Gothic** movement and what it can produce among American youth today. Luke Woodham, age 16, after stabbing his 50-year-old mother with a butcher knife in his home, drove his white Chevy Corsica up to his high school. He then took a .30-.30 rifle from **beneath his trench coat** and opened fire, wounding seven schoolmates and killing two. According to *Time*, October 20, 1997, p. 54, Luke Woodham belonged to a **Gothic cult group** called "the Group." Shortly after the murder of the two teenage girls, Justin Sledge, a 16-year-old friend of Woodham who was dressed in a **black trench coat, black shirt**, and dark glasses, disrupted a prayer vigil for the victims and later notes were pasted up in the town of Pearl declaring in Greek letters "Luke is God."

Then, one month later, Denver, Colorado, in 1997 was to experience a **new Aryan** rash of Skinhead crimes. Back in November 1997, two Skinheads traded gunfire with police during a 20-mile car chase. Captured suspect Jerald Dean Allen flashed hate tattoos and announced

[81]*Time*, February 24, 1997, p. 68.

"I am fighting for my cause." A week later, Matthaeus Jaehnig, age 25, and another White Skinhead, in a similar incident murdered police officer Bruce VanderJagt. According to *Time*, December 1, 1997, p. 53, Jaehnig had been a longtime member of an Aryan group in Denver calling themselves the Denver Skins, who brazenly attended the slain officer's funeral and a few days later, someone deposited a dead pig inscribed with the name Vanderjagt near the slain policeman's station house.

In another Denver murder sparked by racial hatred, swastika-tattooed Nazi named Nathan Thill, then age 19, shot defenseless Oumar Dia to death, and a nurse's assistant, Jeannie VanVelkinburgh, was paralyzed from her waist down after Thill opened fire on them. Carl Raschke, a professor at the University of Denver who tracks hate groups, told *Time* the following about the White Supremacist groups today: " 'These people don't have to know each other. **They click on the same Websites**, they listen to the **same music**, they **know the code**.' Last week, he surmises, they began a 'game of chicken' with city authorities. Denver residents fear the game could take more tragic turns before it's over." Unfortunately, that is exactly what happened.

Michael Carneal, age 14, fired off 12 shots killing three and wounding five of his classmates at Heath High School in Paducah, Kentucky, in December of 1997. It was brought out, however, that Michael Carneal was not a Goth and he wasn't into drugs or crime or cults. He never dressed in black or wore upside-down crosses, and he had never before fired a gun. According to *Newsweek*, December 15, 1997, pages 30, 31, Michael had suffered from the effects of teasing and he felt small and powerless, but he was going to show the world how powerless he was. This is also what led to the psychopathic massacre at Columbine High School which we shall look at in a moment. As we shall see, kids today are brutally mistreated and are divided into different hate factions in public schools.

Human beings are natural imitators. We do not want to admit it, but we copy each other. It is as natural as drinking water to follow the Jones' and to try to keep up with them. The Hippie will say that this is not true, but how does a dropout learn to be a dropout instead of a Jones? He learned it from another Hippie! **What kind of example**

did James Dean with his cigarette dangling from his mouth, or Elvis Presley, John Wayne, or Frank Sinatra leave us? Who set the example and encouraged masses of people to smoke or to rebel against Christian morality? Was it not encouraged from the heros of the entertainment field and by our parents who copied them?

In the average American household, the children, their parents, the granddaddy, and the grandmamma watch at least 30 hours of television per week. Everything from homosexuality to mass murders to cannibalism is recorded in the memory bank of the brain as they waste away their remaining hours before the TV set. Both natural law and the Bible teaches **that by beholding, you will become changed**. Would you let a mass murderer baby-sit your children? Would you want your children to hang around witches, crooks, and drug addicts? Would you encourage your children to learn the curious arts of witchcraft? Would you allow your children to be sent to a school which trains little minds to know what it would be like to kill people? Of course, most Christians would say, "Never!" However, the above is what television and the movies and especially the computer games you give your children encourage your young, as well as you, to do while you and your family live out each murder scene or sexual encounter shown on the screen. No? Look at today's headlines in the newspapers at how children have murdered their schoolmates in the halls of their own schools. Where did they learn to do these things?

Some may say, "We don't allow our children to watch certain violent television programs or movies which promote permissive sex or the use of drugs." OK, but what about Spiritualism? Very few there are who recognize that **Walt Disney cartoons and movies have been promoting Sufism, magic, sorcery, and other occult sciences right under the noses of Christian parents**. Nonsense? Well, look at Mickey Mouse. What does he often dress as? What does he often portray? **Mickey Mouse is a sorcerer.** He is often dressed like a male witch. Do you remember seeing him wearing a pointed hood with the crescent and pentagram displayed on it? What does he do? He hypnotizes brooms to sweep for him or works magic spells to get what he wants. Another cartoon character we need to look at is **Cinderella**. Who appears to Cinderella? A mysterious fairy godmother appears. What does she do? She takes her wand, touches the kin, and it becomes a golden carriage. How did she do this? Was that done by the power of God? It is called white magic in occult circles. Parents, take another look at the Disney's *The Lion King*, *Pocahontas*, *The Hunchback of Notre Dame*, and *Aladdin* books and movies you have given your children to read and watch. In these books, you will find the promotion of the same deceptions of Spiritualism, as we studied earlier, which are condemned by God in Deuteronomy, Chapter 18.

As pointed out, Sufism (Islamic mysticism) is the most powerful order of Oriental Spiritualism on earth. The Sufi masters made their way throughout the Old World as musicians, poets, storytellers, and miracle workers. They are believed to have, like Buddha, become a perfect human being, possessing supernatural power and superhuman qualities.[82] These supernatural powers and superhuman qualities were articulately and cunningly promoted through the writing of fairy tales. The Sufi teacher Idries Shah who points out in his book, *The Way of the Sufi,* on page 38 that **Kabbalism and Sufism are identical**, also points out how Islamic mysticism had inspired some of the most popular children authors. In his above documented book, Shah states how William Tell's legend of Switzerland, the cult of the 'Peacock Angel,' and the tales of Hans Christian Andersen were borrowed from the Sufi poets.[83] It was Sir Richard Burton, the Sufi master who visited Brigham Young in 1860, who was a secret agent for the British and translated the Muslim mystical adventures entitled *The Arabian Nights*, *Tales of Hindu Devilry,* and *Vikram and the Vampire.*[84]

What do the television programs *Bewitched* or *I Dream of Jeannie* teach your children to do? What about the Muslim tale of *Aladdin*? **The Sufi masters learned ages ago how they could promote their form of Spiritualism through poetry and music. Now, it is vividly portrayed on the Big Screen and TV, as well as in popular children's fairy tale books.**

There is just one more thing we need to look at, and that is these **TERRIBLE VIDEO AND COMPUTER GAMES**.

[82]***The Encyclopedia of Religion*, Vol. 14, ed. Eliade, 1987, p. 118.**

[83]***The Way of the Sufi*, Shah, p. 20.**

[84]***The New Encyclopaedia Britannica*, Micropaedia, Vol. 2, 1997, p. 668.**

According to *Time*, May 3, 1999, page 31, as Eric Harris and Dylan Klebold prowled the halls of Columbine High School with their bombs and guns, they could be heard laughing as they sought out their victims. The murderers were without pity. **"Survivors said they treated it like a video game." Liberal** mothers and fathers, have you taken a **look** lately at these vicious video or computer games that your children are allowed to act out in their imagination?

If you are not aware of the character-destroying computer games the youth of today are playing with, just take a look at the **number-one computer game magazine entitled *Computer Gaming World*.** I was just made aware of this hideous magazine in December of 1996. An ad for your child between the ages of 13–19 is on the back cover of the December 1996 issue of this magazine. The name of the computer game is "*Crusader: No Regret.*" The ad goes on to say: "The explosive sequel to *Crusader: No Remorse.*" *PC Gamer* said in the same ad, "**The most brutal and addictive gameplay around**." An ad promoting the computer game entitled "*Killing Time*" is also shown in this same magazine.[85] The ad shows how the viewer uses the shotgun to kill doleful beings in a haunted mansion. There are six windows in the display ad showing the viewer that he has the shotgun in hand. **He aims and fires the shotgun at his foes and shoots them as if it actually happened.**

An ad for a computer game entitled *Killing Giant Human Beings* is also shown in the above magazine. The ad says, "In prison interviews, **psychopaths** often speak of the incredible feeling of power that comes from killing another human being. You're a lot closer to being interviewed than you'd like people to know."[86] **This game lets the player feel what it would be like to be a psychopath as he slays his victims.**

According to *The Daily Herald*, April 26, 1999, Provo, Utah, p. A3, the two young men who massacred 12 students and a teacher at Columbine High School (Eric Harris, age 18, and Dylan Klebold, age 17) were **obsessed** with **violent video games**. Eric sent venomous

[85]*Computer Gaming World*, December 1996, pp. 20, 21.

[86]*Ibid.*, December 1996, p. 83.

messages on the Internet back in 1998 allegedly prompting others to murder a classmate. Parents do not know or do not care about what their children are learning while they freely search the Internet. On the front cover of *U.S. News & World Report*, March 22, 1999, there is staged a young teenage girl pretending that no one is looking while she is talking on the telephone in the privacy of her own bedroom with her computer sitting on her bed and using a mouse to search her computer. Her mouse pad is a miniature **Ouija board**!

The killings which have recently taken place within high schools by Goth or Nazi skinhead groups have been caused by disturbed children who have been watching violent movies or TV shows, searching the Internet for Web sites promoting violence, playing computer games, and/or who have been listening to **"gangsta rap"** and **death-rock music**.

To the unconverted, the rock group, Led Zeppelin, is still one of the most popular rock'n'roll groups of all times, and their song, "*Stairway to Heaven*," is one of the most popular songs ever produced as well. Many high schools have ignorantly used "***Stairway to Heaven***" for the theme song during their proms. However, listen to some more of the lyrics of this song:

"Then the **PIPER** will lead us to **REASON** – And a new day will dawn for those who stand long – And the forest will echo with laughter – And it makes me wonder....

"Yes there are **TWO PATHS** you can go by – But in the long run – **THERE'S STILL TIME TO CHANGE THE ROAD YOU'RE ON** – Your head is **HUMMING** and it won't go–**IN CASE YOU DON'T KNOW – THE PIPER'S CALLING YOU TO JOIN HIM**."

However, in case you don't know, **SO IS JESUS!** The King of kings and Lord of lords is calling those who have been fooled into following Pan to turn to Him. Those who are called by Christ will find that they do not fit anywhere in society today. Have you ever felt that you did not fit in or that the world is against you? A man or a woman may have all the riches that this world has to offer, but still be miserable day by day. Jesus said of them that He has called:

"If ye were of the world, the world would love his own: but because ye are not of the world, but I have chosen you out of the world, THEREFORE THE WORLD HATETH YOU." John 15:19.

Have you come to the place in your mind where you have had enough of the degraded lifestyle your peers have pressured you into doing? Have you reached a point in your life now where all this glamour, self-glorification, and excitement coming from Hollywood and the Music Industry and sport hero's are no longer mesmerizing you?

It is true that "there are **TWO PATHS** you can go by," as the song, "*Stairway to Heaven*," sings, and it is true that the **prince** of this world or the **Piper is calling you**, but this **false shepherd** does not care for his goats. The Piper enjoys leading his goats to destruction. While this Piper's music leads his goats to rebel against the Good Shepherd and to commit crime, murder, fornication, and/or to use drugs, many go down into untimely graves with AIDS, an overdose of drugs, or by being murdered. While the **Piper** leads his followers to take drugs, they may be led into crime to get them and then this same Piper may turn you in to suffer the consequences. Nevertheless, there is another voice the reader may come to recognize if he diligently seeks it.

"The thief cometh not, but for to steal, and to kill, and to destroy: I AM COME THAT THEY MIGHT HAVE LIFE, AND THAT THEY MIGHT HAVE IT MORE ABUNDANTLY.

"I AM THE GOOD SHEPHERD: the good shepherd giveth his life for the sheep. But he that is an HIRELING, AND NOT THE SHEPHERD, whose own the sheep are not, seeth the wolf coming, and leaveth the sheep, and fleeth: and the wolf catcheth them, and scattereth the sheep.

"The hireling fleeth, because he is an hireling, and careth not for the sheep. I AM THE GOOD SHEPHERD, AND KNOW MY SHEEP, AND AM KNOWN OF MINE." John 10:10–14.

"ALL THAT THE FATHER GIVETH ME SHALL COME TO ME; AND HIM THAT COMETH TO ME I WILL IN NO WISE CAST OUT." John 6:37.

"I JESUS have sent mine angel to testify unto you these things in the churches. I AM the ROOT and the OFFSPRING OF DAVID, and the BRIGHT and MORNING STAR. And the Spirit and the bride say, COME. And let him that heareth say, COME. And let him that is ATHIRST come. AND WHOSOEVER WILL, LET HIM TAKE THE WATER OF LIFE FREELY." Revelation 22:16, 17.

"COME UNTO ME, ALL YE THAT LABOUR AND ARE HEAVY LADEN, AND I WILL GIVE YOU REST. TAKE MY YOKE UPON YOU, AND LEARN OF ME; FOR I AM MEEK AND LOWLY IN HEART: AND YE SHALL FIND REST UNTO YOUR SOULS. FOR MY YOKE IS EASY, AND MY BURDEN IS LIGHT." Matthew 11:28–30.

As pointed out, Satan has deceived the whole world, and his murderous hatred is being manifested especially among the young people he is motivating. Lucifer's main downfall was his self-exalting pride and his beautiful physique. (See Ezekiel 28:17) His proud attributes are clearly seen in those heros of the Big Screen and the heros of the baseball, football, soccer, and basketball arenas. Eric Harris and Dylan Klebold were also mesmerized by the excitement of competitive sports. They were Little Leaguers. However, like most young people, they suffered spiritual wounds from not only being unable to compete well enough among the big guys, but also suffered deep emotional and psychological trauma from the jocks and cheerleaders of the Littleton Columbine High School.

According to *Time*, May 3, 1999, pages 28, 29, Eric Harris and Dylan Klebold suffered terribly by the social elite of their high school. Lying rumors were spread that they were faggots, and, because of this, they were discarded, unwanted, and were stereotyped by the jocks, who sat at their own tables during lunch, as "geeks." It was brought out by *Time* that the ones who were the worst at spreading rumors and lies about Harris and Klebold were the athletes (jocks) and their cheerleaders. Not only did they suffer deep emotional wounds from their cruel mouths, but they had rocks and bottles thrown at them as the jocks passed by them in cars. Before the massacre, *Time* said their graffiti written in the boys' bathroom warned, "Columbine will explode one day. Kill all athletes. All jocks must die."

Jesus promises us spiritual power to endure the cruel voice of the Dragon as he speaks through the mouth of the gossip. We are to go to Christ with our troubles and give Him our burdens and He will give us rest. Our God is a refuge from the storm of persecution. However, Harris and Klebold never learned how to make God their shield and buckler and fortress. They had completely given themselves over to the Destroyer to be used by him. This writer believes that they had actually programmed themselves to become psychopaths by their own obsession for violence via computer games and by searching the dangerous hate Web sites found on the Internet. Unless the heart of man is controlled and kept in check by the Spirit of God, he or she will continue to reflect our worst enemy's attributes in both words and deeds. As long as the high schools continue to make competitive sports, sex, popular music, and self-exaltation the central theme among the student population, the longer these hideous crimes will continue. Practically the whole world is following the Pied Piper; even those who claim to be Christians are jocks or are like them.

However, very soon Jesus will put an end to the plans and purposes of this Pied Piper and those who continue to follow him. The prophets in the Old Testament and the apostles in the New Testament foretold what the Creator of this world is about to do:

"For, behold, the Lord cometh out of his place to punish the inhabitants of the earth for their iniquity: the earth also shall disclose her blood, and shall no more cover her slain." Isaiah 26:21.

King David prophesied, "Our God shall come, and shall not keep silence: a fire shall devour before him, and it shall be very tempestuous round about him." Thc apostle Paul prophesied the manner of Christ's Second Coming and said, "And to you who are troubled rest with us, when the Lord Jesus shall be revealed from heaven with his mighty angels, **In flaming fire taking vengeance** on them **that know not God**, and that **obey not** the gospel of our Lord Jesus Christ: Who shall be punished with everlasting destruction from the presence of the Lord, and from the glory of his power." 2 Thessalonians 1:7–9. The prophet Joel said, "Alas for the day! for the day of the Lord is at hand, and as a destruction from the Almighty shall it come." Joel 1:15. The apostle Peter prophesied, "The Lord is not slack concerning his promise, as some men count slackness; but is longsuffering to us-ward, not willing that any should perish, but that all should come to repentance. But the day of the Lord will come as a thief in the night; in the which the heavens shall pass away with a great noise, and the elements shall melt with fervent heat, the earth also and the works that are therein shall be burned up. Seeing then that all these things shall be dissolved, what manner of persons ought ye to be in all holy conversation and godliness, Looking for and hasting unto the coming of the day of God, wherein the heavens being on fire shall be dissolved, and the elements shall melt with fervent heat? Nevertheless we, according to his promise, look for new heavens and a new earth, wherein dwelleth righteousness." 2 Peter 3:9–13.

This promise of the destruction of the wicked and the world by Jesus Christ is twofold. The Hebrew prophets in the Old Testament and the apostles in the New Testament both warn that there shall be two cleansings of the inhabitants of this world who have chosen to reject the salvation of Jesus or refuse to obey His Gospel. This cleansing of the living wicked from the earth shall occur at Christ's Second Coming and then again after the thousand-year Reign of Christ in Heaven. There are two resurrections. The first shall be for the saints of Christ, and the second shall be for those who rejected the Gospel's call. It is here that Satan and his evil angels who deceived the inhabitants of this world by the use of mysticism will also meet their final destruction.

In between the first resurrection of the saints and the second resurrection of the wicked, the saints will reign with Christ Jesus for 1,000 years in Heaven. Again, this is not on earth (which the majority of Christians believe), but in Heaven. During this 1,000 years, Satan will be bound to this empty world without anyone to deceive, for the saints at this time are in Heaven with Christ and the wicked were destroyed at Christ's Second Coming.

The prophecy about the Dragon (Satan) being bound to this earth with no one to tempt during the Millennium is in Revelation 20:1–3.

"And I saw an angel come down from heaven, having the **key of the bottomless pit** and a great chain in his hand. And he laid hold on the dragon, that old serpent, which is the Devil, and Satan, and bound him a thousand years, And cast him into the bottomless pit, and shut him up, and set a seal upon him, **that he should deceive the nations no more, till the thousand years should be fulfilled:** and after that he must be loosed a little season." Revelation 20:1–3.

As pointed out so many times, Satan is this Angel of the Bottomless Pit out of which mysticism derived. It says here that an angel from Heaven had a "**key of the bottomless pit**" and a great chain in his hand. The Destroyer is to be locked up in his abode from which he has been operating. This abode is symbolized as the Bottomless Pit, and Satan has claimed that he is the god of this world.

Hence, this world shall be his prison for 1,000 years with nothing to do but think about all the carnage he has caused among both the Heavenly angels and mankind.

"Blessed and holy is he that hath part in the **first resurrection**: on such the second death hath no power, but they shall be priests of God and of Christ, and shall reign with him a thousand years. And when **the thousand years are expired**, Satan shall be loosed out of his prison, And shall go out to deceive the nations which are in the four quarters of the earth, Gog and Magog, to gather them together to battle: the number of whom is as the sand of the sea.

"And they went up on the breadth of the earth, and compassed the camp of the saints about, and the beloved city: and fire came down from God out of heaven, and devoured them. And the devil that deceived them was cast into the lake of fire and brimstone, where the beast and the false prophet are, and shall be tormented day and night for ever and ever. And I saw a great white throne, and him that sat on it, from whose face the earth and the heaven fled away; and there was found no place for them.

"And I saw the dead, small and great, stand before God; and the books were opened: and another book was opened, which is the book of life: and the dead were judged out of those things which were written in the books, according to their works. And the sea gave up the dead which were in it; and death and hell delivered up the dead which were in them: and they were judged every man according to their works.

"And death and hell were cast into the lake of fire. This is the second death. And whosoever was not found written in the book of life was cast into the lake of fire." Revelation 20:6–15.

As pointed out in Volumes One, Two, and Three, this hellfire which the Old and New Testament prophesies about shall come from Heaven, not from some secret place under the earth (hell) of which both Catholic and Protestant leaders scream to their congregations. The hellfire shall cover the whole earth! Fire is God's purifying agent; He will cleanse the world of its sins and pollutions by the use of fire.

"Nevertheless," says the apostle Peter, "we, according to his promise, look for **new heavens and a new earth**, wherein dwelleth righteousness." 2 Peter 3:13.

This new heaven and new earth is where Christ's Kingdom will reign forever, not in this present sinful world. Today, it is here that the Protestant Christians, the pagan New Agers, the Muslims, the Roman Catholics, and the Jews of the flesh are under a **strong delusion**. This ushering in of a one-world religion with a one-world communal government via Plato's Atlantean Plan a.k.a. Age of Aquarius a.k.a. New World Order has and will deceive the very elect if possible into thinking that this effort shall usher in the long-expected millennium here on earth. At the height of this false excitement, Satan will personate Jesus. However, those who can hear what the Spirit is saying to the churches do not have their affections wrapped up in the things of this present world, "but now they desire a better country, that is, an heavenly: wherefore God is not ashamed to be called their God: **for he hath prepared for them a city**." Hebrews 11:16.

"Therefore also now, saith the Lord, turn ye even to me with all your heart, and with fasting, and with weeping, and with mourning: And rend your heart, and not your garments, and turn unto the Lord your God: for he is gracious and merciful, slow to anger, and of great kindness, and repenteth him of the evil.

"Let the priests, the ministers of the Lord, weep between the porch and the altar, and let them say, Spare thy people, O Lord, and give not thine heritage to reproach, that the heathen should rule over them: wherefore should they say among the people, Where is their God?" Joel 2:12, 13, 17.

Jesus' last call to the wicked and those who have been deceived by the philosophies of mysticism (Babylon the Great) is found in Revelation 18:1–5.

"And after these things I saw another angel come down from heaven, having great power; and the earth was lightened with his glory. And he cried mightily with a strong voice, saying, Babylon the great is fallen, is fallen, and is become the habitation of devils, and the hold of every foul spirit, and a cage of every unclean and hateful bird. For all nations have drunk of the wine of the wrath of her fornication with her, and the merchants of the earth are waxed rich through the abundance of her delicacies.

"And I heard another voice from heaven, saying, **Come out of her, my people, that ye be not partakers of her sins, and that ye**

receive not of her plagues. For her sins have reached unto heaven, and God hath remembered her iniquities." Revelation 18:1–5.

Those who heed this warning and have repented and received Jesus of Nazareth as their only Redeemer and Saviour have this promise:

"And I saw a new heaven and a new earth: for the first heaven and the first earth were passed away; and there was no more sea. And I John saw the holy city, new Jerusalem, coming down from God out of heaven, prepared as a bride adorned for her husband. And I heard a great voice out of heaven saying, Behold, the tabernacle of God is with men, and he will dwell with them, and they shall be his people, and God himself shall be with them, and be their God.

"And God shall wipe away all tears from their eyes; and there shall be no more death, neither sorrow, nor crying, neither shall there be any more pain: for the former things are passed away. And he that sat upon the throne said, Behold, I make all things new. And he said unto me, Write: for these words are true and faithful.

"And he said unto me, It is done. I am Alpha and Omega, the beginning and the end. I will give unto him that is athirst of the fountain of the water of life freely. He that overcometh shall inherit all things; and I will be his God, and he shall be my son.

"But the fearful, and unbelieving, and the abominable, and murderers, and whoremongers, and sorcerers, and idolaters, and all liars, shall have their part in the lake which burneth with fire and brimstone: which is the second death." Revelation 21:1–8.

INDEX

A

B

C

D

E

F

G

H

I

J

K

L

M

N

O

P

Q

R

S

T

U

V

W

Y

Z

TWENTY-NINE YEARS IN THE MAKING! PERHAPS THE MOST UP-TO-DATE AND FULLY DOCUMENTED STUDY WITHIN FIVE VOLUMES ABOUT THE THREE-FOLD UNION OF THE SECRET SOCIETIES OF THE ILLUMINATI, THE PAPACY, AND THE APOSTATE PROTESTANTS THAT YOU HAVE EVER READ IN YOUR ENTIRE LIFE! TAKE A PROPHETICAL AND HISTORICAL JOURNEY THROUGH THE AGES FROM 2200 B.C. UP TO THE YEAR A.D. 1999 AND VIEW, WITH YOUR OWN ASTONISHED EYES, THE REAL AND TRUE-TO-LIFE BATTLE BETWEEN THE FORCES OF GOOD AND THE FORCES OF EVIL. TRULY SEE FOR YOURSELF HOW THIS TERRIBLE STRUGGLE IS ABOUT TO REACH ITS CLIMAX!

Vol. 1	**Vol. 2**	**Vol. 3**	**Vol. 4**	**Vol. 5**
261 pages	**304 pages**	**288 pages**	**383 pages**	**383 pages**
$9.95	**$10.95**	**$10.95**	**$11.95**	**$11.95**

Please allow $1.50 per book for POSTAGE AND HANDLING

Send your order to the following distributor below:

PLEASE ALLOW 3 TO 6 WEEKS DELIVERY